A Sensitive Independence

McGill-Queen's Studies in the History of Religion
G.A. Rawlyk, Editor

Volumes in this series have been supported by the Jackman Foundation of Toronto.

A Sensitive Independence

Canadian Methodist Women Missionaries in Canada and the Orient, 1881–1925

ROSEMARY R. GAGAN

McGill-Queen's University Press
Montreal & Kingston • London • Buffalo

© McGill-Queen's University Press 1992
ISBN 0-7735-0896-1

Legal deposit second quarter 1992
Bibliothèque nationale du Québec

Printed in Canada on acid-free paper

This book has been published with the help of a grant
from the Social Science Federation of Canada, using
funds provided by the Social Sciences and Humanities
Research Council of Canada.

Canadian Cataloguing in Publication Data

Gagan, Rosemary Ruth
   A sensitive independence
   (McGill-Queen's studies in the history of religion; 9)
   Includes bibliographical references and index.
   ISBN 0-7735-0896-1

   1. Women missionaries – Canada – History. 2. Women
   missionaries – Japan – History. 3. Women missionaries
   – China – History. 4. Methodist Church of Canada –
   Missions – History. I. Title. II. Series.

   BV2418.G34 1992   266'.7   C92-090092-5
   73246

All illustrations in the book are published by
permission of the Archives of the United Church of
Canada, Victoria University, Toronto.

Typeset in Palatino 10/12 by
Caractéra production graphique inc., Quebec City.

To Sarah, Jamie, Becky, Abby,
and David

Contents

Preface and Acknowledgments

This book's immediate origins lie with a doctoral dissertation undertaken for McMaster University in an effort to fulfil a scholar's ambition to contribute in some small way to the historiography of Canadian women. However, my personal curiosity about missionaries pre-dates by far the more academic purposes for which the project may have been conceived.

My maternal grandmother's house in London, Ontario, had a spare bedroom that served as an attic. As a child I always looked forward to a trip up the narrow stairs to the third floor, where the accumulated detritus of several generations lay packed away in a multitude of trunks and boxes. Besides the usual letters, photographs, and newspaper clippings there were quilts, paintings, and pieces of embroidery – the handiwork of an assortment of maiden aunts – Orange Lodge regalia, and a variety of mineral samples collected by my grandfather, a prospector in northern Ontario. Best of all was the tissue-lined box containing an ivory silk and lace Edwardian wedding gown, which seemed to me the epitome of elegance and beauty. One day my cousin and I were allowed to try it on. To my disgust it fit her perfectly, but I could barely move in it.

No one ever said much about the bride who had worn the dress for a few hours on a hot September day in 1909. For many years all I really knew was that my great-aunt Cordelia Dunkin had married James L. Stewart, a missionary whom she met while she was attending Alma College in St Thomas, Ontario, and that she had died, probably of cholera, en route to the Canadian Methodist mission in Szechwan. I did not quiz my older relatives too closely because it seemed that almost half a century after her death an aura of sadness and bitterness was still attached to the story. One thing I understood: the episode had been a great personal tragedy and a time of spiritual trauma for a devoted family whose Methodist roots could be traced back to the days of John Wesley.

This anecdote of a Victorian woman missionary who died in a foreign country is hardly unique in the records of the Canadian past. Cordelia Dunkin Stewart, who ended her brief life on a houseboat on the Yangtze River and was buried high on a cliff in Chungking, was just one of thousands of Canadian men and women of many religious denominations who, for a mixture of selfish, pragmatic, and visionary reasons, chose to commit their lives to the Christianization of the wider world, most of which was utterly unknown to them. Countless others served in Canada as home missionaries to native people, to the immigrant communities, and to the casualties of an increasingly brutal urban industrializing society. The volume that follows is an attempt to examine the experience of one readily identified group of missionaries, the personnel of the Woman's Missionary Society of the Methodist Church of Canada, which from 1881 to 1925 employed more than three hundred single women as its representatives in Canada and the Orient.

For women in particular missionary work was an enticing and respectable profession whose supportive female atmosphere provided a congenial alternative, albeit sometimes only temporarily, to marriage, a family, and the strictures of a patriarchal society. Yet the missionary experience was far from homogeneous; it was as varied as the personalities involved. Success was very much the consequence of a woman's individual ability to cope with the host society in which she functioned. Some women merely tolerated their term with the WMS; at worst the pressure of the mission field simply overwhelmed them, physically and emotionally, and they abandoned their profession. Other women thrived; they became role models for their peers, serving the WMS for many years. Success and misfortune are intricately woven together in the WMS experience.

It is my regret that in many ways this is a one-sided account of the missionary experience; of necessity it is constructed largely from documentation provided by the missionaries themselves and by the administrators of the WMS, all middle-class, educated Canadian women. At this stage in the evolution of Canadian women's history, when so much of the emphasis of recent scholarship has shifted from elitist chronicles to a more diffuse interpretation, I had hoped to provide a more comprehensive analysis of the relationships between the missionaries and their female constituents in Canada and the Orient. Perhaps in the future the other side of the story will be told if new evidence comes to light. In the meantime my own travels, especially to the Orient, convince me that, in the best of all possible worlds, the ideal of a universal sisterhood transcending race and class existed, even though the WMS missionaries were sometimes incapable of articulating or achieving it.

After so many years of work on this project I have accumulated a large debt to many people whose help and advice can never be appropriately repaid. As a "mature" student returning to graduate work, I was first encouraged by A.F. "Pat" Thompson of Oxford University, then Messecar Professor of History at McMaster University. Under his guidance and perhaps against his better judgment, a quantitative examination of the characteristics and behaviour of the Diehards in the British House of Lords became an unlikely methodological test case for this study of WMS missionaries. I am very grateful to Harry Turner of the McMaster History Department for agreeing to supervise the thesis that produced this book and to Richard Rempel and Harvey Levenstein for their always insightful, sometimes acerbic comments at the thesis stage. I especially thank Joy Parr, who, as external reader, made many critical suggestions that facilitated the transition from an academic exercise to an acceptable manuscript. The manuscript was improved and sharpened by the comments of readers for McGill-Queen's University Press and the Social Sciences Federation of Canada. In its final stages the book benefited immensely from Susan Kent Davidson's astute editing. I also wish to acknowledge the encouragement and support extended by Don Akenson and George Rawlyk of McGill-Queen's University Press throughout the publication process.

Throughout my years of research I have been helped by archivists across the country, who provided everything from uncatalogued documents to first aid. I especially wish to thank the staff of Pine Hill Divinity School, Halifax, Diane Haglund of the United Church Archives at the University of Winnipeg, and Bob Stewart, who oversees his domain from "Heaven" at the United Church Archives at the Vancouver School of Theology. Closer to home, Jean Dryden's splendid staff at the United Church Archives, located at Victoria University in Toronto, never complained about what must have been hundreds of requests for materials related to the WMS. They are simply a wonderful group to be involved with.

In April 1989 I was fortunate to be a part of a civic delegation from Hamilton, led by Mayor Robert Morrow, that visited Hamilton's twin cities of Fukuyama, Japan, and Mansha'an, China. In Tokyo Mrs Yasuko Miyake and her daughter Kaori made it possible for me to visit the Toyo Eiwa Jo Gakko, the first WMS mission school established in the Orient. My appreciation goes as well to Gladys Rogers and Merrill Brown, United Church workers at the school, who took time from their busy schedules to give me a tour of the school and the missionary section of Aoyama Cemetery, a memorable sight during blosson time. My experience in China was somewhat circumscribed by events in Beijing that spring. Like the missionaries I did take a short trip on the Yangtze River. Most importantly, my own reaction to being so far from home during a political upheaval gave me a deeper appreciation of the WMS missionaries' apprehension about the future.

Finally, I wish to thank my immediate family and friends, who have been infinitely supportive of my work but must have been bored to tears by my conversation during the past few years. We are all tired of missionary jokes. I dedicate the book to my children, Sarah, Jamie, Becky, and Abby, who were deprived of motherly care but not fast food during the creative process, and to my husband, David, the best friend I could ever have.

Rosemary Gagan
October 1991

NOTE ON SPELLING

Like others who write of China during this period, in order to avoid much confusion I have simply retained the spelling of Chinese place-names that was used by missionaries at the time.

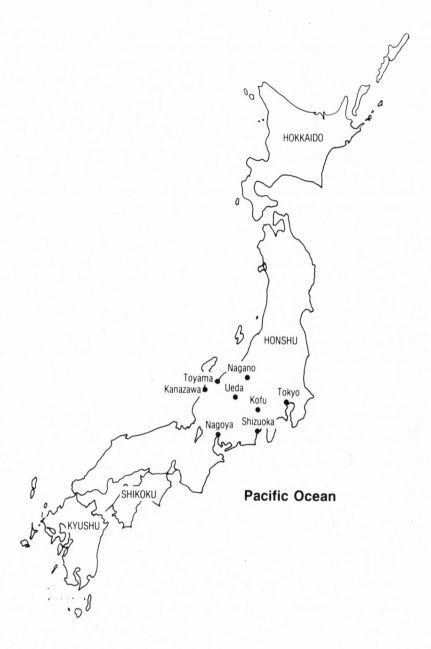

HOKKAIDO

HONSHU

Nagano
Toyama
Kanazawa Ueda
Kofu Tokyo
Nagoya Shizuoka

SHIKOKU

Pacific Ocean

KYUSHU

WMS mission stations in Japan 1882–1925

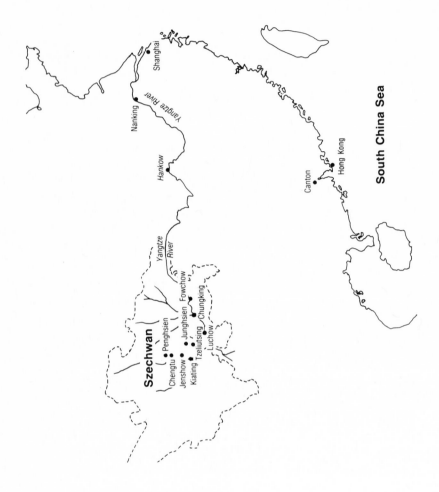

wms mission stations in Szechwan 1893–1925

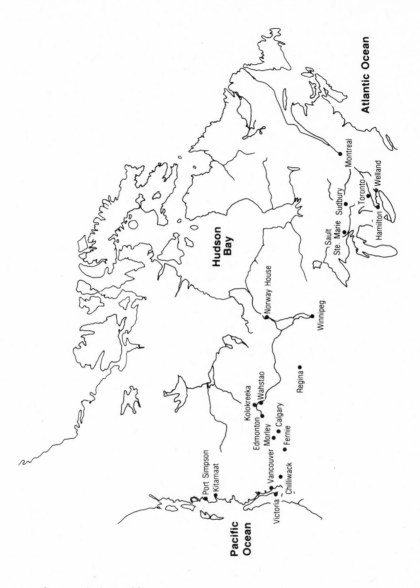

Atlantic Ocean

Montreal
Toronto Welland
Sudbury Hamilton
Sault
Ste. Marie

Hudson
Bay

Norway House

Winnipeg

Regina

Kolokreeka Wahstao
Edmonton Calgary
Morley
Fernie

Port Simpson
Kitamaat
Vancouver
Chilliwack
Victoria

Pacific
Ocean

wms home missions 1882–1925

A Sensitive Independence

CHAPTER ONE

The call of duty

In August 1886 twenty-one-year-old Agnes Wintemute left her comfortable home in St Thomas, Ontario, to take up a position half-way around the world in Tokyo as just the third overseas representative of the Woman's Missionary Society of the Methodist Church of Canada. When she had the time to reflect she was almost overwhelmed with misgivings about the magnitude of her decision, but for the next six years Wintemute worked tirelessly as an activist for Christianity, Canadian Methodism, and her employer, the Woman's Missionary Society, to improve the spiritual, social, and educational circumstances of Japanese girls and women. When her marriage in 1893 to Harper Coates, a Canadian Methodist General Board of Missions representative, forced her resignation from the wms, Wintemute voluntarily continued her pursuits on behalf of Japanese women. But along the way she became an outspoken critic of the manner in which the Methodist Church managed its missionary affairs and treated its missionary personnel.[1]

Agnes Wintemute Coates challenged in particular the widespread misconceptions about the fundamental qualities required by missionaries. She questioned the familiar assumption that a missionary "must be very *good*" and that "*clever* people should not go off to waste their talents on Indians or Orientals, but ought to stay [in Canada] where they will be appreciated and can climb the ladder to success and renown." Why, she wondered, should the missionary "be good and a lawyer or doctor or business man be clever?"[2] From her own experience with the wms Coates recognized both virtue and intelligence as critical to a successful missionary career, especially for women. Her former colleagues provided ample proof that these attributes were not mutually exclusive.

The impression persists of women missionaries as essentially self-less spinster "do-gooders" whose careers were a noble but not altogether satisfactory substitute for love, marriage, and children. In literature the female missionary has been depicted as either a drab figure, like Edwina Crane, the Anglican missionary in *The Jewel in the Crown*, a "plain somewhat horse-faced woman"[3] admired for her self-sacrifice but not her charm, or as a romanticized heroine like Gladys Aylward, whose life was fictionalized in *The Inn of the Sixth Happiness*. Stereotyped portrayals like these have obscured the reality of an occupation taken up by thousands of women throughout the world, including several hundred Canadians from many denominations, who joined the far-reaching late Victorian Protestant missionary crusade directed at the "Evangelization of the World in this Generation."[4] This volume is an attempt to contribute to the demythologizing of the missionary enterprise by examining the experiences of the personnel of the Woman's Missionary Society of the Methodist Church of Canada from 1881 to 1925, to strip away the layers of sentimentality that have tended to obscure the durability of these women, and to reinstate Agnes Wintemute and her associates in the front ranks of the small but significant minority of late nineteenth- and early twentieth-century Canadian women who chose a career and rejected the thrall of conventional attitudes towards woman's place in the ordering of society and households.

However anachronistic the missionary ideal has become in our secular global village, where the collapse of Western imperial ascendancy has thwarted wholesale attempts at redemption, a century ago and less missionary work provided a singular opportunity for ambitious unmarried Canadian women who preferred, either permanently or temporarily, a professional career to the Victorian ideal of domesticity. In an era characterized by limited career opportunities for women,[5] a missionary calling enabled women to support themselves, to earn respect and authority as experts in mission affairs, to gain public recognition and adulation for their accomplishments, to discharge their profound personal obligations as faithful Christians, and to lead an independent existence, often in exotic circumstances only imagined by their more domesticated sisters. Within the atmosphere of public and private religiosity of late Victorian Protestant Canada, whose church-going populace was determined to transform the nation and the world, an occupation that, devoid of its sacred objectives, would have been censured as inappropriate for well-bred women became instead a vehicle for their liberation.[6]

From its inception in 1881 until 1925, when the formation of the United Church of Canada effectively ended its separate existence, the

Woman's Missionary Society of the Methodist Church of Canada (henceforward WMS) employed more than three hundred single women to staff its network of mission stations in Japan, West China, and across Canada. The formal recruitment policies defined by the society's administrators, themselves able and decisive women determined to establish and maintain the WMS's autonomy within the patriarchal Methodist Church structure, appealed particularly to educated young women from the small towns of Ontario and the Maritime provinces. Daughters of the parsonage and the mercantile and professional classes, usually with some experience in the work-force as teachers, doctors, and nurses, and often at an age beyond which marriage was a statistically receding probability, were especially attracted by the overtures of the WMS.

The existence, however, of social and educational differentials among the recruits contributed, partly by design and partly through circumstances in the mission field, to the emergence of a hierarchical division of labour within the WMS, which consigned the least-qualified recruits to work with native peoples and recent immigrants in Canada, and the most accomplished, socially as well as intellectually, to the politically more visible, and more appealing, stations in the Orient. These disparities help to explain why some women became career professionals, remaining with the society for thirty or forty years until their death or retirement, while for others a few years of employment merely bridged the gap between dependence upon parents and the establishment of their own households. Social and educational attributes appear to have influenced not only where and for how long women served the WMS but the quality of their individual experience as missionaries in the field, their adaptability, and the degree of self-sufficiency they realized, singly or collectively, as the situation might dictate. In short, distance from the centre encouraged administrative ability and fostered independence.

Yet for every woman who persisted as a WMS missionary, two dropped by the wayside, evidence that Canadian Methodist WMS missionaries did not lead charmed lives. The popular missionary rhetoric of the day and the society's own publications tended to sanctify women missionaries, often representing them as martyrs patiently accepting whatever God might send their way. This sanitized version of missionary life, effective perhaps in evoking sympathy and financial support for the missionary cause, deliberately sidestepped issues that might provoke criticism and controversy about the appropriate role of the missionary. In reality, compromises and reduced ambitions in the face of the harsh and demanding circumstances of the mission field impeded the women's success both in evangelizing and in alleviating the suffering of their constituents. Some women soon became disillusioned by a career that did not conform to their naïve and blinkered expectations of a gracious and congenial way of life. They resigned as soon as their initial term was finished, sometimes before, while a few women who proved totally incompetent were discharged. But, despite personal hardship and professional frustration, if they remained with the society long enough many women became satisfied, often enthusiastic and elated, with the new opportunities their work afforded, and they were proud of their own ability to adjust to the most unusual of circumstances.

Among the many things pertinent to the WMS missionaries that interest the historian, their social, economic, educational, and occupational backgrounds provide evidence about the distinctive characteristics common to a group of predominantly middle-class women pursuing professional careers when female employment outside the home was largely the province of single working-class women and marriage the preoccupation of the majority of women of all classes.[7] Their experience in the mission field elucidates the relationship between their qualifications and training and the opportunities available to them to define and control the direction and quality of their professional lives, especially the degree of independence they sought and realized in a world and, more particularly, an institution dominated by men. At the same time, an examination of their backgrounds and the catalysts steering these women towards Canadian Methodism's missionary enterprise contributes to an understanding of the impact of religion on Canadian women during the late nineteenth and early twentieth centuries and to a recognition of the centrality of religion and spirituality to Canadian women's everyday existence. More specifically, this study extends the history of the Methodist Church of Canada, which has until recently been written largely without reference to the role of its female members, who, as the nineteenth century progressed, assumed an increasingly vital function in their church at the local and national level as laywomen, and paid employees. In their own way Methodist women helped to shape the pious and self-disciplined society that sustained the missionary movement in its heyday.

While the male missionary has been better, if not well served on an individual basis with biographies of James Endicott and Robert McClure and collectively in Alvyn Austin's *Saving China* and Hamish Ion's *The Cross and the Rising Sun*,[8] the current attention to women's history and its parent, social history, is steadily generating a comparable historiography pertaining to women who opted for a religious vocation. In particular, several studies of Quebec women who entered Roman Catholic orders, notably Marta Danylewycz's *Taking the Veil*, have appeared.[9] Danylewycz argues that for many Quebec women the religious life proved a highly satisfactory option to the domestic tyranny that might otherwise have been their lot: "Entering a convent could well mean overcoming the disadvantage of being a woman in a man's world."[10] In *New Women for God: Canadian Presbyterian Women and India Missions, 1876–1914*, Ruth Brouwer examines the evolution of one area of Canadian Presbyterian women's overseas missionary enterprise, the interaction between women at the home base in Canada and those in the mission field, and specifically the "richly rewarding" life that the women realized in central India.[11] For the most part, however, Canadian Protestant women pursuing religious vocations have not been included as part of the small but significant contingent of late nineteenth- and early twentieth-century working women with whom they identified. In so far as historians have been concerned with late Victorian and early twentieth-century Canadian women in the workforce, their attention has focused on women at the bottom of the class structure – millworkers, prostitutes, and domestic servants – who of course represented the majority of working women. Those at the top, professional career women, the doctors and lawyers, and those in the middle, the teachers and nurses, have been subjects of scholarly investigation primarily as victims of a male-dominated society.

Similarly, Canadian historians' past preoccupation on the one hand with the cult of maternal feminism, the seedbed of social reform as societal housekeeping, and on the other with the failure of a more radical variety of feminism to advance the cause of suffragism has overbalanced historiography on the side of middle-class wives and mothers, for whom social activism and philanthropy were compatible and agreeable avocations, but not a livelihood.[12] Certainly women's missionary work, with its emphasis on love and concern for the less fortunate and the transmission of Western ideals of womanhood, was grounded in a nurturing or social form of feminism. But its exponents in the mission field did not inevitably interpret their own situation and career goals in the same mothering context as they did those of their constituents. Their experiences as women employed by a religious institution that circumscribed women's roles often presents striking evidence of their conflicting motives and their ambiguous perceptions of their work and aspirations.

Like other Canadian women moving into the public sphere as workers, professionals, or volunteers, wMs missionaries wisely capitalized on their allegedly superior feminine attributes to advance their individual and collective career goals. If necessary, the wMs exploited to the full the domestic imperative and women's moral superiority to reconcile public opinion to its feminist ambitions. But as career women seeking to establish their credibility and autonomy within a traditionally male structure, the WMS missionaries were often far removed from the ideal of Victorian or Edwardian womanhood that society and their church expected them to replicate. Rather than passively accept the demeaning tokenism so often accorded women in the public spotlight if their behaviour coincided with society's traditional ideas about women's sphere, the WMS's administrators and missionaries alike preferred to rely on their own professional credentials and attitudes as they struggled for an equality built on their competence to perform the same work as men. Joy Parr's taxonomy, which recognizes women whose "characterisations of self were not 'maternal,'"[13] seems in many ways applicable to the perspective of the WMS personnel.

None of these observations about the missionary as career woman is meant to imply that a majority of the WMS missionaries were not sincere, idealistic, and altruistic promoters of the Methodist Church's evangelical designs. But it seems clear that, as professional women, the missionaries distinguished between the often impossible objectives of the Methodist Church and their own needs and aspirations as working women, a situation that the society, with its congruous nature, was able to accommodate. For WMS missionaries there appears to have been little contradiction between serving God and their employers and pursuing their own ambitions as self-supporting, independent women. In the field the WMS personnel took their assignment to better the material and spiritual quality of women's lives seriously; they universally deplored the low social status of their female constituents in the Orient and the suffering of Canada's native and immigrant women. As part of their mandate they fought to expand women's prospects through education, medicine, and, ultimately, conversion to Christianity. Moreover, when their male colleagues tried to restrict them to the narrow boundaries of so-called women's work – for instance, in Japan in the 1890s – the women acted quickly to safeguard their territory. Against this backdrop of passionate concern for other women and for their own prerogatives, then, the WMS missionaries were feminists.

Undeniably, however, they were removed from the more strident, radicalized feminists who defied contemporary standards of behaviour. When the opportunity for marriage presented itself, many missionaries abandoned their developing careers to establish their own households. Love may have been the incentive behind these unions, but in the long run marriage probably still afforded women more security for the future than a career. Nor did the missionaries use their positions as respected women either within their local communities or nationally to promote Canadian women's rights. Hence, within the framework of North American women's history their concerns sometimes emerge as narrow and restricted, possibly even selfish in many respects. While some of the women whose volunteerism fuelled the WMS – Sarah Rowell Wright, for example – were impassioned advocates of universal suffrage,[14] in public at least the WMS personnel did not advocate suffrage either to advance their own interests or as a blanket corrective for women's problems. Nor did they actively lobby for a voice on their own Methodist Church councils. The WMS might have praised Lady Aberdeen as an embodiment of Tennyson's adage, "Kind hearts are more than coronets," but it rejected the overtures of her pet organization, the National Council of Women, which hoped to forge an alliance of all the major women's groups in Canada to further women's public interests, especially suffrage.[15]

In the final analysis the WMS missionaries, as neither the most rampant and politicized feminists nor merely passive apologists for woman's "proper sphere," seem to belong to the company of exceptional late nineteenth-century and early twentieth-century women who, to cite Martha Vicinus, "prided themselves on their independence both from the narrow community of domesticated women and from the new vocal feminists. They had made their way in the world by hard work, perseverance, and determination, and they were convinced that others could do as well, if only they would try."[16]

That missionary work emerged as one of a limited number of careers accessible to Canadian women in the late nineteenth century was precipitated by at least two interrelated circumstances: first, the strong impulse on the part of Canadian evangelical churches to join their British and especially their American counterparts, who by mid-century had launched aggressive missionary ventures both within their own countries and on foreign territory; and, as a corollary of this fervour, the drive by Canadian Protestant women to form their own denominational missionary societies. By the time the WMS was constituted in 1881, Methodists in Canada were already on their way to establishing a substantial reputation as conspicuous champions of the rapidly expanding missionary movement. This ardent enthusiasm for missions was logical behaviour for Canadian Methodists who traditionally traced the origins of their church to missionaries from Great Britain and the United States who had transported Methodism to Canada at the end of the eighteenth century. Writing in 1911, S.P. Rose praised the Methodist Church, "born of missionary zeal," for its continued adherence to "the ideal of John Wesley ... 'I look upon the world as my parish.'"[17]

Methodists in Canada first undertook their own missionary work in 1824, when one of the several branches of Methodism, the Methodist Episcopal Church, directed its attention to the conversion and moral reform of the native tribes of Upper Canada.[18] After the Methodist Episcopal churches of Canada and the United States officially separated in 1828 and William Case assumed the general superintendency of the Methodist Church in Canada, more explicit plans were drawn up for the evangelization and Christianization of the Indians. By 1838 missions to the Indians were operating as far west as Fort William, and the following year a station was opened in connection with the settlement at Norway House in present-day Manitoba.[19] Canadian Methodist missionary work among the Indians in British Columbia was started in 1859 by four ministers who were sent to attend to the spiritual needs of the miners in the Fraser Valley but ministered to the Salish in the vicinity as well. Over the next two decades Methodist missions were set up at Victoria, Nanaimo, and Chilliwack, where the Colqualeetza Institute, an industrial school, was opened in 1886.[20] In 1873 George McDougall established a base at Morleyville, Alberta, to minister to the Stoney tribe.[21]

Methodists of the day took pride in their missionary work among native peoples, not so much for the improvement it might bring to native people as for the benefit for white Canadians. In particular they believed "that the government of the native tribes of Canada has been rendered comparatively easy by reason of the loyalty to the crown which the Methodist missionary has taught the Indian to recognize as part of his obligation to the Christian faith."[22] This form of social control became even more evident in the 1890s, when the Methodist Church's emphasis in Indian missions shifted from a humanitarian concern about "ignorance, immorality and disease"[23] to the less altruistic expedient of domestic and industrial training for young native people so that they could be more easily assimilated by Canadian society.[24] By the turn of the century, however, missionary work among native peoples was declining, usurped by the government's increased responsibility for Indian affairs and eclipsed by the demands of the growing overseas missions in the Orient and Methodists' renewed interest in "nation-building, home-building and church-building" in the face of the Laurier government's aggressive immigration program.[25]

Methodists generally believed that immigrants who accepted evangelical Protestantism, with its emphasis on moral virtues, especially sobriety, would immediately be transformed into responsible Canadian citizens. If the dissolute Eastern Europeans entering Canada did not abandon their wicked ways in favour of a less boisterous and more abstemious existence, many Methodists feared, the social and religious citadel of their church might topple.[26] Left alone, a profligate foreign-born population could destroy "the hopes that patriotic Canadians legitimately cherish" for the nation's future.[27]

Establishing missions for immigrants also gave Methodists a chance to compensate for their inability to convert the Roman Catholic French-speaking population of Quebec. For many decades Methodist missionary work in the province of Quebec, first begun in 1856, was considered a fundamental part of Canadian Methodism's evangelical commission.[28] It was, moreover, a facet of Methodist evangelical activity where women's help had been welcomed. Much of the evangelization in the Montreal area was conducted under the auspices of volunteers and Bible women of the Ladies' French Missionary Society, founded in 1878.[29] In the long run the endeavour was a disappointment at best. On the eve of the First World War the Methodist Church readily admitted that its enterprise among the French in Quebec was "the least encouraging of all the fields of activity in which the missionary zeal of Canadian Methodists finds expression."[30]

By 1880 the Methodist Church of Canada had also established a foothold in overseas missionary work. In time, its missionary operations outside Canada's borders would attract far more attention, money, and personnel than home missions. But in 1873, when suggestions first surfaced that the Methodist Church should launch overseas missionary ventures, possibly in Japan, home missions and the future of the several branches of Canadian Methodism were still of paramount concern to many Methodists. Consequently, the initial proposal by the Wesleyan Methodists for a mission in Japan drew sharp criticism from some church members who alleged that "home missionaries were struggling along with very inadequate stipends; many Indian tribes were still unreached; the calls from new settlements in our own country were loud and frequent, and the vast French population of the Province of Quebec was scarcely touched by Methodist agencies." Alexander Sutherland, general secretary of the Missionary Society of the Methodist Church of Canada from 1878 until 1910, was not surprised that under the circumstances "some were inclined to say: 'We have here only five barley loaves and two small fishes, and what are these among so many?'"[31]

That such powerful opposition to entering the overseas missionary contest was eventually overcome was, in part, the result of the intercession of popular preachers, like Dr Morley Punshon, a captivating British Wesleyan minister whose persuasive endorsement of overseas missions inspired, among others, the first WMS overseas recruit, Martha Cartmell, to pursue a missionary career.[32] In 1873 Dr Davidson Macdonald and Rev. George Cochran were dispatched to Tokyo as the first overseas representatives of the General Board of Missions of the Methodist Church of Canada.[33] By 1880 a church building had been constructed in Tokyo to accommodate the forty-nine Japanese members of the congregation, and evangelistic work was extended to four centres.[34] In short, the support for Canadian Methodist missions was enthusiastic, the crucial initial contact with native people in Canada and the Japanese overseas had been established, and the basic administrative machinery was functioning by the time the WMS added its considerable energy and resources to the Methodist Church's missionary crusade.

Looking back in 1907, the official historian of the Methodist WMS believed that Canadian Methodist women had been "very conservative and slow" to emulate their American sisters in the Methodist Episcopal Church, who had organized a Woman's Foreign Missionary Society in 1869.[35] To excuse the delay the Canadian society explained that "no such baptism of blood," a reference to the American Civil War, had "prepared the women of Canadian Methodism for their work." Canadian Methodist women were motivated by "simply the call of duty, or, as we prefer to say, the call of the Master saying to us, 'Go, work to-day in my vineyard.'"[36] But even without such a mobilizing factor as the Civil War, no large-scale Canadian voluntary organization, religious or secular, and capable of galvanizing women's energies, was conceivable before Confederation. Until at least 1870 and perhaps later the predominantly rural and frontier nature of much of central Canada and the west, coupled with limited transportation facilities, narrowed women's organized public activities and recreation to philanthropy or entertainment within the local community or congregation. Nor were there enough educated and concerned women prepared to direct the complex administrative and financial affairs of a large association.[37]

By the last decades of the century, however, urbanization, industrialization, immigration, and better educational opportunities for women had increased the potential participants in women's voluntary societies and simultaneously created the very visible social and economic problems that women's philanthropic undertakings were designed to relieve. Moreover, in Canada as in Britain and the United

States the growth of industrial capitalism, quite apart from the historical debate over whether it initiated the separation of home and work-place, had intensified the sexual division of labour, furthering the evolution of "home-making as a woman's vocation" and holding up the domestic virtues of middle-class women as a model for emulation.[38] While it posited women's subordination in both the workplace and the home, the cult of domesticity, as Kathy Peiss among others has pointed out, also "made a moral and social duty out of the traditional tasks of housework and child care ... and open[ed] possibilities for female influence and assertion in and out of the home."[39] Like their contemporaries in the United States and Britain, middle-class Canadian women with leisure, learning, and financial resources embraced the "cult of domesticity as more than a domestic presence – as the development of a distinct and important social vocation"[40] that took them "out of the private sphere to reform the world."[41] In this way, Jacques Donzelot argues, middle-class women established a "new continuity" between their domestic duties and their social interests. In the process they "discovered a new missionary domain in which to operate; a new professional sphere was opened, consisting in the spread of the new welfare and educational norms."[42]

Much of women's preoccupation with social housekeeping and the preservation of traditional moral values derived from their spiritual convictions, their church-centred philanthropy and recreation, and from the messages that churches as male hierarchical establishments delivered, through the clergy and religious publications, about appropriate conduct for the growing female membership. Religion gave women "not only a clear definition of their expected sphere but also a very positive, even exalted, role within it."[43] In Canada, then, as in the United States, during the nineteenth century the church became the primary agency whereby women seeking some form of public involvement, social diversion, or domestic liberation could unleash their energies with a minimum of public protest.[44] In particular evangelical Protestantism, which "supported the notion that women were morally superior to men and thus encouraged women to value themselves and their own contribution to social life," was, argues Nancy Cott, one of the antecedents of the late nineteenth-century women's movement.[45]

Although some local Protestant women's church groups – for example, the Halifax Wesleyan Female Benevolent Society, founded in 1816 to help indigent women[46] – were organized in the Maritimes and the Canadas in the early nineteenth century, women's religious and secular associations proliferated in the 1870s and 1880s in the Maritimes and Ontario. These regions had been the sites of impassioned revivals in the 1850s and 1860s, conducted under the auspices of the world-renowned preachers James Caughey and Phoebe Palmer, who encouraged reflection on holiness and sanctification as the route to personal salvation.[47] Canadian Methodist women participated fully in revivals; some, like Eliza Bentley, a prominent Ontario laywoman who published her spiritual diary, identified with Phoebe Palmer as "a kindred spirit."[48] In the 1880s the lingering fires of evangelicalism were reignited by the acclaimed American revivalists of the day, Moody and Sankey, and the Canadian team of Crossley and Hunter. The egalitarian revivalist mood, which sanctioned women's right to participate in religious activities and philanthropic enterprises,[49] extended the opportunities for female lay leadership[50] and galvanized North American women's burgeoning commitment to religious and secular philanthropy. In sum, then, in Canada as in the United States it seems, as Caroline Gifford contends, appropriate "to stop viewing [women's voluntary associations] from the perspective of feminist scholarship exclusively and treat them also as what they were: expressions of strong religious belief and commitment."[51]

Baptist women in the Maritimes were the first Canadian laywomen to inaugurate a separate denominational woman's organization to promote missionary ventures and fund-raising. Prodded by Hannah Norris, whom the society later supported as a missionary to Burma, a local missionary group in Canso, Nova Scotia, in 1870 became the nucleus of the United Baptist Woman's Missionary Union. In 1876 the Woman's Baptist Foreign Missionary Society of Eastern Ontario and Quebec was organized, followed in 1896 by the Woman's Baptist Home Missionary Society of Eastern Ontario and Quebec. Branches were also formed in Manitoba and British Columbia, but because of the higher proportion of Baptists in the Maritimes, most Baptist foreign missionary work, in particular its extensive operations in India, continued to be administered from the Maritimes.[52] The Maritimes also spawned the first organized missionary activity among Presbyterian women. In 1876, a year after Presbyterian church union, the Woman's Foreign Missionary Society of the Presbyterian Church in Canada (Eastern Division) was constituted in Halifax; a western branch was soon situated in Toronto. Shortly after, Presbyterian women began to sponsor women missionaries in central India.[53] The Woman's Christian Temperance Union, the Young Women's Christian Association, the Dominion Order of the King's Daughters, and the Girls' Friendly Society, an Anglican organization similar to the YWCA, were also established in Canada during these decades as evidence of Canadian women's commitment to current social and moral issues.[54]

As class leaders, Sunday school teachers, and evangelists and even preachers, Methodist women had always actively upheld the church's spiritual convictions. Now they became vigorous champions of women's associations, especially church missionary societies.[55] In 1876 the Methodist Episcopal Church in Canada was the first branch of Canadian Methodism to organize a separate women's missionary society. Five years later the larger Methodist Church of Canada, formed in 1874 by the union of the New Connexion and the Wesleyan Methodists, also constituted a women's missionary society. These two missionary organizations operated without reference to one another until the unification of Canadian Methodism in 1884, when they amalgamated as the Woman's Missionary Society of the Methodist Church of Canada.

Because there is so little documentation of the circumstances prompting the creation of the Methodist Episcopal WMS, one is left to speculate that its formation in 1876 was an attempt to compete with the rival Baptist and Presbyterian churches. What records exist indicate that in the summer of 1876 the Woman's Missionary Society of the Methodist Episcopal Church in Canada was officially inaugurated in Belleville, Ontario, the heart of Episcopal Methodism in Canada, under the supervision of Mrs Levi Massey as president and Mrs Albert Carman as first vice-president. Annual membership dues were one dollar, life membership twenty dollars, with an additional prestigious category, honourary membership, of one hundred dollars. A board of managers, comprising the president, vice-presidents, secretaries, and five members-at-large, was to meet annually.[56]

On paper at least the Canadian MEWMS, which agreed "to work in harmony with and under the supervision of the authorities of the Missionary Society of the Methodist Episcopal Church and be subject to their approval in the employment and remuneration of missionaries, the designation of their fields of labour, and in the general plans and designs of the work,"[57] lacked the autonomy of its American Methodist Episcopal counterpart, which only formally applied to its church's general board to endorse the appointment of missionaries.[58] In practice the women's freedom to make self-governing decisions about their work and the direction of their missionaries never became a contentious issue because the society failed to realize its objectives of sending women into the field. In its first year the society organized an auxiliary for the St Lawrence campground (site of Methodist "camp meetings") and had designated $100 for the support of the Methodist Church in the northwest.[59] Three years later most of its receipts of $399 continued to be allocated to the church in the northwest.[60] But from June 1882 to June 1883, with the extinction of the

Methodist Episcopal church as the result of the final union of Methodism in Canada, the society's reported income was only $123.20.[61] When the Methodist Episcopal Church joined with the larger Methodist Church of Canada on 1 July 1884, the MEWMS merged with the thriving WMS of the Canadian Methodist Church without ever having placed a missionary in the field.[62]

By comparison, from its founding in 1881 the Canadian Methodist WMS was a more immediate success, perhaps because of the widespread, if not universal, acceptance by its members of women's value as missionary activists and because of a larger urban population base on which to draw for support. The first official proposal for a Canadian Methodist Woman's Missionary Society materialized at the General Conference of 1878 at the urging of the male agents of the General Board of Missions, who requested the services of women to assist with the missionary work in Japan, where Oriental social taboos and religious practices inhibited Western men from mixing with the female population, especially the upper classes. The General Board was hard pressed to finance this project on its own. Consequently, while a motion was tabled by the conference recommending "that a Ladies' Missionary Society devoting itself exclusively to the work of Christian education [of] our Indians, French and Foreign Missions, would be a valuable *auxiliary* to our present missionary organization" because it was "burdened with debt," the General Board did not "consider it expedient at the present time to initiate a movement that might possibly involve responsibilities which we would be unable to meet."[63] At the time the mere hint of a ladies' missionary association met hostility from many male delegates whose concern over the financial stability of the General Board of Missions led them to question the wisdom of creating a potential rival for Methodists' money. The Methodist hierarchy 's dubious response to women's missionary ventures heralded the beginning of a perennial contest for financial support and patronage that became a source of jealousy and sometimes outright animosity throughout the early history of the relationship of the two mission societies.

Defenders of a separate women's society, Rev. L.N. Beaudry for one, pointed out that in the United States women's missionary societies had stimulated, not impeded, missionary delirium and financial support. John Williams, who became general superintendent of the Methodist Church of Canada in 1883[64] and whose daughter Elizabeth Williams Ross was WMS president from 1897 until 1920, saw little reason for a women's society to hinder the effectiveness of the General Board of Missions, especially when the General Board's program to convert French Canadians to Methodism, already severely curtailed by a shortage of workers and money, badly needed bailing out.[65] When no satisfactory decision about the immediate establishment of a women's society was reached, the matter was referred to a committee with a mandate to launch such an association within the next four years "if, in their judgment, the financial condition of the General Society should warrant it."[66]

There was apparently no further action on the issue until June 1880 at the annual conference in Hamilton, where Alexander Sutherland met with interested Hamilton women, the middle-class wives, daughters, and widows of ministers, doctors, lawyers, and merchants, to discuss the best strategy for organizing the woman's society. As mission secretary Sutherland himself was receptive to a separate women's society and generally remained supportive and sympathetic to the society's objectives throughout his tenure. The WMS later acknowledged that without his "help and encouragement, in the beginning, the Woman's Missionary Society would have found it difficult to overcome the prejudice and indifference of the times, if, indeed, it could have lived at all."[67] A committee of ten women was appointed, first to study the operations of various American women's missionary societies, and then to draft a constitution and by-laws. All sincerely interested women from Hamilton Methodist churches were summoned to a meeting on 23 June, when the first WMS auxiliary was formed.[68] Over the next months numerous gatherings, which consisted of an hour of prayers for missions, followed by a business session, then tea, were held in private homes, at the Wesleyan Ladies' College, and at Centenary, King Street and Wesley churches in Hamilton.[69] During the first year, through voluntary contributions alone the women raised two hundred dollars, which was sent to Thomas Crosby for his work in northern British Columbia.[70]

It has been possible, using census material and local records, to identify 73 of the 101 members of the first Hamilton WMS auxiliary. In general they seem to conform to the historical models of middle-class "club women" with the leisure and financial resources to sustain their extra-domestic pursuits. Their ages ranged from 25 to 67, and the average age was 43. In short, these women tended to be married middle-aged matrons, although the auxiliary also included at least 6 widows and 11 single women, several of whom were teachers. While most married women still had children living at home, the size and age of their families suggest that they were no longer responsible for the care of numerous young children, all the more so because more than half employed servants, leaving them relatively free from onerous domestic obligations. Their husbands' occupations represent a wide range of careers, but most of Hamilton's founding WMS members were married to professionals or business men. More than 80 per cent (50 of 58) of the heads of household fall into the two uppermost socio-economic ranks identified by Michael Katz in his extensive analysis of Hamilton at mid-century, which seems just as applicable for the 1880s.[71] The wives of 4 physicians, 2 dentists, 4 clergymen, 4 contractors, 9 manufacturers, 9 merchants, 3 commercial travellers, 2 shopkeepers, a fire-insurance inspector, a librarian, and a surveyor constituted a majority of the group. But among them were to be found as well the wives of a shoemaker, a tailor, a fireman, a printer, and a brickmaker.

Most importantly, the original auxiliary's roster was reinforced by the names of the wives of many distinguished Hamilton business-men who were themselves prominent Methodist laymen. Eliza Fear-man was the wife of Fred, a merchant and meat packer, member of the Board of Education, the Hamilton Association, the library board, and a staunch Methodist. Nancy Gurney was married to Edward, owner of the Gurney Stove Foundry, a director of the Bank of Ham-ilton, board member of many companies, and a member of Centenary Methodist Church. Emily Lister was the wife of Joseph Lister, a prom-inent businessman, member of the Board of Water Commissioners, a public-school trustee, and a member of Centenary Methodist, while Emily Moore's husband, Lyman, owned the Hamilton Glass Works and the Times Printing Company. Mary Moore's husband, Dennis, was one of the richest men in the city,[72] an iron founder and tinware manufacturer, the director of several banks, and a man with a heavy investment in Hamilton real estate, while Sophia Sanford's husband, William, owner of the Hamilton wholesale clothing firm Sanford, McInnes and Company and renowned as "the Wool King of Canada," was a personal friend of Sir John A. Macdonald.[73] These particular women were privileged members of some of Hamilton's wealthiest families; their affluence translated into the ability to pursue social and religious activism as they chose. It is interesting to note that in the Centenary Methodist church parlour, at least, working-class women, including the WMS members' own domestic help, did not mingle with Hamilton's elite.

Under the guidance of its prosperous mentors the Hamilton exper-iment proved to be a success. In January 1881, in the introductory issue of the Methodist Church's publication the *Missionary Outlook*, Alexander Sutherland took the opportunity to point out that although it would be "premature" to try to form "a General Connexional Soci-ety" at that time, the Hamilton auxiliary's experience indicated that more branches should be organized immediately. Making very evi-dent his views on the sexual division of labour and power within the Methodist Church, Sutherland suggested specific areas for the women's attention – the funding and staffing of the Crosby Home in northern British Columbia and the McDougall orphanage in southern Alberta. If Methodist women assumed responsibility for these teaching and custodial jobs without impinging on the exclusive rights of the General Board missionaries as ordained clergy to preach and receive members into the church, the General Missionary Society would be relieved "of part of its burdens, leaving it free to employ all its energies and resources in fully evangelistic work." Because of the persistent fear that a second missionary society would siphon off funds normally accruing to the General Board, he advised the women's auxiliaries to refrain from initiating any new ventures that might encroach on the General Board's territory. Instead, money that the women raised should be contributed to projects already directed by the General Board.[74] Sutherland's caveat did not escape the notice of the members of the Hamilton Centenary Church auxiliary, who were alert to the resistance in some Methodist quarters to the women's cause.

From the outset the WMS was sensitive to the possibility that, as a women's association within a strongly patriarchal structure that denied women access to decision making and to ordination, their society would be assigned a secondary role in executing the missionary work of the Methodist Church. At the first WMS annual meeting the newly elected president, Sarah Burns, wife of the principal of Hamilton Ladies' College and a founding member of the society, urged Methodist women not to be restrained "because of the ultra conservatism of some touching woman's sphere. As she was the first at the sepulchre to announce the risen Lord, so may she be first to announce to many a heart in our day 'he receiveth sinners still.'"[75] If Burns was typical of the other board members, then some at least of the WMS's founders foresaw a more aggressive role for women as proselytizers within a missionary society designed to finance and supervise women missionaries and their work in the mission field, not to underwrite projects planned and executed by men.

Shortly after Sutherland's statement appeared, the Centenary auxiliary examined the "most vital" question of the allocation of the money they might raise, and specifically whether WMS funds should be channelled into existing missionary projects, by implication under the supervision of the General Board.[76] The women were prepared to defer to the experience of the General Board in some missionary business, but they insisted on their fiscal autonomy. Was it not better, they asked, to "strike out on an entirely new line? Assume all the responsibilities ourselves, and take the burden upon our own hearts and heads, which will force us to our knees, to seek the wisdom from above which is profitable to direct, and the zeal which will surely accompany knowledge and love?"[77] As far as the women were concerned, budgetary control and accountability were the keys to their freedom as an organization. Their tenacity in this regard not only suggests a parallel with the domestic sphere in terms of the connection between money and power in their own homes; it suggests as well that they were shrewd observers of their husbands' business affairs. Whatever the motivating forces behind the founders' determination, when the provisional constitution for a nationwide WMS was delivered in April 1881, the relationship between the new organization and the existing General Board missionary society was only loosely delineated, allowing ample latitude for future dissension or co-operation between the Church's two missionary societies.[78]

As defined in the constitution, the objectives of the WMS encompassed both the evangelizing and civilizing functions of missionary work: "to engage the effort of Christian women in the evangelization of heathen women and children; to aid in sustaining female Missionaries and Teachers or other special labourers, in foreign or home fields, and to raise funds for this work."[79] There was no delineation of financial arrangements and specifically no mention of relinquishing fiscal control. However, in a statement almost indistinguishable from the words of the MEWMS's constitution, the women pledged "to work in harmony with the authorities of the Mission Society ... and be subject to their approval in the employment and remuneration of Missionaries or other Agents, the designation of fields of labour, and in the general plans and designs of the work."[80] As soon as the WMS was on a firm footing, that clause was conveniently ignored.

A board of managers, comprising the elected officers, was given the final authority to review the society's work, to appoint and assign missionaries, and to approve the allocation of funds.[81] It became the power behind the WMS. Three Hamilton women held the highest posts: Sarah Burns was elected president, Mrs F.W. (Lizzie) Watkins Jr treasurer, and Elizabeth Strachan corresponding secretary. Strachan, who served in that capacity from 1881 until her retirement in 1924, assumed wide-ranging responsibility to make ad hoc decisions about the problems missionaries encountered in the field, which usually demanded an immediate solution. She became a respected friend and adviser to the missionaries, and the house she shared with her cousins Elizabeth Ross and Martha Cartmell was designated the "House of Peace,"[82] a haven where exhausted missionaries often spent the first weeks of their furlough.

As soon as the provisional constitution was endorsed, the invitation went out for a general meeting to approve a national society. On 8 November 1881, in a dignified ceremony held at the Hamilton Ladies' College, the WMS was formally brought into existence. Its members accepted a special mandate to support Methodist French missions in Montreal, the Crosby girls' home at Port Simpson, the McDougall orphanage in Morley, Alberta, and to send a woman missionary to Japan. During the evening more than one thousand dollars was raised through the sale of twenty-five-dollar life memberships purchased by prominent Toronto and Hamilton businessmen and clergy for their wives.[83] The immediate response of other Canadian Methodist women to the new society as a way to demonstrate concern for less fortunate women overseas and in Canada was not quite as enthusiastic as that of Hamiltonians. As Harriet Platt, long-time president of the Bay of Quinte branch and a dedicated member of the Board of Managers,[84] observed twenty years later, the excitement of "that memorable meeting in Hamilton" did not "spread like wildfire."[85] "Busy women were not eager to engage in the work. Indeed, the way was, and still is, barred in many places by the prejudice of Christian women – women who look upon the work as optional, something they can take up or let alone. Many of us who now feel *woe is me if I neglect this work* were once conscientiously opposed. We thought there was work enough at home – that one missionary society was enough, and another would only detract from its funds; that the new movement was only a fad and would soon die a natural death. We sinned through ignorance, and we have been converted."[86]

The *Christian Guardian* and the *Missionary Outlook* became active publicists on the society's behalf, reporting the formation of new branches and urging women in other congregations to follow this example. The society's executive had confidently assumed that all Methodist women would support the new venture because women were "called by God to this work."[87]. When it became patently clear that this was not the case, the WMS assiduously promoted the premise, which was the very foundation of maternal feminism, that there were special duties that only women could carry out on behalf of women in non-Christian societies, where "the voice of man can never be heard behind their prison bars."[88] An early WMS pamphlet, *Ten Reasons Why I Should Belong to the Woman's Missionary Society*, explicitly identified the realization of the ideals of womanhood with the advent of the millennium. As women and mothers whose virtues "coincided with the values of the millennium,"[89] it was the responsibility of Canadian Methodist women to recognize that "upon the condition and character of the mothers depends the condition and character of a nation, for in the hands of the mother is the moulding and developing of the character of the children ... to reach and save the mothers is to reach and save the children; and to save the children is to claim the nation for Jesus our King."[90]

Membership brought other benefits, especially for the Methodist Church itself, because the WMS was responsible for "leading the women into a larger experience of the efficacy of prayer and the faithfulness of God, bringing their lives into more harmony with the Divine will, and in sympathy with the compassionate Jesus."[91] Appeals like this, framed as they were in the rhetoric of maternal feminism, Christian imperialism, and Methodist piety, may have helped to attract women whose husbands and families needed reassurance that membership in a public organization would not threaten their own family units or, on a larger scale, Canadian social stability, and would in fact strengthen the status quo. Moreover, these same arguments may have been effective in convincing the Methodist hierarchy that a women's organization backed by a growing female church membership would not undermine its authority, and indeed was indispensable to the Church's prosperity at a time when the Protestant church generally seemed imperilled by an increasingly urban, industrialized, and secular society.[92]

This is not to suggest that the middle-class wives and mothers with the requisite time and money who comprised the membership of the WMS seriously questioned their exclusive commission to extend women's special nurturing and caretaking virtues beyond their own insulated households. But from the outset some of the decisions made by the Board of Managers and the behaviour of the missionaries in the field in defence of their society seemed at odds with "the self-denying exertions"[93] that social housekeeping demanded and more consistent with the ambitions of women determined to broaden the parameters the Church hierarchy imposed on them and to move beyond the "narrow way in which women must be content to work."[94] Perhaps this was because the women agreed with Sarah (Mrs James) Gooderham, who in her aggressive 1884 presidential address cautioned them never to take their role in the missionary movement for granted. "Woman has not ... won her way to her present position of usefulness, in connection with the great work of the world's evangelization, without a pretty severe conflict," she pointed out. "The prejudices against women engaging in evangelistic labors in some of the churches have been so strong that they have raised a formidable barrier in the way of our sisters in these denominations."[95]

The WMS steadily gained momentum. Within a year its twenty auxiliaries – in small Ontario towns such as Uxbridge, Goderich, Paris, Simcoe, and Brantford, but also in large urban centres such as Toronto, Ottawa, Montreal, and Halifax – had nine hundred members who raised almost three thousand dollars.[96] In 1881 the Ladies' French Missionary Society of Montreal, founded in 1878 to work among the French-speaking Roman Catholic population of Québec, merged with the WMS.[97] Four years later, at the annual meeting of the WMS held in Kingston in June 1885, the still small and foundering Methodist Episcopal WMS officially amalgamated with the larger and more visible society.[98] A former administrator of the MEWMS, Mrs Albert Carman, assumed the vice-presidency of the consolidated organization, but there were no significant constitutional changes.[99] On its twenty-fifth anniversary in 1906 the WMS included 946 auxiliaries across Canada with a membership of 26,741, and 545 mission circles and bands comprised of 16,000 children and young people.[100] The even growth continued: in 1916 the society recorded a membership of 44,315 in 1,246 auxiliaries, 616 bands with 20,443 members, 405 circles with 10,616 members, and a total income of $168,916.44.[101] At church union in 1925 the organization had expanded to 61,049 members; its financial assets totalled $687,441.32, while its real estate holdings in the Orient and in Canada were evaluated at nearly $500,000.[102]

Over its forty-five year history the Methodist WMS raised a total of $6,557,333.49.[103] The WMS remained watchful of its financial position and its investments. The society never borrowed money and only expanded its operations when the money to do so was in the bank. Within a year of its inception, when the society had enough funds accumulated to launch its rather ambitious plans, the board hired two women to represent the society in the mission field, which was, after all, the raison d'être of any missionary society. By the end of 1882 Kezia Hendrie and Martha Cartmell were at work as the first home and overseas WMS missionaries.

As single women who had chosen a potentially risky career, Cartmell, Hendrie, and their contemporaries faced a degree of resistance even within their own church, partly because they represented a separate women's society that threatened the existing mission body but also because of traditional attitudes about suitable work for women. Still, by 1881 some, at least, of the earlier prejudice and animosity surrounding the value of single women missionaries had been overcome by Canadian Methodists' increasing familiarity, through the pages of the *Christian Guardian*, with accounts of the exploits and the achievements of women missionaries of other denominations.[104] But this endorsement of women as religious emissaries in their own right had been achieved only very gradually in the face of solid opposition to the infiltration of a traditionally male profession by single women. In the United States in the pre–Civil War period, while widows occasionally were hired by some evangelical missionary societies, single women usually could become missionaries only through marriage to a missionary. To facilitate the deployment of able women whose services might otherwise have been lost, churches sometimes assisted by arranging marriages between single women and suitable male missionaries,[105] but once married the women had no personal status as missionaries. Their only credentials were as missionary wives.[106] Mission boards soon realized, to their displeasure, that especially after children were born, many married women no longer had the time or the inclination to continue the work among women that had been designated their special preserve.[107] Reluctantly, then, the men in the field were forced to concede that single women might have a place in reaching women, especially in Eastern cultures that dictated sexual segregation.

The public continued to resist sending single women deliberately into potentially dangerous situations until the American Civil War, when women's value and ability as nurses under fire was proven. After the Civil War the growth of separate women's missionary societies as sponsors of single women who were attracted to missionary work as a permanent occupation finally empowered American women to serve on a more equal, if separate, footing in the mission field.[108] By the last third of the nineteenth century, "woman's work for woman," which could now be conducted in an almost exclusively female atmosphere, was evolving as a suitable career for well-bred single women. The approbation for women's missionary work as well as the apparent relevance of missionary societies and their objectives to late Victorian women's experience is evident in the proliferation of organizations promoting some aspect of women's missionary activity. Whereas in 1860 there were five large and five small women's missionary boards, by 1900 more than forty boards employing only single women as their agents were functioning in the United States alone.[109] As Jane Hunter points out, by the end of the nineteenth century the initial suspicions about the social impropriety of women's missionary work and the predictions of fiscal catastrophe had become "a beleaguered effort by men of the general boards to retain minority control over a majority of female workers."[110]

The experience of the Canadian Methodist wms and its missionaries supplies an especially fitting illustration of this metamorphosis.

Social, economic, and religious factors may have prevented Canadian Methodist women from joining the missionary crusade until, as one prominent Methodist clergyman put it, the propriety of women missionaries was "no longer a doubtful question."[111] But the WMS's administrative acumen and its missionaries' reputations as messengers of the gospel and champions of improved social conditions for women in other cultures were quickly confirmed, and, like their American counterparts, these Canadian women realized "a new role and status ... within one of the most important movements of organized religion."[112] If in the long run the missionary movement did not fulfil its ambitious commission, for a significant group of Canadian women entering the labour force between 1881 and 1925 the opportunity to become a WMS missionary presented an exciting and potentially rewarding alternative to the Scylla of marriage and the Charybdis of solitary spinsterhood.

Elizabeth Strachan, WMS corresponding-secretary, and Elizabeth Ross, WMS president, (middle row, wearing hats), with WMS missionaries and Japanese Christian women, Kofu, 1905. Back row, left to right, Elizabeth Hart, Elizabeth Alcorn, Augusta Preston, Lottie Deacon. The woman at the end of the middle row can only be identified as Mrs Borden.

Evening meal, mission home, Tokyo, 1910. Standing at left, Isabella Blackmore; seated left to right, Jessie Howie, Kate Morgan, Ila Day, Edith Campbell, Isabella Hargrave, Alice Timberlake, Margaret Keagey, Olive Markland, Mary Ann Chapman.

WMS and General Board missionaries at leisure, Tokyo, Japan, ca. 1890.

Girls setting tables, French Methodist Institute, Montreal, Quebec, ca. 1910.

Sewing class for Italian women, Toronto, ca. 1920.

Alice Belton and her sewing class, Kanazawa Industrial School, Kanazawa, Japan, 1899.

Sara Brackbill, founder of the first WMS girls' school in Szechwan. Photo taken 1907.

Kate Morgan (left) and Ida Snyder (right) with residents of the Chinese Rescue Home, Victoria, B.C., ca. 1910.

Ready for church, Crosby Girls' Home, Port Simpson, B.C., 1910.

Martha Cartmell, first WMS overseas missionary, at the time of her departure for Tokyo, 1882.

Missionaries shipwrecked on the Yangtze River, ca. 1895.

WMS missionaries' residence, Chengtu, Szechwan.

Dr Florence O'Donnell and her chair bearers, Szechwan, ca. 1905.

Dr Retta Gifford Kilborn (back row, second from right) and members of the Anti-foot-binding Society, Chengtu, ca. 1895.

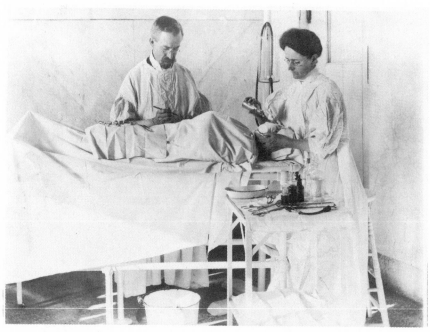

Drs Omar and Retta (Gifford) Kilborn at work, Jungshien Hospital, Szechwan, ca. 1900.

Eliza Spencer Large and her daughter about 1890, Tokyo.

CHAPTER TWO

Here I am, send me

The youngest child of earnest Christian parents, my religious training received careful attention; and my interest in, and sympathy for, those who had heard not "the tidings of great joy" was early awakened – Even while I was myself a stranger to the Saviour's pardoning love. After spending three years at the Normal School Truro, I began teaching, at the age of 17 years. It was while teaching in Oxford village [Nova Scotia] that my concern for my spiritual state became very great … the memory of the many times that I had rejected Christ's offered mercy, filled me with remorse and despair.

This continued for about five months, my distress and hopelessness grow-ing deeper each week. But at length the promise, "Seek & ye shall find" was fulfilled to me … Soon after I was received into the Meth. Church by the Rev. A.D. Morton. I was then 19 years of age. Almost immediately the longing to carry the "message of Peace" to those who knew it not, sprang up in my heart. Doubting, however, my ability for mission work, I gave up all thought of personally entering upon it, as duties at home lay in my path. Since then my time has been divided between teaching and housework at my father's home. So I have had about two years experience in farm housekeeping. I am now 25 years of age – hold grade C license … [T]he conviction that help such as I could give was needed in the Lord's Vineyards abroad, became so strong that I could no longer put it aside … All I have and am I wish to belong to Christ. Gladly will I work in His service in any way or anywhere, if I may but know I am doing His will. As to how soon I can go, I feel I am given but one answer. When the Master has need of me.[1]

This pious submission to the WMS's Nova Scotia branch was Isabella Blackmore's first formal step along the path to a missionary career. It is an appropriate introduction to the following examination of the backgrounds, education, and professional training and piety of the more than three hundred Canadian women who served the WMS as its representatives from 1881 to 1925 because, in its distinctive fashion, Blackmore's letter embodies so many of the social and educational attributes and the religiosity that characterized wms recruits. Her brief chronicle is equally illuminating because it underscores the personal nature of the women's impulses, the obstacles that often delayed their careers, their readiness to sacrifice for their religious convictions, and their ultimate expectation of personal gratification and self-realization in return for a life of service to Christ and his teachings.

It is not surprising that before they met as missionaries the recruits had already shared many experiences. Whether or not the applicants were aware of the nature of the wms hiring policies, the Board of Managers, which acted as a screening committee, held fixed notions about the requisite qualities for success as a wms representative. The board may have advertised in the *Christian Guardian* and the *Missionary Outlook* for its personnel, but a broad public solicitation did not necessarily mean that any woman drawn by the excitement and fascination of the mission field was acceptable to the society's executive. To encourage the qualified and deter dilettantes, the society drafted explicit guidelines concerning age, marital status, education, work experience, moral character, and spiritual commitment. These regulations were published in the society's annual reports, where women contemplating a missionary vocation could scrutinize them.

On paper at least the question of Christian duty received priority. A prospective candidate "must believe herself divinely called to the work ... and assert her belief that she is activated only by a desire to work in accordance with God's will."[2] The board requested verification from a minister of her "Christian usefulness."[3] After 1889 the society probed the nature of a recruit's faith more intensely, inquiring whether she was "inwardly moved by the Holy Ghost to take upon [her] the work of a foreign missionary?" and if she had "an experimental knowledge of salvation through the atonement of Jesus Christ our Lord."[4] A "yes," accompanied perhaps by the dates and circumstances of the conversion, seems to have satisfied the board that candidates had indeed been saved through divine assurance and that, as fervent Methodists, "their sins had been forgiven, [that] they had been accepted by God and could by their own efforts ... find ultimate sanctification, that is, Salvation."[5] The emphasis the society itself placed on its employees' adherence to traditional Methodist doctrine – in particular to the ideal of Christian perfection – tends to corroborate recent historians' arguments about the strong hold that Wesley's original teaching retained on Canadian Methodist theology throughout the nineteenth century.[6]

By the turn of the century the Board of Managers acknowledged that a good education, especially a university degree, professional training, and some experience in the work-force, preferably as a teacher, nurse, or doctor, were also indispensible requirements that could determine the success of the individual's career and the WMS enterprise. The board was explicitly interested in candidates' proficiency in languages and whether they "readily acquire[d] the same." "Financial and executive ability," the "power of adaptation to circumstances," and a record of good health and physical fitness also ranked high on the list of tangible attributes for a model missionary.[7]

From the outset the Board of Managers was forthright about the gravity of the decision to become a missionary, warning applicants that the WMS demanded an absolute commitment to a career defined as "the service of [their] effective years." At the very least recruits were obliged to "give ... five of these years of continuous service, as a single woman, to the work of the Woman's Missionary Society, unless prevented by ill health."[8] Failure to discharge the terms of the contract or resignation for reasons other than illness before the first term was served exacted a stiff penalty: the repayment to the society of a portion of the costs of the outfit and travel, which decreased with the number of years of employment. If the woman had served less than a year, the cost of buying her way out might, for a missionary in the Orient, equal a year's wages.

To realize the maximum years of service and to guarantee some measure of maturity among its personnel, the board also established age limits for recruits. Initially the society accepted only women aged 22 to 30, although the board made exceptions for women over 30 with "a thorough, intellectual training, with a facility in languages, and a remarkable ability for Christian work."[9] The rules were waived quite often, especially for home missionaries; more than 25 per cent of recruits were over 30 when they were hired. The lower age limit was relinquished less frequently; just 2 per cent of the women were under 22. After 1895, in response to the tension and quarrelling in the Japan Mission, which suggested to the Board of Managers that some women had been too young to handle their responsibilities, the minimum age was raised to 25.[10] As a result of these stipulations, the average age of all WMS missionary recruits was 29; overseas candidates tended to be about a year younger, and home missionaries somewhat older, on average 31.4 years of age. In the long run, immaturity was not a crucial problem in the mission field. For WMS candidates, who were several years beyond the average age at marriage of Canadian women during the late nineteenth and early twentieth centuries, the bloom was well off the rose, with middle age and confirmed spinsterhood looming as indisputable facts of their lives and the prospects for marriage and a family rapidly diminishing.[11]

From time to time the board made changes in its hiring procedure, but the basic criteria formulated in the 1880s governed the society's employment policies for most of its forty-five-year history. In short, the Board of Managers solicited mature, clever, tenacious, and devout women who could, as Elizabeth Strachan familiarly phrased it, introduce the women of the world to the "Friend that sticketh closer than a brother" and "purify the home fountain, from which it is hoped will flow clearer and sweeter streams into social, commercial and religious life."[12] The collective demographic, social, educational, and religious background that can be reconstructed for the WMS personnel substantiates the WMS's ability to attract, in the flesh, the archetypal missionary candidate.

In the first instance, the women's geographic origins provided the group with a common identity as central Canadians. Though it may not have been their place of birth, almost 60 per cent of the recruits were residents of Ontario when they joined the WMS. Another 21 per cent had been raised in the Maritimes, including Newfoundland, which, though not yet politically a part of Canada, fell, like Bermuda, under the jurisdiction of the Methodist Church of Canada. Half the Maritimers were from Nova Scotia alone. Of the others, 4 per cent had homes in Manitoba, 5 per cent came from Alberta and Saskatchewan combined, and 4 per cent were from British Columbia. Fewer than 4 per cent – that is, twelve women – recorded Quebec as their home province; seven of them were hired specifically to staff the WMS missions in the Montreal area. Finally, seven women (2 per cent) – three daughters of missionaries in Asia – were from outside Canada.

It was perhaps inevitable, given Canada's demographic characteristics, and especially the distribution of its Protestant population, that Ontario would provide the largest number of WMS recruits. In 1911, for example, 60 per cent of Canada's Methodists lived in Ontario.[13] But it is also important to remember that Ontario, in the period 1890–1914, was the nursery of muscular Methodism, which among other things stressed the Church's evangelical mission to the non-Christian world.[14] By 1910 more than three-quarters of the WMS membership and two-thirds of the society's revenue came from the Ontario and Montreal conferences.[15] Reasons other than demography, therefore, may account for the number of Ontarians among the WMS missionaries.

It is noteworthy that Nova Scotian women are somewhat over-represented in the group, a tendency that shows up most clearly in the structure of the Japan Mission, where 15 per cent of the missionaries were former Nova Scotians. The high proportion of women from Nova Scotia can be partly attributed to consanguinity (there were three sets of sisters and several cousins among the Nova Scotians). It also seems that professional career opportunities for single women in Nova Scotia were more limited than in other provinces, largely because of a surplus of women, especially in Halifax. The "anomalous position the superfluous woman holds" provoked one Halifax female physician, who spoke for other unmarried women in the city who could not find "a place or vocation ... in all this great, beautiful, bountiful universe,"[16] to bring the matter to the attention of a local paper. The tendency of late-Victorian Nova Scotian women to marry late, have smaller families, and to enter the work-force all became matters of public debate.[17] It is also important to recognize the strong historical roots of Methodism in eastern Canada, the heritage of women's Christian voluntary pursuits, and the extensive tradition of good education for women, frequently obtained at denominational schools and colleges, which together may have stimulated Maritime women's curiosity about a missionary career and perhaps gave them an edge in the hiring process.

Just as Ontario-bred women were in the majority, so were women raised in rural areas, villages, and small towns. Only one in four WMS missionaries had an urban upbringing in one of Canada's metropolitan centres, Toronto, Hamilton, Ottawa, Montreal, Halifax, Vancouver, or, after 1900, Edmonton, Calgary, or Regina. Given the increasingly urban character of Canadian Methodism by the closing decades of the nineteenth century,[18] it seems odd that so few WMS missionaries were enlisted from the growing urban middle class. Yet in her study of American women missionaries in China at the turn of the century, Jane Hunter found that only three of twenty (15 per cent) American Board women missionaries from Ohio had been born in urban areas of the state. To explain the dearth of urban dwellers, Hunter suggests that the freedom permitted to rural women as children and their "pioneer spirit" accounts for the appeal of missionary work, with its adventurous undertones.[19] In the case of the WMS, it seems as likely that the high percentage of rural and small-town women reflected a lack of career opportunities outside the home for ambitious women, whose options for the future were usually confined to marriage or a public-school teaching career within the local community.

One of the most notable and conspicuous attributes common to a majority of WMS missionaries was a middle-class social background. That so many recruits were drawn from the middle class is perhaps hardly remarkable, given the nature of late nineteenth- and early twentieth-century Canadian Methodism. The women's backgrounds conform to the prevailing self-image projected by the Canadian Methodist Church of the day, which envisaged itself as an institution sustained by the growing middle class and which hoped to accommodate the *nouveau riche*[20] as a part of the larger constituency it needed to pursue its ambitious dream of expansion both at home and abroad.

The women's middle-class backgrounds can be partially inferred from an examination of parental occupations, usually that of the father. Occupational data were available for the parents of 123 women, that is, a 40 per cent sample, smaller than for other aspects of the women's backgrounds simply because, unless it was noted in biographical files, parental occupation could only be determined from census information, which was not available after 1891.

Thirty-six (29 per cent) of the parents in the sample were identified as farmers or were employed in occupations related to agriculture: miller, sawyer, produce-dealer, and stock-dealer. Thirty-one (25 per cent) were engaged in business and commerce as merchants and manufacturers or as tradesmen, such as tailors and butchers, while four fathers (2 per cent) were labourers and carpenters. But almost half the parents in the sample were professionals: there were several physicians and teachers, but fifty-two fathers (42 per cent) were ministers or, less commonly, missionaries.[21] One in six, then, of all WMS missionaries was raised as "a daughter of the parsonage,"[22] while at least another 10 per cent had one or more close relatives – grandfather, uncle, brother, sister – who pursued a religious vocation. This family legacy was not shared equally by the women in the three major mission fields. Whereas 40 per cent of Blackmore's associates in Japan were related to members of the clergy, 20 per cent of WMS missionaries in China and 19 per cent in Canada had similar connections.

Among the women whose families bore the distinguishing marks of the middle class were Minnie Brimstin, daughter of James, a leading Toronto Methodist layman, described as "the best cutler in Canada,"[23] and Lydia Sherritt, whose father William was a stock-dealer and Conservative member of Parliament for the Ontario riding of North Middlesex, 1900–04. The Sherritt family was, according to WMS records, "well off." Their apparent wealth and ability to provide for their daughter provoked discussion among the WMS executive when Sherritt refused to repay the costs of an extended furlough taken conveniently just prior to her formal resignation.[24] The prominent Nova Scotian Killam family contributed two daughters to the WMS. Ada Killam, who served in Japan from 1902 until 1940, and Dr Maud Killam, who practised medicine for the WMS in West China from 1897 until she resigned to marry James Neave in 1904, were two of the children of wealthy Yarmouth ship owner Frank Killam, a federal member of Parliament from 1869 to 1882.[25] Mary Sherwood, daughter of a Fergus, Ontario, merchant, was raised in a household with servants,[26] as was Florence Wickett, whose father, Samuel, was a prosperous leather manufacturer.[27]

For these affluent women, a career as a means of self-support probably was not crucial to their well-being. But it is evident that for some other WMS missionaries, like the late-Victorian British women examined by Deborah Gorham, "the nature of most middle-class incomes meant that the role of sheltered flowers, or ornaments in the household, was unattainable."[28] Certainly the salary of a minister or teacher could not be stretched to support too many unmarried dependent daughters. After the death of their fathers, as Martha Vicinus suggests, many middle-class daughters "could expect little in the way of an income ... and so had the most to gain from the new educational and job opportunities."[29] In Canada as elsewhere throughout the Western world, by the end of nineteenth century employment for single middle-class "superfluous women" was becoming not just a matter of choice but a material necessity. With this eventuality in mind, the parents of many WMS missionaries seem to have tried to provide their daughters with the best possible education, even if the family had to sacrifice.

If there was a single attribute that separated the WMS candidates from their contemporaries and affirms their middle-class position, it was their degree of education and professional training. Whether Canadian Methodist women generally were better educated than women of other religious denominations is not yet clear. However, Methodists were among the first Protestant denominations in the Canadas and the Maritimes to demonstrate concern for the higher education of young women. The opening of Upper Canada Academy in 1836 initiated the Methodist Church's drive to educate its young women, although when the school was taken over by Egerton Ryerson in 1841, women were no longer admitted.[30] By the last quarter of the nineteenth century, when higher education for women had become a "very respectable cause,"[31] Canadian Methodists were already convinced that educated women might be the panacea for the proliferation of social problems confronting Canada and the world. In an appeal to "intelligent women" to become church workers, teachers, and missionaries, the editor of the *Christian Guardian* observed in 1888 that "the time [had] gone by forever when culture and knowledge were assumed to be the exclusive privilege of the sons of a family." Prominent Methodist clergy and laymen boasted about their enlightened attitudes towards women's education and place in society. This liberalism was invariably tempered by an equally intense conviction that the education of women should sustain them in their "separate spheres" in order to preserve traditional family and national values. Far from providing women with an entrée into male professions, the evangelical Christian objective in educating women was, first, to "enable them to perform the duties of positions for which without it they would not be qualified," and then to give them "mental culture in order that they may be intelligent companions of their husbands, and wise and capable teachers of their children."[32]

Whatever their reasons for educating their daughters – to equip them for marriage or a career – the parents of the future WMS missionaries appear to have heeded their Church's message. Of the 212 WMS missionaries for whom adequate data concerning education were available and who would have attended elementary school between 1860 and 1910, only three candidates, who were relegated to home missionary work, ended their formal education with elementary school. One of them, Margaret Armstrong (born in 1888) of Myrtle Station, a hamlet north of Oshawa, Ontario, who may not have completed even elementary school, was rejected until she had improved her qualifications. After four years as a secretary for the Toronto Bible College, during which she earned a diploma in stenography and bookkeeping from a Toronto technical school, Armstrong was approved by the Board of Managers for a position at Smokey Lake, Alberta, to work among Eastern European immigrants.[33]

The proliferation of diplomas and certificates and the confusion of provincial regulations make it almost impossible to calculate how many of the women actually graduated from high school.[34] But with the exception of the three women already noted, the remaining 209 recruits in the sample appear to have attended high school, some just long enough to earn the minimum matriculation to enable them to register at a provincial normal school as preparation for a teaching career, others graduating with the highest possible credentials in order to attend university. At least 32 women (11 per cent), probably more, left their families during their adolescent years to attend one of several Methodist Ladies' colleges open by the last decades of the nineteenth century to provide a secondary education for the daughters of the upper and middle classes. This is, of course, a telling comment on the social backgrounds of the recruits. Some girls, like Agnes Wintemute, enrolled at Alma College, which opened in her home town, St Thomas, Ontario, in 1877 under the auspices of the Methodist Episcopal Church. Others, or more likely their parents, chose the Ontario Ladies' College established in 1874 in Whitby, Ontario, or the older Hamilton Ladies' College before it closed in 1897.[35] Of the 64 Maritime women, 12 studied at Mount Allison for at least a term as a part of their formal education.

These Methodist ladies' colleges offered a choice of two three-year courses at the high-school level: the Mistress of Liberal Arts program, which emphasized English and classical studies, required two foreign languages, while the less exacting Mistress of English Language program demanded advanced work in English but no foreign language.[36] After 1886, when the Ontario Methodist ladies' colleges became affiliates of Victoria University, some of the courses were accepted as credits towards university degrees.[37] But despite their pretentious labels, ladies' college diplomas were not the equivalent of university degrees. Indeed, the Massey Foundation commission convened in 1921 to investigate the curriculum of Canada's Methodist colleges concluded that their programs tended to discourage women from attending university.[38] The WMS missionaries seem to refute this conclusion. Whereas 23 per cent of all WMS missionaries attended university, 30 per cent of the WMS ladies' college students proceeded to university.

Women at Methodist colleges usually registered for four terms per year. In 1890 Alma College advertised fees of $190 for four terms to cover board, room, lights, fuel, laundry, and instruction in music, drawing, and calisthenics. If desired, riding lessons could be arranged for an additional $15 per twelve sessions. Fees were halved for the daughters of Methodist clergymen. According to Principal Austin, Alma's levy was the lowest in Canada for a comparable education.[39] Yet this elite education for a daughter was far beyond the means of, for example, a carpenter who in 1901 earned twenty-five cents per hour.[40] Mount Allison Ladies' College, in particular, faced sharp criticism and disapproval during the last years of the nineteenth century because of its growing reputation as an elite institution where the girls' clothing was more and more elaborate and ostentatious each year.[41] Although John Reid argues that Mount Allison "could be defended convincingly against the allegation that it was becoming a finishing school for the children of wealthy families," his own research confirms that labourers' children were in a distinct minority.[42] The information available about the parents of WMS recruits who attended ladies' colleges weighs heavily on the side of elitism.

By 1920 Alma College at least had become more versatile, offering preparation for high school, a four-year high-school curriculum, and also a wide range of music, commercial, art, elocution, and household science courses that could be studied for just a single term. Women at Methodist schools had, of course, regular religious obligations: Sunday church services, daily chapel, mealtime devotions, and prayers.[43] And if Alma College was typical, the colleges were frequently visited by missionaries of both sexes discharging the furlough duties that required them to publicize their work for at least three months. After 1908 Alma and the Ontario Ladies' College hosted Methodist Church summer schools, which over the years were both attended and staffed by missionaries. In short, these institutions, like their British counterparts, exuded "a strong reforming ethos"[44] that was likely to generate and sustain more than a passing interest in a possible career as a missionary, while the exclusively female milieu of the ladies' college encouraged a sense of gender solidarity and female autonomy and the ability to thrive within a community of women, all strengths that were carried over into the mission field.

After leaving high school, most WMS missionary candidates continued their education at university, normal, nursing, or other professional schools, or joined the work-force. Fewer than 5 per cent of the sample but probably more than 25 per cent and as many as 40 per cent of all WMS recruits remained at home, assisting on a family farm, caring for younger siblings or ageing parents, perhaps anticipating marriage and their own domestic arrangements or merely marking time until they were old enough to apply to the WMS. More importantly, an equal number of all WMS missionaries (23 per cent) were among the small minority of women of their generation who attended university.

Until the beginning of the twentieth century the Board of Managers did not direct its recruitment campaigns specifically to university-educated women, probably because there were so few Canadian women university graduates to draw on. In 1872 Mount Allison University in Sackville, New Brunswick, and Queen's University in Kingston, Ontario, had opened their doors to women, and three years later the first woman university graduate in the British Empire received her BSC from Mount Allison.[45] In 1877 the Methodist Victoria College, then located in Cobourg, Ontario, admitted women.[46] By 1900 most Canadian universities accepted women, but their numbers on the campus were still limited by academic standards, family finances, and traditional views about women's roles.[47] Although the insufficient data about the educational status of Canadian women make useful statistical comparisons difficult, it is interesting to note that in 1941, a year when a majority of WMS missionaries and their birth cohorts in the general population were still alive to have been counted, only 6 per cent of all Canadian women reported some university as their highest level of education.[48]

The WMS experience in recruiting university graduates does not necessarily reflect the greater accessibility of university education for Canadian women as the twentieth century unfolded.[49] Only 4 (22 per cent) of the 18 women born before 1871 and for whom educational data were available had attended university; 30 (40 per cent) of the 74 born between 1872 and 1885 earned a degree. But paradoxically, among the 90 women born between 1886 and 1900 and for whom there were more educational opportunities, the proportion who attended university fell to 25 per cent. These distribution patterns, among other things, suggest that after 1900 a greater diversity of career options were open to university-trained women, and among those vocational choices, missionary work had become less tempting. However, the WMS missionaries selected for postings in Japan were a glaring exception to this pattern. In their case, women who had earned BAS increased from 22 per cent for those born before 1871 to 44 per cent for women born 1872–85 to 46 per cent of women recruited after the First World War. Because of its strong emphasis on teaching among the Japanese elite, the Japan mission became the chief beneficiary of the university graduates among the WMS recruits.

Predictably, most of the WMS's university graduates from the Maritimes attended the Methodist Mount Allison University, while the Ontario-bred women chose Victoria University, relocated in 1892 to Toronto.[50] Others graduated from the University of Toronto, McGill, and, after 1900, the University of Manitoba. Queen's, a Presbyterian university, and McMaster, a Baptist institution, graduated just one WMS missionary each, although their female graduates made their way into the missionary ranks of their respective churches.[51] For example, 24 of the 100 women, married and single, who were a part of the Canadian Baptist contingent in India before 1922 had attended university, usually McMaster or Acadia.[52] These figures are comparable to the proportion of all WMS agents who were university grads, but less than the 35 per cent of WMS overseas missionaries with similar educational qualifications. It would be misleading to conclude from this slim evidence that high educational levels were the exclusive mark of WMS missionaries. None the less, by any standards, when they were hired, the WMS missionaries were collectively already exceptionally well-educated women, whether the consequence of religion, social class and family wealth, or their own aspirations and determination. Some missionaries continued to improve their educational and professional qualifications, taking full advantage of their furloughs.

Like other women of their generation in North America and Britain, once at university the women tended to follow traditional courses of study. Few departed from the conventional arts programs, especially English or modern languages, which would prepare them for a future career as a teacher as a prelude to the paramount missionary vocation. Among the exceptions, Olive Markland graduated in 1909 from Victoria with a degree in Honours Philosophy, and in 1921 Christina Sturdy enrolled for a year in Divinity at Victoria, even though she had no hope at that time of ordination.[53] No matter what disciplines these young women selected, the university experience itself and living away from home exposed them to influences that could not help but alter their perceptions of themselves and their goals. As Carol Bacchi concludes, university education sparked "an activist frame of mind" in Canadian suffragists because "the spirit of social reform infected the classroom."[54] Even if the curriculum and their professors' observations failed to prick the women's middle-class consciences, there was a proliferation of voluntary philanthropic societies on campus to stimulate their social activism. The future WMS missionaries were energetic participants in the YWCA and the many clubs and associations, some coed, others exclusively female, that were part of the university experience.

Some contemporary accounts suggest that young women students (especially those living in women's residences) did not always take academic pursuits seriously. They were not only a privileged but a pampered and self-indulgent, even frivolous lot. Kathleen Cowan, who resided from 1907 to 1910 in Annesley Hall, the women's residence at Victoria University, and was a friend of several future WMS missionaries, recounted in her diary the particulars and the trivia of the daily life of a small-town girl away from home for the first time. Many young women studied only when absolutely necessary and spent their time (and much money) in the stores and tea shops along Toronto's Yonge Street. Apparently, they ironed their elaborate dresses and curled their hair more than they studied Plato or Shakespeare.[55] Cowan's diary also suggests that if universities adopted a more vigorous role *in loco parentis* than they now exercise, the university was still a less restrictive environment than the family, where the judicious management of time and finances and the mastery of personal relationships fell to the individual.

The Board of Managers appreciated the value of the total university experience as preparation for the "culture shock" of the overseas if not the home mission field. At university women demonstrated that they could accept some responsibility for their behaviour as they began to break the often inhibiting attachments to home, family, and a future defined by domestic responsibility.[56] With some basis the board tended to respect a BA as testimony to intelligence and hard work, not the social status of its holder; judged on these terms, it became an indicator of general aptitude, and specifically of the competence to learn the difficult languages needed for success in an overseas posting. A university education, then, was the yardstick by which the Board of Managers tried to decide who might most competently serve its interests on the world scene. The repercussions of this selective strategy appear to have had a serious impact on the outcome of the WMS missionary venture. Whereas 35 per cent (59 of 165) of WMS overseas missionaries had a university education, just 8 per cent of the women commissioned as home missionaries had been exposed to the college atmosphere. Even within Canada, most university-educated women were sent to stations where they required a second language: Italian, Chinese, Japanese, or Ukrainian.

While most WMS missionaries received an education commensurate with careers as teachers, nurses, or doctors, some recruits, because of their individual aptitude, financial constraints, domestic obligations, or personal preference, took a less academic route to missionary work. About 4 per cent of all recruits attended a business college, and as mission affairs, especially overseas, became more complex, the Board of Managers solicited candidates with business, accounting, and stenographic skills. Musical credentials, too, were endorsed by the board because the society promoted musical instruction to induce upper-class Japanese to enrol their daughters in its girls' schools and because singing was indispensable to the success of evangelical work. Nearly one in four of the women posted to Japan had received some musical training, either privately, as part of the curriculum at a ladies' college, or more formally, at a university conservatory. Olive Lindsay, who went to Tokyo in 1912 (Lindsay eventually became an ordained minister), was representative of her colleagues: she had studied voice and violin for one year and the piano for several more. Etta deWolfe and Ila Day were graduates of the Halifax and Toronto conservatories respectively, while Sarah Fullerton and Sybil Courtice had recommendations as exceptional organists. Their associate Florence Bird had little musical preparation, an obvious shortcoming that the board pondered when considering applications.[57] Their musical accomplishments and, to a lesser degree, artistic pursuits, such as oil or china painting, suggest that, academic achievement aside, many applicants were raised, like daughters of British Victorian middle-class families, "to adorn the household with their skills in music, painting and fancy needlework."[58] The Board of Managers, composed of similarly well-bred women, took all these uniquely feminine endowments into consideration as manifestations of the Western middle-class culture the society endeavoured to transmit.

With the launching of the Methodist West China Mission in 1891, the society began to recruit medical personnel. Nurses were also needed at Methodist hospitals at Port Simpson in northern British Columbia and at Lamont, Alberta. By 1925, 8 per cent of all WMS missionaries and 15 per cent of the West China staff were trained nurses. Until the late nineteenth century, nursing was bereft of the respectability essential for it to be an acceptable career for well-bred women. In Canada as elsewhere nursing, which until the late nineteenth century required no particular educational qualifications, commonly attracted women whose only other options for self-support were domestic service, factory work, or prostitution.[59] In 1874 the first professional nurses' training school in Canada was established in St Catharines, Ontario.[60] Other nursing schools, usually in connection with major urban hospitals in need of a constant supply of cheap labour, sprang up in its wake. Once purged of its disreputable crew, nursing, with its emphasis on women's special aptitude as purveyors of care and comfort, began a gradual evolution into a suitable profession for young women, many of whom lacked the money for a university education.

In 1886 the observant Canadian journalist Sara Jeannette Duncan, perhaps prematurely under the circumstances, endorsed nursing as a "new bread-winning occupation for women."[61] Nursing was attracting applicants from "a well brought up class of Canadian women ... Now that the services of trained nurses are eagerly sought for in every case of serious illness where the expense can be borne, now that many qualities and much knowledge is required, and the fair remuneration of ten and twelve dollars a week is paid for their services, the social condition of the nurses is vastly different from what it used to be ... There are now many accomplished young ladies among the uniformed nurses of the [Toronto] General Hospital, several daughters of clergymen, and one whose father is an English officer."[62] In the 1890s daughters of the middle class may still have been anomalies in the nursing profession, but by 1910 three-quarters of the candidates at Toronto General had some high-school education as the result of campaigns and screening policies specifically intended to restrict access to the incipient profession to a more select group of women.[63] In a volume prepared for distribution at the Paris Industrial Exhibition of 1900, the National Council of Women cited nursing, along with teaching and medicine, as one of the major professions open to Canadian women.[64] After the turn of the century, in response to the increased need for nurses within the growing public hospital system, the nursing profession underwent a rapid expansion. There were 280 student and graduate nurses in Canada in 1901, 5,600 in 1911, when nursing first received recognition in the census as a "profession,"[65] and 30,510 by 1930.[66]

There was, then, an opportunity, especially for Canadian women born after 1875, to train as nurses if, like women pursuing a university education, they had the ambition and financial resources to move to a centre with a recognized school. On one count at least, nursing had the edge over training as a teacher because student nurses received their room and board and a small remuneration.[67] But before 1900 there were relatively few schools of nursing, and entrance to them was competitive.[68] Some WMS missionaries both trained and worked as graduates at large and reputable nursing schools in the United States – for example, Fannie Forrest of Dundas, Ontario, who graduated from Boston University Hospital, Caroline Wellwood from Wingham, Ontario, who trained in Washington, DC, and Martha Barnett of Ottawa and Violetta Shuttleworth, who had done postgraduate work at New York City's well-known Bellevue Hospital.

Mary Assom of Canmore, Alberta, both graduated from and worked at the School of Nursing at the Ensworth Deaconess Hospital in St Joseph, Missouri.[69] Her experience illustrates the problems that Canadian hospitals faced, by the end of the nineteenth century, in attracting good nursing students, who were often lured to the United States because of the excellent career opportunities there for graduate nurses. As one Canadian hospital administrator explained, "The American schools offered far greater attractions, and the girls of good social standing and education, who developed the nursing fad, went to the United States with exasperating frequency. This was not altogether a misfortune, as it gave many clever, ambitious women an outlet for their abilities and numbers of them assumed leadership in the rising profession."[70] Hence, like the university graduates, by the time they joined the WMS, nurses had already severed many familial connections, establishing for themselves an independence and autonomy denied to most women of the time, who were still accountable to fathers and husbands.[71]

Nine WMS recruits were doctors hired specifically to direct the society's medical activities in West China. Unlike WMS nurses, all but one doctor, Maud Killam, trained in Canada. Had she wished, Killam, from Yarmouth, Nova Scotia, might have attended Dalhousie University Medical School, which admitted women in the early 1890s. But presumably because her family could afford it and because of its fine reputation for producing women physicians, she chose the Women's Medical College at the New York Infirmary.[72] After graduation Killam was licensed by New York State and practised at a sanatorium in Santa Clara, New York, before joining the WMS. Retta Gifford graduated from the Woman's Medical College in Toronto in 1891, as did Anna Henry in 1898, Mabel Cassidy in 1902, and Olive Rea in 1903. May Austen and Florence O'Donnell, natives of Halifax, graduated from Dalhousie Medical College shortly after 1900.[73]

At least two WMS doctors took a circuitous route to the medical careers that represented the fulfilment of a lifelong ambition. Lily Snider (MD Toronto, 1918) taught for three years after she received her BA in 1913, and Ada Speers of Brandon, Manitoba, whose father died when she was thirteen, taught for seven years until she had enough savings to pay for a medical education.[74] In her examination of Canadian women medical graduates, Veronica Strong-Boag has identified other women who financed their medical studies with the income from a previous career. Strong-Boag concludes that although most female medical students "seemed to be daughters of ministers, doctors, teachers or farmers, a relationship which placed them, if somewhat precariously, in the middle class," the apparent lack of family financial backing points to "the marginality of [their middle-class] status."[75] The cost of medical training obviously prohibited many women from becoming physicians, but it is also conceivable that in 1910 the suggestion of a medical career did not elicit enthusiastic parental approval. Pressured by the WMS and its Presbyterian counterpart, the Woman's Medical College in Toronto reduced the fees for women who were recognized missionary candidates. In 1897 a severe financial crisis forced the institution to abandon the practice, leaving individual missionary organizations to fill the gap.[76] As a rule the Methodist WMS did not extend financial assistance to needy candidates, not even to the prospective doctors to whom they perpetually appealed. In a unique instance, in 1913, when Speers, who could no longer afford to pay her medical school fees, contemplated dropping out, the WMS paid the bill. But the board made clear that her case was an exception, not a precedent.[77]

Throughout its history, the society had serious difficulty both recruiting and retaining doctors. Seven of the society's doctors were hired before 1910. To the intense disappointment and frustration of the board, in the next fifteen years, even after completion of a modern hospital in Chengtu in 1914, just Speers and Snider were enlisted. More disheartening for the development of WMS medical projects, of the nine, only Henry and Speers made missionary work the lifetime career the WMS expected.

Carlotta Hacker has estimated that by 1913, "at least a quarter of all the women who had studied medicine in Canada had done so expressly so that they could serve usefully in the mission field."[78] If this is so, the Methodist wms failed to attract its fair share of this valuable commodity; until 1913 only 6 (less than 3 per cent) of the 220 Canadian women medical-school graduates opted to become wms missionaries.[79] The shortage of qualified women available and willing to serve as medical missionaries may partially rationalize the wms' predicament. According to the 1911 census, at that time only 196 women doctors were practising throughout the country.[80] The wms administrators made no special concessions to entice women doctors either by subsidizing their medical studies or by offering them higher salaries commensurate with the time and money invested in their education. The board prided itself on providing the finest equipment and modern drugs for its doctors' use in the field, but it simply was not wms policy to offer missionary doctors higher salaries or more benefits than their colleagues, even though as doctors in Canada they would have earned more than teachers and nurses. Few wms doctors, however, took the opportunity to practise in Canada; all but three physicians went directly from medical school to wms postings in China.

This relative inexperience was atypical. wms records indicate that before they became missionaries, three-fifths (61 per cent) of the recruits had already been employed outside the home. These statistics suggest that a surprisingly large number of middle-class Victorian Canadian women, at least from Methodist ranks, prepared themselves for and pursued employment as single wage-earners. Some women, like Martha Cartmell, who became a wms missionary in her mid-thirties, when the opportunity to serve her own denomination finally materialized, had extensive experience in the work-force, while other younger women, especially university graduates, were employed perhaps only a year or two after completion of their education. The 143 women for whom data were available had worked an average of four and a half years; home missionaries who were older had about a year's more work experience, candidates for Japan or China a few months less. In short, although marriage probably was still their goal until they turned to the wms, as self-supporting single women the future missionaries were already involved in the process, to cite a contemporary authority on women's issues, of creating "a sphere of usefulness and happiness second only to that of happily married women."[81]

There is no simple answer to the question of whether Methodist women were overrepresented in the labour force during this period or whether any one occupation attracted proportionately more Methodist women. The Canadian Methodist hierarchy publicly supported women's entry into the work-force as a fitting use for their education, but women were urged to take up occupations that utilized and promoted their traditional nurturing skills. Alfred Reynar, dean of Victoria University, spoke for his peers when in 1889 he applauded "some of the modern activities of woman, such as their work as nurses in times of war and of peace, their visiting and caring for the poor and the sick, their efforts to establish Christian truth and morals at home and to extend them abroad. In these things the new women have shown themselves true women still."[82]

But Rev. Benjamin Austin, who served as the first principal of Alma College from 1877 to 1897,[83] argued that woman's sphere was not nearly so limited as society supposed. Austin, a man with an obvious bias favouring the education and employment of women, tried to convince his female students that they should never "be placed in circumstances such as to make marriage an only refuge from poverty or dependence on ... friends, or from a life of ennui."[84] There were many alternatives. The census of 1881 had recorded 227 different occupations engaging women, and although Austin condemned cheap labour, he staunchly upheld women's right to earn a living in any career they chose, even traditionally male trades. "If a girl can make money by milking a cow, making a horseshoe or packing shingles," Austin contended, "it is quite as respectable for her to do it as for a man."[85] William Withrow, editor of the *Methodist Magazine*, agreed. He "repudiate[d] the idea so commonly entertained that the higher education of woman is only a lure to the gilded bower of matrimony, to enable her to ... win a prize in the lottery of marriage. It has loftier and sublimer ends than these – the development of the noblest part of her nature, the intellect and the affections; the expansion and culture of all her powers."[86] Yet this eloquent verbiage did not translate into sexual equality in the work-force. Even the best-educated and most determined Canadian women faced the harsh reality of sexual discrimination in a male-dominated work-place, and Methodists or not, they gravitated to professions accepted as the special preserve of women.

In particular, women carved out their niche in the teaching profession, where, by the 1870s, in spite of the unmistakable discrepancies in salaries and opportunities for promotion between male and female teachers, women well outnumbered men.[87] Almost half (44 per cent) of all WMS missionaries had attended a normal school, after high school or university, to acquire one of the wide array of teaching certificates available. Others taught without the advantage of teacher training. In all, nearly 50 per cent of WMS recruits had some teaching experience, 125 as public-school teachers, 4 as high-school teachers, and 8 as instructors at private schools. Before they joined the society,

50 (62 per cent) women sent to Japan and 36 (43 per cent) of the China hands had taught in Canada. By contrast, just one in four home missionaries (29 per cent) had been teachers, a circumstance indicative of the lower educational levels among home missionaries and the greater demand for teachers overseas. As far as the Board of Managers was concerned, teaching experience with or without a college degree was no particular advantage in Port Simpson, where sewing, combing hair, and gardening were the order of the day and where the government was responsible for hiring teachers and providing a minimum education for the Indian population.

About two-thirds of WMS nurses had some work experience when they were recruited, through only 3 of the doctors appear to have practised before reaching China, evidence perhaps of the limited opportunities for young women doctors in Canada. A mere 16 (5 per cent) of the candidates reported some business experience, while another 13 (4 per cent) had engaged in some aspect of social and philanthropic work or were deaconesses. Although most of the women who had worked outside the home before becoming missionaries had, as teachers, been employed in a low-paying profession where women seldom received administrative posts,[88] some recruits had attained positions of respect and authority. Elizabeth Alcorn, who spent many years in Japan, had been the head of the art department at Mount Allison Ladies' College. Her friend and associate Myra Veazey, a graduate of the University of New Brunswick, had taught privately in Maine and at the Cookman Institute for Negro Students, one of the first American negro colleges operated by the Methodist Church of the United States, in Jacksonville, Florida.[89] Esther Ryan, another member of the Japan Mission, had been principal of Shawville Academy in Quebec before she joined the WMS in 1913. Annie MacLean had been the principal of two elementary schools in the 1920s, while Muriel Hockey was appointed assistant principal of the Methodist Training School in 1912. May Inglis, a graduate in 1900 from the New England Training School in Boston, was involved with prison work on behalf of several Boston churches.[90] Positions like these, if not always lucrative, allowed women to assert themselves and equipped them for the responsibility of independent decision making in the mission field. The Board of Managers valued candidates who had several years of relevant work experience, but superior qualifications did not earn them a higher salary than their less well-prepared colleagues.

There are no similar details about work experience for nearly 40 per cent of the recruits, probably because they did not hold paid positions beyond their own households. Some women who remained in their parents' homes seemed proud of their ability to work hard; rural applicants especially boasted about their varied domestic accomplishments. For them, taking charge of a household and caring for elderly parents or orphaned brothers and sisters seemed the equivalent of outside employment. Martha Swann of Moorefield, Ontario, "thoroughly [understood] the keeping of a home having assisted during my vacation at my own home and being a close observer while away."[91] As a child Ada Sandell attended to the younger members of her family of seventeen when her widowed mother went out to work in a laundry.[92] Retta Gifford worked on her parents' farm near Meaford, Ontario, before entering high school in Owen Sound at the age of eighteen.[93] To young women raised in a strong Christian tradition that "implied obedience to older kin," the care and responsibility of the family was an integral part of their lives.[94] The members of the Board of Managers who were more or less sympathetic to family obligations regarded domestic experience as useful training for service among immigrants and for the operation of boarding schools among the Indians; but they counted it of little consequence for a post in the Orient, where servants were plentiful and cheap and missionaries were closely scrutinized by the host culture.

Within the context of late nineteenth- and early twentieth-century Canadian women's history the WMS missionaries stand out as an elite company of educated middle-class pious single women. But their educational, social, and career histories, though vital components of the collective WMS experience and factors that, in the long run, contributed to professional satisfaction and career longevity, do not adequately explain the women's momentous and premeditated decisions to change the patterns of their lives, to leave families and friends and familiar surroundings, in some cases forever, and to renounce for the immediate future the possibility of marriage and a family in order to "share in the evangelization of the world in [their] generation."[95]

Becoming a missionary was neither a sudden nor a rash choice. Had there been any impetuosity in the decision, WMS policies and red tape guaranteed that no woman was assigned to the mission field without sufficient time to reflect carefully about her future. This was rarely necessary. For many women, like Jessie Munro, a teacher in eastern Ontario, the actualization of a missionary career was the culmination of a recurring desire, a lifelong dream that they could pursue only after their parents were dead. As soon as Munro's own mother and father had both died, she "covenanted with the Lord that if He called and opened the way," she would go to Japan. With extraordinarily good timing, she saw an advertisement in the *Christian Guardian* appealing for teachers for the WMS girls' school in Tokyo. It was, Munro decided, "an answer to my vow, but so many spoke to me that I began to fear that I was activated by a love of adventure, and determined to think no more about it." Selflessly she prayed not so much that she might be sent as that the best of those who volunteered might be chosen.[96]

For most recruits, reared in the deep-rooted Methodist evangelical tradition, the decision to become a missionary dedicated to the service of God was simply the logical outcome of their upbringing. A religious vocation was a respectable way for a Victorian middle-class single woman whose parents could not support her indefinitely to earn her living and, at the same time, satisfy a strong moral and spiritual obligation to herself, her family, her church, and God. The difficulty for the historian lies in segregating the sometimes conflicting motives – piety, adventure, or economic necessity – that troubled Munro and her associates.

With few exceptions, the WMS recruits were raised in one of several branches of Methodism in Canada: after the union of Canadian Methodists in 1884, they belonged simply to the Methodist Church, the largest Protestant denomination in the country.[97] Methodism, in whatever form, was an integral part of their daily lives. As William Magney has observed, by the mid-nineteenth century, Methodism was "a way of life with deep historical roots in the Canadian past. It encompassed a code of conduct, to which one subscribed with belligerent pride."[98] It was a distinctively social religion, and the Methodists' "characteristic institutions and values ... class meetings, lovefeasts, society meetings, protracted meetings, camp meetings, tea meetings, and even ... family worship, were all meant to create an organic solidarity amongst the membership."[99] By the end of the nineteenth century the Methodist Church had moved beyond its purely religious role in Canadian society to become "the bustling hub of community social activities, whether of a charitable, convivial, or regenerative character."[100] If they chose, Canadian Methodists could be involved in the Church's social organizations from birth to death.

The Methodist hierarchy and membership crusaded vigorously on behalf of those causes that they believed would most benefit society as a whole. The strict observance of the Sabbath and the temperance and prohibition movements, traditional goals of both British and Canadian Methodism, took precedence over other social issues. As Magney, for one, suggests, there seemed to be a "direct correlation between the growth of militancy in pursuit of these goals, and the awakening of a distinctive Methodist spirit of social, political, and economic reform."[101] By the turn of the century many Methodists, as activists on behalf of the nascent social-gospel movement, promoted the notion that "the Church was responsible for more than the spiritual welfare of the individual. The simple Christian gospel truths had to be applied to the whole institutional character of contemporary society."[102]

Methodists gradually relinquished their limited concern for their individual spiritual health to assume a broader responsibility for the material and spiritual condition of, ultimately, all mankind.[103] At the General Conference of 1906 the Church formally acknowledged its obligation to "set up the Kingdom of God among men, which we understand to be a social order founded upon the principles of the Gospel – the Golden Rule and the Sermon on the Mount."[104] For Methodism's faithful, among them the future WMS recruits, brought up to heed and respect their church's pronouncements on religious and secular matters, this millennial vision of God's kingdom on earth was not just an illusory myth but a prospect within their grasp.[105] Beneath the layers of the social gospel, nevertheless, the remnants of Methodism's traditional evangelical doctrines remained, sometimes creating tensions in the Church and its organizations even after the First World War, when the tenets of the social gospel were supposedly solidly in place as the foundation of the Methodist Church's principles.[106] The religious convictions of the WMS missionaries and their methods in the mission field reflect this range of opinion during a critical period of ideological and doctrinal change.

Until 1914 women were denied any official voice in the *inner sanctum* of the Methodist Church; within the history of the Church women were refused ordination. Only in 1936, a decade after the extinction of Methodism per se, were women accepted as ministers by the United Church of Canada.[107] But, because women were widely recognized as paragons of morality and guardians of the Victorian family, the Church willingly conceived a role for them in expediting the millennium. Much of the responsibility for the strength and the extension of Canadian Methodism rested with the family and the home, which had become for evangelical Christians of all denominations twin symbols of morality and a refuge from the encroaching evils of a changing society.[108] Within the domestic sphere the wife and mother was charged with the religious education of her family. Women's obituaries in Methodist newspapers confirm that many women strove to assume "a millennial vocation" as model Christian wives and mothers whose children would live a righteous life.[109]

Although women's role in Canadian Methodism has not been thoroughly examined, there is some evidence of the "feminization" that has been ascribed to nineteenth-century American Protestantism.[110] Canadian Methodist women were active as members of individual congregations; in many churches women comprised more than two-thirds of the membership. During the first half of the nineteenth century, before the Methodist Church became a predominantly urban-based institution, a significant number of women served as preachers and evangelists in addition to their roles as class leaders and Sunday-school teachers.[111] By 1900 participation in Methodist women's organizations, notably the WMS, had given women a broader perspective on the world, familiarizing them with the circumstances of women in other cultures and allowing them to join with like-minded women for more than purely social objectives.

Only a few missionaries, usually the older recruits, seem themselves to have belonged to a WMS auxiliary, but many women noted that their mothers, as ardent champions of the missionary enterprise, had influenced their own career choice. At the farewell service in 1889 for Lizzie and Nellie Hart and Isabella Blackmore, who were leaving for Japan, the trio "paid a high tribute to their mothers' Christian care and raising and the influence of Christian homes."[112] When Ethel Virgo went to China in 1908, the society praised the "godly home" where her "lot was cast" and "the example of a mother who ... was ever ready to stretch out the helping hand to the poor, the needy and the afflicted ones." Converted at sixteen during a Crossley and Hunter revival service, Virgo resolved to become a missionary while she was a student at Victoria University. With a trace of inconsistency for a dedicated and pious woman, Virgo's devout mother opposed her daughter's choice. As it happened, Virgo's mother died, or as the society construed it, she was "given the victory and enabled to let her daughter go even to distant Sinem to tell of the Saviour mighty to save."[113] Other cases of maternal moral suasion among the families of WMS recruits support the impression that in Canada, as in the United States, women's influential role in the child-rearing process was critical to their children's vocational choice.[114]

The upbringing of the many WMS missionaries whose fathers were ministers was even more closely monitored by devout parents. For daughters of the parsonage pressure to conform to rigorous behavioural standards was strong at a time when the minister was sacrosanct and his family members acted out their roles under the sharp eyes of the local congregation, on whom they depended for their daily bread. Childhood habits, especially regular church attendance, were deeply ingrained. For example, at forty-one, Annie Allen, the daughter of a superintendent of Home Missions for the Methodist Church and a WMS missionary in Tokyo, admitted in her diary that she had "done a bold deed and came home after Sunday School without staying to Church – which, of course, will result in many inquiries for my health."[115] It was inevitable that the missionaries would impose similar standards of conduct on their young charges.

Whether or not ministers applied exceptional pressure to persuade their children to follow a religious career is not clear, but clerical families certainly contributed in full measure to swell the ranks of the WMS. Sarah and Elizabeth Hart were two of the eight children of Rev. Thomas Hart, a Nova Scotian Methodist minister. In 1888 Sarah became matron of the Crosby girls' school in Port Simpson; Elizabeth was sent to Japan in 1889. A third sister, Louise, applied for a position as a WMS doctor in China, but because of the unsettled political situation there she switched her allegiance, subsequently spending many years with the Presbyterian mission in central India.[116] The Woodsworth family, too, contributed its share to the Methodist missionary crusade. Rev. Richard Woodsworth, father of Hattie, who went to China for the WMS in 1906, was a cousin of James Woodsworth, superintendent of Missions for the Methodist Church of Canada and father of James Shaver Woodsworth. Richard's second wife, Hattie's stepmother, had herself been a missionary in Africa for twelve years and later undertook deaconess work at Centenary Methodist Church in Hamilton. One of Hattie's sisters was the female principal of Alma College before she married George Blewett, who eventually held the chair in ethics at Victoria University,[117] while another sister was on the staff of Clifton Springs Sanatorium, a popular rest home for missionaries located near Rochester, New York. Though it seems to have been made on her own initiative Hattie's choice of a career closely conformed to family expectations and tradition.[118]

Women like Hattie Woodsworth and Elizabeth and Sarah Hart, reared in a strict, perhaps even stifling Methodist atmosphere, could neither easily nor rashly dismiss their overpowering sense of obligation to their families and their church. Almost from birth the prospective WMS missionaries had been initiated into the social and religious rituals of Methodism through their own attendance at Sunday school, church services, prayer meetings, and revivals and their parents' participation in the WMS, ladies' aid, class meetings, Bible study groups, and administrative councils. For Edna and Ada Speers, who became WMS missionaries in China, Sunday in turn-of-the-century Brandon, Manitoba, was a ceaseless but apparently satisfying round of religious activities and good works. The sisters "joined Prof. Taylor in his Sunday morning visits to the jail, got back in time for the 11 a.m. service, back again for Sunday School at 2:30

p.m., Evening worship at 7 p.m., and singing and refreshments in the Men's Parlour, downstairs, afterwards. And, yes, after Sunday School we had time for a good 'sing' at home, around our own piano before mother called us to supper."[119]

That the Speers's was an orthodox Methodist household is further confirmed by Edna's promise as a child never to "play cards, dance or go to a horse race."[120] These restrictions were part of the "Note" added in 1886 to paragraph 35 of the *Methodist Discipline*, which survived on paper until 1910 but in the Methodist spirit long after.[121] The Speers's social and philanthropic pursuits, which were typical of Canadian Methodists, served to establish and reinforce a particular kind of confining social behaviour. Religious historians have demonstrated how, tangentially, this responsibility aroused "the religious consciousness of the individual" and increased an "awareness of the applicability of Christian principles to his daily existence."[122] But it may also be argued that Methodists' concern about the question of the "Note," their preoccupation with total abstinence and the rejection of what they considered shallow and hedonistic pleasures – the opera, dancing, and novel reading – provide evidence of the persistence of the most distinctive feature of Wesleyan theology, that is, the traditional Methodist quest for perfection,[123] a search that absorbed many of the older WMS missionaries throughout their lives.

As Phyllis Airhart suggests, well into the twentieth century Methodists' pursuit of a holy life produced a particular mode of behaviour.[124] To "avoid the eternal flames" and as a confirmation of their Christian credentials, late Victorian Methodists were expected to confine their social activities to the pleasures that their religion could comfortably accommodate.[125] In 1886, in a volume entitled *Shall We or Shall We Not*, Rev. Hugh Johnston reviewed the social and recreational pursuits that were congruous with Methodism. Much of his advice was directed specifically at young women, as future Methodist wives and mothers. Gambling, card playing, dancing, especially the "disgraceful" waltz, the theatre, but above all the opera, with its "immoral dancing" and scantily clad chorus, were all forbidden pleasures for earnest Methodists.[126] This was not, it must be understood, trifling rhetoric but a compendium of rules that all Methodists were expected to observe. On one occasion in 1898 the *Christian Guardian* apologized for the suggestion in a Toronto newspaper that prominent Methodists, among them Chancellor Burwash of Victoria University, had enjoyed themselves at the Victorian Era Ball held by the city's social lions. "Our people should know," the paper explained, "that while these invitations were received in due course and respectfully, they were also accordingly declined by ministers and laymen alike."[127]

If they could not dance, there was still a lengthy catalogue of leisure pastimes for Methodists: the game of Authors, "fireside games," croquet, lawn tennis, sailing, rowing, ice skating (but not roller skating, which was "vicious and unhealthy"), lectures, reading, and certain symphony concerts.[128] Given what seems, on the surface at least, to have been an inhibited and suppressed mentality (which may have derived as much from Methodists' middle-class status as from their spiritual anxiety), it is hard to refute Goldwin French's conclusion that nineteenth-century Canadian evangelical churches "discouraged the formation of a liberal climate of opinion in which intellectual and cultural diversity would be cherished, and thereby delayed in some measure the attainment of cultural maturity in Canada."[129] These inhibitions infused wms missionary stations at home and overseas, where the women often displayed an uneasiness, verging on an obsession, about their own and others' spiritual and moral perfectibility as the culmination of the Methodist concept of holiness. A "soul ... emptied of sin and filled with God," an ideal articulated in the Methodist Manual of 1893, seems, in fact, to have been the spiritual standard many missionaries set for themselves.[130] For instance, in an effort to observe this "self and social regulation," which, Brian McKillop points out, was essential for salvation,[131] Mary Lamb, a missionary in China, regularly shut herself up in her room for private Bible study, fearing that "unless I keep my own soul in a healthy condition, I don't see how I am going to have anything for others."[132]

These rigid moral directives and the relatively simple Methodist doctrines of universal redemption, repentance, justification by faith, and sanctification[133] were reinforced as the future missionaries themselves became immersed in the Methodist culture. These young women had participated in revivals and prayer meetings; they joined the choir, played the organ, taught Sunday school, and, as their records repeatedly indicate, they became members and officers of the Epworth League.

The first formal Methodist youth organization, the Epworth League was constituted in 1889 to attract young men and women to the church because Methodist membership was faltering.[134] According to a rather clumsily worded statement in the *Christian Guardian* in 1891, the league's aim was "to promote the spirit which, familiarizing youthful workers with the truths of Methodist doctrine and the best methods of spreading them, will energetically follow out into mature life, without likelihood of break or hindrance, the methods and principles taught as essential to the life of our Church ... The stronger the bond between the Church and the young, the more united and continuous will be the force exerted in the uplifting of the masses into the light and liberty of the Gospel."[135] At a time when society generally was beginning to recognize adolescence as a distinct phase of life, the Methodist Church, like secular institutions, accepted a moral responsibility to reform the youth of Canada, especially if, in return, the Church might benefit from their membership and financial support.[136] As the *Guardian* pointed out, "A church in which the interests of the young are neglected, or in which they are not made an integral part of its work and organization, may be said to be divided against itself."[137] Many WMS applicants cited membership and executive experience in the League as a stimulus arousing interest in a future devoted to missionary work. A quick examination of the league's records, however, indicates that within the league's administration, women invariably assumed the offices of secretary or social convener. The presidency was a male bastion.

Within a decade the Epworth League was overshadowed as the exclusive agency promoting missionary activities among young people by a more explicit instrument to excite interest in world-wide missionary ventures in the form of the Young People's Forward Movement for Missions. This society was launched in 1896 by Methodist college students with the blessing of Chancellor Burwash of Victoria University. Designed as an antidote to the growing apathy towards Methodist missionary activities, which had, additionally, been challenged by attacks in West China and by internal tension in Japan (the most visible manifestation of this apathy was the increasing difficulty in raising money for missions), the Young People's Forward Movement became the exclusive preoccupation of Dr Frederick Stephenson, whose own plans to become a missionary in China had been frustrated by the Methodist Church's shortage of funds, and his wife.[138] Originally called the Students' Campaign for Missions, the YPFMM was the first Methodist organization to adopt the successful concept of systematic giving to bolster its financial contributions to the church's missionary needs.[139] A list of the campaigners for 1898 and 1899 contains no women's names, but by 1906 Canadian women, several future WMS missionaries included, had obligated themselves, through the Young People's Forward Movement, to a missionary career.[140]

Stephenson's enterprise played a prominent part in fund-raising and publishing missionary literature for many years. But after 1900 it was in its turn eclipsed by the Student Volunteer Movement, the most powerful and aggressive of the agencies for recruiting missionaries and exciting interest in missions. The SVM, whose origins can be traced to a summer Bible school sponsored in 1886 by the evangelist Dwight Moody and the Young Men's Christian Association, immediately began to take root under the guidance of its first director, John R. Mott, on North American college campuses.[141] By 1891, 6,000 college students, including 320 Canadians, claimed membership in the SVM.[142] The movement's appeal has been attributed to its genesis in the strong currents of revivalism still flowing in late nineteenth-century America; the meetings, with their impassioned appeals for "the evangelization of the world in this generation," have been characterized as latter-day tent meetings, albeit in an urban, collegiate setting.[143]

Unlike the Young People's Forward Movement and the Epworth League, the SVM was interdenominational; it was not affiliated with any one particular church but with the YMCA. It was, moreover, an international organization that held a convention every four years for delegates from colleges throughout the United States and Canada who gathered to hear speakers from denominational missionary societies discuss all aspects of missionary work. Special sessions were always convened to address issues related to women's role in missions.[144] In 1902, when Toronto hosted the Fourth International Student Volunteer Convention, more than four thousand delegates and interested citizens crowded Massey Hall for the mass rallies. The basement of the hall housed an impressive panorama of missionary memorabilia and books as well as the latest fads in the equipment recommended for foreign postings, from stoves and organs to pith helmets and rifles, all designed to whet the appetites of the curious visitors.[145] In Canada the SVM's prestige and credibility was enhanced by its prominent patrons, among them Timothy Eaton, Chester Massey, J.W. Flavelle, Methodists all, and S.H. Blake.[146]

Affiliation with the SVM was open to members of Protestant evangelical churches who had already "accepted certain responsibilities and obligations as an individual Christian, and [were] striving to live up to them through active service in his church, his Christian association and other college activities." If approved, members were then committed, among other things, to "strengthening their missionary purpose, stimulating and helping one another to secure adequate preparation, intellectual and physical for their future work."[147] Above all else, the SVM's objective was to "create a foreign missionary consciousness on the campus."[148] Chancellor Burwash had some reservations about the presence of the SVM on the Victoria University campus. He suspected that it might be dangerous to interfere too openly with the university's existing missionary work, directed by the YPFMM.[149] None the less, in spite of Burwash's less than enthusiastic reaction, the SVM became a fixture of Canadian campus life. By 1919 it claimed responsibility for the pledges from half the men and women who became missionaries; at least fifteen of wms recruits who had attended college belonged to this group.[150]

By contrast with the Epworth League or the Young People's Forward Movement, the svm demanded an unequivocal commitment to a future in missions. Signing the svm membership card meant that "the question is settled and that it closes the door with a click." This agreement could be rescinded only on the condition that the decision to withdraw was "as intelligent, as conscientious, as selfless, as distinctly the outcome of his desire to fully do the work of God and to express most perfectly the surrender of his life as was the case with the original forming of the purpose. In other words, God's leading out of the purpose must be as clear, at least as clear, as was the leading into the purpose."[151] The vow to become a missionary for life, taken even before a candidate was accepted by any missionary society, distinguished the svm's approach to recruitment from the more flexible and informal *modus operandi* of the organizations within the Methodist church. It did not seem to deter prospective missionaries who might have already decided their futures and were eager to sign the svm's pledge. The promise "if God permits, to become a foreign missionary" was for them merely the formalized expression of a private vow, often made years before, and not likely the result of coercion by the svm.[152]

External catalysts such as the Epworth League and the svm no doubt clarified and strengthened the women's resolve. But there were many other considerations that might prompt a young woman to investigate a missionary career. Some women's interest was first piqued when they heard a veteran missionary recount her experiences in the field. For the first group of wms recruits, however – that is, women who joined the wms before about 1895 – there were few Methodist women missionaries against whom they could measure themselves and their aspirations. While reports of the work, sacrifices, and, in some cases, ultimate martyrdom of American women missionaries in India, China, Africa, and the South Seas had appeared in Methodist publications, the first applicants had little of the personal contact with returned missionaries on furlough that later recruits remembered as an especially persuasive influence. Moreover, unless they had intimate discussions with a veteran missionary who chose to speak candidly, the recruits usually encountered Pollyannas who, for the benefit of the wms membership, often tended to ignore or reject reality in order to satisfy the congregations and societies that sustained them in the field.

For some women who no longer anticipated marriage, a missionary career, especially after the overseas stations were well-established with comfortable living quarters, seems to have appealed as a secure alternative to a traditional domestic arrangement. Missionary work offered the companionship that the teaching profession and a lonely boarding-house could not provide. When the death of her mother left her without a family, Mildred Armstrong pleaded fervently with the regional executive to consider her application. "I want so badly to go. I have now no home ties to keep me here ... Since my dear mother has been taken from me, I am quite alone; and my girlish dream – or rather desire has come back to me with renewed force."[153] Armstrong was chosen for overseas service and the Japanese mission became her home for the next forty years.

In one instance, a missionary career became the substitute for a marriage denied by the death of a fiancé,[154] while Alice Jackson decided to apply for a position as sewing teacher at the McDougall orphanage following the death of her dressmaking partner.[155] More often it was a husband's death that induced women to become missionaries. Missionary work was considered an especially appropriate occupation for the widows of ministers or missionaries who were forced to earn their own living. At least ten widows became WMS missionaries. Retta Gifford Kilborn, a WMS physician in West China from 1893 to 1897, re-enlisted in 1925 after the death of her missionary husband; she remained with the WMS until she retired in 1934. Lily Howie Hockin joined the WMS in West China in 1912 after the death of her missionary husband from typhoid. Her daughter, Katharine, later became a missionary for the United Church of Canada. Most of the widows, however, were hired as home missionaries because they lacked the qualifications desired for foreign mission work.[156]

If some parents, themselves ministers or ardent lay activists on behalf of missions, strongly endorsed their daughters' designs to become missionaries, and sometimes, like the Killams, Harts, Speers, Howies, Lawsons, and Josts, contributed two daughters to the WMS, other parents uncompromisingly opposed their daughters' career choice. Paternal authority could be very powerful. Even though applicants were not young girls who required their fathers' permission to become missionaries, the WMS acted very cautiously if there was the slightest family resistance.[157] Parental fears for their daughters' safety as missionaries were not unrealistic, given the unsettled political situation in China, the hazards of overseas travel, and the health problems that women suffered in the mission field. Some women were able, in time, to sway their parents to change their minds; but for others, like Jessie Munro, parental objections or the need to remain at home to care for aged parents ended only with the death of one or both parents. Considering the circumstances of Victorian domestic life, where heavy responsibility with little freedom was the prospect for single women at home, missionary work, which inevitably meant leaving home, must have been very inviting for some women escaping an austere and authoritarian family atmosphere.

Even though neither the applications nor the board's notations about the candidates hints at any obvious dissatisfaction with their previous occupations or personal relationships, Jessie Munro's suspicion that her own motives might be less than selfless raises the perplexing question of whether some women, especially those who wanted foreign postings, were in fact deliberately searching for a life of excitement and adventure not freely available to them in Canada at the time.

The allure of missionary work was heightened, albeit inadvertently, by an overabundance of travel literature, adventure stories, and novels that Desmond Pacey has collectively labelled "romantic escapism."[158] For example, in 1907 J.C. Lambert, author of *The Romance of Missionary Heroism*, asked "whether there [was] any career which offer[ed] so many opportunities of romantic experience and heroic achievement as that of a Christian missionary." He recommended that the "adventurous and stirring side of missionary experience need[ed] to be brought out, and emphasis laid upon the fact that the romantic days of missions [were] by no means past."[159] The closely edited missionary columns of Methodist papers and journals contributed their share to an idealized and sanitized, yet often stirring rendition of life as a missionary. Even in times of extreme danger for its missionaries the Methodist Church persisted, for the sake of financial support, in glossing over the risks involved in spreading the word of God. Missionaries became objects of adulation nationally and within their own congregations; their activities and misadventures were frequently highlighted in local newspapers. WMS missionaries on furlough were feted in their home towns and given a hero's welcome at the society's annual meetings. In all of this there was little to dissuade two or three generations of Canadian women from a missionary career. Rather, the religious life as embodied in such a career tended to become a magnetic force, attracting and pulling women from across Canada into its field.

It is probable that in a few instances the charisma of WMS work was boosted by the respectable, if not exactly lavish salaries that the society paid its employees, especially during the first twenty years. The first overseas missionaries, Martha Cartmell and Eliza Spencer, were hired at $600 per year,[160] while Kezia Hendrie, as matron of the girls' school at Port Simpson, received $400 per year for her services.[161] These salary discrepancies between the fields existed for many years. In 1911 salaries for home missionaries were fixed at $450 for the first and second years and $500 for subsequent years. For missionaries in Japan the first year's salary was set at $500, the second to fifth years $650, and the second and following terms of service $700. Women assigned to China received $500 for their first year, $550, the second, $600 for the third to fifth years, and $650 for the second and following terms. No explanation other than the relative adversity of the work was offered for the higher overseas salaries. Nor was there fiscal compensation for previous related experience or any latitude for individual salary negotiation, even by the doctors. By 1921 starting salaries were uniform throughout the mission fields, and in response to persistent petitions from the employees, wages were increased to keep pace with rampant post-war inflation. Thereafter, all first-year recruits were paid $750; veterans and missionaries on furlough received $900.[162]

It is difficult to reconstruct similar wage scales for other working women. Women teachers employed in Toronto in 1881, for example, might draw salaries equal to those of WMS missionaries. By 1910 a veteran teacher in an urban area could earn as much as $900. But rural teachers' salaries were lower, ranging from about $200 to $600 over the period 1880–1920.[163] This discrepancy may partly explain the preponderance of rural and small-town women among the missionary force. Salaries for nurses at the turn of the century were about $2 per day and $3 for the care of patients with infectious diseases.[164] In 1908 one recruit who had worked in Buffalo as a private-duty nurse reported that she charged $20 per week for her services and "was busy."[165] Most Canadian nurses were not so fortunate. For many recruits, then, a missionary career occasioned a marginal improvement in their financial status. Although the women often complained about the gap between their expenses and their incomes, WMS salaries were higher than those paid by most other Canadian churches. In 1922 single women employees of the Canadian Baptist Missionary Society received $600 for the first two years and $700 thereafter.[166]

A WMS missionary career had other obvious benefits, in particular a furlough every six or seven years, a bonus that a teaching career did not provide. In addition to three-quarters salary, all travel expenses to the mission field and furlough return fares were paid for home and overseas missionaries.[167] Not surprisingly, many women in the Orient took the long way home through Russia or India and the Middle East. To ensure that a recruit had no extra expenses, the WMS

contributed an allowance for personal necessities, books and bedding, and furniture, usually a bed and dresser, which were to become
the property of the society.[168] The society provided housing, ideally
in a mission home or boarding school, and covered most related
living expenses, that is heat and light, for missionaries in the field.

The society seems to have become adept at discouraging mere adventurers, however. James Endicott, general secretary of the Board of
Foreign Missions from 1913 until 1937, for one, placed the impulses
of the WMS missionaries above reproach. After visiting the Orient in
1918, he praised the WMS while suspecting the motives of some misguided missionaries of other churches. There was, he conceded, a
romantic aura attached to missions, but he doubted very much "if
the lure of distant fields was a serious element in leading these
women to offer for foreign mission work. Certainly it is not this
which keeps them there. The mere romance of the work speedily
dissipates, to give place to something much more noble and deeply
inspiring."[169] Endicott's assessment of the WMS can probably be taken
at face value.

The most constant incentive drawing women to missionary work
was, simply, an intense and overpowering impulse to "do service for
the Master,"[170] sanctioned, of course, by the requisite personal call
from God that was the absolute proof of their legitimacy as Methodists. The summons was not, as one might assume, necessarily a
confidential matter, but an experience worth rehearsing to sway others. It marked the entry into a select club of Methodist women who
shared the common bond of the assurance of their salvation and
purpose in life. During the WMS annual meetings, where new recruits
were given enthusiastic send-offs, the candidates sometimes
described their personal communion with God. Other women
recorded the details of their summons to a life dedicated to God's
work in their diaries or in correspondence with the society. The
nature of the call, the submissiveness and passivity inherent in the
response, and the rhetoric of the retelling remained unchanged
throughout the history of the society. Martha Cartmell experienced
her "clear and convincing" call in the midst of a service conducted
by Dr Morley Punshon, the impassioned mission publicist. In Cartmell's case the impulse was so strong "that when we bowed in prayer
I felt myself alone in the presence of my Creator, and I said simply,
'Lord, Thou knowest me altogether and seest the line of my life from
its beginning to the end. Here I am, send me.' I was immediately,
almost overwhelmed by the solemnity of the act and my sense of

utter worthlessness ... I sought to be obedient. I said, 'If Thou has spoken knowing me perfectly, if Thou canst use me, and will make Thy will known to me, I will obey and follow Thee.'"[171]

Cartmell's colleague Agnes Wintemute was invited in the first instance not by God but by her minister to become a missionary. Wintemute, who seemed rather ambivalent about volunteering, prayed for God's intervention to guarantee "that if such were not His will that He would put hindrances in the way."[172] When no divinely inspired impediments materialized, Wintemute, by now thoroughly convinced that God had interceded on her behalf, went to the dentist and then to the dressmaker to plan a new wardrobe suitable, she hoped, for the variable Japanese climate.[173] In the weeks before her departure secret misgivings plagued Wintemute. She lamented in her diary that the "Lord's ways are not our ways," a familiar adage repeated by missionaries in the face of uncertainty, fear, and tragedy.[174]

Other women were far more confident about their belief and commitment. Martha Swann, sent to China in 1900, had been, she assured the board, "moved by the Holy Spirit to the work of a missionary." In her own eyes she was an especially worthy candidate because her sins were "all washed away in the precious blood of Jesus ... [She] had endeavoured to live a consistent and godly life and to let [her] light so shine before men that others might glorify [her] Father in Heaven."[175] Jean Holt, who had been teaching, as she put it, "the strangers within our gates" in Hilltop, Manitoba,[176] approached the WMS in 1914 for a posting to China because she did not believe that "God intended [her] to stay while others could do the work and voices are calling ... from across the waters."[177] Uberta Steele, by contrast, struggled to find God and a sign that she should pursue the missionary career that her membership in the Young Peoples' Forward Movement seemed to condone.[178] Steele subsequently had to surmount an acute spiritual crisis, but it culminated in her application to the WMS. Katherine Drake was another who trusted that "God was leading [her] all along the way." "Is it possible," she asked the board, "that My Master wants me to offer myself to Him for missionary work and is so shutting up other doors?"[179] In the final analysis, then, the myriad of testimonials affirming a determination "to live for others" and a desire to become "a soul winner"[180] suggests that religious considerations, not an excess of late Victorian romantic imagination, were uppermost in attracting Methodist women to the missionary profession.

Inspired by the traditional Methodist quest for holiness, WMS recruits assumed, somewhat selfishly, that by helping and saving others they would secure their own place in the Heavenly Kingdom. It was not, as Barbara Welter has suggested of American foreign missionaries, that they actively sought "death in the service of the Lord" as martyrs.[181] In fact, the possibility of dying in the mission field was not a matter of pressing concern to them for their own sake because as Victorian women they understood and accepted the proximity of death.[182] As practical women they worried more about the expense and the anguish for their relatives at home. Their greatest personal anxiety, as diaries and letters written after they reached their destinations reveal, was their inability to overcome the worldly habits that blocked the path to their own perfection and salvation. Earnest, eschewing frivolity, but not entirely lacking a sense of fun and good humour, these women, like the Jane Addams depicted so sensitively by Christopher Lasch, sometimes seem to have been rebelling against a meaningless and foolish way of life that their society sought to impose on them.[183]

Implicit in the recruits' testimonies are the themes of traditional Methodism. Their emotional affirmations of faith support the contention that Methodism, at least in its British Wesleyan form, was essentially an experimental religion rooted not in "mere theory or speculation or intellectual conviction, but ... the personal knowledge of the 'life of God in the soul of man.'"[184] The WMS, with its regard for the evidence of personal knowledge of God, encouraged this attachment to the historical tenets of Methodism.[185] To ensure that its personnel thoroughly understood and could transmit Methodist doctrine, when the Methodist Training School was opened in Toronto in 1894 to prepare deaconesses, the society required its recruits to enrol for at least a term.

The training school might have represented a forward step in the participation of women in the Methodist Church had it not been for its use as a steady supply of cheap labour, which it produced in the form of deaconesses. Ten years earlier the *Christian Guardian* had strenuously opposed a Methodist diaconate because "the employment of women as deaconesses and teachers ha[d] hardly been tried upon a large enough scale to make one confident respecting the results."[186] By 1894, however, the paper praised deaconess work as "wise and laudable," deserving "liberal support," in particular because of its benevolence to the growing hordes of urban poor.[187] The diaconate soon became an accepted component of the Canadian Methodist structure, and, as John Thomas has noted, "the Laurier boom, the continued patronage of wealthy Methodists, and vigorous explanation and promotion combined to vitalize the work."[188]

The WMS drafted its own course of study "in the presentation of spiritual truth and in the winning of others to Christ,"[189] but the training school program was designed to repair a multiplicity of defects in a candidate's character as well. In one unusual case where Mission Secretary Alexander Sutherland was consulted concerning an applicant's suitability, the woman in question, whose credentials were "very satisfactory as far as her Christian character and ability [were] concerned," was referred to the training school because of "her lack of neatness ... a matter of great importance in any one who goes to work among the Indians, especially if the work be in one of the Homes." A term at the training school was expected to improve the woman's personal appearance and give the Board of Managers "sufficient time to form a definite opinion in the matter."[190] This proved to be the appropriate corrective; the reformed candidate served as a home missionary for thirty years.[191]

The spartan and almost cloistered routine at the home was a harsh introduction to missionary life, especially for women who had just spent three or four years at college, but once there, few women seem to have dropped out. Most women financed their own way, but the WMS was prepared to offer loans, to be repaid in instalments as soon as the candidates reached the mission field. Residents of the home had to pay for room, board, fuel, and lights and were expected "to assume cheerfully [a] share of the general housework."[192] All students were advised to bring religious books but only one trunk, and were required to furnish for their personal use blankets, towels and soap, kitchen aprons, heavy underflannels (with sleeves), overshoes and leggings, and "gossamer and umbrellas, as the work may require one to be outdoors in all weather." Clothing was to be "simple and serviceable, special attention being paid to the comfort and health of the wearer. Dentistry, shopping and dress-making should be attended to before coming that studies may not be interrupted by these matters." Social life at the training school was equally regimented. Callers could be received only on Friday evenings; Sunday and one other evening might be spent outside the home without special consent.[193]

Much of the mandatory curriculum for WMS recruits was expressly Methodist in content. The women were required to study Galbraith's *Manual of Methodist Doctrines*, along with selected sermons of John Wesley: 1. Salvation by Faith; 5. Justification by Faith; 10. Witness of the Spirit; 13. Sin in Believers; 35. Law Established through Faith;

and 40. On Christian Perfection. These sermons are the core of Wesleyan theology.[194] For Bible study, candidates were referred to *Bible Outlines* by J.H. Vincent and the Epistle to the Romans, and they were also responsible for knowing the Discipline of the Methodist Church.[195] In 1899 the WMS expanded the course to include an examination of the entire Bible, Church history, the evidence of Christianity, Christian doctrine, early Christian art, as well as more practical topics for missionaries: elementary medicine, applied Christianity, temperance, and mission financing.[196] By 1921 the curriculum included lectures about the WMS and courses on the lives of Christ and Paul, Hebrew poetry, the philosophy of religion, first aid, physical education, the social customs of China and Japan, and public speaking. The mandatory course in homiletics and evangelism, which included advice for the conduct of public prayers and religious meetings, reflected the distance the women had come from merely telling the simple story of Jesus' love.[197] In short, while still preserving the principles of Wesleyan Methodism, the changing curriculum also kept pace with or was in advance of the evolution of the Methodist Church, which by the end of the First World War had shifted from a preoccupation with individual salvation to earn a reputation as "the most radical religious denomination in North America."[198] At the training school, then, the recruits were exposed to a variety of ideas and methodologies that they could, if they chose, apply to their subsequent work in the mission field.

The final hurdle in the way of recruits awaiting an assignment to the mission field was a thorough medical evaluation. At first the word of a family physician was accepted as evidence that a candidate was in top physical condition, but after about 1890 the WMS designated its own medical examiner and adopted a standardized medical form borrowed from the Women's Foreign Missionary Society of the American Methodist Episcopal Church.[199] This change seems to have been prompted by a suspicion that some women who returned to Canada at the society's expense because of ill health should not have been approved in the first place. The society, obviously, prized a good medical report. The board was convinced that excellent health and stamina were vital, especially when contending with the adversities of the overseas mission fields. In actuality, missionaries in northern British Columbia lacked more of the comforts of civilization, including good medical care, than missionaries in Japan or West China. By 1920 the Board of Managers, which had always tended to equate the

Orient with deprivation, admitted that there was, in fact, "no light work" for those who could not handle adversity.[200]

The doctor examined the candidate's heart, lungs, digestive system, and urinary tract. WMS medical reports indicate a particular concern over tuberculosis; in dubious cases, if family members had the disease, candidates were rejected. Whether this caution was responsible, there were no reported cases of tuberculosis among the WMS missionaries during the society's forty-five-year history. The doctor considered the patient's past illnesses, family medical problems, menstrual history, and vaccination record before pronouncing on her physical condition. A complaint of "occasional flatulence" was no barrier to an overseas posting.[201] But even a complete examination could not preclude serious illness, mental breakdown, or death. Take, for instance, Miss Dingman, an unusually outstanding recruit who survived the perils of missionary work in Africa but died in Canada shortly after her appointment to Port Simpson.[202] Ironically, some women relegated to home mission work because of a less than sensational medical report worked until retirement and lived into their eighties.[203]

The General Board of Missions of the Methodist Church and the mission secretary theoretically had the last word on WMS appointments. Only rarely did the mission secretary impede the WMS selection process, thus confirming the initial autonomy the society had established from male interference in its affairs. At any rate, further evaluation of the candidates by the church hierarchy would have been redundant because the WMS board had already solicited letters from the candidates' employers, usually school superintendents, and from their ministers. The authors of these testimonials (which are available only for women who were accepted) placed a high value on common sense, unselfishness, energy, and perseverance. Critical comments were infrequent, although one or two women were characterized by their male superiors as "timid" or "retiring," in masculine eyes apparently a disadvantage for missionary work. Taken at face value, the testimonials and the WMS' own observations denote a select group of consecrated and devoted women of "sterling character" and exemplary personal lives who were well equipped to handle, with ingenuity and tact, the obstacles of the mission field.[204]

As far as the board was concerned, after completion of their allotted time at the training school most candidates were ready to be sent to the mission field. Usually it was still several months before the recruit reached her post. The logistics and minutia of departure occupied many weeks of the new missionary's time. Because of the uncertainty and ignorance about living abroad and because the society worried about the inconvenience and the money wasted having personal and household goods shipped to missionaries in the Orient, the women tried to leave home prepared for all conceivable circumstances. Martha Cartmell spent several weeks packing her personal belongings for Japan. Her outfit included a coal-oil stove (with five nightdresses tucked into the oven), a desk, a chest, bedding, and cooking utensils. Her clothing inventory, reminiscent of a bridal trousseau, consisted of six new silk dresses, eight skirts (two white), two printed everyday dresses, four suits, six hats, five pairs of boots, three pairs of slippers, and nineteen pairs of stockings. Among her books were Bibles, Wesley's hymns, the poetry of Longfellow and Tennyson, the *Odyssey*, the *Iliad*, Caesar, Herodotus, a juvenile temperance manual, and an assortment of Ontario secondary school-books and readers intended for her prospective Japanese pupils.[205] Friends and admirers deluged her with dozens of gifts, which she carefully listed – a gold watch, gold bracelets, evening shawls to ward off the night air of Tokyo, a bottle of wild strawberry, which may have been perfume but, more likely, was a common remedy for dysentery, and photos of her home town. Cartmell's own fare to Yokohama totalled $221.10; shipping her baggage cost $311.90![206]

On 23 November 1882 a final farewell was held for Cartmell at Centenary Methodist Church in Hamilton. She was presented with a purse containing two hundred dollars from well-wishers as a gesture of admiration and deference for a woman who already was a local heroine. During the evening "all the speakers expressed the most profound sympathy with Miss Cartmell in the noble duty which she had undertaken, while they expressed their joy and satisfaction that this new missionary movement had been inaugurated and that such a worthy instrument had been selected to advance the objects of the society."[207] In keeping with Victorian convention, which frowned on women speaking in public, Cartmell's cousin, Rev. Donald Sutherland, responded on her behalf.[208]

This was probably the last time Cartmell relied on such a proxy; once in Japan she soon learned to speak up for herself. The next day she relinquished the security and comfort of her home, her teaching career, and her close-knit circle of friends and family to journey to "the Mikado's Kingdom" to work for the Woman's Missionary Society.[209] Over the next forty years three hundred more women would follow a similar route to WMS missions at home and abroad. Like Martha Cartmell's, their lives would be transformed by their confrontation with unfamiliar cultures and environments and by their individual and collective efforts to make missionary work a viable and rewarding career.

CHAPTER THREE

The spirit of a sensitive independence

In late December 1882 Martha Cartmell arrived in Tokyo to begin work as the first WMS overseas representative. During the previous month she had travelled more than eight thousand miles, first by train from Buffalo to San Francisco (until the Canadian Pacific Railway was completed in 1885, it was necessary to take the American route to the west coast), then by steamer across the Pacific to Yokohama. To accommodate Victorian etiquette, which censured not just women speaking in public but well-bred women travelling alone, the WMS had made arrangements at Buffalo for Cartmell to accompany a party of American missionaries also en route to the Orient. The group, which included two women whom Cartmell wryly characterized as "not ... so good looking, but ... decidedly practical Christian workers,"[1] travelled to Omaha, then to San Francisco to board the steamer *City of Tokio* for the two- to three-week voyage across the Pacific.

The vessel was just one of many passenger ships that, by the 1880s, regularly ferried missionaries, businessmen, diplomats, and adventurers to various destinations in the Orient. Their more worldly and hedonistic fellow travellers regarded the missionaries as a piously self-righteous lot who inhibited the anticipated levity and festivity of a prolonged ocean passage. For instance, in the summer of 1887 on a voyage across the Pacific with her astronomer husband to observe an eclipse of the sun in Japan, Mabel Loomis Todd, a woman with a far more permissive outlook than any missionary, found herself, to her chagrin, among "a funny collection of passengers, certainly. Every one is a missionary of some sort – minister or doctor, wife of one ... They can't and won't play whist, they drink no ale, only ginger pop, and they have prayers ... every evening, and sing hymns for recreation."[2] For their part, unless they were seasick, a common enough complaint, missionaries enjoyed the voyage. Neophytes were especially appreciative of the advice proffered by veteran missionaries with whom they became acquainted. But in spite of her own congenial and sympathetic companions, even before she arrived in Omaha, Cartmell was overwhelmed by the acute homesickness and doubts about her ability that invariably troubled wms missionaries leaving home for the first time.[3]

Cartmell's emotional response to her challenging situation is hardly surprising. As she made her way to Japan, the middle-aged schoolteacher at last had the leisure to reflect on the drastic change in her life. She recalled how she had kept her decision "in secret to God" before she was given the opportunity, through employment with the wms, to reveal it "to mortals."[4] Once in Tokyo, Cartmell was somewhat reassured by the warm welcome she received from Dr Davidson Macdonald, the patriarch of the Canadian Methodist mission in Japan, in whose home she was to board, and Mrs C.S. Eby, wife of a General Board missionary. Mrs Eby's first priority was to initiate Cartmell into the delights of Japanese cuisine at a Tokyo restaurant. With a degree of both stoicism and optimism, Cartmell conceded that the food looked very appealing, but "some peculiar flavour made it less palatable than it will be by and by."[5]

In spite of her intention to adapt to the unfamiliar Japanese culture, Cartmell and many of the eighty other wms missionaries who arrived in Japan over the next forty-five years never became completely or comfortably acclimatized. Their mandate to Christianize Japanese women did not necessarily require their own conformity to Japanese ways. On the contrary, it could be useful to keep one's distance from the host culture. As a way to impress upon their Canadian audience the defects in Japanese society that Christianity would repair, many missionaries berated Japanese food and domestic habits, politics, morality, and religion as irritating, offensive, unprogressive, and of course heathen. Some of these denunciations were rooted in westerners' ignorance or misunderstanding of the historical implications of Oriental habits. But another reason for the difficult adjustment may have been the prevailing image of Japan that these pioneering missionaries carried with them from Canada. Their perception of Japan was probably shaped in the first instance by the extensive travel and periodical literature of the day, which in the 1870s and 1880s especially tended on the one hand to romanticize Japan, emphasizing its stunning landscapes and untamed nature, but on the other to condemn the country's moral indifference and licentiousness.[6]

Over the years the women's complaints ranged from the trivial – sitting on the floor and the scarcity of some Western consumer goods

– to a wholesale indictment of Japanese civilization and the Japanese people. If their situation as missionaries in Japan became tolerable, even satisfying, the women's own ability to sustain their middle-class Canadian behaviour and customs within the Japanese milieu was largely responsible. As the WMS mission developed and the missionary community expanded, personal adjustment became somewhat easier. But the kind of misgivings that Cartmell suffered in the 1880s continued to perturb women who arrived forty years later. Sadie Tait's self-doubt and cultural shock on her arrival in Japan in 1917 hardly differed from Cartmell's initial response. Infused as they were with Christian passion, the women had difficulty recognizing and ultimately conceding that they were, as one of them admitted, "on the outside of Japanese life, and to a certain extent must be content to remain so."[7] This was because most Japanese regarded the missionaries with indifference, suspicion, or hostility as interlopers, as Western imperialist intruders who, collectively at least, threatened the Japanese national identity. With some justification, even as late as 1925 WMS missionaries felt uneasy and culturally isolated in Japan.[8]

Distressing as it was for the individual missionary, this alienation was not an insurmountable barrier to WMS work. In time the missionaries carved out a niche within Japanese society from which they operated relatively freely, administering some of the most prestigious girls' schools in the country. The WMS Japanese mission is all the more remarkable for the degree of autonomy that its personnel achieved as highly qualified and self-reliant professional Western women in a country whose patriarchal social structure thwarted most attempts to redefine women's subordinate role within the family. The WMS workers' diligence earned the respect of the small but apparently influential Japanese Christian community.[9]

By the time Cartmell arrived in Tokyo, the General Board of Missions of the Methodist Church of Canada had already been evangelizing and teaching there for ten years. In 1873, as part of an extensive modernization policy designed to bring Japan recognition and respect from the West, the emperor Mitsuhito, who took the name Meiji, meaning "Enlightened government," began to institute social and political reforms to vitalize Japanese society. These measures included the removal of the Tokugawa edicts, which had prohibited the preaching of Christianity in Japan. Almost immediately Western missionaries, among them Dr Macdonald and Rev. George Cochran of the General Board of Missions of the Methodist Church of Canada,[10] who interpreted the loosening of restrictions as a victory for Christianity, rushed to Japan, determined to make up for lost time.

The missionaries met little opposition to their message because, encouraged by the government's less insular outlook, the Japanese, in particular the samurai class, had become intensely curious about all aspects of Western culture and technology. To implement its program of social improvement and modernization, in the 1870s the Japanese government had hired "scores of Occidental experts and teachers at high salaries in order to attract real talents, and since ... they paid for these people out of their own meagre financial resources, they utilized them to the fullest."[11] The ambitious Japanese middle class aped Western cultural and social mores. Japanese men began to abandon the traditional topknot for more practical Western haircuts, while the modern young men about town could be seen "eating beef, sporting umbrellas and big 'turnip' watches. Women learned to use the new sewing machines to turn out western-style dresses with large bustles."[12] University students studied Western literature; translations of J.S. Mill and Samuel Smiles seemed to hold the formulae for successful competition with the West.[13]

Missionaries were appreciated as the source of much of this new learning. Consequently, for a brief period in the 1880s Western missionaries, financed by their own constituencies were, if not always eagerly welcomed for their proselytizing and Christian message, widely tolerated because of the exceptional Western education they offered to the children of the ambitious Japanese middle class.[14] The WMS rode into Japan on the crest of this serendipitous wave of interest in all things Western. The reception would not be repeated in the following decades.

By 1880 Christianizing Japanese women had become a matter of urgency among Canadian Methodists. While Japanese women's lives were somewhat less restricted than those of their Chinese sisters, Oriental social convention none the less barred male missionaries, including medical practitioners, from any form of contact, even evangelization, with women, especially of the upper classes. Moreover, their limited success in proselytizing Japanese men was influencing the General Board missionaries to apply prevailing North American attitudes about the role of women as moral guardians of the family to the Japanese. They argued that if Japanese women were exposed to Christianity, they would in their innate capacity as virtuous wives and mothers then awaken the rest of the household and deliver them to the Methodist fold. The General Board missionaries began publicly to reprimand their church for its negligence in this area of missionary endeavour. As George Cochran explained, "Nearly every mission had a girls' school, under the care of Christian women, sent out and sustained by special funds. I have felt it as the one defect in our mission to Japan that we have nothing of the kind."[15]

As much as women missionaries were sought as a necessary complement to the Methodist contingent, Cochran and his colleagues never recommended that they should be hired by a separate woman's society; the men had anticipated that women missionaries would be employed as part of their jurisdiction. Financial difficulties, however, prevented the General Board from adopting Cochran's proposal. In the meantime, Canadian Methodist women formed their own exclusively female missionary organization. It seems likely that the General Board's dashed hopes about the subordination of women missionaries fostered some of the consequent animosity and sexual tension between the men and women of the Japan mission.

As a woman missionary Cartmell was, in fact, a latecomer to Japan. In 1882 fifty-two woman missionaries were at work throughout the country, with seven girls' boarding schools under their supervision.[16] The Methodists believed that they faced a distinct disadvantage by opening work in regions where other churches had already begun evangelizing and were operating schools. In Japan the rivalry and competition among churches for converts and pupils was keen and remained so until at least the first decade of the twentieth century, when Protestant missionaries generally recognized the fiscal senselessness of duplicated services and turned to more co-operative ventures.[17] Ignoring her male associates' recommendation that as a woman she ought not to do too much,[18] Cartmell slowly and cautiously began her work with the aid of an interpreter. Within a few months she reported that she was "entering any open door to usefulness and influence," helping in the Sunday school, teaching English to a group of young men, conducting women's meetings, and visiting the sick.[19]

Cartmell's WMS champions in Canada provided generous financial support. In addition to her annual salary of six hundred dollars and her extensive outfit, she received private donations to expedite the opening of the anticipated girls' school and the metamorphosis of Japanese women.[20] (The practice of sending donations to individual missionaries was banned by the Board of Managers a few years later when it warned missionaries that all funds must come from "the proper official authorities.")[21] Cartmell's happiness and well-being so far from home worried her Canadian mentors, perhaps all the more because she was a cousin of Elizabeth Strachan, WMS corresponding secretary, and Elizabeth Ross, another prominent Methodist laywoman who became WMS president in 1897. But as a rule all WMS missionaries were greatly admired by the society's members, many of whom harboured their own secret ambitions to have pursued a missionary career. As an expression of their respect, for instance, whenever a missionary entered a WMS meeting, auxiliary members always stood.[22] Canadian Methodist women remained proud of their ability to raise sufficient money to ensure that their agents were as secure and content as circumstances would permit. At the end of her first year in Tokyo, Cartmell could report that "comforts surround me" and her own lot was not an especially hard one. It was not more financial support that she requested, but prayers to advance her work among Japanese women.[23]

Success, as measured by Cartmell's ability to implement the WMS' scheme for a girls' school, came relatively easily. In October 1884, just two years after Cartmell arrived in Tokyo, the first WMS girls' boarding school, the Toyo Eiwa Jo Gakko (Oriental-English Japanese Girls' School), was officially opened in the Azabu district of Tokyo. Although the society's original intention was to operate a day school, Cartmell insisted that a boarding school where "girls could be kept under constant Christian influences" was preferable to permitting them to return at day's end to the anti-Christian atmosphere of their homes.[24] Before she could open the school Cartmell had to petition the Japanese government to ensure that her plans coincided with its regulations, set up in 1871, to develop an educational system based on that of the United States. In keeping with the modernization policy, education for both sexes was made compulsory, although girls were not required to remain in school as long as boys and after 1879 boys and girls beyond the elementary level had to attend separate schools.[25] In 1872 the government had itself founded the Tokyo Girls' School.[26]

Cartmell's request was granted, and when the General Board offered her a piece of land adjacent to its new boys' school for the substantial sum of one thousand dollars, Cartmell, to the astonishment of the Board of Managers, accepted the proposal so that she might launch her project at once. Fortuitously for the society, Sarah Gooderham, WMS president, had just advised Cartmell "not to waste time and money on day schools but to begin a boarding school at once," adding that she would personally contribute "even to the lessening of [her] principal in the bank."[27] According to WMS tradition, the letters crossed in the Pacific, an incident that the society interpreted as proof of God's mysterious ways.

With Macdonald's assistance, Cartmell supervised the construction of the school building, designed to accommodate two missionaries in their own apartments, twenty boarders, and fifty-four day students. It opened with just two girls in residence, but before the school year ended in 1884 the building was so overcrowded that without an addition students would have had to be turned away. The society agreed to construct a second building on the same property to accommodate two hundred fifty students and four missionaries.[28] Although, as other missionaries in Tokyo warned her, the Japanese would "watch and test both us and the methods employed,"[29] Cartmell's fears that the WMS school would not be accepted by the Japanese were not realized.

Cartmell's achievement in establishing the Toyo Eiwa Jo Gakko in the face of language barriers, "idol worshippers," and the Japanese suspicion towards Westerners was rehearsed over and over in the annals of Canadian Methodism.[30] In 1930, when she was eighty-five, she was canonized as one of the "seers of the early period who read the signs of the times and advocated education for girls who would play a big part in the coming era"; her struggle "would live forever in the life of the Christian Church."[31] In spite of its overriding hagiographical tone and some perhaps predictable exaggeration of the Japanese antipathy towards Westernization, the appreciation of Cartmell's fortitude seems deserved and, certainly, hard earned. While the Japanese government may have extended compulsory education to girls, there were "no attempts to promote, at the same time, the requisite changes in attitude to get parents to pay for the education of daughters."[32] Moreover, the government's response to most missionary-inspired social changes, such as shorter hair or less gaudy and ostentatious clothing, that might affect women and their relationships within the family remained largely negative.[33] Hence, for a Westerner to gain popular support for a girls' school in Tokyo was exceptional. But by her own admission Cartmell inched her way to this eventual success; years later, she admitted that several months elapsed before she was invited into a Japanese home.[34]

For more than two years Cartmell was the sole WMS agent stationed in Japan. The society had deliberately avoided rapid expansion overseas because the board reasoned that "there was more danger in precipitancy than in delay."[35] In the long run, perhaps this course was judicious; but for Cartmell being on her own in the school was unsettling, especially because she put herself under extreme pressure to succeed. Although she appears to have been acquainted with other missionaries in Tokyo, she did not write about any one special friend or confidante. To add to her sense of isolation, she was constantly depressed by the "utter helplessness and inability to do anything that oppresses the missionary just entering a new field. Everything is strange, you are separated from those you wish to attract to yourself by race prejudices, habits and customs, which if not respected widen the breach, and more particularly by the language." Even the arrival of Eliza Spencer, a Brantford, Ontario, teacher and the daughter of a former editor of the *Christian Guardian,* to take charge of the administration of the girls' school did not alleviate Cartmell's obsession with her own "inability to reach more of the women of the churches, and through them the neighbors and friends who knew not the Gospel."

Convinced that "her lispings of the language" had hindered the evangelical work that was her personal preoccupation, she apologized to her Canadian supporters that "the feeble effort [she] was making in the weekly Bible Class seemed so futile."[36] To facilitate her evangelizing, Cartmell, following the example of women missionaries of other churches, hired a Japanese Bible woman, who began under the supervision of a Japanese preacher to visit women in their homes. Within a short time, the larger share of wms evangelization was being conducted by Bible women, whose simple Bible stories and lessons were, Western missionaries believed, "a most effective means of reaching the native women in the midst of their own households."[37] When her failing health permitted, Cartmell drafted a course of study for the four Bible women she had engaged, at a minimal salary, as soon as her work was "sufficiently successful to justify ... doing so."[38]

Although Cartmell increasingly concentrated on evangelizing, she remained committed to the girls' school as the route to Christianizing middle-class Japanese women. If sometimes she was discouraged about the overall prospects for Christian missions in Japan, Cartmell wrote optimistically about the school's future and the value of education for Japanese women. "No matter what these dear girls may be called upon to endure, in consequence of the contrast between the present of wonderful privilege and the future of necessary privation," Cartmell was sure that their wms schooling would "enable them nobly to accommodate themselves to the changes of circumstances ... and the world [will] be the better for their having lived in it."[39]

Girls' schools were women missionaries' first line of attack on the Japanese social and religious practices that they believed had rendered Eastern women "unwelcome at birth, untaught in childhood, enslaved when married, accursed as widows, unlamented when they died."[40] Like other Westerners in Japan, the wms agents were convinced that "the doctrine of 'triple obedience' to father, to husband, and when old to son" had had "disastrous consequences" for the country.[41] They believed that Japanese women could not realize their potential as moral guardians of the home or achieve the ideal of womanhood as defined by the Western "cult of domesticity" if they were denied both public and private responsibility and respect. Living for even a few months in the still feudal and patriarchal country provoked a strong emotional response from the missionaries about the treatment of women. They challenged the restrictions on Japanese women's personal freedom, their inadequate education, the arranged marriages, the extent of prostitution and male infidelity, and in particular the limited opportunities outside the home for the girls whom they were carefully grooming to be more self-reliant than their mothers.

The wms argued that from their privileged position Canadian Methodist women could not possibly comprehend the suffering of women "where the religion of Christ is unknown. For them, no light of homelife has ever shone. *Slaves* to brutal masters – not loving and beloved *wives* – have they been. Even motherly love – that precious and most enduring of all earthly loves – has been crushed and bleeding under the direful superstition of their so-called religions."[42] There can hardly be a clearer evocation of the Victorian "cult of true womanhood and domesticity," of the message of maternal feminism and its centrality to the gospel of Christian social reform as espoused by Canadian Methodists of the day, or of the wms's sense of *noblesse oblige* and duty to Oriental women than this assertion, which epitomized the society's perspective about its role in Japan. Fifty years later the wms's view of Japanese women was substantially unchanged. A history of the United Church's Japan missions written in 1931 concluded that "the freedom and individuality of Japanese women had been sacrificed on the altar of the family system, the result of the ethical teachings of Confucianism which flourished for six hundred years, and to this Buddhism had added its oppression of women. Socially and religiously their development had been hampered. Instead of self-expression, the tradition for women was self-effacement. Her virtues were negative – modesty and unobtrusiveness."[43]

Recent examinations of the status of women in the Meiji period substantiate these contemporary opinions. If anything, the Meiji reforms reinforced women's already submissive role within the family structure. "The moral code that became widespread during the Meiji period enjoined the wife to be the first up in the morning, the last to go to bed, to take her bath only after her husband and all his family members had bathed, and to devote herself in every way to her husband and his family."[44] To sustain this patriarchal family pattern, government-sponsored women's education aspired to "produce the good wife and wise mother for the maintenance of the family system."[45] Employment outside the home was not condoned for well-bred women.[46] After 1868, while 40 per cent of Japanese boys regularly attended school, 10 per cent of girls entered the educational system. Even then, cooking and sewing took precedence over science and mathematics in their curriculum. Most women's education continued to be carried on within the confines of the home as preparation for marriage and family life.[47] Only in 1911 were Japanese women given access to university education.[48] In Japan, as Cartmell explained to the WMS in 1885, "*A woman's place was in her home.*"[49]

The majority of Japanese women did not challenge tradition, but in the 1880s a handful of feminists who believed that education was the key to improving women's status "rejected the past and accepted the challenge of a changing Japan in which they would play larger and more significant roles."[50] Their spokesperson was Kishida Toshiko, founder of the Kyoto Women's Lecture Society, whose first meeting in 1883 was attended by more than two thousand women.[51] The incipient feminist movement shrivelled after Kishida's arrest in 1884; the Liberal party, which had promoted the women's lecture societies, dissolved, leaving Japanese feminists ideologically isolated and their educational plans without financial support.[52] In the absence of other arenas for women's reforming impulses, Christian mission schools like the Toyo Eiwa Jo Gakko filled the void by "offering intellectual challenges and a humanistic view of women to their Japanese students" and by helping to moderate, if not revolutionize, traditional Japanese attitudes about women's place in society.[53]

The WMS Tokyo girls' school adopted a broad curriculum encompassing mathematics, sciences, history, and instruction in English. Academically, socially, and morally, the Western influence was strong and pervasive. Mathematics was the only subject taught in Japanese. By graduation, girls were expected to have acquired "a reading and writing knowledge of Chinese, having taken their Japanese history and literature in Chinese, and facility in reading, writing and speaking English."[54] Science, specifically biology, was also a conspicuous feature of the curriculum. To generate interest in the subject Cartmell requested and received a microscope from Canada. The girls were fascinated by the slides she made of a flea, a mosquito, a moth, a fish scale, and sugar.[55] The primary-course required three years' attendance at the school, the full course eight, after which students, according to the WMS, should have skills comparable to Canadian children entering the second year of a high school.

Many middle-class parents sent their daughters to mission schools because the programs were more comprehensive than the compulsory government education for girls, which covered only the four years from ages six to ten;[56] some parents even approved if their daughters became Christians along the way. For others not especially attracted to Christian doctrine, mission schools were simply the most convenient route for their children to follow to obtain an excellent Western-style education. But in the mission school Western education and Christianity could not be segregated. The girls were required to attend several religious services on Sunday: Sunday school at 9 a.m., preaching at 10 a.m., prayer meeting at 4, English hymn singing from 5:30 to 6.00, and finally an evening service at 7 p.m.; daily Bible lessons were compulsory.[57] The low ratio of baptisms to the total number of students registered in wms schools suggests that many Japanese parents may have successfully inoculated their children against the proselytizing that was an integral part of the curriculum. Of the two hundred fifty students enrolled at the Tokyo school in 1885,[58] seventeen, by Eliza Spencer's accounting, became Christians – "exotics, transplanted from a heathen soil to a Christian garden."[59]

Whatever the motives of those Japanese parents who sent their daughters to a mission school, in its first years the Tokyo school was well received, and to the surprise of the society it became a remarkable financial success. The board had not intended the school to be a charitable institution for indigent students, but neither had it expected it to earn profits from the fees, which were allocated specifically to pay for board and the salaries of the Japanese teachers. In 1887 the income from Japanese sources covered all the operating costs of the school as well as the expenses of the five or six supported girls the society subsidized, and money was left over.[60] For its part the wms paid the salaries and expenses of its own employees and some costs of construction and upkeep.

The society attributed its early prosperity in Japan to the social position of its students, the daughters of the "higher classes" who were attracted to the Tokyo school. To the satisfaction of the missionaries, the board, and society members in Canada, the majority of the Tokyo schoolgirls belonged to very wealthy families, evidenced, the missionaries reported, by their fine silk clothing.[61] Among the early pupils in Tokyo were two princesses, the daughters of Marquis Hirobumi Ito, who was prime minister of Japan four times between 1885 and 1901, and the daughters of other high-ranking public officials and military officers. A few girls from poor families had their fees paid as "supported students," a practice that spread when enrolment slipped. As shrewd business managers the board members ensured that the society's investment was repaid. After graduation, supported students were required to serve the wms for two years as Bible women or teachers.[62]

The missionaries interpreted their affluent students' presence as part of God's purpose. "It was," wrote Eliza Spencer, "the Master leading when this school was established here, where its students can do so much to support themselves ... we can by their influence and money do much toward hastening on the time when from one end to the other of this beautiful land the 'Glad Tidings' shall have been preached."[63] While this sentiment might seem merely the expression of the women's elitist philosophy and upbringing, it was also a measure of their astuteness and missionary *realpolitik*. Cartmell and Spencer at least grasped quite quickly that in Japan, a society where change of any sort – political, social or cultural – could not be effected without the endorsement of the governing classes, the success of their mission depended on the good will of those adjacent to power. There was no resistance to this philosophy because WMS missionaries felt most comfortable working among women and girls of their own class, if not race. Abby Veazey found culture and refinement to be exclusive to the upper class; she and the others who frequented Tokyo's slums in the course of their evangelizing detested "the crowding about them of the dirty, ill-kept, unwashed children, and ... they had to pray hard that they might not mind the smells and sickening dirt around them."[64] The women slowly overcame their aversion to the circumstances in which some of their constituents lived. By 1912, while graduates of WMS girls' schools still included "the princess representing Japanese royalty at the British Coronation, ... the guest of honour at the right hand of our beloved King," also among them was "the happy, busy young wife of an earnest Christian washerman whose piles of fresh well-laundered linen is evidence of his doing no unimportant part of the world's work."[65] But the elitist image the women cultivated for their schools, especially in Tokyo, remained conspicuously at odds with their more burdensome work among the destitute and helpless in Japan's increasingly bleak industrial areas.

Organizing the Tokyo school and assuming total responsibility for the future of WMS missions in Japan eventually took its expected toll on Cartmell's stamina. Her deteriorating health began to alarm the Board of Managers. The exact nature of Cartmell's medical condition, if a physical problem existed, was unspecified and would not, in any event, have been the subject of public discussion. There was only a vague reference in the *Missionary Outlook* to "the Japan head," an ailment that some missionaries attributed to language study.[66] According to the doctors in the mission community, the disorder was the result of overwork and strain; the proposed cure, several weeks of rest in the cooler mountain regions.[67]

Cartmell was devastated by the diagnosis. In a private letter to her family, which, like other pieces of correspondence between missionaries and their Canadian relatives, inexplicably appeared in the *Missionary Outlook*, she confided that she feared "the worst form of head trouble. It is only when I think I am eating the fruits of my own doings, and that I am forced to rest when I ought to be working that anguish comes ... I cannot bear you should write, 'I know you were working too hard,' and I know you won't if you know it will pain me ... The praise of men has not been what I have sought and I cannot take it ... If I have done wrong, the Master's forgiveness is all I crave, and the forgetfulness into which He will cast my sin."[68]

Cartmell's excessive guilt seems consistent with the symptoms of a nervous breakdown. Her own analysis of the situation appears on the surface to imply a rather serious breach of conduct on her part, but that anything of the sort occurred is unlikely. Had Cartmell sinned in any literal sense, the indiscretion, as a later case involving a WMS missionary in China confirms, would never have been mentioned publicly and she would have been recalled immediately. Probably in response to Cartmell's situation, a sympathetic observation about the burdens of missionary life was published in the *Missionary Outlook*. The editor reminded readers that missionaries were merely "men and women with the same infirmities of body and mind as our own, and with far greater trials and temptations. They are placed in circumstances where the weakness of the flesh is sorely tried."[69]

Cartmell did not respond to the prescribed rest; early in 1887 she was furloughed to Canada.[70] By 1890 she had recovered her health, rejoining the WMS as an adviser to home missions in British Columbia; in 1892 she returned to Japan as an evangelist unencumbered by the administrative tasks that she had found so taxing. Three years later, in the midst of the chaos in the Japan Mission, Cartmell resigned to care for her ailing sister and retired permanently to Hamilton, where she lived with her cousins. She remained a WMS activist, addressing missionary circles and corresponding with her former WMS colleagues and Japanese pupils and friends almost until her death in 1945 at the age of ninety-nine.[71]

While accolades were given to her as the successful architect of the Tokyo school, Cartmell's response to praise remained self-effacing. Ten years after her return to Canada she was still haunted by the persistent fear that she had not known the Lord as she should; that she "did not exercise the self-control that would convince others of the grace I was conscious of – because I would talk of my fear of making mistakes when there should have been no fear."[72] Self-doubt and uncertainty, Cartmell believed, had contributed to her personal collapse. More probably, the obligations she assumed on behalf of the WMS in a culture totally unfamiliar to a middle-class, middle-aged

Victorian Canadian spinster in a male-dominated mission community were simply too onerous for a woman about whom a fellow worker said, "I believe God never put a sweeter soul in human form."[73]

Despite Cartmell's qualms about the future of WMS missions in Japan and her own part in them, the society itself was confident that an infusion of recruits could strengthen and extend the work. When Cartmell left Tokyo in 1887, three WMS missionaries remained to oversee the mission. Two of them, Spencer and Agnes Wintemute, if not quite the antithesis of Cartmell's reticence were at least more opinionated, self-reliant, and confident, qualities that became unmistakable in their encounters with the men of the mission community. Under Spencer's capable direction a second station was opened in 1887 in Shizuoka, a city about 130 miles southwest of Tokyo. In this case a delegation of influential Japanese businessmen approached the WMS about a school in their municipality. If the WMS were willing to administer the school and pay the missionary teachers, the Japanese would assume responsibility for all other expenses.[74] The society accepted the offer. The joint venture was bolstered by a donation of one thousand dollars from two Toronto women.[75] Early in 1888 Mary Jane Cunningham, an experienced teacher who had just arrived from Halifax, became director in Shizuoka, where she remained for most of the next twenty years.[76]

At first, the Shizuoka school building failed to meet Cunningham's rather pretentious expectations because it was only a Japanese home, albeit that of the deputy governor of the city, not the substantial Western-style structure she had anticipated. Still, the missionaries were pleased that in Shizuoka, too, their pupils were the daughters of the elite. Cunningham became an enthusiastic activist on behalf of Japanese women. Never a timid woman, she took the opportunity on at least one occasion to hector civic leaders about the need for better education for Japanese women. Her "audacity – standing up and telling the governor and other official men of Shizuoka that their wives were inferior to American ladies," astounded F.A. Cassidy of the General Board, who, Cunningham reported, "was afraid that they would be offended, but no such thing. My 'lecture' quite pleased them."[77] Eventually Cunningham's lack of respect did "provoke comment from Japanese," necessitating her recall in 1908;[78] but in the meantime her feminist statements were endorsed as promoting the WMS cause.

During its first fifteen years the society sent twenty-three women to Japan; in 1896 fifteen of them remained as a nucleus that shaped and determined the nature of WMS missionary work there. Furthermore, the women's meticulous accounts of their encounter with Japan, published in the various Methodist missionary journals, and their talks to WMS auxiliaries during their furloughs introduced the Canadian WMS membership to an unfamiliar culture. Through monthly WMS mission-study groups, Canadian women began, within the context of a supportive, exclusively female dialogue, to empathize with women of different races and gradually to reject some of their ethnocentric opinions.

In some instances auxiliaries might target individual missionaries for a more personalized correspondence. Much as the society expected the missionaries to contribute detailed letters to its publications, the women regarded correspondence for public consumption as a tedious chore. Some, on grounds that they did not have the time, provided only the minimum expected of them, while others simply did not write very frequently. Often the letters were repetitious; newcomers' first impressions of Japan rarely varied. Based on the missionaries' accounts of the beauty of Japan and its lush foliage, Methodist readers must have pictured the Japanese mission stations as agreeable locales in which to live and work in spite of the frequent manifestations of the unpredictable climate – earthquakes, typhoons, and tidal waves.

During her two years of language study in Tokyo in 1886 and 1887 Agnes Wintemute kept a diary that documents the normal routine of missionary life and registers her own particular delight and frustration as she began her career. At the girls' school missionaries and students alike operated within a highly structured and disciplined atmosphere. Daily activity was rigidly regimented. Breakfast was at 7. For Wintemute and other "novitiates" on the mission staff, three times a week the hour from 8:30 to 9:30 a.m. was set aside to study Japanese under the supervision of a Japanese teacher. Each evening before dinner there was an hour of Bible study. On Wednesday afternoons the women visited Japanese homes seeking an audience for their stories about Jesus; on Friday afternoons from 3:30 to 6:00 the mission house was open to visitors, usually Japanese women more curious about how the missionaries lived than about Christianity. In the intervals between duties those missionaries who were designated as teachers instructed English classes, while others, on their own or with Bible women, evangelized among Japanese women in urban and rural areas of the country, sometimes staying overnight in local inns in order to spread God's word. This rigorous schedule none the less allowed time for leisure activities: croquet, horseback riding, and lots of reading. Wintemute kept a list of the books she had read after leaving Canada. It included many contemporary novels (which might not have been approved Methodist reading) as well as the classics: *Ben Hur, Nicholas Nickleby, Letters from Hell, Adam Bede, Looking Backward*, and books by the popular evangelist Dwight Moody.[79] Some volumes were probably from the mission library and were available freely to all the women in the mission community.

Like Cartmell, the women could not legitimately complain of physical discomfort or material deprivation because they had brought with them so many trappings of middle-class Canada. They were, however, still acutely aware of the distance that separated them from Canada, from their homes and families. The arrival of overseas mail was eagerly anticipated, although as a veteran recalled, if it was delivered on Sunday, it was not opened.[80] Because responses to letters might take up to four months to reach Japan, the news of deaths and illness among family and friends was received with a stoical acceptance. Wintemute looked forward to news from home with "a strange mixture of ... anxiety, joy, surprise, pleasure and sorrow." When an account of a relative's death arrived, she responded predictably: "Thus one is taken and another left. Oh, to be ever prepared to meet our God."[81]

While they are valuable sources to document the operation of the Japan mission, Wintemute's diaries reveal equally her discouragement and doubt about her suitability for missionary work, misgivings that had surfaced even before she left Canada. The first anniversary of her decision to go to Japan was, for her, a day "when a person would lose all heart, if he did not truly believe that in some way or other there was a providence in everything."[82] Disheartened after a very frustrating afternoon of home visitation, she confessed that "on Wednesday afternoons ... I would rather stay at home, but after I go I am always so glad; and I almost believe it does *me* more good than the people whom I visit."[83]

Her first trip to the mountains for the summer vacation opened Wintemute's eyes "to the most wretched squalid looking places that [she] had seen in Japan." She pronounced Katatsui, a village where the party stayed overnight to observe the same eclipse that brought Mabel Todd to Japan, so immoral that "Dante should have visited ... before he wrote his Inferno."[84] Most nineteenth-century Western missionaries in Japan shared her revulsion at Japanese attitudes towards nudity and public bathing. In rural areas in summer, men, women, and children often wore only a *koshimaki*, a piece of cloth about two feet wide tied around the lower body.[85] Wintemute was especially unnerved by the public baths, where "people of both sexes bath[ed] promiscuously," and by the openness of the houses, where one, as she delicately phrased it, could "see all."[86]

In time Wintemute become reconciled to Japanese culture and sexual mores. After her marriage in 1893 she resigned from the WMS, but until the 1920s, when she rejected Methodist doctrines in favour of a variety of unorthodox movements, she continued to work with Japanese women on a voluntary basis and was so attached to her adopted land that she remained in Japan throughout the Second World War until her death in 1945.[87]

Others in this pioneering group were more encouraged than Wintemute by their efforts to win Christian converts and to recast Japanese society. Kate Morgan's first year in Japan was "the brightest and happiest in my religious experience, for never before have I felt such entire dependence on God and so little able to do anything in my own strength ... Is it not wonderful that the very men who last year were opposed to Christianity have now built a school where it is to be taught?"[88]

By the end of the 1880s, however, WMS correspondence suggests that the work was not proceeding as smoothly as the society or the missionaries expected because of Japanese scepticism towards the government's modernization policies. The most striking evidence of the current bitterness towards the West was a sharp decline in enrolments at mission schools. Now out of fashion, Christian schools were suspect as instruments of Western imperialism designed to erode conventional Japanese values. Girls' school were denounced for neglecting the "special characteristics" of Japanese women and because they were "'insufficiently protective' of traditional Japanese virtues." "Foreign women," it was argued, "in addition to making every effort to convert paying students to Christianity, filled their heads with subjects totally inappropriate to the reality of women's lives."[89] Publicly, the WMS missionaries attributed the diminishing attendance to a depressed Japanese economy, not to the heightened Japanese nationalism that produced "successive waves of chauvinism."[90]

Mary Jane Cunningham, for one, conceded that the antipathy to the girls' schools was related, if not to a reaction against Westernization generally, then to the indisputably Christian character of the mission schools. As she explained to the board, "People complain that such a strong religious influence is thrown round the girls that those who enter the school as boarders are almost certain to become Christians. At first there was little or no objection to Christianity. It was something Western, and there was such a craze for anything from the West."[91] In Kofu, Wintemute confronted the hostility of people "who [were] not as advanced as those of most of the provinces," Buddhists and "others who hate[d] Christianity."[92] Faced with falling enrolment at the girls' schools, the wms Council in Japan could not justify the appointment of any new workers for 1890.[93] Possibly to conceal the reality of the situation, it moved that the Board of Managers publish only a general financial statement for the year.[94]

During the 1890s Christianity became increasingly distrusted as the advance guard of Western imperialism, especially because most Protestant missionary organizations had "national titles prefixed to their names, such as the American Methodist, the Anglican, the Canadian Methodist ... Suspicious minds thought that these bodies enjoyed political support in their several countries."[95] Among the educated elite who were the most likely converts, Christianity, now denounced as "unJapanese,"[96] faced strong competition from the ideas of Herbert Spencer, Charles Darwin, and English empiricism, which had become firmly entrenched at Tokyo University.[97] Finally, in 1894, the war with China galvanized public sentiment against the West. While they were satisfied with the peace arrangements, the Japanese resented the intervention by Russia, France, and Germany in the negotiations.

The consequences for the Christian church and missions in Japan were devastating. In some instances enrolment at mission schools dropped by more than 50 per cent.[98] The wms experience from 1881 to 1895 reflects these general trends. Whereas in 1886, "without any effort on our part, from thirty to forty women would gather around us to hear the word of God," by 1893, according to Eliza Spencer, "only by constant, untiring work ... can [we] get a half dozen to hear us ... Seven years ago everything foreign was sought after, and, in order to study us and be like us, they endured our teaching of a God whom they knew not of. Now foreign ways are not things to be desired ... the harvest of souls does not appear."[99] After the years of success, rejection and the restrictions on missionary work were hard to accept.

To consolidate its position in Japan, in 1889 the wms had opened a third station in Kofu, midway between Tokyo and Shizuoka, again with the financial backing of local businessmen.[100] By 1898, 134 students were registered at the school there, and in 1900 Kofu boasted a larger enrolment than the Tokyo school. But from 1890 until 1900 there was little growth in wms educational concerns in Japan because of the mounting hostility. Instead the society decided, in 1892, to open a station in Kanazawa, an industrial city on the Sea of Japan, where the women challenged the effects of urban industrial poverty for the first time. In this situation the customary techniques of door-to-door visiting and women's meetings were ineffectual as means to introduce the poverty-stricken women of Kanazawa, who "worked from early morning until long after lamplight at silk embroidery seven days in the week," to Christianity.[101] Because most parents were unable to pay the minimal fees charged by government schools, let alone the expenses involved in sending their children to a mission boarding school, the WMS opened a night school and a Sunday school for factory girls. The missionaries in Kanazawa also rented a house in the slum district where young children were paid to make matches and handkerchiefs, although this scheme ran into difficulty when the Sino-Japanese war seriously disrupted commerce, including the match trade.

The women were not welcome in Kanazawa. Cunningham was "mocked to her face, [and] called [a] foreign devil," as "those teeming thousands, to whom she had brought the most important message in the world" rejected her attempts to help them.[102] Fifteen years passed before the missionaries were able to do their work without harrassment.[103] While Abby Veazey assumed the predominantly working-class populace resented the missionaries simply as foreigners, it seems as likely that the women were relegated to the peripheries of Japanese life after 1890 because of their sex.[104] And to compound the WMS's difficulties in the face of the threatened marginalization of the work in Japan, the strains of disharmony, which climaxed in 1895 with an official investigation of the Canadian Methodist Japan mission stations, began to be heard.

In 1890 the rift between the WMS and the General Board missionaries in Japan was just emerging; its course was complicated by disputes among the men over salaries and authority within their own mission, while the woman disagreed about their allegiance to their putative leader, Eliza Spencer Large, now the senior WMS agent in Japan. Because she was such a capable administrator, the Board of Managers had decided, in spite of its own rules to the contrary, to permit her to carry on as principal of the Tokyo school after her marriage in July 1887 to Alfred Large, a General Board missionary. Their engagement had been a well-kept secret even from Spencer's female colleagues, no doubt because of the reasonable suspicion that she would be relieved of her duties and dismissed as soon as the news became public. In a testimony to Spencer's executive ability and also as a strong endorsement of Christian marriage, the board unexpectedly gave "a hearty consent, believing that benefit may arise as the pupils have a somewhat near view of the privilege accorded by Christianity to women as the companion of man."[105]

On 18 July, wearing the traditional white gown and veil, Eliza Spencer married Alfred Large in a ceremony performed by Rev. Hiraiwa Yoshiyasu, one of the Japanese Methodist preachers.[106] They were attended by many schoolgirls. The following day the entire mission staff, newlyweds in tow, departed on the annual summer trek into the mountains beyond Yokakawa, taking with them all the comforts of the mission compound, servants, beds, and dishes included.[107] The marriage apparently rankled some of the Methodist mission community. Agnes Wintemute recorded her disgust at her associates' malicious reaction. "I really did not think that Christian people could be capable of getting up such detestable gossip as I have reason to believe from to-day's disclosures is being started in this compound."[108]

With Eliza Large entrenched as the director of the Japan mission, the women began to build their own administrative structure and to define their needs and aspirations as professional missionaries. Until 1886 the men of the General Board and the women of the WMS in Japan appear to have discussed, albeit informally, most matters of mutual concern. But in 1886 the General Board in Japan inaugurated its own mission council. The women were not invited to the meetings. This was, perhaps, neither unusual nor unexpected, given that the WMS was not represented on any Methodist council in Canada.[109] But it appears that the women's exclusion from the General Board's mission council was a deliberate affront, not just an oversight. In a report written in 1894 for the General Council's investigation of the Japan Affair, Dr Macdonald, the veteran General Board representative, recalled that "after [6 February 1886 the women] never received any notice of our meetings ... In the constitution of the Council no provision was made for any representation of the Woman's Missionary Society workers." Without directly suggesting that the WMS ought to have been included on the council, Macdonald conceded "that the ladies did not withdraw from us, but we seem to have, unwittingly, dropped them."[110]

After consultations with the Board of Managers, in September 1888 the women set up their own council, designed to evaluate their particular work, to impose uniform standards throughout the mission stations, especially a common school curriculum, and to determine the stationing of personnel. It met monthly under the direction of a secretary-treasurer and a recording secretary, usually veteran missionaries.[111] An executive council, based in Tokyo, was designated to handle emergencies. The annual meeting, which in later years was held at a resort hotel, became a happy reunion where the women shared their experiences, discussed their problems, and simply enjoyed themselves in more luxurious surroundings than usual. But it was also a vehicle for the gradual redefinition of their profession as a self-regulating enterprise and for making decisions without reference to the work of the General Board of Missions. For example, in September 1890, as a protest against their heavy workloads and because there were now thirteen experienced missionaries in the field, the women petitioned the board to raise salaries from $600 to $700 per annum for the first five-year term and to $800 for each subsequent term. They argued that second-term workers who had mastered Japanese were likely to remain with the WMS and therefore required higher salaries in order to save for retirement. The very nature of overseas work, whereby "all alike [gave] up the social privileges and opportunities of advancement they enjoyed at home,"[112] made a raise essential; the women had to purchase books they would not otherwise have needed, and, to intensify their financial predicament, their busy schedules allowed no time "to economize much either in the way of clothing or household expenses, since we are expected to give to the Society not only a limited number of hours daily, but our whole time, except what is necessary for rest or recreation."[113] The request was later rescinded when donations to the society seemed to be dropping off, but it nevertheless demonstrates directly the women's willingness to assume collective responsibility for their future within a vocation with many liabilities and risks.

In April 1890 the women's almost chronic anxiety about their status as Christian missionaries in Japan was heightened by the murder of Alfred Large, a terrifying incident that disrupted the Japan mission and unnerved the missionaries. Just a few months earlier Eliza Large, now the mother of a year-old daughter, had somewhat ruefully indicated to the readers of the *Missionary Leaflet* that her life in Japan had become pretty dull. Day-to-day activities assumed a predictable pattern. "I see almost nothing outside our own grounds; shopping and exercises are about the only calls that take me farther than the gate."[114] A few weeks later the same readers were horrified by her next communiqué, a painful rehearsal of the murder of her "darling" husband by Japanese thieves during the night of 4 and 5 April. It was a traumatic shock that completely destroyed any complacency the mission community might have developed towards its position in Japan.[115] Cartmell urged Canadians who might have thought the work in Japan was "romantic and sentimental ... to command the situation now."[116]

The murder can be reconstructed from Eliza Large's letters and from accounts published in Tokyo's English-language newspapers, although the journalistic versions tended to be critical of Alfred Large's fearless response. Thieves broke into the Tokyo girls' school late at night, bound up the watchman, and, because they needed keys to open the safe, allegedly the repository of a large quantity of silver, set off in search of Eliza Large. The robbers made their way into the Larges' bedroom. Alfred Large "sprang up" and "proceeded to action at once. Unhesitatingly [the robbers] struck at him with their swords and then made for the doors."[117] Alfred was killed; "[Eliza] received a slash which laid open the right side of her face, and seeking to grasp one of the assailant's weapons, the two first fingers of her right hand were almost cut off and the third finger deeply wounded."[118] The facial laceration was severe, a slice to the bone, extending two inches across the right eyebrow and down her face for four inches. Her right index and middle fingers were amputated. An inquest recorded that her husband suffered at least twelve wounds, three to the head. At Eliza Large's insistence, Nellie and Lizzie Hart, who witnessed the assault, carried Large to his bed and administered ammonia to a man they knew was dead.[119]

One newspaper insisted that the murder was not provoked by "anti-Christian fanaticism or ... some sentiment of hatred towards Mr or Mrs Large." The intruders had not planned to kill Large, nor had he been struck until he began to resist. The paper nevertheless conceded that "the absolute immunity enjoyed by foreigners in Japan from all personal violence during this past twenty years invests this sad event with peculiar interest. But burglaries with violence are common everywhere, and in Japan, the sword, freely used, is not an infrequent adjunct to robbery." The admonition ended with a last disapproving observation about the Larges' behaviour. "What could be less likely than that a gentleman and a lady, finding two men standing over them with naked swords, would dream of offering violent opposition to the commands of their assailants."[120]

When Eliza Large had recovered sufficiently to describe her loss, she dismissed the many tributes to her courage, fixing instead on her intense grief, which she couched in the popular Victorian metaphor of heavenly domesticity. "This earth is not my abiding place. Heaven is my home. My loved one is there. My father, brothers and sister are there and best of all, my God and Saviour is there. What a joyful homecoming I shall have someday."[121] The ordeal earned her a year's furlough at full salary to recuperate in Canada. Emerging from seclusion to attend the WMS annual meeting in Toronto in October 1890, Eliza Spencer Large dramatically "came forward draped in black on the arm of Mrs Willmott" to speak, in true missionary style, not of her own unfortunate circumstances but about the development and expansion of the girls' schools in Japan.[122] Apparently the strain of such displays caused a relapse, and in December she retreated to Clifton Springs sanatorium in upper New York State, a spa for furloughed or incapacitated missionaries.

As a matter of interest, its director, identified only as a Dr Foster, prescribed prayer as the remedy for a variety of physical ills. But he also encouraged "the fulfillment of the Union between Christ and his people as the Bridegroom and the Bride, as typified in the Song of Solomon." According to one source his female patients allegedly stripped naked so that the betrothal with Christ might take place in the literal sense.[123] Large's treatment followed the traditional rest-cure for neurasthenia first described in 1873 by the American neurologist Silas Weir Mitchell. Like thousands of North American women, Large was subjected to six weeks of isolation during which she saw neither family nor friends and was not allowed out of bed or permitted to sit up, write, sew, or read. Not surprisingly, during such a confinement female patients might gain as much as fifty pounds and often became very dependent upon their male doctor.[124] By July 1891, because of, or in spite of, the course of treatment, Large had recovered, and with two new recruits in tow she returned to her position in Tokyo.[125] For the time being the WMS had gained a respected heroine. A few General Board agents thought otherwise. Large's furlough was later characterized by the most vociferous General Board combatant, F.A. Cassidy, as "the golden period of pleasant relations between the missions."[126] But the disagreements between the men and the women in Japan had been simmering even while Large was in Canada.

During that time the WMS council in Japan was defining its rules to meet the exigencies of the field. Establishing the boundaries of their respective areas of work, disputes over whether the women should help the men whenever their services were requested, and personality clashes – in effect, power struggles among the veteran missionaries on both sides – emerge as the most conspicuous causes of conflict between the two mission bodies. The confrontation over authority and power (a word often used by both sexes) should not have shocked the Methodist hierarchy given the circumstances in Japan, where men and women with, in all likelihood, limited social relationships and little experience working with members of the opposite sex contended fiercely for the meagre harvest of Japanese souls on whom all their jobs depended. Yet Methodist administrators were reluctant to admit that their competitive and jealous missionary employees, their commitment to the ideals of Christian endeavour notwithstanding, were any different from other men and women. In the inhospitable Japanese environment, where the missionaries' social and recreational activities were limited almost exclusively to the Methodist community, where the women were acutely aware of patriarchal attitudes and the men took female submissiveness for granted, petty quarrels and idle gossip grew to alarming proportions. The women's determination to protect their work and careers stimulated an aggressive feminism directed at the General Board missionaries, who seemed oblivious of the intensity of the women's drive for autonomy and its centrality to their professional identity.

Evidence of the escalating tension between the two missions after 1890 can be gleaned from several sources, notably the WMS Japan Council minutes, which recorded, as far as the women were concerned, the most inflammatory incidents, and from reports and testimonies of the final inquiry. The circumspect and guarded manner in which the women described the events – perhaps because they suspected, correctly, that their letters might become public – sometimes makes it difficult to determine just how the members of the WMS community, which normally condemned any potentially controversial conduct, reacted to the web of accusations gathering around its personnel. Yet what is clear is that much of the dissension was occasioned by the repeated requests from the men of the General Board for assistance from WMS representatives. In September 1891, for example, C.S. Eby and J.W. Saunby asked the WMS Japan Council to loan the General Board a woman to serve as an evangelist at the Central Tabernacle Church in Hongo, a Tokyo suburb about four miles from the school, and for two more women to teach at the Kanazawa boys' school. The WMS refused unless the General Board in Canada approved the request and the recommendation came to the WMS through the proper channels, that is, from the secretary of the General Board. In the interests of developing their professional status, the WMS would no longer tolerate ad hoc arrangements between the missions, although the women were careful to assure the men that WMS plans for inaugurating new work would continue to be referred to the General Board for its approval as the constitution required.[127]

The General Board must have complied because the WMS eventually provided Lizzie Hart for the Tabernacle and Cunningham to teach in Kanazawa.[128] But Saunby then demanded that Cunningham teach more than the daily hour that had been agreed upon. When the WMS Japan Council, on Large's instructions, insisted that Cunningham should do no more, Saunby relieved her of all teaching duties, putting her status as a foreigner in Japan in jeopardy because she was required to teach some English to be eligible for a document enabling her to remain in Japan. Since the wms did not conduct formal English classes in Kanazawa, Cunningham suggested approaching the Presbyterians about teaching opportunities. In retaliation, Saunby threatened "to expose the [wms] ladies to the Presbyterians in such a way that they would in no case take her in." A compromise was reached, and Cunningham continued to teach for the General Board.[129]

In another upsetting incident for the women, the General Board tried to persuade the women to permit Japanese ministerial candidates to teach in wms Sunday schools, where, in deference to Japanese social custom, the society absolutely refused to employ male teachers for the female students.[130] To make matters worse, some General Board missionaries insisted that the wms Sunday school members be included in their records, an arrangement that the women immediately construed as direct interference with their designated work. As the solution, the women simply withdrew all their Sunday schools from the returns.[131] There were also differences over the objectives of the wms's Herbie Bellamy orphanage in Kanazawa when it opened in December 1893.[132] The argument was symptomatic of the ideological rift between the two mission boards, which would widen as time passed. Whereas the General Board stressed traditional evangelism, not the "humanism of Jesus," and seemed "loath to accept the validity of less familiar ideas" as a way to Christianize the Japanese,[133] the wms missionaries were far more willing, perhaps because of the success of their schools, to move into unknown territory to achieve their purpose. Dr Macdonald opposed the orphanage plan "as a pampering" inappropriate for the Methodist mission, which trained the Japanese "to go forth and take up their work."[134] As far as the women were concerned, the home was the logical extension of their work among the poor in Kanazawa and it seemed politically vital because of the Presbyterians' success in this same field.[135]

At the fifth annual Japan Council meeting in July 1892, attended by Sarah Gooderham and Elizabeth Strachan, who were on a tour of wms missions in Japan and western Canada, the women made a conspicuous effort to promote a good working relationship with the General Board, which now alleged that the wms had ignored the discipline of the Methodist Church of Canada and failed to give the men "rights that are theirs."[136] For their part, the General Board Council appointed three men to confer with the wms Council "with a view to a harmonious adjustment of the work, and a satisfactory understanding between the workers."[137] No rapprochement resulted. As the

WMS Council minutes tersely noted, "the main difficulty apparently [was] that the women were not under the control of the Council of the Japan Mission of the Methodist Church of Canada."[138]

Complicating the issue of just who ultimately determined the disposition of WMS missionary work in Japan was the women's suspicion that the men disliked – probably hated – Eliza Large because she was able to consolidate the other women behind her. In a dramatic gesture just before Gooderham and Strachan left Tokyo, Large tendered her resignation. When her colleagues pledged their support, the Board of Managers refused to accept it, citing her "superior executive ability, strict adherence to duty and her earnest devotion to the work" as critical to the mission's success.[139] This gender solidarity did not improve relationships with the men. Six months later they blamed the unproductive bid to attract women to the Hongo Tabernacle on Lizzie Hart, "a nice but utterly inexperienced girl ... getting more good from the Tabernacle than giving."[140] The WMS withdrew its workers from the Tabernacle and demanded substantiation of the General Board's grievances through a full-scale investigation attended by all members of both missions.[141] Davidson Macdonald, as recording secretary of the General Board Council and unofficial *pater familias* of the Japan Mission, discouraged this strategy, fearing "unnecessary publicity to matters which belong[ed] to the two missions only."[142] The WMS Council insisted that only an open hearing could vindicate its organization and agents.[143] In a final attempt at reconciliation, possibly because the WMS had stalled on a request from the General Board to inaugurate work in Nagano,[144] Macdonald assured the WMS that the General Board had not "the slightest wish and intention to interfere with [their] ... autonomy as a mission."[145] This time the women responded amicably enough, agreeing to "put the past out of sight and memory" in order to solve the mission's problems.[146]

At this point, when it seemed that a compromise might be reached in a reasonable manner, Rev. F.A. Cassidy, stationed at Shizuoka, sent Large a letter that "had the effect of arresting further progress in the way of reconciliations, and stirring up very bitter feelings." What indeed may have been, as Cassidy later maintained, a sincere demonstration of good will was interpreted by Large and her allies as an offensive personal insult, all the more so because the letter arrived on the anniversary of her husband's death. To ease Eliza Large's apparent paranoia, Cassidy had suggested that "the phantom that has embittered your life is 'self-protection.' As a lone lady in a hard world this has formed one of the chief elements of your anxiety."[147] Widowhood had made her "more than ever a lone woman in a hard world" who was suspicious of the men of the General Board; unless she abandoned the notion that she had enemies everywhere, "there [was] no hope of ... remaining here with comfort to yourself or profit to the work."[148]

The letter, which Large considered "neither gentlemanly nor Christian-like," received no reply;[149] instead, she forwarded copies to the WMS Board of Managers and to Mission Secretary Alexander Sutherland. Cassidy tried to make amends in several contrite letters to the Japan Council. But his insistence – compounded by his unfortunate phraseology – that he was not "at war with a lot of hopeless shrews" but "in a bad tangle with a lot of noble and respectable ladies who are working for the glory of God, and who are my sisters in the Gospel" merely aggravated the tension. The WMS Council prohibited its workers in Shizuoka from communicating with him.[150] Finally, in May 1893, the WMS accepted Cassidy's apology, but in the meantime Large had again tendered her resignation, once more declined, over the failure of the Hongo Tabernacle, which was now attributed to her excessive control over the WMS workers.[151] Any fragments of congenial social and business relationships between the two missions dissolved. The continual squabbling compelled John McArthur to seek a transfer to the new Methodist mission in West China because Large had accused the General Board of dishonesty, of squandering missionary funds "for the devil."[152] As a sign of her disgust with the men, Large had refused to shake hands with General Board representative William Elliott, who, she believed, was influenced by rumours about her sharp tongue.[153] Elliott generously blamed her spiteful behaviour on a nervous condition, but he considered "it would certainly be better every way to pay her to stay at home than to pay her to work here."[154]

By March 1893, from his vantage point in Canada, Mission Secretary Alexander Sutherland had identified Eliza Large as a leading cause of dissent. Even though "personally, [he would] be very sorry to have [her] leave,"[155] he was emphatic that she should be removed. The WMS staunchly supported Large in spite of persistent tales, never satisfactorily disproved, about her cruelty and her abrasive personality and rumours that she had "caused ill-health" to one of her associates, Hannah Lund, who had recently died at Brantford, Ontario.[156] The women were equally quick to deny that their alienation from the men was rooted in any personal enmity and antagonism. They had merely acted "in defense of their work." Yet, if "outwardly friendly relationships" between the two groups prevailed, the WMS certainly sought "no ground for closer friendship."[157]

An impassioned vindication of their collective reputation and an endorsement of Eliza Large was sent to the Board of Managers with this demand for immediate action: "We indignantly resent the idea that a band of women mostly experienced in Christian work before leaving home should be so lacking in strength of character as to submit to unjust treatment of themselves or stand passively by and see it imposed upon others; or should be so lacking in integrity as to refrain from expressing our conscientious convictions on all vital points. We protest against Mrs Large's being held personally responsible for the actions of the Council ... We would deny most emphatically the very serious reports now carried in Canada that Mrs Large's treatment of various members has been cruel or even unkind or such as is calculated to injure the health of her fellow workers."[158] The board did not interpret the message in the same light; when the school year ended, Large was relieved of her duties "in order to restore harmony."[159]

In a counter-attack the council members fired off a second irate letter, this time challenging the Methodist concept of justice and soliciting the support of their wms sisters in Canada. It was a vigorous and dynamic assertion of their rights as missionaries.

Does God ask us to come here, offer to Him our all for the good of His work, and after spending the best years of our lives in His service, does He desire us to submit to be called home before we know the charges brought against us or have had opportunity to defend ourselves against them: With our hearts bound up in the work we have left, with health, reputation and fitness for work in Canada impaired or gone, yet most of us are obliged to work for our daily bread. It may be a legal thing to do, but ... Does God ask us to do this? ... the meanest British subject cannot be condemned before a law-court until he has been made acquainted definitely with the charges preferred against him and until he has had an opportunity to defend himself. But a missionary, the herald of Christ, *can* be condemned without even being told what wrong she has committed.[160]

The letter did not reach its intended audience. The controversy culminated in October 1895, when the "Japan Affair" came before the General Board of Missions of the Methodist Church of Canada. The concerted efforts by the Church and its missionary organizations to suppress rumours about the Japan Mission had failed. Before the hearings got underway, the chaos in the Canadian Methodist Japan Mission was already familiar to the Canadian public through the pages of the *Christian Guardian* and the *Globe*.[161]

Prior to the official investigation that was convened essentially to examine the operations of the General Board, not the problems facing the wms, the wms conducted its own review because four senior missionaries, three of whom later reconsidered and returned to

Japan, had tendered their resignations and were on furlough in Canada. The inquiry disclosed, among other things, Large's abuse of her colleagues by hypnotism and the extent of her cruelty to Hannah Lund, whom, it appears, Large confined to her room with a diet of only bread and water, allegedly because she might have diphtheria.[162] Large confessed that she and Lund had continued to quarrel after they had returned to Canada on furlough, a circumstance confirmed by Sarah Burns, a former WMS president who had visited Lund's home. Burns, who disliked Large, "did not leave [Lund's] home with the impression [that the] ... perfect harmony that Mrs. Large had spoken of existed."[163] The WMS missionaries present at the hearings agreed that the situation was "almost more than [we] could bear,"[164] but they remained loyal to Large. Isabella Blackmore, for one, knew that under the circumstances she had "done what was right, and as I know Mrs. Large had done what was right as far as she knew I felt it was useless for me to go back."[165] The last months before the hearing had been intolerable and unproductive; the disagreements among the missionaries, already an embarrassment "to the parties themselves and to the officers of those Societies at home ... [became] known to many of the people in [Canada] and to many of the natives in Japan."[166] For Martha Cartmell, it was "a tempest ... raging here. It seems as if Satan has been let loose to rend and destroy the Church."[167]

Although the investigation was intended to cover the issues that had precipitated the resignations of six men, the all-male tribunal felt obliged to explore the uneasy relationship between the two mission bodies. During the questioning the WMS and General Board missionaries introduced some new evidence about personal enmity, especially between Cassidy and Eliza Large, but most of the testimony was all too familiar to the parties concerned. The failure of the General Board's initiative in Hongo was much discussed. So was Nellie Hart's association with Cassidy, who had pressured her to accompany him on overnight trips, arguing that a Western woman would attract a large audience for his evangelist meetings.[168] Hart had declined on the grounds that the junkets involved travel on Sunday. Nevertheless, the tribunal persisted in quizzing her about the sensitive question of the sexual impropriety in Cassidy's request. "That thought never came into my mind," Hart replied.[169] The tribunal's inference was that Hart should have been shocked by the undertones of Cassidy's proposal and was immodest in not assuming Cassidy's suggestion was improper.

Eliza Large was the chief WMS witness. Her testimony disclosed more personality clashes, among them a spiteful feud with Agnes Wintemute. She alleged that Wintemute prejudiced the other women against her; in return Large sent back her invitation to Wintemute's wedding.[170] Large was evasive about her relationships with her colleagues of both sexes, preferring to steer the questioning to the Hongo Tabernacle issue, which, she contended, confirmed "the evident desire on the part of some of the agents of the General Board to get control of the work of the Woman's Missionary Society."[171] By the end of the probe at least one member of the tribunal was thoroughly disgusted by the "trifles" that had "humiliated [the] Church from ocean to ocean."[172]

The tribunal voted (with one dissension) that Cassidy and Eby, who were, in fact, the men incriminated by the wms for intervening in the women's work, should be recalled for the time being. Nor did Sutherland consider it wise for Large to resume her position,[173] because if missionaries "cannot help quarrelling over things that ought not to set children quarrelling – it does become a question whether they ought not to be brought out of the field."[174] As Sutherland astutely concluded, the bitterness among individual missionaries had "begun in little sparks of misunderstanding that, fanned by the breath of gossip and tale-bearing, kindled smouldering fires of mutual suspicion and dislike, and rendered more difficult the adjustment of wider differences." The friction between the two councils generated by these personal vendettas was aggravated by "the persistent endeavor of certain [men] to dominate the work and workers of the Woman's Missionary Society." If the men "could not agree with lady missionaries, they had still the alternative of quietly letting them alone."[175]

In a confidential report written after an official inspection of the Japanese missions in 1898, Sutherland reiterated his confidence in the women as "faithful workers ... rendering our beloved Zion a very noble and valuable service."[176] But, he pointed out, even the most faithful missionaries had make mistakes. "The Methodist Church ... [was] running a two-wheeled vehicle without any connection between the wheels but the invisible bond of piety and good sense, which are not always present in large quantities. The riders on the separate wheels sometimes make vaulting sprints and dash into collision."[177] The wms was partly responsible: "Its workplans, not of a set purpose but of an unguarded evolution, greatly accentuated and increased the difficulties ... and may in some instances have even been the occasion of their development. The spirit of a sensitive independence did not conduce to harmony and cooperation."[178]

Sutherland's seems to be a fairly accurate analysis of the situation. The wms missionaries, cut off by a three months' delay in communication with Canada, had acted on their own initiative in order to

safeguard their work and defend their reputations. As they understood it their foremost obligation was to their own society and their
charges in Japan, not to the men who believed that the women should
always be ready and pleased to assist them. For the women, acqui-
escing to their male colleagues was not part of God's plan. Cassidy
in particular was obsessed with the notion that the women were
"primed with the idea of independence, and with a latent prejudice
against the missionaries of the General Board and charged to resist
any encroachment by the missionaries of the Gen Board."[179] He
claimed that WMS president Sarah Gooderham fostered "the same
ambition for absolute independence ... she encourages it in the ladies
in every possible way."[180] One member of the tribunal blamed the
structure of the Methodist Church: "The friction ... would never have
happened, if men and women had been placed upon an equality
long ago in the Methodist church, and we had no Women's Missionary Society."[181] His proposal for a joint society was an impractical
ideal given the inexperience on both sides in working and communicating with members of the opposite sex and the women's fears of
compromise as a prelude to surrender of their control over matters
of WMS jurisdiction. Thousands of miles from their homes and the
people they might have consulted, the women imagined that they
were easy targets for their male associates, who expected them to
submit meekly to their demands.

Implicit in the WMS responses are the voices of determined women
challenging the hierarchical ordering of Victorian society, which, in
spite of its allusions and deference to women's unique qualities, continued to endorse patriarchal authority in the home and the work-
force. Even the pious missionary proved vulnerable to the sexual
tensions and jealousies that often resulted when women successfully
invaded a previously male preserve, all the more because of the isolation, anxiety, and personal misgivings kindled by the unfamiliar
surroundings and the indifference to Christianity in Japan. Both societies were reluctant, perhaps ashamed, to admit that the quarrel was
rooted in personal differences; the women and men preferred to
define the problem exclusively in terms of their respective work of
salvation, which, in the eyes of the church, its membership, and God,
was beyond reproach.

The WMS petitioned Sutherland to reinstate Eliza Large. Even
before the hearings had ended he denied the request. This time the
WMS Board of Managers relented, acknowledging that Sutherland was
acting in the best interests of both missions in Japan. In reality there
was little else the WMS could do because it had no constitutional
authority to act further.[182] The status of Eliza Large continued to pose

a dilemma. In a letter to Elizabeth Strachan, Large reaffirmed her divine call to work in Japan, outlining plans to return independently. She was "forced to take this position ... under protest, but realizing my *duty* and hearing my Father's voice saying, 'Behold I have set before you an open door'; I dare not do otherwise."[183] A few months later Sarah Gooderham, now "out of harmony" with the society over Large's situation, resigned as president to sponsor and accompany her friend to Japan, where they worked for several years on behalf of the WCTU.[184] WMS records indicate that Eliza Large later moved to Pennsylvania, where she took up fruit farming until her death in 1933.[185] At regular intervals she petitioned the WMS for financial help. She was finally given a pension in 1909, when the Board of Managers took pity on her "straitened circumstances." Bitter to the end, Large insisted that "the WMS no less than the General Board ... had wrecked her life and that of her daughter."[186]

In the aftermath of what Methodists termed the "imbroglio" – an appropriate word denoting a "confused entanglement" – the WMS tried to repair the damage to its mission community in Japan. Explicit consultation procedures were set up between overseas field secretaries and the home base in Canada. Policies were also adopted to settle personal disputes in the field. In an addendum to the requirements for candidates, each mission was designated as a "little community in which the will of the majority should rule. Each member of it should do her utmost to promote its peace and unity, and to submit gracefully and not merely because she cannot prevail. She should keep herself well informed as to the work and policy of her associates, in order that her estimate of their needs and rights may be fair and comprehensive, and that of her own just and unselfish ... she has always the right of an appeal to the Board of Managers, but her strength will be in that 'charity that thinketh no evil, which suffereth long and is kind,' and in quiet waiting upon Him who makes 'all things work together for good to them that love Him.'"[187]

By 1898 Isabella Blackmore, though still pleading for Large's return, believed that "peace and confidence like that of the old days before the mission trouble, are coming back to us."[188] But the WMS administration in Canada and the missionaries in the field had been severely tested and their vulnerability exposed. Aggravating the problem was the uncertainty surrounding the WMS West China Mission, which was suffering physical attacks of a more tangible and life-threatening nature. To direct attention to the society's plight and to vindicate the missionaries, who, the society feared, might be condemned for their outspoken conduct, a metaphorical editorial in the *Outlook,* implicating the wider WMS membership in the affair, explained how "the mission ship, whose sails and pennons bear the mystic letters, WMS, has at times sailed near dangerous shoals and sand-banks, but, thank God, has never drifted out of her course! The 'Captain of our Salvation' has ever been aboard, guiding and controlling the ship. But, by far the greater number of the ship's crew have right loyally yielded obedience implicit and free to their Captain."[189] Ten years later the official history of the WMS affirmed that "there was no stain on the character of any of the missionaries, and that they personally retained the confidence of the Mission Board and, we believe, the favour of God."[190]

Whatever message the society might have wanted to convey about the episode, the affair and the ugly accusations surrounding the missionaries altered the future course of the Japan Mission. Among other things the WMS concluded that some of the younger employees in Japan had been immature. They needed "experience in life and work! The average girl of 24 is *very* young … too young to be a real strength to the work."[191] Hence, with a single exception, after 1896 all women dispatched to Japan were over the minimum age requirement of twenty-five. For several years following the friction, women designated for Japan seem to have been hand-picked by the Board of Managers or the regional secretaries. Nearly half (44 per cent – 16 of 36) the recruits for Japan from 1896 to 1914 were ministers' daughters, sisters, or granddaughters, chosen because the board perhaps supposed that they would be more mindful of the Church's commands. As well, after 1895 WMS recruits were required to attend the Methodist Training School or an equivalent to acquire the essential theological foundations and, at the same time, to be observed interacting with their future co-workers in an institutional setting. The intensive screening of candidates seems to have paid dividends for the society, at least in terms of length of service. The thirty-six women hired between 1896 and 1914 remained in Japan an average of 24.4 years; two-thirds of them reached retirement. These statistics themselves point to the women's deep commitment to their profession and support their own observations about the relatively satisfactory nature of employment in Japan once the WMS's "sensitive independence" was no longer in dispute.

After 1896 the WMS operation in Japan began to grow again. In November 1900 a new school building opened in Tokyo. By 1903 the school had reached its capacity of 145 boarders.[192] It is, however, difficult on the basis of the reports sent from the Japan mission field to analyse the relative success of the society in either its educational or evangelical work. The annual statement drafted at the end of the school year July 1899, for example, reported 179 boarding pupils and 187 day students. Yet the average daily attendance of 218 was far below the number of girls who could be accommodated, suggesting that many day pupils attended school sporadically. During the year 9 baptisms were recorded, none at the Tokyo school, although 42 girls were listed as attending classes to prepare for the eventuality. The evangelistic department made 5,030 visits to homes in Tokyo, Shizuoka, Kofu, and Nagano. Again, the harvest of 29 baptisms seems meagre.[193] The missionaries now understood that conversion to Christianity was an excruciatingly slow process. Minnie Robertson, a teacher at Kofu, rationalized the mission's failure to baptize more schoolgirls: "If all the girls do not turn out as we would like to have them," Robertson explained, "this we are sure of, they are better for the time spent here, be it long or short. Some day there will be a rich harvest from the faithful sowing that has been done in past years and is still being done all over the province. We are waiting and praying for it."[194] In short, in Japan the civilizing aspect of missionary endeavour was becoming a logical and essential complement to the wms evangelical work.

In Kanazawa the wms opened a free school to provide a rudimentary education for working-class children and also as an opportunity for missionaries to visit Japanese women in their homes. The Kanazawa experiment is one example of the wms's willingness, in the face of their limited achievement, to adapt to the situation at hand, to move out into the community rather than continuing to expect the Japanese to conform to more traditional missionary methods. The Kanazawa school initially catered to fifty boys and girls who, the missionaries complained, "knew nothing of obedience and order, who had never been confined in a class before; dirty, repulsive, ignorant, ungrateful and disrespectful."[195] The curriculum differed from that of the girls' schools in Tokyo and Shizuoka. Each morning the children received a Bible lesson and instruction in reading, writing, and counting. In the afternoons the girls were taught delicate embroidery techniques. Their handiwork was shipped to Canada to be sold by the auxiliaries. The society retained the substantial proceeds. Boys made envelopes, on the piece-work system, for Japanese factories.[196] The wms operations in Kanazawa were closely scrutinized by the Japanese. Buddhist priests there first warned parents not to send their children to the school, then hired young men to harass those still in attendance. [197]

In Nagano, a Buddhist stronghold where the wms began working in 1897, the missionaries confronted even more overt opposition to their girls' school. The school's opening was deferred for several months because the WMS was unable to hire Japanese teachers with the required government certificates. In contrast with the Tokyo school, attendance at Nagano was barely adequate. Pupils came only because of a renewed interest in learning English, not from any burning impulse to become Christians. By 1902 enrolment had dropped to twenty. A kindergarten was started as an alternative to attract the younger children, while the missionaries reverted to traditional evangelism and itinerating in hopes of appealing to the Japanese women. In Motto, one of the villages serviced from Kanazawa, even evangelistic work was halted when the Buddhist priests forced the inhabitants to sign a petition barring Christians from their village and forbidding anyone to rent a house that might be used for missionary work.[198] The Nagano mission station was temporarily abandoned in 1902 when the school was closed by government regulation.[199] The enemy had been "by no means silent," wrote Laura Wigle. "In many ways he shows his presence, but our cause is the stronger and our God will prevail."[200] By 1900 the missionaries conceded that they were most successful in urban centres among the "people of wealth."[201]

Many women found the cultural distance between them and the Japanese hard to fathom. Abby Veazey, at Kanazawa in the 1890s, could not accept that the Japanese were not eagerly awaiting the Christian gospel. Instead of an enthusiastic and receptive populace the women confronted "degradation, poverty, misery and filth in equal degrees."[202] Workers outside Tokyo were particularly grateful when their leave was due, but in some cases a furlough in Canada merely sharpened the contrast between East and West. After her year back in Canada in 1893, Cunningham described her disillusionment and the challenge of readjusting to life in Japan. Her catalogue of complaints was comprehensive: "The halls of school seemed narrower. The dresses, too, of some of our ladies wanted making over badly; they were decidedly not in style. One of your missionaries was reduced to the state of having no hat, and for some months had been wearing a cap which I had discarded two years ago. Everything was musty for Shizuoka is rather damp in summer ... the Shizuoka spiders were so large and I disliked them even more than I used to. It seems to me as if I never could get reconciled to the thought that I must live here for seven long years."[203] Cunningham nevertheless became acclimatized and four years later reported that the Shizuoka school had become a great evangelistic centre where it was a pleasure to live and work.[204]

In 1897 the second and subsequent terms of employment were lengthened from six to seven years, further confirmation that continuity of service in the field was crucial to effective missionary work. Most women endorsed the additional year between furloughs as a necessary sacrifice, but Isabella Blackmore questioned its benefits out of concern for her family in Canada. At the same time she applauded the Board of Manager's decision to pay expenses incurred in the event of a death in the field, a calamity these realistic women had already foreseen. According to Blackmore, they had "all thought more or less of the inconvenience to others if we should not have on hand enough money to cover expenses at the time of our death and some have endeavoured to always have sufficient money available for the purpose."[205] Blackmore perpetually worried about her financial affairs. In a letter to Elizabeth Strachan she endorsed the suggestion of a rest fund for the missionaries because her heavy financial burden prevented her from putting aside any money for the future. "I *must* contribute to my mother's support, my sister's daughter *must* be helped to get something more of an education than their country home affords. I have a debt which must be diminished."[206] In 1902 a rest fund was established for retired missionaries and women who needed more than one furlough year to regain their health. The Board of Managers allocated some of the society's assets to the fund, while the missionaries themselves contributed ten dollars annually. Annuities were then issued at an annual rate of ten dollars for each year of service; in 1919 the rate was increased to fifteen dollars after fifteen years' employment. No pension was ever awarded until at least twelve years were completed, although in some exceptional cases the Board of Managers assisted women who could no longer work.[207] Blackmore, who died in 1942, drew on the fund for seventeen years.[208]

After 1900 the Methodist Church's growing preoccupation with social reform and education began to reach its overseas missions. Because most older Japanese women were still illiterate, Bible study groups designed to convert them were generally quite ineffective. While the wms continued its work with women, the Christian education of young children seemed to be the key to future success in Christianizing the Japanese. Consequently, kindergarten work became central to the wms work in Japan for the next two decades. It reflected, if somewhat belatedly, Methodists' changing attitudes towards children, who were no longer assumed to be tainted by original sin before the age of reason.[209] Some of these ideas infiltrated the mission field, although Elizabeth Crombie recognized that by establishing kindergartens the mission was merely following the wisdom of Ignatius Loyola, who believed that the years before six were critical for moulding young minds.[210] Yet anxious as the women were to "save helpless children" through their orphanage and kindergarten work, their principal emphasis was on the indoctrination and discipline of their young charges, "to lead them to Him whose jewels are the little children that love Him."[211] The girls taken in by the Herbie Bellamy orphanage were trained to become "useful women" and, as the author of a history of wms orphanage work, possibly Cartmell, recommended, to be obedient and "thankful for the kindness of those supporting them (such a good rule!)."[212]

In time the wms became more sensitive to the material as well as the spiritual and moral welfare of Japanese women, especially the prostitutes and the large numbers of women now employed in factories.[213] But the opportunities to move into new spheres of missionary work were restricted both by the constraints of Japanese society and by the personalities and preferences of the missionaries themselves. For every woman like Annie Allen who was intrepid enough to enter the cotton and silk factories in search of converts or to frequent the haunts of prostitutes to rescue the fallen women of Tokyo, there was another like Alice Timberlake who reminded her colleagues that "the true aim of missionary work [is] to preach the Gospel. Nothing else can support one in the trial and disappointment which are sure to come. Nothing else can give the joy which comes alone to those who tell others of Christ."[214] This rather egocentric theme was echoed by Margaret Armstrong, whose reflections about her career were published as part of an extensive campaign to attract recruits for Japan at a time when the West China mission was challenging Japan for both funds and candidates.

What I have *tried* to teach is a Living Christ, a Saviour who saves us every moment of every day … It is no easy thing to give up home, perhaps, and friends, and one's own land, and the pursuits one enjoys, to go to an unknown country – to spend hours and days and months and years studying a difficult language – to learn customs, which, at first appear foolish – to be, to all intents and purposes a *child*, having none of the privileges and happy responsibilities and pleasant associations that come to one after graduating from normal school or college, and on beginning to take one's place as a *woman* in the church life and social life of the town or city in which one lives. It is no life of ease and luxury to which I entreat you to come. It is a life of cross-bearing. But, oh, how near the Master comes! He lifts us over the roughest places, giving us such secret joy in His presence that the cross does not hurt us. [215]

To the frustrations of their demanding professional activities in Japan were added the challenges of individual self-preservation in an alien environment. Japan, as Armstrong perceived it, was permeated with "subtle temptations ... which never assail us in our native land. They are in the air, and they come to you with all the insidiousness of the serpent gliding from under some bank of fragrant blossoms. Don't imagine that temptations will not beset a missionary! I doubt not that in the hereafter, when the great battles of the world are made clear to us, some of the greatest will be found to have been fought in the breasts of us on the mission field."[216] What these temptations were was left to the reader's imagination. The women were, however, assailed by an assortment of identifiable problems; the most urgent was their bad health, which they attributed to living in Japan.

From Cartmell's arrival in Tokyo, the missionaries' physical and mental health was a major concern to the individual, the mission community, and above all the Board of Managers, which bore the ultimate responsibility for the women's medical expenses, including the cost of a return trip to Canada, and might lose a valuable worker. Of the eighty-one women who went to Japan before 1925, two died on active duty, one of them from surgical complications. Three others died on furlough while still employees of the society, or so shortly after their resignation that it is probable their illnesses began in Japan, prompting their return. Eleven women were obliged to resign because of chronic health problems, one from mental illness, and two others were transferred to the more beneficial climate of British Columbia, where they continued as home missionaries. Overall, WMS missionaries in Japan sustained an approximate death rate of 3.3 per 1,000 person-years of service in the field, compared to the thirty British, Canadian, and American missionary groups in Japan analysed in 1933, which had a death rate of 7.6 per 1,000 person-years of service.[217] In this case the data belie reality. Letters from the field suggest that illness in many guises plagued the missionaries and frustrated their work.

The women's ailments were a source of speculation, gossip, and alarm within the mission community to a far greater extent than in West China or Canada, where sickness was merely an annoying inconvenience temporarily disrupting the normal pattern of work. For one young woman who suffered a nervous breakdown and was sent home to Canada, the affair took on a very mysterious and secretive aura consistent with the stigma attached to mental illness. Her companion was counselled by Blackmore to "understand that the course which seems to you one of 'secrecy and evasion' is the only one possible under the circumstances. In cases of sickness it is often impossible to give details to outsiders, and I think a hint to your friends that nervous trouble is usually aggravated by questions will be sufficient to keep them from asking about her health."[218] Another woman, suffering from similar but obviously less serious nervous problems, cured herself by riding a bicycle, "which has the advantage over walking as an exercise, in that she [could not] think about her work while riding."[219] Other illnesses were not remedied so easily.

Many missionaries frequently were quite unwell, suffering from health problems that were seldom fatal but seldom completely curable either. In the absence of modern analgesics, headaches and menstrual cramps became incapacitating nuisances.[220] Correspondence between the mission secretaries and the home base exposes a litany of complaints – disabling migraine headaches, menstrual irregularities and pain, suspected tuberculosis, carbuncles, bowel trouble, gall bladder and gynaecological surgery, and at least one mastectomy. Most of these disorders were not reported in any missionary publication even if they occasioned the recall of the victim. It is interesting to consider as a possible explanation for some of the women's less serious ailments Lee Chambers-Schiller's suggestion that in the face of professional frustration, nineteenth-century American women reformers had a tendency to "retreat into illness." "As negative, self-destructive behavior, whether conscious or not," she argues, "[illness] did serve in a positive way to meet some of the spinster's emotional needs. It provided an opportunity for respite from the taxations of reform work, from the inner conflict associated with so public and unfeminine a role, and from the demands of family and social obligation."[221] Certainly in the Japan Mission, the sympathy of colleagues and the special pampering invalids received may have helped to relieve the frustrations of an occupation that could be unrewarding and lonely.

Female illness was a private matter, but from the perspective of the WMS, death was not. A missionary's death provided an opportunity for an outburst of public emotion and sympathy. When Hannah Lund, the WMS's "first missionary to go home," died in 1894, the society showed no hesitation in releasing the details of her last days as an inspiration for other Methodist women.[222] Lund's death was depicted in glowing terms as "a climax. Her face seemed to shine as if the glory of heaven had already dawned upon her."[223] Ten years later, when Alice Belton died unexpectedly in Japan following surgery, her bravery in the face of intense suffering and her life struggle against "adversity, against pain, against self" were similarly celebrated.[224] Though Lund and Belton had not died in true martyr's fashion at the hands of those they were seeking to convert, as far as the WMS was concerned they had none the less sacrificed their lives for the Christian cause.

The litany of grievances about the inhospitable climate, sickness, the dearth of converts, and the apathy of the Japanese to Christianity that so often accompanied reports from the Japan field tended to inflate the apparent adversity and strangeness of Japan, where, in comparison to other mission fields, the women generally did not suffer from material deprivation. Poverty and hardship were not prerequisites for the propagation of Methodist doctrines in Japan. Indeed, as spinsters the women may have found that their circumstances were more congenial than if they had remained in Canada. As soon as the society's finances and modern technology allowed, the WMS homes and schools were provided with running water, indoor plumbing, central heating, and electricity at a time when these amenities were notably absent in many parts of Canada and certainly were not available to WMS missionaries in northern Alberta and British Columbia. A case in point is the hot-water boiler sent, in 1907, from Gurney's in Hamilton to Kofu at the cost of $1131.[225] Expensive as it was, the practice of transporting the material comforts of middle-class Canada was not discouraged. To the contrary, a recommendation from the outfit committee in Japan in 1897, based on fifteen years' experience, enumerated the essentials that should be shipped out from Canada. Bedding, towels, pictures, ornaments, books, a half-dozen dinner knives and forks, dessert knives, forks and spoons and teaspoons were indispensable to a well-managed middle-class mission home. The missionary's wardrobe was more perplexing because the extremes of climate necessitated a variety of clothing. Photos show Eliza Large wearing a fur wrap, an apparent luxury, but justified, according to the WMS, because it was "serviceable." Dresses could be made inexpensively in Japan, but underflannels (in Japan probably worn only by missionaries) were hard to obtain, perhaps because the Japanese were smaller than Westerners. To guard against a shortage, the society warned that "in coming to Japan one cannot be too well provided with warm underclothing." Kid gloves, however, were superfluous, and at any rate mildewed in the damp summers.[226]

The WMS missionaries could not be accused of obsessive vanity, although some women were quite meticulous about their personal appearance. A few kept up with the latest in North American ladies' fashion but, as good Methodists, tempered with practicality any desire to be extravagant. Augusta Preston asked her mother to send her a "white waist instead of [a] corset waist ... They are quite expensive [but the cost was justified because they] appear to be serviceable."[227] Three decades later, when a long-awaited salary increase was approved for the missionaries struggling to cope with inflation in Japan's post-war economy, Minnie Robertson's first purchase was "a blue serge school-dress, the first winter garment I have bought since my return five years ago."[228] Unlike their counterparts in China, the women had no desire to emulate what might be termed native dress. As far as the WMS was concerned, the bright kimonos and elaborate coiffures of Japanese women were irrefutable evidence of immorality. On one occasion Agnes Wintemute exchanged clothing with a convert for a photograph, but the Canadians preferred their Western clothes and prayed that their students could be persuaded to dress less garishly.[229]

The missionaries' concern for appearances was not fed by demands imposed by an active social life beyond the Methodist mission compound. Although the women developed some social relationships within the Japanese Christian community, women outside Tokyo might be quite remote from both Westerners and Japanese. With the exception of the concerts, teas, graduation ceremonies, and elaborate Christmas and Easter celebrations offered for the benefit of the pupils, their families, and converts, the women had little social life. Nor is there, in contrast to West China, evidence that, after the Japan Affair, they fraternized with the men of the General Board of Missions and their wives. The various activities associated with the schools, the women's groups, the occasional WCTU or revival meeting, and the missionaries' personal interest in some of their talented and dedicated students filled their days and, by their own admission, provided enough satisfaction. If there are hints that some women were beset by loneliness and unrelieved boredom, most in time became resigned to the solitude of missionary work, to living, like Harriet Jost, stationed in Kofu in 1900, "ten months of the year with nothing more exciting to break the monotony of everyday life than the Church service or the occasional literary meeting of young school girls."[230]

Under these circumstances, any visit from Westerners was savoured. When the Hon. Sydney Fisher, Canadian minister of Agriculture and Commerce, called on the Azabu School in 1903, a special musical program was prepared by the schoolgirls and the children in the WMS orphanage.[231] Royal guests invoked a more enthusiastic response. As soon as the rumour leaked out that Arthur, Prince of Wales, intended to tour Japan, Isabella Blackmore persuaded the wife of the British ambassador to arrange for the prince to inspect the Tokyo Girl's school. Before his arrival the excited WMS missionaries were invited to examine his hotel room to ensure that everything was correct. They made the bed and proudly set up the tea tray with the silver that Elizabeth Strachan had presented to the mission. In a display of imperial sentiment Cunningham pronounced the visit "a great event for 'us Britishers.'" But what impressed her most was the report that although there were five kinds of wine on the table, in response to the many toasts the prince "simply raised his glass to his lips."[232]

As a rule, these sorts of comment about contemporary events were infrequent. The women's interest in current affairs appears to have been circumscribed by the implications for their work. Instead of provoking any apprehension about their safety, the Russo-Japanese War, which erupted in 1904, seems to have been a diversion, adding variety and excitement to the routine of the WMS mission community. The women seized on the war as a unique opportunity to gain new converts. The Shizuoka regiment, which suffered heavy casualties, became the special focus of their attention. Cunningham visited survivors in hospital, while "Miss Howie, accompanied by her Bible woman and two others, took her autoharp and sang hymns to the men."[233] The invalids' response was not documented. As a further demonstration of their sympathy for the community, the women went to the railway station whenever troops were sent off to the front. In Tokyo the missionaries dutifully attended the funerals of twelve Japanese officers, while the schoolgirls made "comfort bags," which included Bibles, for the soldiers at the front.[234] Lizzie Hart credited the war with "open[ing] a new door" for the flagging WMS effort.[235] The WMS's concern for the fate of the Japanese had "made the people count us as friends."[236]

Although the war provides an example of how the women tried, given the opportunity, to extend the range of their work, their attention still remained fixed on the dismal prospects for Japanese women, especially the urban factory workers. In 1910 Jessie Howie was granted permission by the factories' foremen to conduct evangelizing meetings among the female employees of the Sapporo Beer Company and the Calico Weaving Company.[237] By 1919 the WMS missionaries in Tokyo had personal contact with 3,527 women in thirty-four factories; the society also bought a small home near the ocean where ill and exhausted female industrial workers could recuperate.[238] Annie Allen, who had arrived in 1905, began rehabilitation work among prostitutes in the red-light district of Tokyo.[239]

But interest in these social-service schemes was not the *sine qua non* of every WMS missionary. As Augusta Preston, who seems representative of the older women steeped in nineteenth-century Methodist rituals and doctrine, put it, "one longs to give [the women] better conditions of life and above all a vital knowledge of the only Love that can adequately redeem and save, individually, morally, industrially."[240] Despite the Methodist Church's ostensible transformation from an introspective evangelical church whose members were preoccupied with their own salvation to a more broad-minded and accepting institution intent on improving the spiritual, moral, and physical state of Canada and the world, even women sent to Japan between 1914 and 1925 and who were, presumably, enlightened about the tenets of the social gospel approached their work in much the same manner as their predecessors.

Nourished by ageing WMS missionary personnel, the old notions about the heathen nature of Japan persisted, if they did not invariably dominate, within the missionary community. New arrivals to the mission field were still warned not to study Japanese in the evening, to avert an attack of 'the Japanese head,' and about the peculiar effect of the climate.[241] Some women recruited after 1910 – Sadie Tait, for example, who admitted to enjoying Japanese foods and was adept at using chopsticks – were more inclined to try to understand and embrace Japanese culture.[242] After the First World War there were fewer complaints about minor discomforts such as sitting on the floor, so distasteful to the earlier arrivals. But at the same time the tolerance of the younger missionaries appears to have been offset by the conservatism and truculence of the older, more powerful and influential women like Preston, who remained obsessed with improving the quality of Japanese hymn singing until she retired just before church union.

Well into the twentieth century the schools remained the backbone of mission work in Japan, probably because the majority of the recruits were teachers (twenty-one of the twenty-four who arrived after 1914 had teaching experience in Canada) for whom evangelizing was a sideline. But by 1910 both the General Board and the WMS missions in Japan, which were on a more or less firm footing and running smoothly, were eclipsed in size and financial support by the more fascinating West China Mission. Over the next fifteen years competition for funds and staff became fierce. The familiar and rather prosaic problems of Japan, such as the white ants eroding the mission stations, were no match for the tales of attacks by bandits and the revolutionary upheavals or the fresh hopes of Christianization emanating from China. Perhaps Canadian Methodist women, even the Board of Managers, had simply become indifferent and bored by the missionaries' impressions of a country that, even in 1914, Ada Killam censured as "a land of shrines and temples" where "most of the people have religious faith ... that is ignorant, essentially selfish, not essentially moral."[243]

It is hardly surprising that life and work in the mission compounds were disrupted very little by the First World War. The women were insulated from daily news of the progress of the war; when they did receive information, it was out of date. Isabella Hargrave found that ignorance about the course of the war had its benefits because "we miss much of the tension that follows from the effects of the war on things in general." When news from home finally did arrive, it was upsetting because "the suffering in all directions [was] beyond expression."[244] For Margaret Keagey the war brought a challenging adventure. In November 1918 Keagey, a former social worker who had spent ten years in Japan, was approached by the Red Cross to assist with relief in Siberia, then overflowing with Europeans in the wake of the Russian revolution.[245] Reluctantly, the Japan Mission Council granted her permission to leave.[246] The Board of Managers was even more hesitant about committing an employee to such a risky scheme, even though one board member at least commended it as a valuable service contributing to the stabilization of Russia.[247] Keagey reached Omsk in January 1919, where, wearing the standard army-issue sheepskin coat and fur hat, she travelled by sleigh to investigate refugee cases, thoroughly relishing the change.[248]

If the war itself did not bring hardship or acute anxiety to the missionaries in Japan, the post-war years more than made up for what the women had been spared. For the first time the women responsible for budgets and disbursements encountered severe financial limitations and the stark realities of rampant inflation. The price of rice soared so high that the mission began seriously to consider alternatives to the students' staple diet.[249] The servants employed by the mission, newly aware of their potential as industrial workers, demanded higher wages. Apparently quite oblivious of the inappropriateness and incongruity of her comments, Robertson, as corresponding secretary of the mission council, complained that the servants had become "insolent in their independence seeing that they can leave us any time for a better wage." To make matters worse, the coolies, too, were guilty of assertiveness and self-interest. "The spirit among that class," Robertson protested, had become "quite equal to that of their class in other countries. This certainly is the labourers' epoch in the progress of evolution."[250] By 1920 Robertson was frustrated by what she, like countless middle-class North American women, referred to as "the servant problem." To add to the already uncongenial atmosphere, fears of declining contributions because of hard times in Canada prompted a warning from the board that the mission must curtail its spending.[251]

The financial crisis dealt a demoralizing blow to the mission. Rumours of a salary cut excited a strong reaction from Blackmore, not so much on her own behalf, because she was now free of debt, but for "the younger women – some with heavy responsibilities, the last year was a series of makeshifts in the hope that this year would bring some relief. The Bonus was very welcome but for most it just went into a hole [of debt] and did not fill it … I hate any appearance of a kick about our salaries, but I think our younger women at least must have a little help."[252] Robertson, who as treasurer admitted that it was demeaning to complain so often to the board about the mission's financial state, understood that the solution depended on shrewd financial decisions in Canada. But without salary increases the women had become "as shabby as it is possible to be and yet be fairly decent. I heard one member of my family shivering over the stove say 'Can't buy woolens on my present salary,' and yet not one of us but feels she is much better off than many another and is willing to 'get along' till prices change and living is easier."[253]

The problem was temporarily alleviated when the board began to allow for the high losses incurred as a result of the soaring exchange rates. By the end of 1921 Blackmore, as custodian of the mission's assets, had discovered the challenges of dickering over bank drafts,[254] although any favourable exchange was to be returned to head office. The board began to keep a close watch on the financial situation in Japan because the term "sundries" appeared too often and because of unanticipated expenditures.[255] In absolute frustration, the next treasurer, Robertson, confronted the board. Although she wanted to be businesslike, she refused to compromise her ideals. "We are all busy *missionaries first*, and accountants, to the best of our ability, after … We deal not in commodities that can be labelled and priced, but in human energies which cannot always be estimated accurately in dollars and cents."[256]

Her letter struck a responsive chord; an assistant was appointed to help with the budget, which in 1923 had been $120,958.48, and to administer a special fund allocated to repair the Tokyo mission after the calamitous earthquake of September 1923.[257] The WMS structures had escaped relatively unscathed from the devastation, which killed perhaps as many as one hundred thousand in the city[258] and severely damaged the General Board mission compound. But the disaster left the WMS mission in Tokyo depressed and shaken because many of the women's Japanese friends and acquaintances had been killed.[259] The impact was far-reaching. In the long run the earthquake generated a more sympathetic and compassionate attitude to the Japanese on the part of the missionaries. Among other things they admired "the skill with which relief has been organized, the kindness of the people, the ready assistance of one to another, the absence of looting and the cheerful fortitude of the people under this *tremendous* calamity."[260] Ironically, as the missionaries themselves had to concede, the catastrophe and the high demand for female labour in the reconstruction process created "more freedom and opportunities" for Japanese women than the combined efforts of all the missionaries in Japan in the previous half-century.[261]

In spite of financial restraints and the rivalry with West China, the WMS work in Japan continued to develop in the post-war period. In 1918 the Woman's Christian College, a joint venture sponsored by several Protestant churches, was opened, although the collegiate departments of the Toya Eiwa Jo Gakko were closed to avoid competition with the new institution. In 1919 the training class for kindergarten teachers, originally established at Ueda, relocated in Tokyo, while in 1920, as a way to expand its activities among industrial workers, the WMS opened a community centre in Kameido.[262] It was not a time, however, for self-congratulation, because attendance at the girls' schools generally dropped during the post-war years. Some missionaries blamed the American mistreatment of the Japanese in California.[263] WMS members in Canada prayed for "an awakening at home," in effect, a revival, to rekindle interest in missionary work,[264] while the missionaries in the field sent assurances that, in spite of the American affront to the Japanese, they were "amazed at the continued courtesy and kindness we invariably receive," which they interpreted as an indication of "the deep spiritual hold the religion of Christ has upon the people."[265] But such optimism about the growth of Christianity in Japan did not convince the board to acquiesce to the Japan Mission's requests for more workers. Only two of the sixteen candidates recruited in 1924 and 1925 were assigned to Japan. Quite possibly the careless accounting had prompted a decrease in favours from the board. At church union the mission staff in Japan numbered forty-three. By then, many veterans had retired – Gussie Preston, Lizzie Hart, and Isabella Blackmore, each after thirty-six years' service. Fourteen seasoned missionaries, with an average of fifteen years in Japan, remained to oversee the transition from Methodist to United Church jurisdiction.

Working for the WMS in Japan had occasioned a wide range of responses from the eighty-one women stationed there between 1882 and 1925. A few, like Annie Allen, moved away from the cloistered classroom to strike out on their own in social-service work, where they thought they could be helpful as harbingers of the social gospel's message of universal brotherhood. The majority, however, were more comfortable with the traditional modes of teaching, conducting women's meetings, itinerating, and as one bluntly put it, "preparing bait."[266] In 1922 former WMS president Elizabeth Ross was gratified that "the Japanese say Canadian women have a mother quality of winning power."[267] Perhaps because they realized that a maternal demeanour appealed to the Japanese, the Canadian women tended to cast themselves in precisely that light. Their letters home frequently included references to the peaceful life in the mission homes, a domesticity that they hoped the Japanese would discover and emulate; the members of the WMS mission community saw themselves as a family unit. Harriet Jost wished that her own family and friends could observe the bustle of an active mission station, where "every room is useful and every room is constantly in use. The house is so *comfortable* throughout without being extravagant, and could not be better suited to our needs."[268] Even living alone, which was not ordinarily approved by the WMS, was described by one intrepid worker, who probably enjoyed her privacy, as a "life of single blessedness."[269]

Usually the women had companions, and the relationships they formed in the field brought them great satisfaction. Despite some patronizing of newcomers by veterans, the mission stations seem to have been the closely knit communities the women themselves described. Robertson may have frowned privately when, within a few months, Annabel Swann and Clara German resigned to marry. She believed that "they ought not to mix the WMS with their nuptial affairs." Nevertheless she supported their decision. Middle-aged spinster that she was, she still believed that "young people ought to get married, it is the natural thing to do." In a letter to her old friend Martha Cartmell she conceded that "perhaps you think I won't be nice to Miss German – Oh yes, I will, but it is too late to discuss this to her edification."[270]

Such camaraderie or sisterhood as was generated within the mission compounds was probably among those intrinsic factors contributing to the higher average length of employment for the WMS missionaries in Japan. By choice or chance, in Japan attrition from marriage was low, 20 per cent compared to 40 per cent in West China. While spinsterhood may have been the inevitable result of demographic conditions in a country where suitable husbands did not present themselves in large numbers, the WMS missionaries in Japan seem to have been less inclined, perhaps because of the Japan Affair, to socialize with other members of the missionary community, preferring the companionship of their colleagues and female students. For the WMS one of the benefits of this low marriage rate was that thirty-three of the employees of the Japan mission (40.7 per cent) remained with the society until retirement, some, like Sybil Courtice, enduring internment during the Second World War.[271] Nearly 40 per cent of these particular women had spent at least thirty years in Japan; half the women sent to Japan after the First World War had careers spanning thirty to forty-seven years.

While extrinsic factors, that is, improved communications with Canada and a relatively comfortable lifestyle, and personal considerations such as good friends and freedom from family pressure and responsibilities obviously influenced an individual's decision to remain in Japan, a return to the statistical data adds another dimension to an understanding of the career patterns of the WMS missionaries in Japan. For example, the employees of the Japan Mission were clearly distinguished from other missionaries by their kinship with the Methodist hierarchy. While 25 per cent of all WMS missionaries had relatives within clerical ranks, more than 40 per cent of those in Japan were related to clergymen. Half the women who stayed in Japan for more than thirty years and who consequently directed mission affairs were "daughters of the parsonage," a designation that in the case of Japan seems to have justified all the confidence the Board of Managers placed in it. Why these women from clerical families had longer employment histories is not entirely certain. While they may have been more submissive to the authority of the Church, it seems probable that, because the rigorous Methodist way of life was familiar to them, they were better able to cope with the adversity and frustrations of their jobs. As well, the Japan Mission was the recipient of a large percentage of women from the Maritimes. Twenty-three (28 per cent) women in the Japan mission had been raised in the Maritime provinces; their careers averaged twenty-nine years and nineteen of them had careers of more than twenty years' duration. Again, there is no easy explanation for their persistence, but limited job opportunities among Maritime women may have heightened the attractiveness of a missionary career, while religious awakenings and revivals, combined with the vigour of the Methodist church in the Maritimes, may have had an impact that manifested itself in the strong religious dedication of these particular women.

At least eighteen (22 per cent) women of the Japan Mission had attended a ladies' college, compared to 11% of all WMS missionaries. This discrepancy raises another question – that is, whether previous exposure to an exclusively female institutional environment could expedite the adjustment to the missionary milieu and, simply, whether women who had already experienced living within a community of women were more compatible. Finally and most significantly, the Japan Mission, with its emphasis on teaching and high-calibre girls' schools, was the beneficiary of a much higher proportion of university graduates than the other wms mission fields. The careers of the twenty-five members of the Japan Mission who had attended university averaged twenty-seven years, compared to eighteen years for their colleagues with no university background. This paradigm of career longevity, repeated in the other mission fields, seems to indicate that college graduates were more career-oriented than women who had not attended a university. The corps of career missionaries in Japan also helps to elucidate why the drive for professionalization, with its concomitant employee benefits, and for administrative change was launched by the Japan Mission Council. As the case of Ila Day illustrates, the personnel of the Japan mission placed a high premium on their independence and personal freedom, which their status as foreign missionaries sustained.

In 1911 Day, a thirty-one-year-old graduate of the University of Toronto Conservatory of Music and a music teacher at the Tokyo Girls' School from 1908, resigned to marry D.M. Perley of the West China Mission, who had been evacuated to Japan during the 1911 revolution. After the danger in China had passed, the newlyweds returned to West China. A few months later Perley reported to the General Board that his wife had suffered a breakdown. It was not, as sometimes happened, attributed to the often insufferable climate of West China. Rather, Ila Day Perley's problems were blamed on "the suddenness of the break with the old life in the wms." The cure: "a time of rest in the old surroundings of Japan."[272]

The treatment was not effective. After consultations with Blackmore and Hargrave and the doctors in Japan, the couple was advised to return to Canada, where Ila Perley was institutionalized. Her husband reported to the mission secretary that she believed she had "made the fatal mistake of her life in leaving her work in Japan and marrying. She ordinarily professed no personal antipathy to me except as I happen to stand in the way of her freedom."[273] Three years as a missionary in Japan had had an indelible effect on Ila Day, affording her a distinct identity as a woman missionary and making the adjustment to any other way of life, especially one where she apparently had to accept the authority of a husband, almost impossible. For Day and her colleagues, a strong sense of Christian duty did not preclude a concern for their own interests.

Again and again wms missionaries in Japan remarked on their serendipitous career choice, which combined professional gratification and Christian service. Elizabeth Alcorn's departing pledge, "If I had twenty lives, I would lay them all down for the women of Japan," could have been repeated by dozens of her associates in Japan,[274] just as the enthusiastic testimony of an anonymous WMS evangelist, travelling by bicycle to spread the Gospel, captured the women's satisfaction with their vocations. "As I told ... the story, and watched [the] wondering, listening faces, I would not have changed places with anyone in the world."[275]

CHAPTER FOUR

Face to face with the devil and his works

Encouraged by the initial success of its venture in Japan and by the enthusiastic patronage of its membership in Canada, the WMS was impatient, after a decade, to explore the feasibility of a second overseas field. Once again, the General Board's decision ultimately determined both the timing and the location of the next WMS base.[1] The growth of Canadian Methodist operations in Japan and the Japanese appetite for Western culture were reason enough to encourage the General Board to consider expansion. But its ambitions were also fuelled by mounting public pressure from Methodists for their Church to compete more vigorously with its Presbyterian rival, which in 1888 had set up a mission field in Honan. Consequently, in 1890, when three persistent and resolute young men from eastern Ontario, Rev. George Hartwell and Drs Omar Kilborn and David Stevenson, volunteered their services expressly for China, the General Board could no longer delay a decision if it wished to sustain its image as an aggressive champion of the missionary crusade.[2]

The WMS was not excited about opening a station in China. In fact its board had already considered Syria, where several American women's missionary societies were active, as its second foreign field.[3] When the General Board ratified Szechwan, a province deep in the western Chinese interior, as the next territory to be Christianized by the Methodist Church of Canada, the WMS was not even formally consulted.[4] Nevertheless, the Board of Managers, in this case adhering to the letter of the WMS constitution, deferred to the General Board's judgment, accepting the "providential provision of men and money, which preceded the decision to open work in China," as a sign of "the Divine will in the selection of a second foreign field."[5] During the next sixty years both mission societies paid an enormous price for the choice, as measured by the heavy financial outlay for travel and living expenses and by the more elusive human costs of the emotional and physical suffering on both sides of the Pacific that was an inescapable consequence of missionary enterprises in China. At the time, however, Szechwan's isolation was not regarded as a drawback; its reputation as "practically virgin soil for missionary work" only intensified its appeal as a challenge and an adventure to the evangelical Protestants – Canadian and American Methodists and Presbyterians, the China Inland Mission, and the London Missionary Society – who chose Szechwan as their precinct.[6]

Western missionaries had been granted access to China's interior by the Treaty of Tientsin, signed in 1858 to conclude the Opium Wars, but the two-thousand-mile journey inland from the coast had deterred Protestant missionaries from infiltrating Szechwan until the late 1870s. The aggressive non-denominational, British-based China Inland Mission (CIM) opened the first Protestant mission station in Szechwan at Chungking in 1877 and a second in Chengtu in 1881. In the same year the Methodist Episcopal Church (U.S.), whose agent, Rev. Virgil Hart, became an adviser to the first Canadian Methodist missionaries in Szechwan, also began work in Chengtu.[7] If the WMS supported the mission in Szechwan because of "the leadings of Providence,"[8] the board also anticipated that China would furnish an opportunity for the society to establish its first medical mission. Because Japan already had a relatively efficient health-care system in place by the last quarter of the nineteenth century, limiting missionaries' chances to engage in medical work, the WMS's overseas activity had been confined to teaching and evangelizing. Medical work among women and children as a way to cultivate the critical initial encounter with Christianity had become such a valuable weapon in the arsenal of other women's missionary societies that Methodist women were impatient to send medical personnel to China, where women who would not consult a male doctor were otherwise lost to the Christian cause.[9]

The WMS had not anticipated any difficulty in hiring a female physician for China, but this expectation was perhaps unrealistic, given that by 1891 just thirty-six women had graduated from Canadian medical schools.[10] When no doctors responded to the society's overtures, the board put the best face on its disappointment. But the women wondered if they had "devot[ed] too little time to prayer? or too much to human machinery and methods."[11] It was a consideration that the crises of the China stations would prompt repeatedly in the following years. In the meantime, if the WMS wanted to be a part of the first Canadian Methodist contingent to China, the society had to be satisfied with Amelia Brown, a woman with no medical qualifications, as the first WMS missionary in China.[12] The Board's frustration and ten years of such departures may account for the restrained farewell given Brown, which was, in spite of popular curiosity about China, less publicized than Martha Cartmell's goodbyes a decade earlier.

Brown left Toronto in early October 1891 with Virgil Hart, his wife and daughter, Dr David Stevenson, and two newlywed couples, Dr and Mrs Omar Kilborn and Rev. and Mrs George Hartwell. The party crossed the Pacific on the new CPR steamship *Empress of China*. After a month-long voyage that included a brief stop in Japan to observe the Ainu in their native habitat, the group disembarked at Shanghai early in November.[13] Brown's first chronicle of her journey appeared in the January 1892 issue of the *Missionary Outlook*, whose cover featured a photograph of the very attractive young woman. Although she was busy studying Chinese and preparing for the arduous expedition up the Yangtze to Szechwan, Brown warned her employers that her stay in Shanghai could be prolonged because of rioting in Hunan province and along the lower Yangtze. The British consul who was responsible for the safety of Canadians in China had decided that although the men in the party might proceed to Chengtu, women should remain in coastal areas until spring.[14] There were no more published communications from Brown, nor does correspondence between Brown and the Board of Managers survive. Instead of writing on her own behalf, Brown apparently designated Hart to explain the uncomfortable circumstances in which she had become involved, which jeopardized the increasingly uneasy alliance between the General Board and the WMS.

Without consulting either mission board (as the WMS later implied they ought to have done), early in 1892 Dr Stevenson and Brown announced their engagement. Alexander Sutherland was hardly surprised by the news; he simply advised Hart "to let matters take their course."[15] This suited the General Board, which really preferred that Stevenson begin his work with a wife to care for him and relieve him of the petty matters involved in running a Chinese household. Equally important for the harmony of the missionary community, Stevenson would not impose upon another missionary family.[16] As a final advantage, the marriage alleviated a potentially embarrassing and awkward situation for the missionaries. The Chinese, who were puzzled and disgusted by single women travelling with married couples, usually interpreted these entourages as *ménages à trois* or worse.[17]

To appease the WMS, whose reputation hinged on Brown's competence as its first agent in China, Sutherland decided that the General Board should reimburse the wms for Brown's travelling expenses and that Stevenson personally was liable for repaying his wife's past wages.[18] There was no apparent precedent for the arrangement, but once in place this procedure was adopted whenever wms employees resigned to marry men from either the Methodist General Board or the other churches represented in China. In this way, even before marriage a missionary wife's indebtedness and dependency on her husband and his employer was secured.[19] If the wms was inconvenienced and irritated by Brown's marriage, the General Board was not. A General Board enthusiast later interpreted the marriage as evidence of the co-operation and accord between the two organizations, explaining how "early in the history of Canadian Missions ... the Woman's Missionary Society [came] to the aid of the General Society in matters matrimonial – a precedent that was more than once followed in after years."[20] Marriages between missionaries became endemic to West China. Over the next thirty years almost half (42 per cent) of the wms West China missionaries married, usually another Canadian Methodist missionary and often before completing the first term.

The numerous resignations eventually created serious problems in West China. Full of ambition and financially secure, the wms over-extended itself, with the result that some stations had to be temporarily closed and missionary operations severely restricted because of the eventual shortage of personnel. The propensity for missionaries in China to marry largely explains why the average length of service for women in West China was sixteen years, five years less than for the wms missionaries in Japan. As good Christian women brought up to accept the notion that marriage was preferable to spinsterhood,[21] the Board of Managers did not, indeed could not forbid its employees to marry in spite of the pledge they had signed to the contrary. But because so much valuable time and money raised by the women of Canada was expended on missionaries who, in some cases, left before they had spent a day productively serving the society, the board seems to have suppressed as far as possible details about the marriages in West China. Brown's case was typical. The official wms history merely noted that the marriage took place in Shanghai, "consent having been asked and received by cable."[22] It was not a source of pride for the society.

While the General Board party made its triumphant entrance into Chengtu, boasting dubiously of being the first missionaries to arrive wearing European-style clothing,[23] the wms was beginning its search for a doctor all over again. This time the advertisements drew, if not a flood of applicants, at least one suitable candidate, Dr Alfretta

(Retta) Gifford, a farmer's daughter raised near Meaford, Ontario. A graduate of the Toronto Woman's Medical College in 1891, Gifford had practised medicine in Owen Sound, Ontario, for about a year.[24] In January 1893 the society also hired Sara Brackbill, coincidentally attending Owen Sound Collegiate Institute to improve her teaching credentials, to accompany Gifford.[25] In their capacities as teacher and physician, these two women, who would spend virtually the rest of their lives as missionaries in West China, shaped the direction of WMS work there.

Fortunately for the society both women were exceptionally diligent and able correspondents. Their letters, published in various Methodist journals, restored the society's slightly tarnished public image after Brown's defection while giving thousands of Canadian women their first opportunity to read about China, a country even more enigmatic and remote than Japan as far as Canadians were concerned. Gifford in particular produced detailed commentaries about Chinese society as it appeared to her, that is, from the perspective of the missionary interests with which she identified as soon as she arrived in China. She became impatient to leave Shanghai, where rapacious Western business ventures had become a fact of life and missionary work was "retarded ... by the example of dissolute foreigners."[26] She was "thankful every day that [her] work [would] be in the interior, away from the influence of the large foreign element which abounds in the Treaty Port."[27] Unlike so many Westerners in China who sanctioned "the prevailing view ... that trade and Christianity marched together to mark the spread of Western civilization,"[28] Gifford deliberately seems to have tried to distance herself from other foreigners, especially Western businessmen, whom she considered to be merely self-serving. The Chinese understandably were less able to make this distinction. Their persistently hostile reaction to any foreign presence – missionaries, diplomats, or businessmen – was an insurmountable and often unfathomable obstacle for the society and its agents.

Candid discussions of Chinese attitudes towards Western missionaries in general or to the Canadian Methodists in particular are conspicuously absent from the women's accounts of their first months in China. Instead, they were preoccupied with purchasing furniture, medical equipment, and provisions for the mission station in Szechwan. Possibly because the WMS was still sensitive to the debate over a separate women's society, the missionaries' letters may have deliberately avoided issues that might provoke unwanted criticism and controversy about the obstacles to their work. Only many years later, in the 1920s, did the Canadian Methodist missionaries directly face the Chinese response to their presence, recognizing their own ignorance and misunderstanding of Chinese culture and society. Katharine Hockin, daughter of a wms missionary in West China and herself a United Church missionary, has observed that "all missionaries from abroad arrived, knowingly or not, burdened by the excess baggage of 'imperialist history.' Because their hands were so full, they were not free to reach out to the poor but proud Chinese on terms of human equality."[29] To the baggage of "imperialist history" must be added, in the case of the wms missionaries, their rather elitist but parochial backgrounds and outlook and their limited exposure to the social realities of Canada's industrializing cities, let alone the squalid lives of an Oriental feudal peasantry. Understanding required a heroic suspension of disbelief.

This narrow perspective on missionary issues may explain why, instead of exploring the confrontation of Eastern and Western ideologies and the missionary's part in the encounter, Brackbill and Gifford's first letters from China focused on their day-to-day activities as fledgling missionaries in Shanghai. They concentrated on studying the Mandarin dialect, not spoken in Shanghai but, they were told, universally understood in Szechwan. Six months of study made them comfortable, if not completely fluent, with the language. As well, Gifford visited other women doctors in Shanghai hospitals to observe their surgical procedures and to learn how to set up a dispensary in Szechwan.[30] Among other things, the pair had to contend with the coldest winter in more than three hundred years. To their chagrin, they were still wearing winter clothing late in April.[31] But after a few months of acculturation they began to ponder the position and treatment of the Chinese women whose misery they had come to relieve. Gifford was especially incensed by the arranged marriages and, as a physician, by the practice of footbinding. As she saw it, the solution to that outrage was simply "example as well as precept ... Very often when the foreign teacher attempts to point out the sinfulness of the practice, she is met with the reply 'foreign woman bind her waist.' They do not understand the difference between a neat, close fitting dress and a tight one, as they wear all their garments so very loose. If we would exert the influence we wish over these women, we must discard corsets and everything approaching them."[32] Photographs suggest that Gifford probably ignored her own sensible advice.

Gifford was also concerned about her professional status as a woman doctor. In response to a complaint from the General Board, which was paying its male doctors $500 per annum, the wms Board of Managers had reduced Gifford's salary of $600 accordingly. When Gifford lodged a protest, the board reinstated her salary and, moreover, decided to pay the rent for the women's house in Chengtu until the WMS had built its own quarters.[33] There was apparently no further grievance from the General Board, which then increased its doctors' salaries to match Gifford's. But as a rule, wage equality between male and female missionaries was the exception. In the Methodist case, General Board salaries for both its single and married men were higher than WMS wage scales, replicating wage differentials in Canada but also reflecting the fact that most male missionaries were remunerated as ordained clergy.

In November 1893 Brackbill and Gifford were finally ready to leave Shanghai. Because Szechwan was so far from the coast, where Western goods were available, missionary societies urged their employees to be well supplied for their first months in the Chinese interior. Westerners in China, who generally had unrealistic notions of their own needs, were unwilling to relinquish the comforts and luxuries of their former existence in spite of the problems that transporting these accoutrements two thousand miles upriver might involve. Brackbill and Gifford were no exceptions. Their preparations left little room for a possible accommodation to the Chinese way of life or any personal discomfort if they could avoid it. Before their departure they had been "obliged to purchase lamps, dishes (bed-room, dinner and tea-sets), chairs, clocks, stoves, springs for bed, etc., as it is impossible to get the least foreign articles, even a pair of shoe strings, up there. We have also been purchasing supplies both for the journey up, and something to last for a time after arrival. Sugar, soap, flour, butter, spices, canned fruit as the bottles are needed for after use, canned meat for the journey, vinegar, salt, pepper, mustard, etc., all have to be purchased in Shanghai."[34] The women joined the second contingent of General Board missionaries: Mr and Mrs James Endicott, Dr Hare, and Omar Kilborn, now a widower, who travelled from Chengtu to escort them to Szechwan. To avoid expense and the inquisitive Chinese who crowded the inns for their first glimpse of a Westerner, wherever possible the party stopped overnight at mission stations along the way.

Any voyage on the Yangtze was a potentially frightening ordeal because of strong currents and rapids and the constant threat of attacks by the robber bands that roamed the river banks. Until the 1930s, when personnel and supplies could be flown in, the river remained a challenge for travellers to Szechwan. Not unexpectedly, Gifford and Brackbill met misadventure during the passage through the spectacular but treacherous Gorges of the Upper Yangtze, where their houseboat "struck a rock, filled in about fifteen minutes and sank." The group was able, as Omar Kilborn later recounted, "to get near a sloping bank and get ashore ourselves, along with all easily movable articles and furniture from our rooms ... Providentially, our small house-boat was right at hand, so we were able to have a sheltered sleeping place. Next day our cargo of boxes was slowly fished out of the sunken boat, and in forty-eight hours after the accident the old craft again stood upright on the water. In the meantime we had purchased coal, built fires on the sand, set up drying poles, and commenced drying bedding, clothing, and books."[35] Gifford and Brackbill lost their books, along with a crate of gifts and a cake that had been "entrusted to [them] by the mother of a prospective bride."[36]

The river journey ended at Chungking, where the party hired sedan chairs for the four-hundred-mile trek to Chengtu, which took another two weeks. At Chengtu, Brackbill and Gifford rented a house near, but not in, the General Board mission compound, which already boasted two school buildings, several missionary homes, a chapel, and a bookroom. The women immediately began to outline their plans for a girls' school and a women's hospital, although, for the time being, they were powerless to initiate their designs. Rigorous as it had seemed, their language instruction was totally inadequate to permit them to communicate even their most basic needs. Consequently, both women spent several more months studying local dialects in order to bridge the gap between, as Gifford put it, "the book language and the colloquial."[37]

Similar frustration over their inability to speak and write Chinese plagued succeeding wms missionaries. The Board of Managers assumed, often mistakenly, that a well-educated candidate could learn a highly complex and exacting foreign language without difficulty. Like countless other Western missionaries, many wms missionaries never became fluent enough in Chinese to feel confident about speaking in public;[38] others blamed the long hours of trying to master the language for their bouts of ill health. The Board of Managers made no provision for recruits to study either Chinese or Japanese before leaving Canada, nor did the society administer even rudimentary tests to determine if a recruit had the capacity to grasp such a complex language. Well into the 1920s missionaries continued to complain about the inadequate language preparation, which limited their effectiveness and undermined their self-assurance.

Brackbill and Kilborn wrote cheerfully enough about Chengtu, a city of about five hundred thousand, which they preferred to Shanghai partly because of its wide streets.[39] But their sense of alienation from Chinese society because of their sex, nationality, and calling became an increasingly persistent theme in their letters. Because walking alone in Chengtu made them nervous and uncomfortable, they travelled, as did the upper-class Chinese women with whom they identified, in closed sedan chairs. Gifford defended their actions, reasoning that "no respectable woman of the better class ever walks; another reason is our foreign dress attracts so much attention and calls forth so many remarks."[40] Amelia Brown Stevenson, now living in Chengtu with her husband, questioned their timidity and uneasiness, pointing out that "the ladies of the CIM and CMS societies travel about as freely and easily as the men, and are winning their way into the hearts of the people. Why not the ladies of the WMS?"[41] Gifford and Brackbill continued to use sedan chairs. No doubt they feared the insults and taunts of the Chinese, but they also conformed to Chinese views about the proper conduct of well-bred women to avoid alienating potential converts.

The society did not challenge their caution. Single female missionaries were open to close scrutiny by the Chinese. If they wished to alleviate Chinese suspicions about their character and morals, Western women had to be painstakingly correct in their behaviour in a sexually segregated society where all but the poorest peasant women were confined to the home to safeguard their virtue. Until the revolution "it was deemed desirable that women should have no public social relations with men, and ... within the household relations between the sexes from adolescence onwards were supposed to be marked by avoidance."[42] As the indomitable Victorian traveller Isabella Bird Bishop (who coincidentally accompanied a party of Canadian Methodists on the Yangtze in 1896) explained, "The fact of a young unmarried woman living anywhere but under her father's roof, exposes her character to the greatest imputations, which are hurled at her in the streets ... The Chinese etiquette ... tends to propriety, and though to our thinking tiresome, no young foreign woman attempting to teach a foreign religion can violate its leading rules without injury to her work."[43] It was a particularly serious breach of Chinese etiquette for women missionaries to receive men in their homes or to call at a Chinese house without the company of a Chinese Bible woman.[44]

It was too sensual a theme for Brackbill and Gifford to raise for their audience in Canada, but foreign women's reputations were also questionable because the Chinese thought it "scandalous for a woman to be seen in a tight bodice, or any other fashion which show[ed] her figure,"[45] while "long skirts suggested an absence of underclothing" to the Chinese, who were accustomed to women dressed in jackets and trousers.[46] The thorny question of how missionaries in China should dress, which had first arisen when the representatives of the British-based China Inland Mission adopted Chinese-style clothing in an effort to shed some of the Western paraphernalia that they concluded distracted from their evangelizing, continued to stir up controversy within missionary communities into the twentieth century. The CIM's chief spokesman in China, Hudson Taylor, considered it "an advantage not to have the [Chinese] women's attention distracted from the message to the dress of the missionary."[47] The men of the CIM let their hair grow, braiding it in the traditional Chinese queue. These attitudes towards dress were not popular among Canadian Methodists, especially Virgil Hart, who appreciated the value of a woman wearing Western dress as an inducement for a good crowd.[48] A few women, Dr Maud Killam of the WMS for one, became short-term converts to Chinese fashions. And most WMS missionaries delighted in purchasing Chinese silks, linens, embroidery, and decorative objects for themselves and their friends in Canada.[49]

If Brackbill and Kilborn showed no inclination to adopt Chinese styles, they were none the less conscious of their appearance and comfort. Because of the extreme heat and cold in the variable Szechwanese climate they needed a variety of clothing, including "as heavy underclothing as we wear at home ... heavy dresses for the winter and plenty of light ones for summer ... several pretty prints as well as white ones ... [They advised] anyone coming out to bring a good supply of lightweight woollen guernseys. Many wear wool next to the skin all summer, as it removes to a great extent the danger of chill from sudden change in temperature."[50] Even under the most adverse circumstances these Victorian women seemed loath to compromise their femininity. Some of the preoccupation about their wardrobes arose probably not so much from concern for their health, as they claimed, but in response to the attention of the male missionaries with whom they were in frequent social and business contact.

In spite of the Chinese social taboos that the women observed as respectable ambassadors for Christ and the dearth of Western material possessions, Szechwan was not the wasteland the women had anticipated. The province was only slightly smaller than Ontario but with a much larger population, estimated in 1905 by the British consul at forty-five million. The weather was generally better than in Canada, although in Chungking, one of the "furnaces" of China, by June temperatures soared to 95°F.[51] Then missionaries retreated to the cooler mountain region or their cellars.[52] Canadians in Szechwan drew parallels with Florida.[53] One of the most fertile agricultural regions of China, Szechwan produced an exceptional range of fruits, vegetables, and grains. Chengtu, always at the centre of Canadian Methodist missionary activities in China, was unique in the province because of its good supply of beef, better than "the cities where there [were] no Mohammedans, for they only are the beef butchers." An inventory of food stuffs available to the missionaries included chicken, duck, geese, beef, mutton, goat, fish, wild fowl, pork, Irish and sweet potatoes, carrots, turnips, beans, celery, cabbage, eggplant, cucumber, peas, onions, radishes, and "of course rice ... as the Chinese cook it, big grains and dry, not soft as it is cooked at home ... popped rice, wheat and corn ... whole wheat flour for breakfast food, pudding, brown bread and gems [muffins]." The abundance of fruits, "cherries, mullberries, apples, apricots, pears, peaches, figs, grapes, persimmons ... pomelas [like a grapefruit and grown only in Szechwan], and many varieties of oranges,"[54] especially appealed to Canadian appetites.

This bountiful harvest did not curb the flood of complaints about the diet, in particular the strong flavour of the oils in which food was customarily cooked and the monotony of the dishes prepared by Chinese cooks who were familiar only with peasant fare. A few women with unrelenting dysentery had good cause for concern about their meals. But others, like Lena Dunfield, who once fed her dog a Chinese-style breakfast her well-intentioned students served her,[55] continued, even after twenty years in China, to shun Szechwanese cooking, preferring instead imported, and very expensive, tinned food. There were, however, some strange degrees of culinary accommodation. Not a few missionaries developed a taste for Tibetan duck, serving it often but still finishing the meal with a North American chocolate or cottage pudding.[56] Descriptions of Christmas celebrations, replete with plum puddings and mince pies, offer additional evidence of the lengths to which the women went to duplicate a traditional Canadian meal amid the "alien corn."[57]

In Szechwan there were far more vital matters than the strange diet to trouble Western women. Lacking even the most basic sanitation, China, as one woman delicately phrased it, was always redolent of "pig odors."[58] Infectious diseases – typhoid, smallpox, and worse, cholera, which killed Dr Kilborn's first wife, were rampant. For the first time in their lives the WMS missionaries came face to face with the horror of leprosy. Moreover, to add to the challenges the women already faced in surmounting their own prejudices and preconceptions about the nature of the Chinese, many old China hands condemned the shortcomings of Szechwanese society as the outward manifestations of the moral corruption of an unusually unstable and evil people.

Denunciations of Chinese morality, such as Dr Hart's searing catalogue, in the *Methodist Magazine* in 1898, of the obstacles to Chinese missionary work, did little to dispel any image that Canadians, future missionaries among them, might have of the Chinese as other than hopelessly degraded heathens. Hart's imperialistic invective perpetuated the comforting notion of Western superiority:

The Westerner teems with energy, is full of progressive ideas, and is much out of harmony with the do-as-little-as necessary Chinaman as a leviathan ironclad in the midst of a fleet of junks ... His laws are not perfect, their execution a hundredfold worse, his officials are rapacious and pitiless toward the weak, his schools are better than none but lamentably deficient in every direction. The religions and philosophers are practically dead, materialism reigns triumphant and the voice of conscience is stifled in dungeons of despair ... Streets and houses are filthy beyond description, harbouring every kind of vermin and germ imaginable. The moral filth is ... greater than the physical. The common language, of both men and women, boys and girls, and indiscriminately used, could not be viler ... beggary is a profession adopted by scores of thousands, poverty is widespread, wine drinking is universal, and opium smoking almost so, footbinding universal, and the terrible evil of infanticide taints the whole moral life of the people. The social evil has driven out all modesty from society. The officials take no steps to deal with these great evils, and the burden of reform in all directions becomes more and more the missionary's imperative duty.[59]

Publicly at least, the WMS missionaries in the field were less judgmental than Hart. In 1905, for instance, the society's history observed that "not so much the vices of the people as their weakness ... makes the work of regeneration all but hopeless."[60]

Until the turn of the century WMS educational, evangelical, and medical activities in China were directed specifically towards the traditional goal of Christian missionaries, that is, winning individuals to Jesus Christ. Although the WMS's special commission remained the conversion of Chinese women and, through them, other family members, adult intransigence convinced the society and its workers of "the absolute necessity of beginning with the children."[61] Following the Japanese missionaries' example, the women gradually began to address China's enormous social problems by applying their energies to children, in particular young girls, whose existence was so irrelevant in nineteenth-century Chinese society. The appropriate care and nurturing, the women hoped, would produce grateful Christian wives, mothers, and teachers. From the outset Sara Brackbill conformed to this principle by opening a boarding school where girls could be educated in a totally Christian environment.

For her part, Retta Gifford was optimistic that a modern women's hospital in Chengtu could relieve the all too obvious suffering and provide the means to evangelize a captive audience.[62] Her ambitions were abandoned for the immediate future in May 1893, when, after only two months in Chengtu, Gifford married Omar Kilborn. The Board of Managers did not demand Gifford's immediate resignation because, as a doctor, she was indispensable to the new mission's success. The WMS dared not risk the public humiliation of another missionary who married before her work was really underway, nor could the board waste the time and money involved in recruiting a successor. Instead, in an unusually strongly worded statement, the board chastised Gifford for her breach of contract, "but considering all the circumstances ... consent[ed] to the marriage and the continuance of Dr Gifford in our work for her term of five years if her full time can be given to medical work among the women and children of China."[63] Gifford was penalized for her disloyalty to the society. From the date of her marriage her salary was reduced to three hundred dollars per annum, probably on the assumption that, as a married woman, she would not be able to give full attention to the WMS.[64]

After their marriage the Kilborns were sent to open a station at Kiating, about 120 miles south of Chengtu, where Retta Kilborn set up a dispensary for the WMS. When they returned to Chengtu two years later, her plans for more extensive women's medical facilities were finally put in motion. In the meantime she had a son while carrying on her WMS work. In 1898 she completed her term, but despite her seemingly exemplary contribution the society did not suggest she continue as a WMS employee. Instead, like so many other missionary wives Kilborn carried on her work as an unpaid volunteer, assisting at the Canadian Methodist hospitals and dispensaries and writing for missionary publications. When her husband died in 1920 she accepted a full-time position as a doctor for the General Board, but after one term she transferred to the WMS of the newly created United Church and practised in Szechwan until her retirement in 1934.[65]

Within eighteen months of Brackbill and Gifford's arrival in Chengtu the Board of Managers was satisfied enough with their reports to advertise for a second physician, a teacher, and a nurse to train Chinese women in simple medical procedures and health care. Gifford had already learned that Chinese assistants, if properly supervised, could be both labour- and cost-efficient.[66] Only the nurse, Jennie Ford, was hired. In March 1895 she reached Szechwan, where she assured the society "all is peace and quietness," even though the potential risks of the Sino-Japanese War had almost kept her at home.[67] The dispensary where Kilborn and her Chinese assistants performed minor surgery, most often to treat eye problems, skin diseases, and complications from bound feet, and gave out medicine was operating at full capacity. Ford became Kilborn's right hand. In contrast Brackbill's educational work among girls had begun more modestly than she expected, with a day school instead of a boarding school, which would have required an expensive building, a large staff, and parents willing to pay for their daughters' education. Brackbill was, none the less, gratified by the attendance.[68]

The women's eagerness about the prospects for Christianity in China was soon dampened. By 1895 Szechwan had become a potential powderkeg in the wake of China's defeat during the Sino-Japanese War, which had broken out in August 1894. In any event, the presence of Westerners in their country was increasingly taken as an insult by the Chinese,[69] who had been forced by the Treaty of Shimonoseki to capitulate to the Japanese, to surrender Taiwan, the Pescadores, and the Liaotung peninsula in southern Manchuria, to open more ports to foreign traders, and to allow Japanese nationals to manufacture and trade in their country.[70] The Western powers took exception to Japan's attempt to control the sea route to north China. Russia, France, and Germany intervened, forcing Japan to relinquish the Liaotung peninsula in return for a larger indemnity. Russia then moved into the territory, building a naval base at Port Arthur and a rail terminus at Dairen. Britain seized Weihaiwei on the Shantung peninsula as a naval station. Germany and France also used the situation to establish strategic bases and to secure the rights for railway construction inland. "As the predatory spirit sharpened, talk of the partition of China was increasingly heard."[71] By the early summer of 1895 it was apparent to some Westerners in Szechwan that their situation was growing very precarious. Fearing the worst, Retta Kilborn turned to "the One who is able to protect us then and now."[72]

Western diplomats delayed in taking action to remove their nationals. Not until the very day that the anti-missionary rioting erupted in Chengtu did the American minister in Peking, Charles Denby, warn the United States State Department that China's defeat threatened to provoke a reaction against foreigners throughout the country.[73] As a rule, British officials were anxious about the safety of their charges, including Canadians, whom they were obligated to protect as British subjects. Their attitude towards safeguarding women missionaries, however, was somewhat ambivalent. Most British diplomats in China regarded missionaries, and single women above all, not as allies in the imperialist enterprise but as nuisances who were usually to blame for the risks they might face. One insightful British envoy in Shansi, who seemed to understand the Chinese perspective on women missionaries, found it "hard to speak temperately of the individual or society that sends girls wholesale into the interior of such a country as China unprotected, practically uncared for, and with most inadequate means ... These poor unfortunate women with the merest smattering of Chinese are being sent about the country ... to pray, play the guitar, and sing hymns in the street, a life that none but an improper woman in China would lead, and which fosters the idea in the native mind that these girls were too bad to be allowed to remain in their own country."[74]

If the British government realized the immediate danger to foreigners in Szechwan, the message that their missionaries were in danger was not conveyed to the Methodist mission societies in Canada. Two years earlier, in a prescient moment, Alexander Sutherland had questioned the expansion of the Methodist enterprise in China: "In view of the strong tendency among the Chinese to suspect foreigners of some sinister design," he wondered if it would be more prudent "to give the people time to become familiar with [our] teachings, motives, and intentions, and when confidence is fully established, additional workers might be sent in more rapidly and with entire safety."[75] What happened in Chengtu in 1895 validated Sutherland's caution, but the Methodist agents on the spot did not have the insight or experience to foresee what was ahead.

The sequence of events of the next months is complicated, to say the least. Simply put, Liu Ping-chang, the viceroy of Szechwan, had been replaced and discredited in 1894 by the governor of Shensi. But Liu remained in Chengtu, where, before his final exit in June 1895, he incited anti-foreign and anti-missionary sentiment as a last display of scorn. Rumours spread that foreigners were plotting to take over Szechwan, that they were criminals fleeing justice and fortune hunters seeking treasures.[76] According to one General Board missionary, "there was a widespread belief that foreign barbarians ate human flesh ... Did the foreigners use parts of the human body to perform their wondrous cures? The use of canned goods, meats, fish, vegetables and fruits aroused curiosity ... Another belief that was very common to all classes was that the foreigners kidnapped children."[77] Women missionaries faced special charges "of eating babies and digging out their eyes for medicine."[78] Yet because Chinese officials had reassured them, the missionaries reported that they felt secure, with little sense of "personal danger, as Chengtu, the capital, was well supplied with military equipment and no trouble could arise unless sanctioned by the officials."[79]

Nevertheless, when the annual Dragon Boat Festival brought crowds into the streets of Chengtu on 28 May, the missionary community anticipated a crisis. Throughout the city placards warned the Chinese to keep their children inside because the missionaries would kidnap and roast them to extract medicine. The day began uneventfully, but as Retta Kilborn reported to the WMS,

About four o'clock … a large crowd gathered in the street outside the compound where Dr and Mrs Stevenson, Dr Kilborn and I lived. Slowly the crowd increased, and some stones were thrown over the wall. As soon as the first stones were thrown, a messenger was sent to the yamen, the residence of the magistrate, with a card asking him to send men to scatter the crowd. The stone throwing increased, and the mob began to pound the heavy gates. Soon the gates were battered down and part of the gateman's house. At this juncture Drs Stevenson and Kilborn faced the mob in the gateway, each with a gun. As soon as the crowd saw the guns they separated and ran a short distance up and down the street, but regained courage and renewed the attack.[80]

The frenzied mob was about to storm the compound when Omar Kilborn fired into the air. The people quickly dispersed. Aided by a loyal former Chinese hospital patient, the missionaries escaped from their compound and, pursued by soldiers, reached the temporary security of the CIM home.[81]

By morning the General Board compound had been completely destroyed. The mob burned Hartwell's new home and headed towards the house where Brackbill and Ford lived. The pair climbed over the back wall, taking with them only a bag of silver. They reached the CIM, but within a few hours it too was under attack. The missionaries then fled to the relative safety of a nearby Chinese home, where they heard "not thirty feet away, and separated only by a mud wall, th[e] … crowd destroy[ing] the China Inland Mission buildings." As Retta Kilborn recalled, "The shouts and curses of the maddened mob, mingled with the crash and roar of falling buildings – it was terrible! We knew not what moment they might find us, and if found probably not one would have escaped alive."[82] Late in the evening the group moved to the *yamen*, the magistrate's residence, the only safe place for them; here the thirty-two men, women, and children spent ten nerve-wracking days in three small rooms.

Stories about the missionaries' nefarious activities circulated in Chengtu. To discredit them even more, the Chinese spattered chicken blood on the ruins of the mission compound, claiming that it was the blood of the children that the missionaries had murdered.[83] David Stevenson and Omar Kilborn specifically were accused of drugging, then killing children to extract medicine from their bodies. As proof, a young boy testified that he had been sedated and confined in a tin box under the floor of the mission chapel. Kilborn denied the incident. But only when he produced his British passport, which stated that British subjects must be referred to the British consul for trial, were the charges dismissed.[84] At midnight on 8 June the missionaries were escorted to boats waiting to carry them to the coast. A month later the party reached Shanghai.[85]

For public consumption Brackbill, for one, tended to make light of the danger. In a remarkable display of humour she joked that "we have no change of clothing and no books, and will be glad to see a home again; but perhaps the Chinese may have some of their homes a little better furnished because of all they have carried off. Could we call this helping to civilize the Chinese?"[86] The quip belies reality; subsequent testimony exposed the extent of the emotional devastation that the rioting had inflicted upon the Canadians. Amelia Brown Stevenson was beaten during the initial escape from the compound; her child was temporarily lost during the ensuing confusion. Usually pacific missionaries had resorted to violence in their own defence, and in the *yamen* several women became very ill. One unidentified woman either gave birth to a stillborn baby or miscarried. The body, as Dr Stevenson reluctantly revealed, "gave us some anxiety. For what if they should find it? As a doctor I was asked to get rid of it and did ... this is disagreeable to write about. In the name of high Heaven what is it to bear these trials."[87] The Canadian Methodist women endured the immediate terror almost stoically, displaying a "capacity for self-control and sublimation" that Peter Gay suggests was characteristic of the late Victorian middle class,[88] but their brush with death left serious scars. Amelia Stevenson suffered a severe nervous breakdown on the way to Shanghai. She and her husband did not return to West China. Jennie Ford's subsequent death in 1897 from meningitis was, perhaps erroneously, attributed by the wms to her horrible experiences during the Chengtu riots.

From Shanghai, Brackbill and Ford travelled to the wms Tokyo mission, where they remained until permission to resume work in Szechwan came at the end of the year. Eventually the Chinese government paid the missionary societies an indemnity covering all loss of property, salaries, and travel expenses. Chinese officials, including the viceroy, were punished for their part in the riots.[89] The wms applauded the action. When the women returned to Szechwan in

April 1896, the Society had raised enough money to purchase property in Chengtu for a girls' boarding school and a missionaries' home. By 1914 the WMS compound in Chengtu encompassed three and a half acres,[90] proof that the fears of those "who predicted that Mission work had been set back years were groundless. The seeming calamity had been over-ruled for the advancement rather than the suppression of Christian Missions."[91] The society's optimism notwithstanding, the attack on the mission irrefutably altered the disposition of the society's work and the lifestyles of the WMS missionaries in Szechwan. The most visible manifestation of the more suspicious, less trusting, but perhaps more realistic outlook the women adopted was the "500 feet of brick wall, twelve feet high, to enclose the property."[92] The wall provided privacy and protection for the women; but it gave them a false sense of security, and at the same time it became a barrier, effectively separating the missionaries and the Chinese, symbolically and in fact.

As Sydney Forsythe has demonstrated in his study of a late nineteenth-century American mission community in China, missionaries "really did not want to enter the Chinese world any more than they had to. Their whole purpose was to get the Chinese to enter theirs."[93] Few missionaries and even fewer women moved beyond their compounds to try to comprehend the dynamics of Chinese society.[94] Jane Hunter draws a similar picture of American women missionaries who, in order to retain a hold on Western civilization, chose to operate within the reconstructed material and cultural milieu of the small midwest towns where they had been raised.[95] To ease the trauma of living in a country where private rituals – hair combing, washing, and defecating – were routinely performed in public, where naked trackers hauled the houseboats along the Yangtze, where full-fledged pitched battles between the armies of ruthless warlords sickened and terrified them,[96] and above all, where foreign women were the objects of abuse, the Canadian Methodist women deliberately distanced themselves from the Chinese society around them. It is tempting to conclude that the "mission-centric" outlook, a perspective that has been seriously criticized in recent years,[97] applies equally to the WMS missionaries. Two examples may serve to illustrate the point.

In 1923, when the WMS Board of Managers suggested employing Chinese-Canadian women as missionaries in Szechwan, the Canadian women in the field resisted. Their objections seem to have arisen from their own experience of relationships with Chinese and Chinese-Canadian women. They did not want to grant Chinese-

Canadian women equal professional standing with WMS missionaries. Nor were Chinese-Canadian women particularly welcome socially as members of the WMS mission family. The WMS West China Mission Council raised questions about "their status on the field? Will they dress the same as we do, and live according to our (Canadian) standard of living, or will they live in the institutions as do our Chinese teachers, nurses and doctors, and eat Chinese food, etc.?"[98] If the Canadian-Chinese women knew their places, received wages according to Chinese scales, and deferred to the WMS missionaries as the Chinese servants did, the Mission Council grudgingly conceded their presence might "help bridge the gulf between the Chinese and the foreigner."[99] But the missionaries were still uncomfortable with suggestions that the Chinese women should move into the mission homes as their intimate colleagues. While their reluctance to recognize educated Chinese-Canadian women as their sisters in God's work seems to imply that the missionaries believed only *bona fide* messengers – that is, professionally qualified recruits – could bring Christianity to China,[100] their elitism inevitably raises the uneasy question of how the WMS missionaries approached the poor and uneducated Chinese women whom they had chosen to serve, and just how committed they were to the society's ambitions to deliver Chinese womanhood from the restraints imposed by Chinese society, if their response to a close association with Chinese women born and educated in Canada was so negative.

A different sort of problem was posed by Mary Foster's unusually familiar relationship with her Chinese tutor. Foster's fate became an object lesson for any newcomer who might have questioned the women's circumspection about mingling with Chinese society. Foster's destruction began when she got too close to the Chinese. Her attachment to her male Chinese language instructor progressed far beyond the sentimental relationships between Western missionaries and Asians that Jane Hunter has described.[101] After eleven years of evangelical work in Kiating, several of them spent living alone with no other Westerners for company, Foster had to be furloughed home because of what the WMS publicly referred to as recurrent ill health. In fact, Foster suffered a severe nervous breakdown. The Board of Managers rejected her petition to be reinstated after a recovery period; it refused to accept any responsibility for her behaviour, nor did it expect its missionaries in the field to "endure the anxiety incident to the risk of [her] return to that land which tries the nerves of the very strongest."[102] But Foster, who seems to have been independently wealthy, soon reappeared in Szechwan, where her conduct prompted her former colleagues to appeal for her immediate return to Canada. The women were reluctant to discuss the matter openly, but a letter from George Hartwell to Sutherland described how Foster's "state of mind of three years ago was returning. It largely surrounds a former teacher whom she claimed was in sight of Heaven her husband."[103] To make matters worse, Foster was riddled with guilt for crimes she thought she had committed against the Chinese – cutting off heads and digging out eyes. The doctors who were consulted feared that she "might during such spells take life."[104]

Foster was subsequently escorted to Shanghai by several WMS missionaries, under restraint and at the expense of the Methodist Church. Her catastrophe alerted her colleagues to the narrow path separating the necessary place of the individual Chinese, as tutor and friend, in the "making of a missionary,"[105] from the insidious effects that China and the Chinese might have on the mental, emotional, and sexual stability of the unwary Occidental. Keeping up the barriers that separated the Westerner and the Chinese was crucial; as John Fairbank has pointed out in a review of Hersey's *The Call*, if missionaries "became too Chinese in their habits and outlook, they might lose the missionary impulse."[106]

The women's understandable caution about the Chinese did not inevitably produce an obsessive attachment to the mission compound. If they could do so without anxiety, the women left the security of the grounds to walk in the streets or to hike into the nearby countryside, sometimes accompanied by the schoolgirls. These were excursions that, in later years, the women liked to recall.[107] When their freedom was restricted by the hostility of the Chinese, they complained bitterly. Then their neat compounds, rose gardens and vegetable plots, Canadian-style meals and tennis games became an essential counterweight to those aspects of existence over the wall that Lena Dunfield, for one, equated with the sixteenth century.[108] Not surprisingly given their sequestered living arrangements, the women came to regard a "naturally cheerful disposition and good common sense" and an interest in cooking as crucial qualities for their future co-workers.[109]

Only rarely did the women allow the Canadian public glimpses into the more upsetting aspects of their existence. Even then they displayed a toughness that might not have been expected of middle-class women reared in Victorian Canada. An excerpt from Sara Brackbill's letters demonstrates her ability, albeit after ten years' seasoning, to adjust to the grim realities of her surroundings. "Sunday morning while passing the Parade Ground on our way to church I was surprised to see the body and head of a man who had been beheaded a few days before, lying beside the path. You may be sure I brought the children back by another street."[110] Coolheadedness, accompanied by perhaps a degree of nonchalance towards the violence around them, was just one characteristic that time spent in China fostered if the women remained long enough. It was usually preferable, however, that Canadian audiences read about the neat and clean schoolgirls making their own clothing and learning to embroider their shoes instead of the seamier aspects of the work and the missionaries' personal misadventures at the hands of beggars, purse snatchers, bandits, and mud slingers. For example, while the annual report for 1902–03 recorded the deaths of eight of the nine babies who had been taken into the Jennie Ford orphanage, the women in the field seldom alluded to such deaths in their correspondence with the society.[111]

This selectivity in reporting raises an interesting question. By dismissing or denying the alarming aspects and the outright failures of their work in China, did WMS missionaries perhaps deceive themselves into believing that theirs was a happy and rewarding life? Or were they simply very carefully and deliberately protecting their careers by editing what the home front might detect about the realities of the situation in West China? Certainly Elizabeth Strachan exercised a heavy editorial hand on news directed to her that was in turn to be presented to the membership. At the same time, the Board of Managers made no attempt to evaluate the circumstances of their missionaries in West China; consequently, the missionaries' version of events was usually taken at face value. Some of the society's executive inspected the stations in Japan and in Canada, but probably because of the expense and because the board members were ageing, none of them travelled to China before the First World War to assess the circumstances of the stations and the employees. Only other workers in the field might have disputed Lottie Brooks's effusive assertion that "the home life is delightful and the whole missionary community is *so* nice, and I am very fond of my work."[112] As a result, the recruiting campaigns launched periodically for university graduates for the Chinese missions were based on the rose-coloured recommendations of the women in the field, whose assurances that a flood of new recruits was the remedy for China's endless problems may have misled the more credulous candidates.

A case in point was Lena Dunfield, a Manitoba farm girl who had graduated from Wesley College a year before her arrival in China in 1904. Dunfield thought that repression of the sights, sounds, and smells of China was the only way she could retain her sanity. In a diary that is instructive because of the use of male gender forms to refer to her own female experience, Dunfield confessed that she simply avoided thinking about the bleak surroundings of Kiating. "When the missionary gets within his own compound he is glad enough to blot out as far as possible the memory of what he knows too well exists. I am too anxious to preserve my sleeping ability to harass my mind in recounting the horrible at this time of night."[113] The difficulty was that closing their eyes and minds to their grim surroundings precluded careful reflection by the women about why they had come to China. Perhaps, as women educated in late Victorian Canada, the missionaries simply lacked the requisite analytical training and historical knowledge that might have enabled them to adopt a more objective view of their work and the Chinese. As it was, as dedicated evangelical Methodists the women presumed that their ambition to transform Chinese society through Christian doctrine was ample justification for their presence in an inhospitable and bewildering country.

The decade from the arrival of the first WMS missionaries to the conclusion of the Boxer Rebellion was marked by repeated unsettling events that made the women's work doubly difficult in the already hostile environment. Whereas the WMS missionaries in Japan seized the opportunity to establish a degree of professional and institutional independence unusual among working women, even professional women in Canada, the explosive nature of Szechwan and the overt enmity to missionary work had a tendency to inhibit the women's pioneering instincts. As a result they remained dependent on the society and the men of the General Board, on British administrators, and on the limited tolerance of their antagonistic Chinese hosts for the security of the precarious foothold they had established.

In these circumstances it was unlikely that their perceptions of their work, of their purpose, or of their special call as women missionaries would ever rise above the garrison mentality that the actuality of life in China made necessary and desirable. Consequently, they appear less aggressive and innovative than their colleagues in Japan, though no less ambitious or idealistic about their missionary sphere. To promote their own interests, in 1898 the women organized a mission council, modelled after the Japan council, to administer the increasingly complex operations in Szechwan. Following the society's policies, the council held an annual joint session with the General Board to co-ordinate future development in Szechwan. In this forum the women quickly learned to defend their own ground and to resist suggestions from the men that they bolster the work of the General Board, which the women were only too eager to point out was "always in debt."[114] In West China, however, the women's assertiveness did not provoke the same antagonism between the sexes as it had in Japan. Both societies heeded the lessons of the Japan Affair, so that the annual meetings in Chengtu were valued as supportive dialogues and social events, especially by women outside Chengtu with limited contact with Westerners.

The arrival in 1897 of Dr Maud Killam and a second teacher, Mary Foster, brought the number of WMS missionaries in Chengtu to four – Ford, Brackbill, Killam, and Foster – a close-knit group, as Killam put it, "sisters – ... congenial when we have been sent so far from our dear, dear brothers and sisters in Canada."[115] These missionary pacesetters took very seriously the special obligation that they believed they had as women, to deliver Chinese womankind from the bonds of centuries-old social convention rooted in the errors of Confucius and Buddha. However, their own understanding and tolerance of Chinese women was acquired very slowly. Killam was surprised, even puzzled, that the women she met during her house calls could be pleasant yet so completely oblivious to her Bible stories, and she was always irritated that whenever she entered a Chinese home she was offered the customary waterpipe to smoke opium.[116]

More than any other aspect of women's inferior status in a patriarchal society, the missionaries agonized over the all too visible consequence of infanticide, the countless baby girls, perhaps 10 per cent of all female babies, abandoned to die by the roadside.[117] In an extraordinarily moving letter to the WMS membership Jennie Ford recounted how she had adopted a baby girl left in a ditch below the mission compound

just because it had the misfortune to be born a girl ... when they do die the dogs eat them. We hesitated about bringing her in at first, because of the awful stories they tell about our eating babies and digging out their eyes for medicine, etc; but we quickly concluded the course the Master would take, and had her brought in. Such a bundle of dirty, vermin-infested rags you never saw, and from under a dirty cap two great black eyes staring wide open ... We quickly gave her warm milk and stimulants, and, getting her out of the dirty rags, put her in a hot bath ... and kept her in a basket by the open oven door all day ... But in a week of feeding on good milk we had a bright baby, not yet two months old, weighing now seven and a half pounds. We called the officials in and told them of the child, and that we would care for it. Proper papers were made out, so there can be no trouble, and her parents cannot claim her when she grows big enough to earn a little money. Of course we have no authority from home to do orphanage work; but this one I have adopted, and will bring her up, trusting that some day she may perhaps take my place when I am obliged to quit work; and she may more than fill it because of being native born.[118]

When Ford died a few months later, the society opened a small orphanage in Chengtu in her memory.[119] A few other girls were "adopted" by the missionaries, but it was closer to a form of sponsorship because the children continued to live in the orphanage, not in the wms mission home. As the orphanage system grew, adoptions became infrequent.[120]

In 1897 the girls' school in Chengtu, a three-storey brick structure designed to impress the Chinese, and a mission home were constructed under Brackbill's watchful supervision. The school's enrolment of forty-three day pupils and fourteen boarders was a personal disappointment to Brackbill as principal, although her stipulation that girls must unbind their feet before they could be admitted was partly responsible. In addition, parents were required to sign a contract outlining the terms of their daughter's entrance: how long the girl was to remain in school, that she would not "be betrothed without [wms] consent," that in the event of sickness or death no trouble would be made, and finally, that the wms's "government [was] not to be interfered with."[121] In short, the wms demanded *carte blanche* to shape the girls as they chose in their new environment, and the missionaries did not tolerate any parental interference in their Christianizing processes.

The wms agents regarded the crusade against footbinding, the most conspicuous and debasing physical manifestation of the degradation of Chinese women, as their most concrete and realistic challenge. The zealous Brackbill boasted about the hours she spent knitting socks designed to prevent further injury to her students' damaged but now unbound feet.[122] According to Isabella Bishop, footbinding was almost universal in Szechwan,

except among the Manchu or Tartar women and those of a degraded class ... and the shoe of even the poorest and most hard-worked peasant woman does not exceed four inches in length. Though in walking these "golden lilies" look like hoofs, and the women hobble on their heels, I have seen them walk thirty *li* [10 miles] in a day, and some have told me that they can walk sixty easily ... I have never seen a hospital in China without some case or cases not only of extreme danger to the foot or great toe, but of ulcers or gangrene involving absolute loss by amputation. It is fashion, of course. Hitherto a Chinese woman with "big feet" is either denationalized or vile; a girl with unbound feet would have no chance of marriage, and a bridegroom, finding that his bride had large feet when he expected small ones, would be abundantly justified by public opinion in returning her at once to her parents.[123]

Footbinding was commonly initiated when a girl was between four and nine. One Chinese woman whose feet were first bound at the age of seven recalled that, because they hurt so much, for two years she had to crawl on her hands and knees. In her case the procedure was completed when she was thirteen.[124] Footbinding created "a deep cleft across the sole of the foot and between the heel and toes, which are forced together."[125] Graphic photographs of the distortion of women's feet appeared regularly in missionary literature to stimulate donations.

Like other Western women in China who condemned footbinding, Doctors Gifford and Killam joined the Anti-footbinding League, which had been organized in 1892.[126] The league's concern seems to have coincided with, but apparently did not trigger, the Chinese government's own efforts, after the defeat by Japan in 1895, to improve the situation of women as part of a general reform program. The Chinese court, too, took up the issue; in 1902 the Empress Dowager issued a formal anti-footbinding edict.[127] But it was ineffective. Hence, the league continued to attract Western women and government officials, usually in the treaty ports, who at very least were able to create a negative image of footbinding. But as Alison Drucker points out, "the foreign and Christian roots of the anti-footbinding campaign had to be renounced in order for victory to be achieved."[128] In 1911 the new nationalist government abolished footbinding with some degree of success. Still, it remained a disturbing problem for the missionaries in the hinterland. In some parts of Szechwan anti-footbinding campaigns, directed by a few women whom the WMS missionaries considered "progressive," were just getting started in 1916.[129] The private erotic attachment to bound feet could not be legislated away, so the custom of footbinding, especially in rural Szechwan, where it always was strongest, lingered into the 1920s as "a symbol of Chinese opposition to foreign rule."[130]

The WMS anticipated that after graduation most students from its schools would become teachers or Bible women attached to the WMS mission. With this in mind the schools were designed "to weave religious thought and Christian endeavour in with their every day work, so that in the children's minds the one will be inseparable from the other."[131] The curriculum and regimen were copied from the thriving WMS Japanese schools. Chinese teachers were hired to teach Chinese characters and language, leaving the missionary responsible for "all other subjects, such as arithmetic, algebra, geography, history, physiology, botany, astronomy, English, calisthenics, nature study, and music," which were usually taught in Chinese.[132] In time the WMS realized that further professional training was essential for the first-rate teachers they wanted. Because a normal school was too ambitious a venture for the Canadians to undertake alone, it became a co-operative project sponsored by the Baptist, Methodist Episcopal, Friends, and Canadian Methodist missions in the region. In January 1915 the Union Christian Normal School opened, with Alice Estabrook of the WMS as the first principal.[133] By the 1920s more than thirty graduates from WMS normal schools were teaching in mission schools.[134]

A permanent connection to the missionary community after graduation appears to have attracted more young women in China than in Japan, probably because of the lower social status of Chinese students at Christian mission schools.[135] Before 1900 the majority of the students in Chengtu were from poor families "often glad to get rid of them."[136] By 1902, four thousand women were studying at Christian mission schools, but they continued to be drawn from among the poor, not the middle class.[137] After the revolution in 1911 and increased governmental emphasis on the benefits that educating women would bring to China, the WMS girls' schools attracted a wider clientele. In 1915 the missionaries at Kiating seemed to derive satisfaction from pointing out that their school now catered to girls "from the better class ... daughters of officials, silk and silver merchants and teachers."[138] For the WMS class barriers were no easier to surmount than racial barriers; but with twenty years' experience in the country the missionaries realized that if Western notions about social improvement were to have any impact on China, those women closest to power were their most useful allies.

After an auspicious beginning, WMS medical work advanced less smoothly than the educational operations because of the cost of equipment and facilities and a chronic shortage of doctors, which in the long run thwarted WMS visions of a network of medical facilities throughout Szechwan. Of necessity, WMS medical work remained concentrated in Chengtu, where, after serving an apprenticeship with Retta Kilborn, Maud Killam was established as the resident physician at the dispensary. Initially public response was gratifying;[139] but by September 1899, rumours that all mission property in the vicinity would again be destroyed forced Killam to limit her work.

Brackbill predicted that the Roman Catholic missions in the area would be the primary target of Chinese hatred, but other missionaries were realistic enough to recognize that the Chinese did not make a distinction between churches. In response to the hostile mood of the region few patients ventured to the dispensary.[140] The women no longer left their compound unless they were concealed in sedan chairs, and all mission property was heavily guarded by Chinese soldiers.[141] In June, while travelling from Kiating to Chengtu, Lottie Brooks was threatened but not harmed by robbers.[142] Five months later, en route from Shanghai to Chengtu, Minnie Brimstin and Anna Henry were robbed at the CIM mission home in Ichang, where thieves stole trunks containing their linens and underclothing.[143] Brimstin put on a brave face for friends at home, to whom she reported that she had "never felt better in [her] life,"[144] but before the message reached Canada, China had erupted with the terror and confusion provoked by the Boxer Rebellion.

The most vicious assaults against the foreign presence in China were centred in the province of Shantung. But encouraged by the Empress Dowager and the conservative elements in the court, who were intent on eradicating all vestiges of foreign imperialism, the Boxers attacked Westerners everywhere. The WMS missionaries provided little commentary on the sources of the rebellion. Though they may have recognized that most foreigners whom the ordinary Chinese encountered were missionaries, they seemed none the less convinced, if only for their Canadian supporters' sake, that the mantle of Christianity absolved them personally of the taint of Western imperialist ambitions.

The missionaries' refusal to implicate themselves or their cause, in the false belief that the Boxers wanted only to rescue China from the encroachment of foreign capitalism, was common, even though it should have been clear to them that the Chinese had reason to resent any and all foreigners who had entered China uninvited.[145] Recent analyses of the rebellion suggest that the sect's fanaticism was both anti-foreign and anti-missionary in nature and that the Boxers, who associated Christianity with the other odious aspects of Western imperialism, were explicitly anti-Christian in their activities.[146] Whatever the Boxers' impulses, before the rebellion was put down by the military intervention of foreign powers, 231 foreigners, almost all missionaries and among them two Canadians, and countless Chinese Christians were murdered and their bodies hideously mutilated.[147]

On 15 July 1900, as British subjects the Canadian Methodists in Szechwan were ordered by the British consul to proceed "with all possible speed to places where they might have British military or naval protection."[148] Because gunboats were not yet stationed along the Yangtze, this meant travelling all the way to Shanghai.[149] The Canadian Methodist mission stations were evacuated and closed.

Foster, Brooks, and Killam returned to Canada on early furloughs; other WMS missionaries spent the next months in Tokyo, while Brackbill remained in Shanghai as liaison for the society.[150] The Boxers' savage attacks, which included castration and slashing off breasts, terrified and sickened the Canadian women, who sought solace in divine will. Their faith was profoundly tested. Why, asked Lottie Brooks, would God "allow such atrocities! Why? ... we must believe that it is for some good purpose, that all things, even such things as this will be for the good of Christ's Church on Earth."[151]

The British consul general disagreed with the missionaries' version of the events. Because single women living alone in out-stations had been murdered, he threatened "not to allow married ladies to return to the interior before five years and unmarried ladies – never."[152] By the end of the year he had yielded, granting the women permission to travel to Chungking; but when they arrived, he would not let them continue to Chengtu. They took refuge with the members of the Episcopal Methodist mission while awaiting further orders. The consul's caution was justified; Chungking still echoed with threats against missionaries. In June, "dodgers" from the north arrived in the province, urging the people to "rise and massacre all the foreigners."[153] Only the vigilance of the British consul prevented serious violence.

The missionaries' repeated requests to friends in Canada for "prayers to be kept faithful to our charge"[154] at last seemed rewarded in September 1901, when their passports were granted. Even so, the women returned to Chengtu in closed sedan chairs to avoid provocation.[155] Remarkably, in their absence the WMS compound, which had been under surveillance by civic officials, was not disturbed. Again, the society quite willingly accepted an indemnity of 5,680 *taels* from the total of 450,000,000 to be paid by the Chinese government.[156] The school and dispensary in Chengtu reopened immediately, but Foster's visits to women in the outlying villages were not resumed because of continuing unrest.[157] Yet even in such discouraging and risky circumstances the Board of Managers proposed a second station in Kiating, to complement the General Board's projects there. Ignoring the controversy about single women on their own, the WMS sent Mary Foster to Kiating to offer women's Bible classes and to teach in the General Board Sunday school.[158] By 1905 two women were stationed in Kiating, directing informal study groups for women and girls and operating a school with eight boarders and twelve day students.[159]

When the Boxer uprising was settled and an uneasy peace restored to China, the board tried to comply with the women's request for more workers because it agreed with them that China still held tremendous potential for Christianity. But after a decade of energy and misfortune, there were just seven WMS missionaries in West China: four teachers, who also conducted most of the evangelistic work, two doctors, and a nurse. From 1902 until 1910 Szechwan enjoyed a relative calm, and for the first time the WMS work progressed uninterrupted. In 1906 a third station was opened at Jenshow, another of the General Board stations, seventy miles south of Chengtu. The society purchased property, built a wall and a small mission house where about twenty girls attended a day school.[160] By 1910 the Jenshow station included the usual imposing mission house and girls' boarding school. The decade also saw completion of a new girls' boarding school in Chengtu, with a well-equipped gymnasium to introduce the students to the benefits of Western-style physical culture.

More generally, Canadian Methodist missionary work in Szechwan seems to have benefited, after the Boxer Rebellion, from increased co-operation among the several Protestant missions in the region, motivated by the need to economize and present a united front to the continuing indifference and hostility, especially to the less utilitarian, purely evangelical aspects of missionary work. In 1906, for example, delegates from several Protestant missionary societies in Szechwan formed a committee to centralize primary education for boys and girls by "means of a uniform course of study, similar textbooks, and common examinations," a system designed both to save money and to compete with the Chinese government's newly opened schools.[161] The long-range objective of Protestant educators in Szechwan was the creation of a Christian university for graduates of the region's elementary and secondary mission schools. The WMS sent representatives to the requisite conferences to help set these plans in motion. The outcome was the opening of West China Union University in 1910. Originally offering courses in arts and sciences, the university expanded to encompass faculties of religion, medicine, education, and dentistry.[162] In 1924 women were granted admission as students in arts and medicine.[163]

In spite of the comparative political stability in Szechwan after the Boxer Rebellion, the vast expansion that the WMS had anticipated did not begin until the second decade of the twentieth century. One of the principal barriers to progress was the shortage of personnel to service a vast geographic area; until 1910 there were never more than fifteen women at any given time to staff the WMS missions in Szechwan. Although the society had sent twenty-eight women to West China, thirteen had withdrawn. Jennie Ford had died; Mary Foster's resignation had been requested; but the others had left the society's employ to marry, five before their first term was completed. In 1910 the West China Mission was reinvigorated when in that single year eight women, including a doctor and three nurses, were recruited for China. By 1916 there were thirty WMS missionaries in West China: thirteen teachers, five nurses, three doctors, eight evangelists, and a matron of the orphanage. The enlarged staff enabled the WMS to open a fourth station with a boarding school in Junghsien, a city of thirty thousand located to the west of Kiating[164] and another in Tzeliutsing, an industrial city of seven hundred thousand located in the heart of the salt-well district about one hundred and fifty miles south of Chengtu.[165] The society also set up small stations in Luchow, two hundred miles west of Chungking, and Penghsien, a city of fifty thousand, north of Chengtu. By 1925 work was being conducted in nine cities in the province where the General Board was already established.[166]

This explosion of WMS work reflected the renewed enthusiasm in North America for Protestant missionary work in China that had been stimulated by the energies of the Student Volunteer Movement. Whereas in 1889 there were 1,296 Protestant missionaries in China, by 1905 that number had risen to 3,445, including 964 single women. In 1914, of the 5,462 missionaries in China, 1,652 (30 per cent) were missionary wives, 2,176 (40 per cent) men, and 1,614 (29 per cent) were single women.[167] Canadian Methodist demographics were remarkably similar; in 1908 the West China mission reported 49 (36 per cent) missionary wives, 52 (39 per cent) male missionaries, and 35 (26 per cent) single women missionaries.[168] As far as Protestant missions are concerned, these statistics seem to indicate the escalating feminization of missionary work in the face of its increased acceptability as a profession for women, but they also indicate flagging interest in it as a masculine pursuit.

At the height of the West's renewed preoccupation with China, the WMS Board of Managers made a special appeal to "the Methodist young women throughout our Colleges and Normal Schools of Canada" to "offer ... themselves for these posts where the need is greatest," namely, West China. Above all the board wanted "Canada's young women with their Christian ideals and strength of character" as teachers.[169] In response, the number of WMS West China missionaries who had at least some university education, excluding physicians, increased from 5 of 38 (13 per cent) before 1910 to 13 of 46 (28 per cent) for the years from 1911 to 1925. Most of these university-educated women were assigned to teaching positions. Because many university graduates had also attended normal school, the professional credentials of the teachers hired after 1910 also improved. Before 1910, 42 per cent of the recruits had attended a normal school;

after 1910 the figure rose to 64 per cent. By contrast, while 7 physicians were recruited before 1910, only 2 joined the WMS after 1910. The percentage of nurses in the mission force also decreased, from 21 per cent before 1910 to 13 per cent after that time, probably because without more doctors and hospitals, nursing services were not required, especially after the General Board began to hire its own nurses.

It seems, then, that after the first decade of the twentieth century, the education and professional training of recruits increasingly determined the direction of the WMS undertaking in China. The Board of Managers now acknowledged its inability to attract and retain medical practitioners and abandoned its ambitious plan for modern medical facilities throughout Szechwan. Moreover, the similarity of the recruits' education and experience limited the WMS's ability to pursue as diverse a course as it hoped to follow in West China. While the General Board recruited pharmacists, architects, accountants, and publishers to expand the range of its services after the First World War, the WMS, with its cadre of teachers, continued with conventional educational and evangelization programs, partly by choice but also from necessity, even though its agents in China sensed that the country was changing.

Dr Anna Henry, for example, informed readers of the *Christian Guardian* in 1907 that she was indeed witnessing the birth of a new modern China, even if the evidence was "not always [what] we would wish to see. On the Bund [in Shanghai] can be seen the carriages and motors rolling along filled with wealthy Chinese, who look quite contemptuously at the foreigner, especially if he or she happens to be in Chinese dress."[170] The animosity and suspicion of the Chinese middle and upper classes towards foreigners remained as strong as ever. Nor did the Chinese government's interest in modernizing the army, developing industry, and implementing educational reform as part of its effort to emulate its rival, Japan, translate, in Szechwan, into an interest in Western education accompanied by floods of applications for the mission schools or mass conversions to Christianity. In Jenshow in 1908, the women remained "very reluctant about coming to church, as they are in danger of losing the respect of their friends by assembling in the same congregation as the men."[171]

As Michael Gasster has pointed out, the idea that "rapid social change is both desirable and possible" had few adherents in early twentieth-century China, where the notion "that life *should* be very different from what it had always been" was only slowly beginning to be understood.[172] Consequently, the missionaries had to find the evidence of their impact on Chinese society in little victories. Lottie Brooks, for instance, wrote animatedly about her Bible study class, which attracted women from a neighbouring village who made the forty-mile trip in wheelbarrows.[173] When the husband of an incurably ill heart patient calmly accepted the verdict that nothing could save his wife, admitting that Dr Henry had "been very kind to her and I thank you very much," Henry construed his even-tempered reaction as confirmation that Western medicine was becoming acceptable to the Chinese and that missionary doctors need no longer fear being held liable for the death of a moribund patient.[174] From these minor incidents in their day-to-day encounters the missionaries' optimism was forged. But after a decade of relatively uninterrupted, if not exactly triumphant, missionary work in West China, "a deep shadow" fell across the mission field.[175]

Early in 1911 Mission Secretary T.E. Shore had quizzed Charles Murphy, the Canadian secretary of state, about the safety of Canadian Methodists in Szechwan because of rumours of political unrest in that part of China.[176] The under-secretary of state for External Affairs, Joseph Pope, replied in a rather perfunctory way that although he was cognizant of newspaper accounts of unrest in China, "no information regarding these disturbances has reached this department."[177] There matters rested for the next few months. The WMS Board of Managers continued to seek recruits for West China, while the missionaries' letters described their relaxing vacation in the cool mountain region. On 20 September, however, an unusual plea from Elizabeth Ross, WMS president, soliciting prayers for the twenty-five WMS employees currently in West China, who were, she understood, in extreme danger, appeared in the *Christian Guardian*.[178]

From April until November 1911 revolutionary violence, which culminated in the forced resignation of the imperial regent at the end of October and the establishment of a revolutionary government under Dr Sun Yat-Sen, had been spreading throughout China.[179] In Szechwan the situation was complicated by riots associated with the nationalization and foreign financing of the railways. Agitators "sought to give the movement an anti-foreign and anti-Christian attitude placarding places with scurrilous cartoons and wrecking chapels. Anything, past experience showed, might happen under such circumstances, so at the strong urging of the consular authorities, both merchants and missionaries gathered in the larger centres."[180]

The consul general advised that all mission schools should be closed. Reluctantly, the WMS complied; most of the women left their stations, first for the relative safety of the unfinished General Board hospital in Chengtu, then to a resort near Chungking. Here they "lived quietly" and had "delightful climbs over the hills"[181] while awaiting the outcome of the events, which, they were sure, would "all be overruled for the extension of God in this land."[182] None the less, because they must have remembered the fate of other single women at the hands of the Boxers, they were sufficiently afraid that some, like Minnie Brimstin, sent their last letters home. "I am ready to go, and should this be the last message I ever send you, my dear brothers and sisters, it is one of joy and peace through believing in the Lord Jesus Christ. I would not change places with anyone. How one's heart goes out in sympathy to these poor people. I love and pity them to-day, when they are on the eve of a rebellion, more than ever. This is to be expected in a land where Christ is not known."[183]

The women were unable to reassure their families that they were safe because during September and October all communication between Szechwan and the rest of China was broken. Canadian newspapers, the *Globe* in particular, published some alarming stories about the unrest in Szechwan that intensified relatives' fears about their loved ones' safety. Frantic calls from the families of Methodists in China prompted Shore to ask the *Globe's* editor to substantiate his information with the appropriate Methodist authorities.[184]

On 31 October the *Globe*, like other sources throughout the world, reported that the Manchu dynasty had fallen and the viceroy had fled to Shanghai after revolutionary forces had attacked his headquarters in Wuhan.[185] Within a few days central China was in rebel hands. A revolutionary torrent swept the country, and in a month "nine provinces had declared their independence of the Imperial Government, though not necessarily their common adherence to one Revolutionary regime."[186] The imperial surrender forced the British consul general, who now feared that the Chinese army would become uncontrollable, to advise all missionaries in Szechwan to leave for the coast immediately. Had the women refused, the consul would have been responsible for their safety, a burden he seemed unwilling to assume.[187] Both the consul and the British Foreign Office worried that the missionaries might be attacked by revolutionaries or the bands of roving bandits who had taken advantage of the unrest to expand their own criminal activities.[188]

The decision to ask the missionaries to abandon their posts was not taken lightly, but Szechwan was isolated and well known for its tempestuous politics. A familiar adage insisted that "when the Empire is Peaceful, Szechwan is the first to have disorder; after peace is restored, Szechwan is the last to be stabilized."[189] The veterans Brackbill and Brimstin and two senior General Board missionaries remained in Chengtu after the others had left, to place all the children from the orphanage in safe homes and to secure the mission property.[190] Much as he might have wanted these stubborn women to leave with the others, the consul did not exercise his right to arrest and deport them.[191] Finally, when fighting and looting broke out in the streets, the last missionaries left Chengtu, escorted by one hundred soldiers, for Chungking, where they boarded boats for the exodus to Shanghai. Brackbill, a strict and uncompromising Methodist, reluctantly agreed, apparently for the first time in her life, to travel on a Sunday.[192]

Although foreign flags identified their boats, one party was fired upon when the gunboat *Widgeon* abandoned the flotilla under its protection. Later the Canadians lodged a protest against the captain, but charges that he had failed to provide adequate security could not be substantiated.[193] Ethel McPherson of the WMS sent a detailed commentary describing her escape to the London, Ontario, newspaper where she had once been employed. Her version of events did not sidestep the perils of the evacuation:

Boats were secured to leave Saturday, Dec. 9 ... Friday morning we heard shooting and shouting on the Great East Parade Grounds, adjoining the CIM property ... A number of soldiers were firing and presently they dashed down the street past our gate. The firing continued all day and all night and bullets went whizzing through the air all around us. Sometimes they clipped along the tiles on the roof at a lively gait. Soon we learned the first volley was a signal for outright robbery. The public treasury was robbed and the large Government bank ... at dusk the soldiers were looting within three blocks of our compound. ... After lunch we called chairmen to take us, but very few could be had ... We started off afoot. We had gone about a hundred yards when we were met by the soldiers guarding the Si Shen Si street gate who refused to permit us to pass. They stated there was fighting outside the East and North gates and on no consideration must we leave the city. They escorted us back to our hospital gate talking all the while about the danger of leaving Chengtu and offering us asylum ... we slipped out the back gate, half a dozen at a time, and walked through the streets out the East gate and down to the waterfront without the least trouble.[194]

After the party transferred to houseboats at Kiating, the journey became even more hazardous. "Above the city of HoChiang we passed the *Widgeon* at anchor. A little later we were opposite the rebel encampment outside the city. Strange that this place should still be under the Imperialists with a Manchu official. It was under seige and when we came within range from the city wall we were promptly fired upon as was every boat that passed. Several bullets hit our boat and many went through. One embedded itself in a pillow on one of the beds. On the same boat a Chinese oarsman was struck, the lead lodging in his cheekbone."[195] Strangely enough, no Methodist publication was quite as candid about the harrowing escape from Chengtu.

By the beginning of 1912 the West China mission field was completely evacuated, the women scattered. Some remained in Shanghai to study Chinese and work in hospitals or schools. Others travelled to Japan or, if nearing a furlough, home to Canada. Mary Smith compared them to "the children of Israel who, having come in sight of the promised land, were compelled to wander about in the wilderness before they could occupy the land of promise."[196] The exile lasted nearly a year. At the end of April 1912, apparently without consular approval, the first party of General Board missionaries began the journey upriver from Ichang to Szechwan.[197] The consul, who expected more violence in the province throughout the summer, cautioned that no women should return. "The fewer there are in the interior the better, for the summer."[198]

In the past the Canadian Methodists, including the WMS, had criticized what they regarded as the unduly conservative position of the British government towards their work. They often protested the consul's motives in denying them access to their domain. This time, however, the consular warning seemed to originate from genuine concern for their safety, because only weeks before an American missionary from Szechwan Provincial College had been murdered while travelling on the river from Ichang to Chungking.[199] Foreign Missions Secretary Shore agreed that those hoping to return must defer to British authorities; still, he insisted "that no undue conservatism should retard the return of our missionaries beyond a reasonable time."[200]

The women were granted their passports in August. All but one who had fled returned to her post in Szechwan.[201] By Christmas all members of both missions had reached their appointed stations or were en route. Correspondence between the consul and the General Board of Missions seems to suggest that some eager missionaries resumed their work in defiance of consular authority.[202]

The winds of revolution did not sweep away those aspects of Chinese society that missionaries had found so distasteful. Opium use and the ensuing opium suicides, footbinding and infanticide were still there as reminders to the missionaries of their inability to regenerate

Chinese society. But for a few years at least there was "a period of unprecedented open-mindedness to the Christian message and of friendliness to the messengers" in which the WMS shared.[203] Perhaps this was because the messengers had become capable of learning to appreciate China's culture and people.[204] But it may also have been that after the evacuation of 1911 the WMS personnel adopted a more realistic approach to what was possible for them to achieve. Their energy now was directed more towards improving the quality of life in the communities they served than towards the total reconstruction of Chinese civilization, a vain hope under the best of circumstances and a challenge that the missionaries assumed the revolutionary government would take up.

The WMS continued to reassure its Canadian supporters that the society's ultimate goal in China was to win souls for Christ, but it no longer apologized for its agents' attention to some worldly and more realistic matters. As recently as 1901 Maud Killam had been publicly chastised for telling a WMS meeting in Guelph that "the greatest need of China is medical practitioners and hospitals."[205] The Board of Managers immediately corrected her assumption, assuring members that "in as far as the hospital is an educator, it is of permanent value. Otherwise the medical work only clips off the fruit from an evil tree. Truth has its stronghold in the hearts of the youth and the proclamation of truth strikes at the root of evil. So [Dr Killam] would call Christian schools of the greatest need, and place them foremost in laying the foundation of a Christian civilization."[206] Again, in 1908 the society explained that "the purpose of medical missions is not simply philanthropic, although it finds glory in self-sacrificing philanthropy ... The purpose of medical missions is to win men to Jesus Christ by the use of methods precisely compatible to those used by Christ when on earth as the great Succorer of bodies as well as the divine Saviour of Souls."[207]

It was not easy for the traditional Board of Managers to move away from "the original purpose of missions, the salvation of individuals," and espouse "the larger vision of Christianizing society" that the post-Victorian Methodist Church, animated by the social gospel, now seemed to endorse.[208] But in time the WMS officers' attitude towards at least the legitimacy of medical missions changed. In 1917 Elizabeth Strachan conceded just how "much had been accomplished in the breaking down of prejudice by the relief given to many afflicted ones, through unwonted kindness shown by our capable doctors and nurses, instruction imparted, intellects quickened, and in many cases spiritual life received through the power of the Divine One."[209]

When the missionaries returned to Szechwan in 1912, the construction of a woman's hospital in Chengtu, where the WMS medical staff could function separately from the General Board's doctors and where they could introduce nurses' training for Chinese women, was given priority. It was completed in 1915. A large four-storey brick structure, the sixty-five-bed hospital was the equal of any Canadian hospital of the day. Dr Anna Henry described her domain as follows: "The ground floor, or basement, contains the laboratory, drug room, nurses' lecture room, dining-room, etc. On the second, third and fourth stories are wards, public and private ... On each floor are bathrooms, dressing-rooms and diet kitchens. The superintendent's rooms, guest room, sitting-rooms and chapel are situated on the first floor ... there is a suite of operating-rooms and an obstetric ward on the second floor, while on the third are an open-air ward for tubercular patients, a dark room for eye examination and a ward for opium patients. The fourth floor is mainly occupied by nurses in training, of whom there are more applicants than can be accommodated."[210] The first class of Chinese nurses graduated in 1918. Their mentor, Mary Assom, expressed her own special pleasure at their achievement. "I felt I had rather present these first graduates with hospital pins than to be presented to King George or Queen Mary, and I am British to the core and love my country too. But to have the honor of representing our Woman's Missionary Society in the work and labor of love for the King of kings was worth a whole lot."[211]

As the hospital and nursing school illustrate, the WMS missionaries succeeded best when their expectations and their abilities addressed real needs defined by the treacherous currents of modern Chinese history. Like the Union Normal School, the hospital gave visible meaning to the missionaries' commitment to the exigencies of the new China. Dr May Austen summarized these changed attitudes when she confessed that she no longer dreaded and loathed personal contact with her Chinese patients. It seems a somewhat strange admission for a doctor and a missionary,[212] but it hints at the difficulty many missionaries faced in breaking free of the fetters of a middle-class upbringing.

The First World War interrupted the West China mission's now comparatively smooth operations by restricting the flow of recruits, financial support, and medical supplies. The mission station at Luchow was closed until a recruiting campaign that capitalized on the patriotic sentiment that had driven Canada's war effort and urged women to "just as promptly and bravely respond to the needs of our sisters in China and to the call of the King of Kings" succeeded in attracting a number of candidates for West China.[213] During the next three years twenty-one recruits arrived in West China; with adequate staff, the girls' schools were filled to capacity.[214] But as in Japan the mission faced a financial crisis, even though the board appears to have favoured West China, with its limitless potential. The situation in Szechwan reached a climax late in 1921, when an unidentified WMS missionary on furlough in Canada reported to the board that "the missionaries will hold at any cost as it means so much. I get hints in letters that they are making up the deficits of this year with their own salaries ... They would simply *have* to carry things over by their own money as far as it would go."[215] A questionnaire directed to the women in the field sought to confirm whether they had in fact covered shortages from their own salaries. An evasive message regretting that the society "should have been burdened with such pessimistic forebodings from insufficient data" and the assurance "that your West China workers still retain as always, an unbroken confidence in our Home Board, that what is really needed for carrying on the work, will, as heretofore be granted so far as it is in your power to do so"[216] did not clarify matters. Budgetary constraints aside, at the outset of the 1920s the WMS had in place in Szechwan an impressive network of seven stations with a total estimated real-estate value of $188,799.32 and forty missionaries to staff it.[217]

Beginning in 1923, missionary work in Szechwan was again disrupted by political unrest. When the British consul restricted travel within the province in October 1923,[218] the Methodist Church took some initiative and devised an elaborate coding system to identify each employee in case of mishap.[219] In February 1924 a serious incident occurred that the society appears to have tried to suppress. Several WMS missionaries were abducted by bandits from the steamer they were travelling on and carried off to the hills. After giving the bandits all their money – about $450[220] – the women were released, apparently unharmed. The mission secretary, Dr James Endicott, urged the Board of Managers not to send more recruits to China because of the mounting risks. His warning provoked a strong reaction from the women because the General Board continued to advertise for women teachers. No women were sent out at the time, but one WMS missionary was reminded of "that old proverb – 'What is sauce for the goose, is sauce for the gander.'"[221] With funds and staff growing scarce, the WMS began to guard its territories and prerogatives more jealously than in the past, fearing that women's work might be the first to suffer.

Yet even in the face of renewed anti-Christian violence, the women tried to convince themselves and the Canadian public that the opportunity to save the Chinese still existed. Constance Smith's response from Jenshow was typical of many missionaries who, as resolute evangelical Methodists, continued to interpret Chinese hostility as fundamental to God's plan. "No doubt many accounts of the anti-Christian movement in China have reached the homeland. For a time it was uncertain how effective the movement was going to be when the foreigners were being insulted in the streets, and work was being held up. But it has been found," Smith insisted, "that where the greatest pressure was brought to bear the result was a greater interest in the Bible classes."[222]

Smith's rationalization provides just one example of the utopian sentiment that continued to pervade the missionaries' correspondence from the field. The women did not, as might have been expected of first-hand observers, communicate very perceptively about the chain of events that began with the Peking students' demonstration of 4 May 1919, designated as National Humiliation Day because of the treatment of China at the Versailles Conference,[223] and culminated in the reorganization of the Communist Party and the army. Instead their letters fixed on the same concerns they had had twenty-five years earlier. Perhaps one explanation for the women's complacency was that events did not threaten their work as directly as had been the case in the past and would be again in 1926. It is none the less surprising, given their own involvement as student activists in, for example, the Student Volunteer Movement, that they tended to ignore student protests, especially when some revolutionaries had been educated in Methodist schools.[224]

An exception to this narrow understanding was Mary Lamb. Lamb may not have been an especially astute political observer, but she had a habit of asking difficult questions, if only in the privacy of her diary, about the character of missionaries and the nature of their work. Another woman whose family responsibilities had thwarted her career plans to be a missionary (Lamb returned to her home in St Andrews, Quebec, after a year at McGill to assist her mother for sixteen years as the local postmistress), Lamb was hired by the General Board of Missions after the First World War as matron of the school for missionaries' children in Chengtu. She constantly criticized her employer, and when her term expired in 1925, she transferred to the WMS as an evangelist.[225]

When she first arrived in China, the forty-one-year-old Lamb encountered "too much social life" for her liking at Junghsien, where she was sent to study the language.[226] She was transferred to Chengtu, where she became acquainted with the men of the Canadian Methodist mission, "good men" but "not very clever, not very well educated (or perhaps I should say not polished)"[227] and "lacking in the culture that comes from so-called 'good family.' Of course from my democratic point of view this is not a serious lack – the only part of it that really jars on me is the attempt by some to appear cultural ... In fact, they are much as I expected ... They are not sanctimonious or 'pious' but with a tendency of the age have swung a little too far to the other extreme."[228] Excessive frivolity and self-indulgence seemed to her to be especially unbecoming traits for the Canadian Methodist missionaries, and she begged God to deliver her from "the conversations and foreign outlook of Chengtu," from "the idea that one has to spend much time and money on clothes," from "afternoon teas ... [and] card parties." Lamb attributed the worst of the short-comings of the mission community to the natural selfishness of the "Lords of Creation" who represented the General Board.[229] "I am coming to see," Lamb concluded, "that the wms is the place for me ... The wms puts the work first, last and always and pay as they go."[230]

"The work," as Lamb, an evangelical who loved revivalist hymns and had little sympathy for the more liberal element, the social gos-pellers within the mission community, defined it, was "getting as close to the [Chinese] people as we should."[231] She was convinced that Canadian Methodism was "not doing things in the right way."[232] There was, she believed, too great a "gulf fixed between the financial standing of the missionary and the Chinese ... I wonder what will become of our fine houses when the native church needs the mis-sionary no more. It seems to me that our lifestyle should be simpler ... it seems to me as if we laid ourselves open more or less to anti-foreign sentiment."[233] From 1925 until 1942 Lamb attempted, as a wms evangelist, to bridge this gulf by improving the image of the mis-sionary among both Chinese and Canadians in spite of a persistent, nagging fear that missionaries were "living in a 'fool's Paradise' here in Chengtu."[234] It was an old refrain. But there may be no better explanation for the failure of the West China Mission to retain the percentage of career missionaries that Japanese missions did.

Living and working in the "fool's Paradise" drained the women physically and emotionally. The wms missionaries rarely wrote about their illnesses, which, if they did not force their retirement, could severely restrict their work and cause both physical and mental anguish. Even in the 1920s many medical problems, commonly the consequence of the Chinese environment, were not amenable to effective treatment. One woman returned, accompanied by a nurse, because her two-year case of dysentery, which could not be cured in China, had left her so debilitated.[235] Three women died on active duty in Szechwan, two others shortly after they had gone home on furlough. The deaths of Myrtle Wheeler during routine gall-bladder surgery and of Mary Totten Smith in 1919 from influenza might have occurred in Canada, but Jennie Ford's painful death in 1897 from meningitis remained in the women's minds associated with her dreadful experience during the riots of 1895.

Ten other WMS missionaries resigned, six from physical and four from mental disorders that became evident only after they had been sent to the mission field. Several women who remained in China for many years, Brackbill and Doctors Henry and Killam among them, travelled to Canada, the United States, or Japan for more sophisticated medical care, especially for the diagnosis and treatment of malignancies. Most illnesses sustained in China had a genuine physical cause, unlike some of the possibly psychosomatic ailments suffered by the women in the Japanese Mission. But many General Board missionary wives, some of them former WMS employees, also became incapacitated from what was diagnosed as a vague neurasthenia or hysteria that could send them to Canada for gynecological surgery. In sum, about 20 per cent of WMS West China missionaries resigned because of physical or mental breakdown, or died. Even so, the attrition from illness was slightly lower than in Japan, perhaps because adequate medical facilities were close at hand – but another plausible answer may be that many women left the WMS to marry *before* their health became a liability as they grew older.

What does distinguish the WMS personnel in China from their counterparts in Japan was their susceptibility not to sickness but to marriage. It seems a reasonable assumption that until they arrived in Szechwan many of these women had not confronted the choice between marriage and a career. They might have remained single had they not volunteered for China, where, as Mary Lamb's remarks suggest, in a frontier-like community, freed from parental restraints, social and sexual barriers were more readily crossed. Organized as it was to serve different spheres of work that were divided along gender lines, the actual day-to-day operation of the two mission boards did not usually bring the men and women together. But to compensate for this segregation there were countless social occasions hosted by the various missions, other Westerners, and even by the British consul where the missionaries mingled. And the women enjoyed entertaining in their own homes. The *West China Missionary News*, the interdenominational paper published by the missionary community in Szechwan, reported a typical event, "a 'poverty party' given by the ladies of the CMMWMS medical house ... on the evening of March 17, when fun was fast and furious, and laughter chased away care, at least for the time being from the faces of those present."[236] The summer treks to Mount Omei, a resort of forty bungalows shared by the missions in Szechwan as an escape from the oppressive summer heat, brought the sexes into more intimate and informal contact as they played tennis, the favourite missionary pursuit, hiked in the hills, or studied in surroundings as close to small-town Canada as could reasonably be sustained within the core of China. The atmosphere promoted normal courtship patterns, removed from the anxiety of the mission compound. As a result, engagement announcements were always anticipated at summer's end, to such a degree that in September 1923 the *West China Missionary News* lamented that a dearth of single men at Mount Omei the past summer meant only one engagement.[237]

The WMS missionaries in China did not believe that being a missionary consigned them to a life devoid of male companionship. Friendships with men were one of the more appealing features of the West China mission field even for Mary Lamb, who infinitely preferred their company to that of their wives, who were overly preoccupied with domestic affairs for her liking.[238] Sometimes the husbands remained at home when their families vacationed and "ke[pt] bachelors' hall, and ... [got] together [with the WMS] for an occasional game of tennis, or a sing-song, or a read."[239] In one instance when their wives did not return with them to Szechwan after the 1911 revolution, several General Board missionaries in Jenshow reported with amusement how they had received a "W.M.S. haircut ... One [woman] held the comb while the other cut."[240] As a result of the close relationship with the WMS, recent widowers quickly found new partners. The mortality among missionary wives, especially from childbirth, and the concentration of missionaries in a relatively small area gave the WMS missionaries in Szechwan a reasonable chance to marry men with similar concerns and to plan a future dedicated to missionary service, although their late marriages might limit hopes for a family.

Even if marriages between missionaries were an embarrassment to both boards, wedding ceremonies in China were always occasions for festivities within the mission compound. British law required that a civil service be held first; then, if desired, a religious ceremony could follow. The marriage of Lena Dunfield and Orlando Jolliffe, a modest affair, was solemnized by only a civil ceremony, for which the practical bride did not bother to have a new dress because "out here we wear low-necked dresses most of the time – not the kind you see at home – but to the band of our ordinary dresses."[241] Maud Killam's more lavish wedding to James Neave in 1904 included a religious ceremony at the wms home in Chengtu. "The bridal party entered the beautifully decorated parlour to the strains of Mendelsohn's Wedding March, they stood under an arch of bridal roses, having a bell of white roses suspended from its centre; and faced a bank of palms, and other artistically arranged shrubbery. The bride was grace itself, in a dress of cream silk, while the bridesmaid looked pretty in a gown of pale blue. Each carried a bouquet of roses." Except for the firecrackers set off by the Chinese servants, the ceremony was no different than if Killam had married in her home town of Yarmouth, Nova Scotia.[242]

Some wms missionaries who married had no regrets and enthusiastically adapted to the role of wife and mother. Others found it hard to be counted merely as part of the Methodist mission, with no salary or official status, while they continued to work in the same Methodist Sunday schools and women's groups where they had formerly served as single wms missionaries. From time to time the married women tried to sequester specific areas of work, such as directing a school for wives of the Chinese evangelists,[243] but as a rule, like Lena Jolliffe, they passed their time rearing children, making marmalade and apple sauce, arbitrating the petty thievery committed by the numerous servants that Chinese convention required, and playing bridge.[244] The following anonymous poem, no doubt written by wms missionaries, provides a humorous interpretation of the relative merits of the single and the married state from the women's perspective. The facetious verse probably contains more than a little truth. More to the point, it neatly juxtaposes the opposite poles of domesticity and professionalism that the small island of Canadian culture in the depths of Szechwan had brought into such sharp relief.

Oh! single life in China is the happiest of all,
We're centres of attraction for the folks of gossip hall.
We only have to blink an eye, a certain given way,
When lo! the word is passed around, she'll marry some sweet day.
Oh, how I love my independence,
Oh, how I'd hate the married state.
w.m.s. suits me A.1.
For the G.B.'s finest son,
We'll never give up, we'll never give up, we'll never give up our freedom.
Oh boy! they think we're awfully sober,
Oh joy! they think we're awfully staid.
But we've set our minds upon this work,
And not one duty we will shirk,
But show them of what stuff we're made.

Oh! married life in China is the luckiest of all.
Those women who have husbands, sure they never work at all.
They never have to cook or sew, but only sit and spoon.
If everything goes well with me, I'll be a wifie soon.
Oh! how I hate a maiden single,
Oh! how I'd love to have a man.
Anyone will do at all, rich or poor or short or tall.
We'll never give up, we'll never give up, we'll never give up 'till our
death beds,
Oh! boy, if only the courting were over,
Oh joy, if only I had him sure,
I'd put my Chinese books away
And stop my work most any day
And spend the rest of my life in play.[245]

Twenty-nine employees never gave up. They made Chinese mission work a lifetime career. They were not necessarily the best educated missionaries: just 15 per cent of them had any university education. Nor were there the disproportionate numbers of "daughters of the parsonage" that characterized the persisters in Japan. More than half (seventeen) were educators, teaching in girls' schools, kindergartens, or in the co-operatively sponsored normal school. Nine career missionaries were evangelists; two were nurses. Of the WMS doctors, however, only Anna Henry remained in China until retirement. In fact, the average career of the WMS doctors spanned just eight years, compared to fourteen for all WMS employees in China. All but two doctors resigned specifically to marry. One who did not, Olive Rea, left at the society's request when she confessed that she had rejected conventional religion for faith healing and, as a consequence, could no longer practise Western medicine. She disagreed with the Methodist Church's position on baptism on the grounds that immersion was the "only true form." The society denounced Rea's non-conformist views as "confusing, disturbing, and inimical to the best interest of the work under our care."[246] Rea immediately joined the "Gift of Tongues" people working in Yunnan, later marrying one of their missionaries.[247]

The numerous resignations among WMS doctors may have no logical explanation. None the less, it might be asked whether a physician's proximity to the suffering of the Chinese, coupled with the inability to cure lepers, suicidal opium users, victims of footbinding, and desperately sick children, quite simply was more than these women fresh from medical school, where they had received little enough practical training in the treatment of standard illnesses, could bear. Strong and determined as they were to pursue a medical career at a time when women were an unwelcome anomaly in a traditionally male profession, as physicians in China they often felt powerless in the face of filth and deadly diseases that defied medical intervention.[248] Under these circumstances the women could not perform the miracles expected of them by the Chinese or their Canadian patrons.

Educators and evangelists, by contrast, were farther removed from the misery of Chinese society. They believed that collectively and individually their exertions were making a difference, at least in the lives of the Chinese women and children with whom they came in contact, even if it was only teaching them basic Chinese characters as a step towards literacy or helping them to earn a minimal living through sales of their exquisite embroidery. These missionaries rarely doubted that their own presence was legitimized by their fervent desire to Christianize and improve the condition of Chinese women. That their benevolence and reforming impulses threatened one of the world's most ancient cultures did not disturb them. As they understood it, the WMS missionary crusade was the logical vehicle for their personal piety and their confidence about the relevance of the Methodist church "to the spiritual development of the world."[249]

Elizabeth Graham, appreciated when she joined the society in 1916 as "a model of fidelity and industry, not brilliant but [with] solid, substantial ability and unwavering pluck,"[250] was one woman who served the WMS in China until retirement. Even on the eve of another eruption of anti-foreign violence in 1924, Graham, who had just opened a new primary girls' boarding school at Luchow, remained excited about her vocation. "I cannot put into words the joy I am having day by day in this work … To me the greatest and most wonderful work in the world is the privilege of close contact with human lives, and especially precious is the opportunity of moulding daily, it may be to only a very small extent, the lives of these young growing girls. I could ask no greater boon from my Heavenly Father's hand. My cup is running over."[251] For women like Graham a missionary career provided a more than satisfactory alternative to marriage and motherhood within the wider context of Christian service to Chinese women.

In sum, the women responded to their responsibility in China much as one might expect of daughters of the Canadian small-town middle class who had not wholly thrown off the effects of their Victorian upbringing. They recognized the realities of Chinese society and dealt with them matter of factly in the course of going about the everyday business of attending to the bodies and spirits of their charges. For public consumption, with the connivance of their employers in Canada, they put the best possible face on their situation, often concealing the risks they took in the name of Christ, in spite of the fact that a few thousand missionaries struggling to infiltrate an inhospitable population of two hundred and fifty million Chinese was improbable from the outset. Beneath this façade of courage and optimism, their private diaries and correspondence are riddled, not unexpectedly, with anxieties, hopes, and contradictions that must have been the subject of intense discussions in the confines of the compounds within which they chose to live and where they strove to sustain an image of the world they had left in the midst of one they could scarcely comprehend. In China the members of this small but tenacious company of Canadian women experienced and came to terms, each in her own distinctive way, with a society they could hardly have imagined. It was "an encounter of mind with world"[252] that could be appreciated only by their colleagues, who, like Jennie Ford, were convinced that in China they had come "face to face with the devil and his works."[253]

CHAPTER FIVE

No serious risk in sending her to Pt. Simpson

When the WMS was founded in 1881, its executive committed the organization to the support of missionary work for women and children not just in the overseas fields they envisioned opening in the Orient but also in Canada, where the Methodist Church had already established a network of mission stations from Port Simpson in northern British Columbia to Montreal. This dual mandate was by far more comprehensive and costly than the blueprints of other Canadian and American women's missionary societies, whose work was usually defined in terms of either home or foreign missions, seldom both.[1] Throughout the WMS's history, neither the board nor the missionaries seriously challenged the demanding double obligation, even when the heavy financial burden impeded the growth of missionary operations or when, in the twentieth century, public interest in overseas missions eclipsed interest in work at home.

In the society's first decade home missionary work was allocated a larger share of the budget than the nascent enterprise in Japan. As the Japanese Mission and the new field in China gained momentum, promising the transformation of a future generation of Asian women into the Christian women that the society prayed for, the board directed more money and personnel overseas than to missions in Canada, where the visible results were less dramatic, the mundane work less liable to capture members' imaginations and hence induce them to open their purses. In 1893 the expenditures for home and overseas missions nearly balanced; the work in Japan and Amelia Brown's journey to China together totalled $16,645, while the outlay for work on three fronts in Canada, in Montreal, Victoria, and northern British Columbia, came to $15,737.70.[2] But as time passed, the gap widened. In 1918 two-thirds of the society's allocation of $318,242.89 went overseas.[3]

The discrepancy in the disbursements on home and foreign mission work was apparent to anyone who examined the society's annual reports. What was less accessible to WMS members at large, and perhaps not readily understood even by the executive, was the magnitude of the disparity that extended to the backgrounds, education, and professional training of the missionaries themselves. To help to maintain its image on the international front, the board siphoned off the most qualified and experienced applicants to represent the society overseas. The less accomplished and, not coincidentally, frequently less competent and career-oriented applicants remained in Canada, and when the need for home missionaries was very pressing, stipulations about age limits were frequently ignored. In short, much of the apparent success and respect that accrued to the WMS missionary work overseas was secured at the expense of home missions.

If the testimony on the applications is an accurate indication of their personal goals, WMS missionary candidates were almost unanimous in their conviction that God had called them for service expressly as foreign missionaries. It became the responsibility of the Board of Managers then to determine who to send abroad and who to retain for work in Canada. With few exceptions the most educated women – doctors, university graduates, and experienced teachers – and the daughters of clergy and families connected to the Church hierarchy, in short, women with the apparent hallmarks for success in a lifetime missionary career, were assigned to the Orient. It does not seem mere chance that Martha Cartmell, cousin of Elizabeth Strachan and Elizabeth Ross and niece of Rev. John Williams, who in 1885 became general superintendent of the Methodist Church of Canada,[4] Maud and Ada Killam, the accomplished daughters of a prominent Nova Scotian family, and Esther Ryan, McGill graduate and minister's daughter, received overseas assignments while Kezia Hendrie and Alice Jackson, both dressmakers, and Mary Fitzpatrick, whose only academic credential was a grade eleven certificate, remained in Canada.

Even the applicant's physical condition could become a decisive factor in allocating positions. Women with exceptional medical reports were preferred as candidates for the foreign mission stations, where, it was assumed, only the fittest in every sense would survive. Paradoxically, living and working conditions in Port Simpson and northern Alberta were usually harsher and more spartan than any situation that the women encountered overseas. In reality, illnesses forced the resignations of just as many, if not more missionaries at posts in Canada, where the environment supposedly posed no hazard to the women's well-being. The most tangible proof of home missionaries's inferior status was their salaries. Presumably because they faced fewer hardships, were closer to their homes and families, and were less educated, home missionaries were paid lower wages than their overseas counterparts during the society's first two decades.[5]

These factors together contributed to the excessive turnover of home missionary personnel. Whereas one in three overseas missionaries resigned before completing her first term, more than half (51 per cent) of home missionaries resigned within the same time period. While more than 30 per cent of overseas missionaries remained with the WMS more than twenty-five years, only 18 per cent of home missionaries, most of whom were appointed to urban centres, worked for a comparable length of time. Moreover, once in the field, few home missionaries seemed as infatuated with their work or as convinced that it would be a lifetime career as women sent abroad. Although their applications do not exhibit any apparent difference in the sincerity or intensity of their initial dedication to a missionary career, home missionaries quickly became disillusioned. Their letters from the field are striking for the absence of the idealistic vision that drove foreign missionaries.

To the scholar's disadvantage, the dichotomy between the two aspects of missionary work extends to the employee records that the society kept. With the exception of census material, which was available equally for both groups of women, materials to document the experience of overseas missionaries are more comprehensive than those extant for home missionaries. This is partly because after the secretarial duties were divided in 1909,[6] as corresponding secretary for foreign missions, Elizabeth Strachan kept close tabs on her flock, while the correspondence between the secretary for home missions, a position with a frequent turnover, and the workers in the field has largely disappeared. Some files for home missionaries contain nothing but the location to which the woman was assigned. If a candidate had no particular academic laurels and no previous career, there was little else to note. There is none the less sufficient evidence to confirm the variations in career patterns and experiences between the women employed in the various facets of mission work across Canada and those who were sent to the Orient.

In some ways home missionaries' backgrounds differed little from those of their overseas counterparts. Over half the home missionaries came from Ontario, while 7 per cent were from Quebec. Most of the Quebec women were francophones assigned to the WMS French missions. Similarly, 6 per cent of home missionaries were from British Columbia, again hired specifically to staff missions in that province.

Like overseas missionaries, the majority of home missionaries had been raised in small towns and rural areas. But their social surroundings must have differed because fewer parents of home missionaries were professionals.[7] Just 11 per cent of home missionaries had fathers who were ministers or missionaries, compared to the Japan Mission, where more than 30 per cent of the women were the children of clergymen. This variation in the women's social and economic status helps to explain in part the dissimilarity in home and overseas missionaries' educational qualifications. Only 11 of the 140 home missionaries (8 per cent) attended university; 8 graduated. A further 10 (7 per cent) were trained as nurses, while 25 were normal-school graduates.

The more relaxed policy towards hiring home missionary recruits meant that these women were an average of three to four years older than overseas missionaries. As a consequence of their age, the women averaged five years' previous working experience, about a year more than foreign missionaries. But to offset their longer experience, very few home missionaries had held responsible positions in the work-force. Several women had been employed in business offices, and about 20 per cent had been teachers, but generally their educational deficiencies circumscribed their access to job opportunities, especially the administrative positions available to university graduates. Nor do they appear to have acquired the executive skills increasingly critical to the operation of a large and efficient missionary enterprise. Yet if many home missionaries were obviously under-qualified by the Board of Managers' own standards, and over-aged as well, they were accepted to the WMS corps if they agreed to work among the French, the Indians, or immigrant groups in their own country instead of hoping for assignments in the more prestigious mission fields of the Orient.

Because so much of the relative satisfaction or discouragement that home missionaries derived from their work appears to have hinged on the location to which they were assigned, the home missionaries have been divided into five smaller groups encompassing WMS French work in the Montreal area, rescue work among the Oriental immigrants in British Columbia, missionary activity in eastern European immigrant communities in northern Alberta, inner-city missions, and finally WMS missions among native people in British Columbia and Alberta. This seems a somewhat arbitrary division based on the various ethnic groups to which the WMS ministered, but it is one that most effectively underscores the dichotomies, especially in employment patterns present even within home mission work.

In general, urban mission work, especially in Montreal or Toronto, required fewer adjustments to an inhospitable physical environment than a posting in northern British Columbia or Alberta, a consideration that by itself goes far towards explaining why WMS urban missionaries tended to remain in the society's employ longer than women stationed in northern and western Canada. Among those missionaries with relatively lengthy WMS careers were the women who staffed the society's missions in the Montreal area, whose employment averaged 13.6 years. If their careers were only slightly longer than the average of 12.2 years among all home missionaries, their persistence is nevertheless remarkable, because French mission work, which received scant publicity, was hardly one of the society's triumphs. It was at best an onerous obligation the WMS shouldered, not without complaint, when it would have preferred to abandon the field for more glamorous and productive ventures.

WMS missionary work in the Montreal area was part of the larger Ontario-directed Methodist crusade that had been launched in the 1850s to convert Quebec's Roman Catholic, French-speaking population to Protestantism. Fifty years after the improbable task had been taken up, Alexander Sutherland charitably characterized Methodist French missionary work as "an interesting though not remarkably successful department."[8] The WMS inherited its particular obligation in Quebec from the Ladies' French Missionary Society of Montreal, organized in 1878. Before its amalgamation with the WMS in 1881, the Montreal society had already employed at least one Bible woman and provided financial aid to the French Mission Church and the French Methodist Institute, a secondary school operated by the General Board for the re-education (a euphemism for conversion) of French-Canadian Roman Catholic children.[9] In 1885 the WMS opened its own girls' school, which accommodated twelve boarders as part of the institute in Montreal;[10] the next year, when a larger building was needed, the school was relocated in Actonvale, fifty-five miles from Montreal. Three years later the two mission boards agreed to consolidate their efforts; they opened a new institute in Montreal, and the Actonvale school was abandoned. By 1890 the WMS was spending almost five thousand dollars per annum on French missionary work.

The Board of Managers tried to convince Canadian Methodist women that the conversion of Roman Catholic Quebec was their special responsibility and burden. A classic editorial published in the

Missionary Outlook in 1887 warned that "others will look after Japan, if need be; but, we, women of Canada, alone have the French-Canadians *given us of God*."[11] Pronouncements like this, which characterized the society's response to the so-called evils of Catholicism, were, however, hardly exclusive to Methodists and must be recognized as part of the widespread paranoia that infected late Victorian English-speaking Protestant Canada. Through its publications the WMS regularly directed vociferous attacks at Roman Catholics, whose presence was, as J.R. Miller has pointed out, perceived by Protestants "as inimical to the social well-being and material progress of any state, including Canada."[12]

Like most other English-Canadians of the day, WMS members would not have questioned the General Board of Missions' hypothesis that "the greatest problem which the Dominion of Canada has to face is the attitudes of its French population, not because it is French, but because it is intensely anti-Protestant and anti-British."[13] The following indictment of Roman Catholicism, which came as late as 1900, from Mrs Gordon Wright, a prominent WMS member and the sister of Newton Rowell, who argued that French mission work should be the society's highest priority, is the embodiment of the virulent anglo-Canadian sentiment that blamed the Roman Catholic Church for Canada's failure to attain national greatness. "As a nation and as a people we can never rise and develop as we should in those sections where Roman Catholicism, with her dwarfing influences, holds absolute sway. Why should we not become more deeply interested in the work of bringing our fellow-countrymen to a knowledge of the true light without the immediate intercession of priest and virgin? ... Why should we not spend more freely of our means on a work so closely touching ourselves as Canadians as this? ... The people are aweary of their bondage."[14] The answer, as Methodist mission societies understood it, was more schools like the one already operating in Montreal to promote not "bigoted proselytism, but ... education based upon a study and knowledge of the Word of God."[15]

From 1885 until 1925 eleven women were employed to develop WMS interests in the Montreal vicinity. Their individual backgrounds and former work experience are the least well documented of those of any group of WMS missionaries, largely because responsibility for the administration of much of the French work appears to have been shouldered by local auxiliaries. As a result there was little direct correspondence between the individual workers and the Board of Managers. Seven women in the French work recorded Montreal as their home; their surnames seem to confirm that they were francophones. The others came from Ontario, New Brunswick, and Nova Scotia.

Although one woman had been a teacher before becoming a missionary, apparently none of them had attended university. Three were widows, but little more can be reconstructed about their backgrounds or their motives for seeking employment as missionaries.

Most WMS workers in the Montreal area were assigned to the French Methodist Institute. The institute admitted both Roman Catholic and Protestant students, but "the preference [was] given to boys and girls from Roman Catholic homes, in the hope that they [would] exert an influence upon those homes that cannot otherwise be reached."[16] Applications were carefully screened to secure young people who the two mission societies thought were the best prospects for conversion. The institute prepared its students for entrance to university or to McGill Normal School. Classes were usually taught in French, another reason why most WMS missionaries were from Quebec. The female students were groomed for the future in a manner that the WMS considered appropriate and sensible for young women. Because the missionaries realized that most of the girls would marry and that "nearly all [would be] obliged to take up housework, sewing, etc.," girls were given, in addition to their academic studies, training in domestic skills, especially "plain cooking, practically in all its branches, from the preparing of a cup of tea or coffee to the cooking of meats, vegetables, etc., and the making of plain cakes and puddings."[17] Under the direction of Isabel Masten, the matron of the girls' school for twenty years, "singing, sewing, and housekeeping, a happy combination of feminine accomplishments" became the indispensable core of the girls' curriculum. As far as Masten was concerned, rudimentary domestic training was absolutely vital because for some girls "the proper care of their persons and their rooms, as well as any kind of order about the house was as unfamiliar as the work of the class-room."[18]

The daily regime and discipline at the institute seem to have been more strictly ordered than in WMS schools abroad. The children were required to do chores that servants performed in the Japanese and Chinese missions. An odd gender division of labour prevailed. "At 6:30 every morning the bell rings, and at seven o'clock everyone must be in the study room. At 7:30 breakfast is served ... From 8:00 to 8:45 the school is like a bee-hive, yet everything is done with the greatest precision. Of course all the pupils have to make their own beds, sweep their room, class-rooms and corridors. The boys peel the potatoes, polish the knives and carry the ashes. The girls wash the dishes and tidy their own department. At a quarter to nine everything must be ready for inspection. After prayers the daily class work begins."[19] Reports like this give the impression that the institute

was managed more like a charitable institution than the elite boarding school it purported to be. The rigid program did not deter applicants. The institute's facilities were always stretched to the limits, and
each year students were turned away. But in spite of the Methodist
Church's soothing euphemisms about the ultimate objectives of the
institute, Roman Catholic parents were wary about enrolling their
children because, the WMS was convinced, of pressure from conniv-
ing parish priests, who wielded the ultimate weapon of excommu-
nication. Of the eighty-seven pupils registered in 1895, for example,
less than a third came from Roman Catholic families.

. In 1906 the WMS decided to expand its responsibilities in Montreal.
In accordance with the prevailing stress on shaping the minds of the
very young, the society opened the French Protestant Home, an
orphanage where abandoned children could be cared for in a Protestant environment in the expectation that they would be delivered
permanently from the errors of Catholicism.[20] The society also funded
and staffed two mission schools in the east and west ends of Montreal
for children whose parents wanted them to have a Protestant education but could not pay "the fees of the ordinary public schools, low
though they be ... they are reduced to the alternatives, either of the
influence of the Roman Catholic schools, or the gross ignorance
resulting from no tuition."[21] With Lillian Bouchard in charge, the West
End Mission gradually evolved into the Syrian Mission School. In
1912 the WMS purchased a building in the Syrian community,
adapted it to conform to Montreal's requirements for school buildings, and staffed it with two teachers.[22] While the school offered a
Protestant education for Syrian children, it was also the venue for
WMS missionaries to visit Syrian homes in the vicinity, establishing
personal contact with the families as a preliminary step in their possible conversion to Methodism.

Bouchard's concern for her pupils went beyond that expected of a
regular classroom teacher or even a missionary. Through her home
visiting she assumed, in effect, the function of a social worker, giving
advice and practical assistance anywhere she could to recent immigrants. Above all she hoped to improve the quality of public health
and child care in an area with an abysmally high infant mortality
rate.[23] At the school Bouchard directed a thorough health program
for the children of working mothers with little time for their maternal
obligations. These children were "naturally dirty ... because they
know no better." Bouchard initiated a system whereby "certain pupils
came on certain days about a quarter to eight, and [she] devoted the
time until nine o'clock in bathing them well with plenty of soap and
water."[24] The doctor who periodically visited the school noted an

immediate improvement in the children's health and credited Bouchard with the transformation.

While Bouchard meticulously tended the children's minor injuries, burns and abrasions, she also insisted that the children under her care, raised as they were in "a culture of poverty,"[25] should have an opportunity to be happy. From private donations she purchased "swings, see-saws, skipping-ropes and games, also a few goldfish and some plants"[26] to brighten the drab atmosphere of the mission. Bouchard was a very sympathetic and kind teacher. Unfortunately, the reports that the society demanded at quarterly intervals from its mission stations reveal very little about the nature of other women's experiences beyond the essential particulars about their daily work as matrons and teachers. Probably because most were native Montrealers who did not reside within a distinct mission community, the women did not rehearse their private activities, which were conducted quite separately from their work. In this sense, for them missionary work was not so much a way of life as a daily task.

By 1910, whatever enthusiasm French missionary work had generated was clearly flagging. Methodist goals in Quebec were unrealized, and the overseas fields, where hopes of successful conversions were still high, seemed far more deserving of Methodists' financial support. The wms was astute enough to recognize that its appointed task in Quebec was futile. This frustration may help to explain why the better-educated recruits were not squandered on the French mission. It was left, then, to local women, who became not the professional missionaries who dominated the foreign fields but rather matrons and friends to the young people in the schools and social workers within the wider immigrant community that the wms served. They were not strong activists for their particular cause, not so much because their interest in the work was perfunctory but because they usually acted as caretakers, not innovators, and because ordained ministers employed by the General Board directed the institute, which was the foundation of the mission. The wms missionaries dutifully filed their reports but rarely made suggestions for improvements, requested additional funds, or urged expansion. There was not, it would appear, in French missionary work much opportunity for women to take the initiative. Almost from its inception French mission work was an anachronism with little potential to become a rewarding, long-term career for an ambitious woman. As Rev. Paul Villard, principal of the institute, recognized in 1919, any woman whom the wms sent to teach at the institute would find "the work more ungrateful and harder [than] similar work would be in China or Japan."[27]

In the long run the WMS missionaries made little lasting impression on the vast Roman Catholic population that the Methodist Church hoped to enlighten. For the most part the WMS and its agents in Quebec were simply ignored by the French-Canadian population, for whom they were just another symbol of the odious Anglo-Canadian presence. In 1925 only Bouchard was employed in Montreal, where she remained until her retirement in 1942. None of the women involved in French mission work resigned to marry; one woman left because of ill health, while another was dismissed after a year because her work as matron of the French Institute was unsatisfactory.[28] The others appear to have left because they were getting old and decided to retire. When this happened, they were not replaced because of the dwindling public regard for the work, which failed to capture the imaginations of the society's members. Though publicly acknowledging its special nationalistic assignment to eradicate "the most solid, thoroughly organized and aggressive type of Romanism to be found in the world,"[29] the WMS preferred to invest its home missionary resources elsewhere with more visible and immediate results. After 1900, as proof of its continued commitment to home missionary work and to renewing the quality of Canadian life, the society turned its attention and assets to the flood of recent immigrants, who, the Methodist Church argued, must be purged of their European habits and religions and indoctrinated in English-Canadian Protestant values. The society prayed that they would not prove as recalcitrant as the French.

The society was first introduced to the immigrant problem in 1885 when the Rev. J.E. Starr alerted the Board of Managers to the "nefarious traffic" in Chinese girls brought into British Columbia specifically as prostitutes.[30] Incensed residents of Victoria were attempting, under the guidance of local churches, to eliminate the "social evil," not so much to help the Oriental women as to purify their own society. The WMS threw its weight behind the project, hiring Annie Leake, a Nova Scotian teacher, as matron of a rescue home to be financed and administered by the society. The following year the society allocated fifteen hundred dollars for rescue work. By 1925 the WMS had employed eighteen women missionaries in this particular branch of their urban missionary work.[31]

From time to time the force was augmented by missionaries from Japan or, less commonly, West China, who spent a year or two assisting in Victoria while they were on furlough or regaining their strength before returning to their overseas posts. Five of the mission's permanent employees were from Victoria and nine from Ontario. There were no university graduates among the group, although five women had considerable teaching experience and others had engaged in social or philanthropic activities. Lily McCargar had worked with Chinese boys in her home town, Moose Jaw, and understood Cantonese, the language spoken by most Chinese in Victoria at the time. Margaret Eason had experience at a Vancouver Chinese and Japanese kindergarten, while Grace Baker was previously employed by an institute for the blind in Halifax. Elizabeth Staples of Durham County, Ontario, housekeeper of the rescue home for twenty years, had worked as an assistant nurse in Kansas, as a deaconess, and at the St John's orphanage prior to joining the WMS at the age of forty-six in 1917.[32] Like Staples, several of these women were middle-aged, well into their forties, when they were hired. In fact, the average age of the eleven women for whom data were available was thirty-seven, possibly because the board preferred mature women for this particular type of work, which involved contact with the more sordid side of life.

Chinese rescue work offered a variety of unique challenges for the women assigned to Victoria. The missionaries' major responsibility consisted of wresting prostitutes from an immoral environment, to be rehabilitated by the society as Christian wives and mothers. By the late nineteenth century, especially in Britain, saving fallen women had become an acceptable altruistic pursuit for middle-class women and, less commonly, men, whose susceptibility to the wiles of prostitutes somewhat tainted their philanthropic gestures.[33] Women, however, as the British reformer Josephine Butler argued, were able "as pure wives and mothers, as members of religious congregations ... [to] defend their public actions in the name of morality and religion."[34] The WMS vehemently attacked the Canadian government for its failure to enforce the existing laws against what the society judged one of the worst forms of criminal activity, whereby up to two hundred Chinese girls and women were ferried annually to Canada to be sold into prostitution or slavery.[35] In the absence of government intervention the WMS dutifully appropriated the twofold burden of rescuing defenceless women from their oppressors and, at the same time, of preserving the sanctity of the family from the unspeakable social evil.

Annie Leake and her associates proved to be militant and dogged rescuers. Hoping to commandeer the girls and women as they disembarked, the WMS personnel regularly met the steamships arriving from China. Other women were rounded up from "the haunts of vice" in Victoria's Chinatown and taken to the home for protection, while a few arrived of their own accord.[36] Because these girls might fetch a price ranging from $250 to $1500, their owners did not let the rescue home have them without a fight, often before the court. In many instances the WMS ensured that the owners were served with a writ of habeas corpus to appear in court, where the girls were given the choice of going to the rescue home or returning to their master. If a girl chose the sanctuary of the home, the WMS was then required to take out legal guardianship papers.

The society protested that they had lost many cases because a Chinese owner could "spend money lavishly ... buying witnesses to swear just such evidence as he thinks necessary in order to regain his chattels."[37] Charges of corruption were common. The missionaries, who assumed that the Chinese women would instinctively prefer to live in the rescue home, were unable to grasp why some women might return to their owners. In the society's eyes the men were always the guilty parties. Oblivious of the strong economic and demographic factors that encouraged prostitution on the west coast and to the profits that accrued to the prostitutes themselves, the WMS defined the issue almost exclusively in moral terms, as a problem that could be solved once and for all if the Oriental women found Christ and were then transformed into virtuous wives and mothers.

During the first five years of WMS rescue operations in Victoria Leake worked alone on behalf of women who otherwise, she believed, could "live and die in a Christian country without an effort being made to offer them the bread of life."[38] Her temerity in confronting the courts and the Chinese procurers elicited widespread sympathy from the WMS membership. Leake planned to educate the girls she brought to the home, hoping ultimately to train them as missionaries who could return to China.[39] She soon realized, however, that she needed an assistant, preferably a woman who spoke Chinese, to carry on a door-to-door evangelization program throughout Victoria's Chinatown, whose population approached two thousand.[40] The Board of Managers responded by sending Martha Cartmell, then in Canada recuperating before returning to Tokyo. Cartmell, of course, spoke no Chinese, but the board assumed that her knowledge of Japanese society qualified her to understand the Chinese as well. She was not an entirely inappropriate choice. At the very least her own experience in Japan had given her the compassion to empathize with Chinese immigrants. Her calls, nevertheless, were seldom very fruitful, although if she was invited into a Chinese home, she took advantage of the occasion to teach the women to knit and to introduce them to some Bible stories. She found the contact with the girls in the rescue home more satisfying because of their honest desire "to do right, though the training and discipline of life seem hard sometimes."[41] Their accounts of life in China and their heart-rending portrayals of infanticide especially touched her.

Cartmell's sympathy and patience at a time when Oriental immi-grants were treated with extreme contempt as unwelcome intruders and the source of moral and social evil appear quite exceptional. Her forbearance seems to have set the tone for many other WMS workers in Victoria. Instead of condemning Oriental behaviour and habits as immoral and wicked, Cartmell tried to find "proofs that God has 'made of one blood all nations of men,' and that 'the Gospel is the power of God unto Salvation' for all alike." Taking a firm stand against Canadians' anti-Chinese prejudice, she allowed that "work among the Chinese is slow and difficult, because of their conservatism fos-tering everything Chinese." Her years in Japan had convinced her that "where they do yield they appreciate, or at least improve under instruction."[42]

Yet understanding as she was, Cartmell's altruism contains a cer-tain ambivalence and indecision about the propriety of the WMS work among the Chinese prostitutes. She openly acknowledged her embar-rassment about the nature of the work, which had, she confessed, forced her to abandon her modesty. It was contrary to her upbringing to write to equally proper women about the "innocent little Chinese girls, who have been sold by their parents or stolen by procuresses in China and brought over for the vilest use of abandoned men and money makers. My heart turns sick at the thought of such plain statements appearing in print from my pen. But what avails modesty that only shudders and weeps."[43] Once immersed in the rescue work, Cartmell and her colleagues usually overcame their middle-class ret-icence to adopt a relatively accommodating stance to their charges' ethnicity, and sometimes even to their immorality. But obviously it was not easy.

The society did not implement Leake's plan to reshape the women as Christian missionaries. Instead, the WMS accepted the more mod-est goal of initiating them into the rites of Christian womanhood and transforming them into virtuous wives and mothers.[44] The mission-aries measured their success by the number of women from the home who married Chinese Christians. By 1896 eighteen marriages had been performed at the home; the wives were all "settled in peaceful and reputable homes of their own [and] won away from a state of slavery to which death itself would have been infinitely preferable."[45] Frequently what passed for a social welfare and rehabilitation pro-gram for prostitutes developed on an ad hoc basis. American mission societies were carrying on similar work along the California coast,[46] but there is no evidence that the Methodist WMS sought any external advice that might have been available to them.

Sincere as they were, the missionaries in Victoria had no familiarity with this kind of rehabilitation. Consequently, the missionaries' tentative solutions to the problems they encountered were often ineffectual. Cartmell, for one, was an advocate of strong coffee as a cure-all for one woman who had been "a cigarette and opium smoker, a gambler and addicted to wine."[47] Ida Snyder developed her own technique to wean one Chinese woman from opium. She described how the woman in question, Ah Yute, "was received over two weeks ago and is getting on famously. She had been using opium and tobacco for at least ten years as nearly as we can make out, and is now content with three cigarettes a day and has had no opium for three days. I have given her both since she came to the home, as we were warned it would be dangerous to deprive her of them too suddenly; but the dose has been decreased so gradually that she has not complained, and she affirmed that the teachers are a 'heap good' which shows that so far she is content."[48] Two months later, when Ah Yute was down to one cigarette a day, Snyder wondered whether WMS supporters could "imagine the Matron of the Home doling out the tobacco?"[49] But the episode did not have a happy ending. By September, Ah Yute had fallen by the wayside and was disgraced after she stole Snyder's secret supply of tobacco. Her punishment, which Snyder thought appropriate to the crime, was to consign the remaining tobacco to the stove.[50] Ah Yute's name does not appear again in WMS reports as evidence of success in Victoria.[51]

The WMS's efforts to curb the trade in Oriental women were commended by the Royal Commission on Chinese and Japanese Immigration when it convened in British Columbia in 1901. The commission's report, published the following year, concluded that the Chinese could not be assimilated and that a head tax of five hundred dollars should be levied to inhibit further Asian immigration.[52] At least one WMS missionary who had testified before the commission, Kate Morgan, formerly of the Japan Mission, agreed. Unlike Cartmell, Morgan, who strongly opposed unrestricted immigration as "bad for the country," showed little compassion for the Oriental.[53] As she explained, the Chinese could not be trusted "for truthfulness"; they attended Christian night schools only from self-interest, and "a Chinaman will profess to be a Christian to get a wife." There was no evidence whatsoever that the Chinese would adopt "our mode of life." As far as Morgan was concerned, "they [were] all a menace to the public from their way of living, the way they herd together." The commissioners, who apparently shared her views, congratulated the rescue home staff for their part in stopping the "infamous barter in humanity" that the government was either unable or unwilling to control.[54] In retrospect, there is little doubt that, at a time when the government was not expected to take the initiative for social welfare and the only alternative continued to be private philanthropy, the WMS and its workers provided assistance and support for women willing to defer to the society's point of view. The degree of accommodation some missionaries expected of Oriental women must at times have been extreme.

WMS work in Victoria gradually became more diversified; the society realized that it needed to cast a wider net if it were to bring Chinatown to Methodism, and also because, as more Canadian women settled in British Columbia, the traffic in women declined. In 1897, in response to appeals from the two missionaries at the home, the WMS sent another worker expressly to open a school to teach English to the children in the vicinity.[55] By 1899 the school reported an enrolment of 230 and an average daily attendance of about 30, but when it moved to new quarters to accommodate larger numbers, the WMS turned it over to the General Board.[56] The women then concentrated their efforts once again on the home, whose programs were expanded to involve Japanese women and children. In 1908 a kindergarten was opened, and in 1909 a new building was constructed to serve the enlarged needs of the society in Victoria.[57] The WMS also extended its work to the Chinese and Japanese living in Vancouver and the lower mainland, an area that the women had tried unsuccessfully to service from Victoria. In 1911 the WMS opened Japanese and Chinese kindergartens in Vancouver under the supervision of Gussie Preston, recently returned from Japan.[58] When Jessie Howie, who had also been stationed in Japan, was assigned to Vancouver, she brought her Japanese Christian protégée, Hibi San, to assist her.[59]

To the women's disappointment, the work in Vancouver yielded few Christian converts, not because the Japanese and Chinese women were visibly hostile but because they simply ignored the missionaries' gestures of friendship. Howie blamed materialism for "a spirit of indifference that is deadly to spiritual life." "The Oriental," she observed, "is here to earn a living and not to learn a new religion. Here we have no leisure class, like we have in Japan; all are young and ambitious to make good, and that means to make money. Second, they have their old religion – for here in our midst is a Buddhist temple and a priest in charge – and although under ordinary circumstances many are indifferent to its claims, yet when death enters their homes they turn to the Buddhist priest to bury their dead ... the Oriental knows well the evils of this Christian land, and treats with indifference a teaching that doesn't work out in a practical way in the world around him."[60] By 1919 the society had become less critical of Oriental customs. It pointed out that the work among Orientals had two goals: "First, to give our Orientals a knowledge of God as their Father and Jesus Christ as their Saviour. Second to help them become good citizens of Canada ... through the growth of friendship and understanding ... These strangers from across the sea need help when they come to this new land, and it is our duty and privilege to help them become as the home-born."[61]

This message from the society's annual report was not just misleading propaganda designed to solicit funds. The WMS missionaries in Victoria and Vancouver were among the very few Canadians who tried, if not always from entirely selfless motives, to be compassionate towards Asian immigrants and to protect women from male sexual violence. From 1887 to 1925, 425 women with an extraordinary range of problems were sheltered at the rescue home.[62] For many Chinese and Japanese newcomers the WMS missionaries provided the only friendly contact in a society that was to prove no less hostile as the years passed. That some of these immigrants trusted the women implicitly was borne out by the numbers of their children who attended the classes at the home and of girls who were consigned to the society's care by parents who could no longer provide for them. In personal and community crises many Orientals turned to the "Jesus people" for advice and comfort. For example, risking their own health, the women set up a temporary hospital in a Vancouver school to provide medical facilities for the Japanese during the influenza epidemic of 1918. Two hundred patients were treated within three weeks, and the WMS reported that their 10 per cent mortality rate was the lowest of any hospital in the city. A grateful community gave Howie, who supervised the operation, a gold watch and a tea service.[63] Howard Sugimato, for one, suggests that this sort of good work, and especially the activities of the Methodist Church among the Japanese, "contributed to the general welfare and harmony in the community," creating "a better and more useful immigrant group."[64]

At the time the missionaries had considerable difficulty gauging their effectiveness. Personal satisfaction about their jobs seems even more elusive. The women constantly complained that rehabilitation work was physically exhausting and nerve-racking. They were probably right. Their own sympathetic and humanitarian attitudes notwithstanding, rescue work in the early years sometimes provoked open hostility within the Chinese community in Victoria, who resented any interference in their affairs. Annie Leake complained that as soon as prostitutes arrived, they were "taught to fear [the missionaries] and the Home more than any place in this world or any other of which they might have heard."[65] For Kate Morgan, "one of the hardest lessons ... to learn [was] that of patience in doing work that apparently bears no fruit."[66] For some months she suffered from insomnia,[67] induced by an attack on the rescue home by Boxer sympathizers responding to rumours that Britain was about to divide China.[68] When Ida Snyder returned from her furlough in 1905, she was the first WMS agent in Victoria to contract for a second term, although she feared she would not last another six years.[69]

As much as they protested about the emotionally troubling nature of their work, women assigned to the Chinese rescue home in actuality resigned for a variety of reasons, only some related to the pressure of their occupation. Five of the eighteen (28 per cent), including Annie Leake at the age of fifty-three, left their work to marry. Illness forced two resignations; two women were needed at home, grounds for resignation cited quite often by home missionaries. Elizabeth Churchill left to join the American Presbyterian mission in Canton, probably because she was already fluent in Cantonese.[70] Sarah Bowes resigned at age fifty-nine to become the matron at the Victoria Court House, a position for which her experience in rescue work had well prepared her.[71] Only three women (17 per cent), all hired after 1899, when the mission had passed the pioneering stage and was less preoccupied with the enervating rescue work, remained with the society until their retirement. Their careers averaged twenty-five years. There is little specific evidence, however, to explain why these particular women, all from Ontario, pursued this aspect of WMS work as a career when the average length of employment was just nine and a half years. Generally, few WMS missionaries employed in Victoria and Vancouver appear to have found the work among Asian immigrants as rewarding as converting the heathen on his own territory.

By 1920 there were only four WMS agents working with Asian women in British Columbia, hardly enough to influence the large Oriental community. Gradually, government services began to encroach on the WMS work in Vancouver and Victoria. Restrictive immigration laws passed in 1919 decreased the need to expand the mission.[72] After the First World War the WMS concentrated on the work of the Oriental home and school in Victoria, which now functioned as a meeting place for the women and girls of the community as well as a temporary home for young Chinese and Japanese girls. It closed in 1942, when the eighteen girls staying there became a part of the Japanese exodus from the west coast.[73] But long before, the WMS had ceased to believe that the success of home missions depended on the growth of the disappointing Oriental work. After the turn of the century, like the majority of anglo-Canadians, the membership of the WMS was more anxious about the threat posed to Canadian national life and morality not by the few thousand Orientals on the west coast but by the floods of immigrants from eastern Europe.[74]

The WMS had not been directly involved in the initial Canadian Methodist urban missionary work among European immigrants begun at the end of the nineteenth century in Toronto at the Fred Victor Mission and in Winnipeg at the All Peoples' Mission. But in 1901, when the WMS was approached by the superintendent of All Peoples' Mission for financial support, the board contributed two thousand dollars towards a new building. The society was not asked, it seems, nor did the Board of Managers volunteer, to send any women as missionaries to Winnipeg. Instead, in 1905 the Methodist Church hired deaconesses specially trained for urban missionary work for the missions in Toronto and Winnipeg.[75] From time to time the WMS paid some or all of the salary of a deaconess at the All People's Mission, but the deaconesses were not WMS employees responsible to the society's administrators, and their names were not included on the roster of missionaries.

After 1904 the WMS began to assume a more direct and aggressive role among European immigrants in both urban and rural areas of Canada. Its major undertaking was in northern Alberta, where the stream of immigrants – twelve thousand Ukrainians settled in western Canada in 1898 alone – had aroused the fears of the English-speaking settlers in the region. In 1898 they requested that the Manitoba and Northwest Conference of the Methodist Church petition the federal government to limit immigration from eastern Europe.[76] In particular the tendency of eastern Europeans to settle in blocs, rather than integrating themselves into the existing farming communities, angered the British farmers who were already working the land.[77] The conference refused to intervene, but the problems associated with eastern European immigration caught the attention of the General Board Missionary Society, which responded by establishing a mission at Pakan, in northern Alberta, in 1900 to facilitate the immigrants' adjustment to Canadian ways.[78]

The Methodist Church generally categorized eastern European settlers as an essentially godless people: intemperate, rowdy, unwilling to conform to Canadian habits, and with little or no esteem for the women in their communities. Some of this apparent indifference to morality and religious practice was attributed to a lack of spiritual leadership, because very few eastern clergy accompanied their charges to greener pastures. Dr Charles Lawford, the first General Board missionary at Pakan, adamantly ascribed the flaws that he observed in the Galician character to a misguided belief in the saints and rituals of the Eastern Orthodox church. The Greek Catholic Church, Lawford postulated, was even more backward because its members worshipped the Virgin Mary instead of following Christ's message in the Scriptures.[79]

In the first years of its work in Alberta, the wms sometimes could be equally judgmental. After two years of work in Alberta the women characterized their constituents as "the least desirable of all the immigrants that come to us."[80] Edith Weekes, an employee whom the Board of Managers especially admired, wrote a pamphlet for the society condemning the Austrians' social customs and religion. In it she thoroughly berated "their ceremonial religion, its priesthood, its subservience and superstition, its bowing and crossing, its repetition of prayers to saint and Virgin, its belief in the efficiency of baptism, confession and sacrament to cleanse from sin – if any cleansing be possible, its observance of holidays and fast seasons and its hopeless 'How and whence can we know?' regarding the life eternal."[81] It was, Weekes argued, and the society agreed, the duty of the wms "to make them *Christians* and *Canadians*."[82]

The wms formally initiated its work among eastern Europeans in 1904, when two Ontario women, Jessie Munro, who had been invalided home from Japan, and Retta Edmonds, a trained nurse, were delegated to open a station in northern Alberta.[83] The Board of Managers had already selected a suitable site near Pakan on the north bank of the North Saskatchewan River in the centre of the Ukrainian settlements where Lawford was working.[84] More than 250 families lived in the six hundred square miles surrounding Pakan; most had come from Bukovinia, which had been made a separate province of the Austro-Hungarian empire in 1849. Other settlers arrived from Galicia, also part of the Austro-Hungarian empire, and from Rumania.[85]

The Board of Managers was impatient for the women to dispense morality and Methodism to the immigrant community, but Munro and Edmonds' first priority was to look after their own basic needs. For several months the pair lived in a tent while they supervised the building of the mission station that would double as their home.[86] All the materials and furnishings had to be floated down the Saskatchewan River from Edmonton, one hundred miles away. When completed, the twenty-two by twenty-four-foot structure comprised a schoolroom and kitchen downstairs, two bedrooms, a sitting room, and a hospital room in the upper storey.[87] Even before the mission home was finished, Edmunds and Munro conducted Sunday school classes in their tent. Although they did not complain publicly about their living conditions, three months of camping out were more than enough.[88] The smoke from the fire, combined with dirt and stormy weather, drove them into the still unfinished home.

Just a few days later a Sunday school student arrived expecting them to solve his particular problem. His dilemma was the first of the practical matters that became the substance of the women's work in the community and would demand all the ingenuity they could muster. The boy, Munro reported, "brought some blue jean, with the request that we should cut out a pair of trousers. We had never done the like before and had no pattern, but we had resolved to do anything we could to show our goodwill and power to help, and so said we would try. Finding an old pair of overalls we washed and ripped them, using them for a pattern."[89]

On 1 November 1904 the women officially opened the school, but with just one pupil in attendance.[90] Because the school complied with Alberta school regulations and the WMS teachers' qualifications also conformed to provincial standards, the society was eligible for government grants to fund the undertaking. By January an average of thirteen children were present daily, and Munro hired a local teacher who read and wrote Ukrainian to help the pupils to learn their native language.[91] After a year Munro was forced to resign temporarily because of poor health. She was immediately replaced by two women, Edith Weekes and Ethel Chace, who had been rejected as physically unfit for service in China.[92] The pair were already good friends, and Chace's letters to Weekes, written forty years later, attest to the difficulty and diversity of their work.

Like more than half the women (twenty-one of thirty-eight, or 55 per cent) who served in Alberta, Chace and Weekes were from Ontario. Nine of the group (24 per cent) were native Albertans, and seven (18 per cent) were raised in the Maritimes. While this geographical breakdown corresponds roughly to that for all WMS missionaries, there were proportionately more Albertans than elsewhere, evidence that tends to refute George Emery's inference that the Methodist Church deliberately sent Ontarians to the west as the messengers of evangelical Protestantism.[93] Unlike most home missionaries, however, Weekes and Chace were very well-educated women; Weekes was a graduate in languages from Victoria University and Chace graduated with honours from the University of Toronto and the

Ontario College of Education and had several years' successful teaching experience.[94]

Although their educational standing may not have matched that of the WMS overseas missionaries, women assigned to Alberta were in general better educated, with more extensive employment histories, than other home missionaries. Four (10.5 per cent) of the thirty-eight women who spent most of their WMS career in Alberta had attended university; almost half (seventeen) were trained teachers, and four others were qualified nurses. Four had been deaconesses, and two had been previously employed in social service work. That these women were assigned to Alberta, not to Port Simpson or Victoria, was probably a deliberate decision on the part of the board. In the hierarchy of WMS home missionary work, the society seemed to rank its operations among the European immigrants above the Indian, Oriental, or French mission work, possibly because the promise of success was greater and because of the sheer numbers involved. As a result, the Board of Managers appears to have carefully selected well-qualified women to direct its interests in Alberta.

Their relatively high educational status did not, however, give the women the privileges of foreign mission work. By 1906 the three women at Wahstao, as they called their mission station, were operating a day school, a Sunday school, a night school for men and boys in winter, women's meetings, and English language classes. When the weather permitted, they made house-to-house visitations in a horse-drawn wagon. They considered themselves fortunate to have the services of a twelve-year-old boy to tend the horses and a young Ukrainian woman who helped with housekeeping and served as their interpreter.[95] The women had to learn Ukrainian on their own because the WMS made no special provisions for language study by allocating funds to hire a language teacher. Weekes, who was fluent in German and had readily mastered Ukrainian, compiled an English-Ukrainian dictionary for the benefit of the Methodist missionary community.[96]

But neither a working knowledge of the language nor the family life that the women tried to create within the mission house could alleviate their feelings, not so much of homesickness but of alienation within their own country from a closed society that they did not understand and that did not welcome them. Chace remembered "how strange all our surroundings seemed ... The mudded houses and farm buildings, not very pretentious in those days, the strange costumes, sheepskin coats, head shawls, and homespun clothing were scarcely more curious than the open prairies and parkland with copses of white poplar."[97] Alberta's climate was an added serious impediment to missionary work and personal comfort. In winter travel was restricted because of the severe snowstorms, and the women suffered constantly from the cold inside their home. It was impossible to keep warm on sub-zero nights, when "you used to fill the box stove with big-wood at bed-time and close off all the drafts; then in the middle of the night you came down to find nothing but a few glowing coals, when you would fill it up again ... When our thermometer registered no more than 40 below we guessed at the lower temperature by the thickness of the hoar-frost that coated everything in the kitchen as soon as the morning kettle began to boil."[98] Chace eventually adjusted to the climate, which she accepted as "healthy"; missionary life in Alberta was, she concluded, probably no "harder to bear physically than life in Japan or China."[99]

In 1908 the Alberta government opened a school that the WMS teachers agreed to staff; it operated from May to October, and school attendance increased. The society applauded the public school as "the surest weapon that can be used against ignorance and bigotry."[100] The missionaries hoped that if parents were responsible for its financial support, they might be more willing to educate their children. More importantly, the public school freed the women to concentrate on the spiritual needs of the area's residents, although the WMS continued to operate a small mission school for a few boarders in winter.

In March 1912 Ella McLean reported from Wahstao that the community finally appeared to have accepted the mission. The proof: "People come to our home on all kinds of errands, for letters to be read and to be written, for toothache and other ills to be cured, for garments to be cut out, to learn how to can fruit, to borrow money, sealers, flat-irons and umbrellas, and to sell all manner of farm and garden produce."[101] However, when the women tried go to Ukrainian homes to conduct evangelical services for the women of the community, the results were only marginally rewarding even by the enthusiastic and hopeful missionaries' low expectations. The Ukrainian women understood little English, while the missionaries had agonizing difficulty speaking Ukrainian. Chace's first meeting in a Ukrainian farmhouse was, by her own admission, a complete disaster. As she recalled years later,

Singing and reading passed off very well then an interruption occurred. From a dark corner, made darker with a heavy gray blanket, a hen walked out. She was quite inoffensive, just tired of close confinement. But she evidently had not been alone under the blanket, and the ray of light that she let in deceived her male companions into thinking that the dawn had come. You know what roosters do at dawn. Well they did it. There may have been seven of them or seventeen; it sounded more like seventy ... Every Ukrainian word that I had memorized so carefully fled from me, and I broke into violent perspiration as I looked in vain to the women for some interest and inspiration. They looked as if they cared not a whit whether they heard me or the roosters and I had to hurriedly close the service in deepest embarrassment.[102]

As the missionaries soon realized, Ukrainian women, whose lives were characterized by "the harsh drabness of labour" and subservience to their frequently brutal, uncaring husbands, had little time to waste on leisure activity.[103] The immigrant children responded more quickly to the missionaries' earnest overtures.[104]

In 1909 a second mission station was opened sixteen miles northwest of Wahstao at Smokey Lake. The women named it Kolokreeka, a Russian word meaning "beside the creek."[105] They had originally wanted a Ukrainian word to do with light to match the Cree "Wahstao," but "every known word for 'light' meant also coal-oil, which did not seem to be a very suitable title."[106] Weekes and Ella McLean were sent to staff it. In 1911, when McLean and her co-worker Phoebe Code took in four children for the winter, parents in the district suggested that the wms open a boarding school. Within a few years it housed thirty children.[107] In addition to their other duties the women at Kolokreeka conducted Sunday morning worship services if there was no minister present, even though the ordination of women was not condoned by the Methodist Church hierarchy.[108]

In 1912 Chace was moved to Chipman, an English-speaking community in the centre of immigrant settlements, where she lived with the Methodist minister's family and visited women in their homes and taught Sunday school. But in 1916 she was transferred to Edmonton, where in 1908 several Edmonton women, including Margaret Sherlock Ash, a former wms missionary from Victoria, had taken an interest in the predicament of young immigrant women who had left their families to find work in the city as waitresses, domestics, or, if all else failed, as prostitutes. A volunteer committee rented rooms where they held Bible classes and sewing groups for the newcomers, who, they contended, needed the "watchful, friendly effort of Christian workers."[109] The classes were so successful that the women appealed to the wms to engage a permanent employee to extend the work. When the society agreed, Ash rented a house that she hoped would become an uplifting force for every Ruthenian girl in household work in the city. To this end we have classes in English reading, that they may learn to read the Bible ... We have tried to make it homelike, restful and attractive, a place in which the girls are always sure to find a welcome and a friend ... In order to get acquainted with girls we have visited many hotels. To some we have gone again and again, for we have learned that six visits to one hotel produces better results than one visit to six. Much time has been given to girls out of work. To these we give a night's lodging for ten cents, and meals at ten cents each. Of course, sometimes this charge has had to be remitted. We advise them about places and try to find respectable places for them and to induce them to prefer such.[110]

A large, modern and comfortable home owned by the society opened late in 1912; in 1915 it provided shelter for nearly one hundred girls, thirty-one of them steady boarders.[111] As part of their crusade against immorality the missionaries in charge of the home made every effort to regulate the girls' leisure activities.[112] Not the least of Jessie Munro's concerns was a rumour that Ruthenian girls had been seen at Socialist meetings, where "ignorant men speak against all religions and do much harm." Munro concluded that she was fighting with the devil for possession of the girls. "Cheap picture shows, low theatres, public dance halls, restaurants of ill-repute are all his agencies, and now these Socialistic meetings."[113]

Rural immigrant behaviour was equally subject to the missionaries' disapproval, and equally misunderstood. Staunch prohibitionists, the women missionaries took up arms against the eastern Europeans' drinking habits. Alice Sanford, stationed at Wahstao in 1910, could not come to terms with "the moral standards of a people who drink and dance, or buy and sell, on the Sabbath day, yet consider it very wrong to even sew a few patches on a day set apart in memory of some saint, or of some less well known event in the history of their church."[114] To combat these vices and to compete with the popular public dances, the missionaries held their own "soirees" where "old-fashioned games" were played.[115] Temperance Sundays became a regular feature at Wahstao "to counter evil influences." On one occasion Chace boasted that fifteen of the twenty-one men at church signed the pledge against "drinking, smoking and profanity."[116] But the women were unable to influence the habits of more than a handful of their neighbours. A few months later they attended a local wedding and "wish[ed] we hadn't," a reference to the drinking and carousing that were always a part of Ukrainian celebrations.[117]

The women were at their best when they assumed the roles of social service workers, not the guardians of the public morality. Their correspondence and diaries suggest that WMS missionaries stationed in Alberta had a far different perception of their function than the society's workers in Japan and China. Significantly, there are fewer references in their writing to the pressing obligation to win souls for Christ and to attempts at direct unadulterated evangelism. Nor did the women brood over the aggregates of potential converts or their own failure to win the eastern Europeans to Methodism. The women at Wahstao were, in fact, reluctant to offer any hard statistical evidence of "the success in leading young people ... to become disciples of the Lord Jesus" because there had been so few converts.[118] They were usually satisfied if they could help immigrants adapt to Canadian ways and if they were able to give the children and young people the advantages of a Canadian education.

In northern Alberta as in Victoria, the WMS missionaries provided services that no one else, including government agencies, offered. They were well aware of the void they filled in the region. For example, while acknowledging that the WMS purpose was still "individual regeneration and salvation," in 1917, at the sixth annual convention of Ruthenian workers, Chace insisted that the missionaries in Alberta should also meet "the need for social service ... Each worker could apply her talents to the best advantage either as a teacher, housekeeper, social service worker or evangelist."[119] In 1918 the women aired their concern about "the urgent need for a certain kind of work suited to the peculiar needs of the place, that could well be described as YMCA work."[120]

Some General Board missionaries who appear to have resented the trust that the immigrant communities placed in the women suggested that one of their male representatives should work with the women, ostensibly because of "the low esteem put upon women by these people."[121] But even most of the men praised and respected the women's persistence and involvement. Chace for one was commended as "a splendid woman, a woman of splendid executive ability, a capable woman, who is just pouring out her life. Miss Chace will die many years sooner than she should because of the sacrifice she is making out there at Wahstao – and there in those foreign settlements ... that woman's life will be shortened; she is grey – she is broken down – because for the love of those people ... her whole soul is in it – There is no reserve."[122]

The Ukrainians themselves remained more impressed by the women's willingness to accommodate them than by the Christian message that, as missionaries, the women tried to deliver. George Vernon, an early settler in the vicinity, recalled how in 1918, at the height of the influenza epidemic, the women at Wahstao converted their mission home to a hospital. Chace was, Vernon noted, "no slouch." She was as orderly and as organized a person as one could find, although something of a prude.[123] Caring for the sick in a house that was without electricity, running water, or indoor plumbing and was a mile from the nearest telephone was an endless job. Chace described one particularly exhausting day during the epidemic as "Black Monday – easily the blackest day I ever knew ... The cow complained bitterly that she was not milked, and we needed the milk so much too. There were the fires to keep up, medicines to dispense, soup to make and whatever else needed cooking, and ten patients to serve. To speak to the doctor meant a run of over a mile to the phone and back, but it had to do done."[124] But if the Ukrainians appreciated the women's hard work and cheerful concern, they did not repay the WMS by joining the Methodist Church. Whatever rewards the work brought were never measured in Methodists.

The dearth of converts failed to deter the women working in the west, many of whom apparently were quite satisfied with their careers in Alberta. Chace, for example, remained in Alberta until she retired in 1943. She was, as Elizabeth Ross put it after a visit to the field in 1911, "a B.A. wiping up the floor, caring for [her] own horse, driving eight miles through intense cold to visit one house."[125] Ten others (26 per cent) worked for the society until they retired. Their careers averaged 30 years, compared to the average of 12.7 years for all WMS missionaries assigned to Alberta. Ten women resigned to marry ranchers, ministers, or missionaries they met through their work. One woman resumed a teaching career; another joined the Alberta Department of Neglected Children, a position for which missionary work had obviously equipped her. Three died on duty and another three were forced to resign when they became ill; although these casualties seem to have derived from random illness, there was proportionately higher attrition from sickness and death in Alberta than among the WMS missionaries in China.

The women seldom stayed in the same mission station throughout their careers but, like their foreign counterparts, were shifted from one posting to another as need dictated. Perhaps variety made their calling more interesting, and helps to explain why a relatively large proportion of these women made missionary work in Alberta a lifetime career. The isolation and hardships seemed to challenge some of the women, and their strong friendships and pride in their independence enabled them to cope with extremely daunting situations. At the same time, their education and work experience appear to have made them more flexible than their less well-educated associates who staffed the Indian missions. Finally, because they were not overly obsessed with gaining converts, they may have been less frustrated than the women in Victoria, who measured achievement by the numbers who claimed to have become Christians. The grateful response of the immigrant community, not the occasional conversion that so often proved to be in name only, was the source of whatever satisfaction WMS missionaries in northern Alberta derived from their work.

The perspective of the other WMS missionaries designated to work among recent immigrants in cities and towns across Canada was likewise marked by an interest in helping and teaching the casualties of Canada's increasingly serious urban and industrial social problems. The women were not, it is important to note, among the most vocal social activists dedicated to changing the nature and structure of Canadian society; for the most part the WMS urban missionaries were satisfied with traditional Methodist evangelical and educational measures to try to ameliorate the destructive consequences of increased immigration and urbanization. The WMS began its inner-city immigrant work in Toronto at the Elm Street mission in the heart of the city's Italian community. From 1911 to 1925 five women were employed in three Toronto missions to staff kindergartens, Sunday schools, night schools, and mothers' meetings. Later a woman was hired to work in the Hamilton Italian community. But to the despair of the WMS, the Italians, like other immigrant groups, turned to the missions predominately for English classes, not for the "cultural soirees and hymn singing" designed to bring them to Christ.[126]

At about the same time, the WMS sent Hannah Paul, who had already been employed among the Indians in British Columbia, to the immigrant mining community in the Crows' Nest Pass area. Paul settled first in Frank, but after the devastating earthslide in 1912, she relocated in the nearby town of Fernie. Eventually she devised a scheme to spend a week in Fernie and the next in Natal and Michel. Like the women in northern Alberta, she provided assistance wherever she could with the expectation that her example would improve the lives of those in the vicinity. But she appears to have been more comfortable with conventional solutions for the immigrants' problems. Most of her messages to her employers focused on drunkenness, which she was determined to eliminate and which the Board of Managers agreed was "the great enemy of the community."[127]

Within its traditional parameters, WMS urban missionary work provided useful services and recreational outlets for the people within its reach. A typical week's activities recorded by an anonymous missionary working in an urban area with a large ethnic population, probably Edmonton, included: "Sunday. two sessions of Sunday School total average attendance 105. Monday aft. classes in Eng. for the women – the men attend night school in the Coll. Inst. evening – Jr c.g.i.t. – 'Wide Awake Group'- Tuesday aft – Baby Clinic – aver. attendance 20–25, Doctor and city nurse are in charge, after school Mission Band and Kitchen Garden. evening – c.g.i.t. 'Golden Rule Group'. Wednesday Aft – Women's Meeting. Thursday Aft. Eng. Classes Frid. Eve. Sr. c.g.i.t. – 'Blue Birds' Remainder of time spent in paying calls or receiving callers."[128] But whether women like Paul and others stationed by themselves in towns like North Bay, Welland, Copper Cliff, or Sudbury were able to provide much support for the many immigrants in their constituencies seems more problematical.

The immigrants' reactions to the women's gestures on their behalf are not well-documented, and it is difficult to know whether they distinguished clearly among the various denominational and philanthropic groups so eager to minister to their needs. Could a sick woman who spoke no English understand that a wms missionary was an agent of God while a public-health nurse was merely a municipal employee? Moreover, even in cases when their work might have benefited and expenses been reduced by increased co-operation with either the General Board or another Protestant church, the women were reluctant to become too closely associated with the General Board missionaries. Consequently, the work of the Methodist Church as a whole may have suffered, because the two groups appear to have co-operated far less in Canada than they did abroad. In Regina, where Nellie Forman worked alone for many years, only the Sunday school was considered of "much consequence."[129] The women's intensely autonomous stance may have been partly to blame. For instance, in 1925 Annie Hind staunchly endorsed separate wms interests in Welland even after the resident General Board missionary, with whom she might have co-operated, guaranteed that "[his] work would not interfere in any way with her work ... for the simple reason that a man could not do the required work among women and girls."[130]

Eighteen women spent most of their years of employment engaged in this diverse urban work; two others began as urban missionaries but were transferred to overseas posts after church union in 1925. The average employment for these twenty women was 21.1 years, the highest of any phase of home missionary work. In addition, eleven of the twenty remained as wms employees until retirement; their careers averaged 32 years. There may be no better explanation for this high survival rate than a comfortable environment, a sense of security, and the relative proximity of family and friends. Based on their own analyses, urban missionaries were the centre of attention in their neighbourhoods, and although they may not always have had close personal friends nearby, they were very much a part of the community. Their presence did not go unnoticed among grateful people who repaid their kindness in produce, eggs, chickens, or whatever else was considered appropriate. In turn, the relatively congenial reception given to these women seems to have encouraged them and contributed to their satisfaction with their work. Because these women functioned independently and in most cases were responsible directly to the Board of Managers, some of their professional fulfilment may have derived from an opportunity to act on their own initiative, largely absent even in overseas mission fields, where a strict hierarchy based on seniority was in place. Finally, as a group these women were better qualified than other home missionaries. At least three (15 per cent) had attended university, and eight (40 per cent) were trained teachers. As an indication of their personal stake in the work, several women used their furloughs to visit Italy or eastern Europe for a first-hand encounter with the homelands of their constituents.[131] Only three women married, which suggests that missionaries in urban areas may have been very career-conscious and less driven by the prevailing winds of maternal feminism to assume the more confining role of wife and mother.

At the opposite end of the spectrum in terms of perseverance were the women assigned to the society's Indian missions in southern Alberta and northern British Columbia, where they confronted substantially more material deprivation and emotional suffering than any other group of WMS workers. Their difficulties were compounded because they were, collectively, the least prepared for their arduous assignments. But even if the outcome of their encounter as missionaries among the Indians was vastly different from that of their colleagues in other fields, some aspects of their backgrounds corresponded to those of all WMS missionaries. Thirty (56 per cent) of the fifty-four women employed in Indian missions were from Ontario, nine (16 per cent) from the Maritimes, and five from British Columbia. Like their associates, most women (74 per cent) for whom the appropriate data were available had lived in small towns or rural areas. Eight (14.8 per cent) had close relatives associated with the ministry, a figure just slightly lower than the 19 per cent for all home missionaries but significantly less than the 25 per cent of all WMS missionaries with clerical associations.

Although records are incomplete for many Indian workers, it seems that only two, Mary Lawson and Lottie Deacon, both Maritimers, had attended university. Deacon, who enrolled at Mount Allison with a WMS scholarship to support her future career, was initially stationed in Japan. She arrived in northern British Columbia by default when the debilitating atmosphere of Japan forced her to return to Canada and a supposedly easier posting.[132] Just seven WMS Indian missionaries (13 per cent), five of whom were stationed at Port Simpson, where the society had some responsibility for the education of native children, had the teaching experience typical of other WMS missionaries. The preparation of missionaries for Indian work seems all the more deficient because only five women appear to have attended the Methodist Training School, where they would have been familiarized with the routines and problems of missionary life, expanded their perception of their roles as missionaries to the Indians, and received an extra infusion of Methodist piety. Five women, three of whom were attached to the Port Simpson hospital, were trained nurses. One woman had been a music teacher, and Alice Jackson, like Kezia Hendrie, the first WMS Indian missionary, was a dressmaker by trade. For the others, there is no record of previous work experience, if they had it; indeed, the society may not have considered time spent in the work-force as a necessary condition of employment in Indian missions. There were, in fact, few occupations that would have armed recruits for the vicissitudes of the remote Indian communities.

Many women stationed among the Indians quickly became disenchanted with their chosen vocation. They hated living and working in semi-isolation among the native people; they excoriated native culture and dismissed native religion as paganism. In short, the degree of personal adaptation and privation required for Indian missionary work seems to have been more acute than for missionaries in Japan or China. In turn, the recurrent resignations and the abbreviated careers frustrated any long- or short-term designs the Board of Managers might have had for the future of the society's Indian missions.

In the 1880s the Methodist Church was optimistic about the prospect of converting and assimilating native people. As soon as the WMS was functioning, it assumed a substantial financial obligation for work with Indians. Its special interest was Thomas Crosby's work in Port Simpson because his wife, a native of Hamilton, was a close friend of several board members. In fact, Kezia Hendrie, a dressmaker for a Brantford department store who became the society's first emissary to the Indians, was hired as matron at the newly opened girls' school at Port Simpson not by the WMS but by Crosby, who had been working since 1871 as the first full-time Methodist missionary in northern British Columbia.[133]

When the WMS allocated five hundred dollars as Hendrie's salary, she was designated their agent.[134] But while Martha Cartmell's departure as the society's first foreign missionary was publicized and apotheosized, Hendrie's journey, in the autumn of 1882, to the British Columbia wilderness went almost unnoticed.[135] This was in part because Hendrie was not a prolific correspondent, perhaps as a consequence of her rather limited education and the heavy demands of her work. For several years Mrs Crosby supplied the society with the necessary details about the mission. From these letters it seems that Hendrie's duties as matron consisted of the upkeep and administration of the home and teaching the girls basic housekeeping skills. Because the girls attended the nearby public school, she was not responsible for their academic training.[136]

By 1885 Hendrie had thirteen girls under her care. "Many things in connection with the 'Home' [were]," she complained, "very trying and unpleasant," but she had learned "many precious lessons and [was] getting better acquainted with Jesus."[137] Hendrie's own salvation was especially important to her, all the more so because, as a former class leader,[138] she must have been intensely influenced by the Methodist ideal of Christian perfection. The climax of her term in Port Simpson was her own spiritual awakening, "a gracious spiritual blessing which the better fitted her for her missionary labours." The transformation occurred when "one morning Kezia wandered alone into the woods and kneeling beside a log spent many hours in communion with God. The power of the Holy Spirit came upon her in a wonderful way. When she returned to the camp the girls soon recognized a change in her appearance ... Kezia told them the Spirit of God was present in power and bade them gather in her tent for prayer ... a sense of the presence of the Lord was felt by all." But her strong faith did not make supervising the girls either easy or personally rewarding. Hendrie was extremely distraught when, as she discreetly put it, the "large girls became so reckless and dissatisfied that several ... left without permission."[139] Back in their communities, the girls' inevitable fate was early marriage, an outrage to Christian principles that the home had been founded explicitly to prevent.[140]

In an attempt to improve "spiritual and temporal" conditions, Hendrie met with eager and interested girls and women in the native community once a week, but the gatherings proved more useful in relieving the monotony of her own life as matron; there was little discernible change in the native women's habits.[141] One of Hendrie's rare success stories was Annie, a woman "with a sinstained soul and a disease-stricken body" who had returned from Victoria, apparently to die.[142] As a friend recalled, "When Kezia first went to see [Annie] ... she turned to the wall her face, which a sense of shame had led her to cover. Hoping by kindness to awaken some response to the love which yearned to tell of a Christ who had given his life to save not the righteous, but helpless, hopeless sinners, Kezia took her flowers and tempting morsels of food ... as the story of the love of God was told, weeping for her sins Annie listened and believed. Being assured of forgiveness she longed to die and passed away happy in the knowledge that the sins which had been 'as scarlet' were 'as white as snow.'"[143]

At the end of 1885 Hendrie resigned to marry Edward Nicholas, a General Board missionary at a nearby Indian village whom she had met shortly after her arrival.[144] The couple remained in northern British Columbia for many years. There was no comment from the society about the marriage, and Hendrie was immediately replaced by Agnes Knight of Halifax, whose academic credentials were little better. Knight introduced a very strict disciplinary code to keep the girls in check. "We have," she wrote, "bedroom, dining-room, kitchen and washroom rules, also general rules, or a timetable giving the hour for everything, from the rising-bell to bed-time."[145] She also assumed a special obligation to protect the older girls from the promiscuous life led by the Tsimshian in the area.[146] In 1887, when Knight became seriously ill, a second worker, Sarah Hart, also from Nova Scotia, was hired to assist in caring for the twenty girls then in the home. Thereafter the home continued to be supervised by at least two missionaries.

The WMS also supported an Indian mission station at Chilliwack, British Columbia, and the McDougall orphanage at Morley, Alberta. Grants of two hundred to seven hundred dollars were made to Morley, but the WMS did not hire a worker there until 1904, when Hannah Buehler of Kitchener, Ontario, was appointed to help the Indian women in the area. Two years later the WMS sent a former Japanese missionary, Margaret Laing, a nurse, to the Morley hospital, where she remained for four years.[147] Buehler held meetings to persuade the native women to "mend their ways"[148] and give up their indigenous customs. Her efforts, she reported, were successful: "Some of the women are anxious to have tables, pretty dishes, make cakes and puddings," and they were becoming more thrifty. However successful Buehler may have thought she was at introducing native women to Canadian ways, when she resigned to serve independently as an unpaid deaconess in the same vicinity, the society abandoned its enterprise at Morley.[149]

The society's missionary work at the Coqualeetza Institute in Chilliwack was more extensive. In 1885 the society gave four hundred dollars to help the General Board to establish an industrial training school for Indian children. The following year it contributed two thousand dollars towards a new building; when the structure was completed, the board hired Lavinia Clarke as matron. Four women spent brief terms at the institute. But by 1900 the services of the WMS missionaries had been withdrawn, although the Board of Managers was still willing, if necessary, to provide financial help to the General Board to maintain the institute.[150] In 1889 the society opened a second Indian girls' home in Kitamaat, a native community 160 miles southeast of Port Simpson. Over time, at least seventeen women worked here as matrons, teachers, and dressmakers.[151] The society also supported nurses at Hazelton and Bella Coola in British Columbia, and in 1913 Alice Jackson was sent from Kitamaat to Nelson House in northern Manitoba to establish a mission for native people in the area.

While the missionaries' educational deficiencies and their limited exposure to the world of work may have made their jobs more difficult under the best of circumstances, the inhospitable environments of Port Simpson, Chilliwack, and Kitamaat made the experience even harder and more disagreeable. In 1906 the Methodist Church smugly pointed to Port Simpson as the most progressive and advanced of all Indian settlements in British Columbia: "The Indians, of whom there are some 800, representing eight or ten tribes, are Methodists. In addition to a fine church, a mission house, our Boys' Home, the Crosby Girls' Home, and a hospital, this village boasts of a fire hall, two stories high, with a tower; a two-story drill hall, a sash and door factory, a shingle mill and a turning mill, both worked by water power, and an excellent brass band."[152] All this was quite accurate, but during the early period of the WMS mission's existence, life at Port Simpson had few of the advantages of Tokyo or Chengtu, where the women formed close friendships among their colleagues and the larger European community.

Elizabeth Long's trials at Kitamaat in 1899 were typical of the exigencies of Indian mission work. The first mission home had outdoor plumbing; the water supply from a nearby stream had to be carried uphill for half a mile, and sometimes in summer the stream dried up entirely.[153] If Japanese and Chinese boarding schools lacked little in the way of physical inducements to encourage parents to send the children to Christian schools, in sharp contrast, many children at the Coqualeetza Institute slept on the floor. The native parents promised to provide all the clothing their children needed, but the society often had to help, and the Indian missions relied on bales sent by wms auxiliaries. Myrtle Burpee appealed to her friends to donate pillows, towels and "every variety of goods and clothing" for the children.[154] These bundles were especially welcome if they did not contain cast-off evening clothes. When used clothing was received, the girls were taught to make it over. There is no evidence that the wms missionaries were guilty of selling or trading the clothing for Indian handicrafts and furs, as some General Board missionaries allegedly had done.[155]

Conditions at Port Simpson improved after 1892, when a new home was built, located just off the Indian reserve, as the women had requested. At maximum capacity the three-storey frame house accommodated forty-five to fifty girls, some orphans and others placed in the home by parents who paid for their care and instruction. But of necessity the regimen in the homes at Port Simpson and Kitamaat continued to be very rigorous for staff and students. For example, the diet for missionaries and students alike was usually little more than adequate. Most Indian schools had their own gardens and cows, but at Port Simpson, where the climate was too severe to sustain much agricultural development, even native foods – salmon, seaweed, fish and game – had to be purchased for the children. The missionaries did not impose their own tastes on the children, largely because, as they had discovered, it was healthier for the girls to eat as they had been accustomed, but also because it was so expensive to obtain other than native fare.[156] Even though they could barely tolerate the stench, the wms missionaries used oolachan grease, a form of fish oil, in cooking because they observed a deterioration in the girls' health if they were deprived of it.[157] The girls themselves were taught to dry and salt fish for the winter. At Kitamaat, in one season they smoked thirty thousand small fish for their own use.[158] The missionaries also, however, encouraged the girls to bake bread and cakes to serve at the tea parties that were a regular feature in the home.

Communication between the missionaries and the native children must have been extremely difficult and frustrating because the girls neither spoke nor understood English when they first entered the home and there were no native teachers at the schools. The missionaries had little if any training in the Tsimshian dialect. Adjustment was mostly on the side of the Indians. The missionaries reported that the girls quickly learned to speak English. As well, the girls were taught to "make and keep in repair all their own garments," and they performed "most of the manual labor connected with the house-keeping."[159]

The guiding principle of WMS Indian institutions was "exact obedience [from] every pupil, irrespective of personal inclination; and to so blend love and firmness, hard work and recreation, that every girl will voluntarily choose the discipline and restraint instead of the free idle life."[160] According to Lavinia Clarke, stationed first at Chilliwack and then Port Simpson, the girls' spiritual welfare should always "take first place ... failure to lead our girls into a true Christian life means failure in all we value most." To this end the girls were instructed every day in Bible history, Methodist doctrines, and catechism, and they regularly attended religious services. But Clarke had to admit that "all [had] not been victory, and our girls have need to be sorry more times than we could wish."[161] Twenty years later an unidentified missionary noted that the work at Port Simpson "ha[d] to be done largely in faith, with the hope that in the future a harvest will be reaped. The worker needs all the love and patience and tact of a mother, and that toward children who not only are not her own, but who are of a different race. All womanly virtues, graces and accomplishments can find scope here."[162] But in spite of the WMS's stress on developing ideal womanly qualities among its wards, some missionaries themselves wanted similar hallmarks of true womanhood.

The women were convinced that the Indians' quality of life, at least judged by Canadian standards, would improve immeasurably if the girls were "better mothers, pure minded, with the grace of God implanted so deeply in their hearts that it will influence their whole lives; mothers who will not be content to bring up their families amidst surroundings which will fill their minds with thoughts of evil even at a tender age; mothers who by cleanliness and industry will make their houses home-like and attractive, not mere stopping places; educated mothers who will see the need of education for their children, and who will do their utmost to give them that advantage, and who will not love them in a blind, selfish way, thinking only of the present."[163] Yet although the society reiterated these arguments promoting the education of Indian girls, the emphasis in the WMS homes was not on scholarship. Little pressure was ever put on the native girls to excel in academic matters, possibly because most missionaries believed that Indians were incapable of academic achievement and, indeed, had no desire or need for higher education.

Given their denunciations of native people, it is not surprising that the women do not seem to have become attached to the girls under their care. They did not adopt orphan girls, as WMS missionaries had done in China. Margaret Butcher, a respected member of the Kitamaat staff, believed that obedience to her was an absolute necessity if she were to succeed with the girls. The children were not "vicious" or "wicked," but, Butcher reminded wms members in 1917, they were still "the second generation from pure heathenism."[164] The reaction of Mrs Redner, who arrived in Port Simpson in 1893, was not unusual: "It [was] much easier," Redner had discovered, "to see the defects than to make any permanent improvement, and I am only surprised that the teachers have succeeded as well as they have with this class of people. Their dispositions and habits are so very different from those of white people that we need not expect the same results from our efforts to improve them."[165] Two months later, perhaps prompted by the Board of Managers, which was always sensitive to public opinion, Redner reported a change of heart. Her job had become more enjoyable because she now had some insight into the problems that her charges faced growing up in Indian society, where "there is so much to keep them down, and such terrible temptations for young girls, that this Home seems to be a blessed refuge for them. They do not appreciate it very much, it is true, but that is nothing to us; our work is for the Master, and I hope will meet with his approval."[166] When she had been at Port Simpson almost a year, the sewing teacher, Ellen Beavis, acknowledged a gradual improvement in behaviour, but it was measured in small things. For example, if she left the sewing room for ten minutes, the girls no longer stole the needles, thimbles, "or anything we might happen to have on our sewing table."[167] Only a few women appear to have overcome the intolerance and aversion that characterized Canadians' attitudes towards native people.

While the missionaries aspired to remake the girls under their care into model Victorian housewives and mothers, they recognized the girls' moral and physical welfare as an immediate priority. The women agreed that removing girls to mission homes was the only possible way to safeguard them from a wretched future such as that faced by an eight-year-old girl who was married to a man from another tribe and sent away from her home.[168] To add to the missionaries' list of grievances, the homes were not adequately financed or staffed to train the girls as the missionaries recommended. Hannah Paul, who was especially concerned about the limited facilities of the home at Port Simpson, begged wms auxiliary members for generous support to Indian missions. "If those at home fully realized the position of these poor Indian girls, as we do who are in the field, that the only way to save them from a life of immorality and make of them intelligent Christian women is by taking them into some such Home as this, where they are shielded from temptation surely the money would be forthcoming to establish homes among other tribes ... I reasoned that if these girls could learn house work, knitting, sewing, fancy work, they could learn at school if they were only interested." Paul, for one, did not think that the Indian girls were inherently stupid. She had "succeeded beyond [her] expectations in arousing in them a desire for knowledge. They have a natural talent for music. They are also very observant and can copy almost anything."[169] Others, like Sarah Alton, disagreed; the Indian girls, who were "not as intelligent as the men," were incapable of formal learning.[170]

The girls' disobedience and immorality, notably promiscuity and stealing, disturbed the missionaries, but it was the sickness in the home that most frequently brought the women to the breaking point. Illness and death became a familiar and unnerving part of every missionary's experience in Port Simpson, as the home was continually ravaged by uncontrollable epidemics of contagious diseases – measles, whooping cough, and influenza. Hendrie was tormented by the deaths of the younger children, especially one, Dollie Robinson, "the most unloving, ill-natured child" that she had ever known but who, in the face of death, had repented her sins.[171] In October 1891 Sarah Hart, whose kindness and tolerance towards the children was envied by the other women, reported that every child in the Port Simpson home had whooping cough. "These last days seem[ed] like a terrible dream." Hart, who had never seen anyone die before, was overwhelmed. After the death of a little girl Hart "could scarcely believe it was death; I had never seen it come before ... when I came into the room and found the woman with the child's body in her arms, it was almost more than I could stand."[172]

Episodes like this left the women emotionally and physically drained. As Redner wrote during an outbreak of influenza in 1896, "the constant watchfulness necessary to properly guard these children leaves but little rest for the body and none for the mind, except time spent in sleep."[173] For Myrtle Burpee, the greatest pleasure of her furlough was "on retiring to know that there will be no half-past five bell in the morning to wake me to another day's routine."[174] Whether the women liked the children or not, they took their responsibility for the children's welfare very seriously, all the more so because of the repercussions that deaths and illness might have in the Indian community, which was already suspicious of missionary medical practices and intervention.

The situation of missionaries in the northern settlements improved only very slowly. When the Elizabeth Long Home at Kitamaat was opened in 1908 after the former home had burned, the women finally had indoor plumbing, with "all sewage ... carried to tide water by a large drain pipe."[175] But the material improvements did nothing to better the atmosphere of the mission homes. Although there were usually four or five women staffing each home, there was little of the intense friendship among the women that was a feature of overseas mission fields, probably because of the frequency of resignations. The camaraderie described by the women in Japan was strikingly absent in northern British Columbia. Quite the contrary – on more than one occasion women were transferred because they did not get along with their associates.[176]

The women organized social activities, especially during the holiday season, for the Indian communities, but they did not really care to become involved with other residents of the area, the majority of whom were rough and ready unattached men. Consequently, the women had to come to terms with their isolation and recognize that a trip to Vancouver was a yearly treat to be taken in the summer when the girls had returned to their families. Alice Jackson, who arrived in Kitamaat in 1900, was one of a few women missionaries who came to appreciate, even enjoy, their isolation. Removed from the company of others, Jackson found it was "natural to turn to something else; that is why I think all nature has a new meaning to me and I enjoy it as never before – the sea, the mountains, and the flowers and trees all seem to be real friends."[177] Jackson adapted well to living alone. She left Kitamaat in 1913 for Nelson House in northern Manitoba, where she spent the next thirteen years working by herself, travelling extensively by dogsled to nurse the Indians in the vicinity, even in sub-zero temperatures. Usually she was "happy and content." There had been, she admitted, "lonely hours, but, for these and all I am deprived of, there have been abundant compensations ... Suffering relieved, a sick one made more comfortable, a mother's fears removed, sad and lonely hearts comfortable and strengthened, sympathy given, hungry ones fed and little children made happy."[178]

The shortage of recreational facilities also meant that outdoor activities and games became of necessity an important part of the routine of Indian mission homes. As J.A. Mangan argues, Victorians believed that organized games and team sports should be "much more than mere entertainment for leisure hours. They were a significant instrument of moral training."[179] Some leisure pursuits were instituted for the missionaries' benefit as much as their charges'. At Kitamaat, for example, in summer the women took the girls camping at a nearby ranch owned by Methodist friends. Elizabeth Anderson Varley, daughter of the ranchers, recalled that for everyone these were happy and relaxing breaks from the controlled routine.[180] Varley's own impressions of the missionaries are worth mentioning. She reminisced about the mission home as the scene of happy Christmas concerts where Santa presented everyone with the requisite candy, nuts, and oranges, but neither Varley nor her brother really liked the women missionaries.[181] As she remembered nearly seventy-five years later, "There were few men who came to the ranch that we children did not like. There were few women from the Mission that we did. Most men teased us, which brought out the worst in us, and this worst was increased against the visiting ladies from the Mission, who tried to counteract the 'bad influence' of the men by imposing disciplined good manners."[182]

The affectations of one missionary at Kitamaat for a period of rest as part of her furlough from Japan were particularly irksome to young Elizabeth. Among her other peculiarities, the woman objected to the use of the word "bull" in front of the children, preferring instead the euphemism "gentleman cow," which she felt was more suitable for civilized and refined conversation. Elizabeth's father, normally polite to all the women from the mission, was "overheard ... to say to [her] mother, 'I find the expression "gentleman cow" disgusting. The children don't have to mention the bull at the table, if it's offensive, but I'll not have either of them saying "gentleman cow.""[183] This misplaced puritanism may seem merely amusing and somewhat ludicrous given the frontier atmosphere of Kitamaat. But far more serious and disturbing, even to the child Elizabeth, was the same woman's unconcealed disdain for the Indian girls and her abuse of young Elizabeth, to whom she briefly gave piano lessons.[184] Obviously this was the way the woman believed children should be dealt with, and while a white child sensed that the woman was odd and nasty, an Indian child might not have understood.

At the schools and homes, work and discipline were always "the law." According to Lavinia Clarke, there was "no place in our economy for idlers."[185] Clarke herself set such a splendid example that in 1902 she was forced to resign because she was "very tired and cannot summon strength to do everything up to the mark I set myself." To the end she remained convinced that her approach had been right, professing that "a life fully consecrated to God, in every relation is the only one, and my word to the sisterhood is to *live* and *serve*. Go, therefore, and teach and Jesus will be with you even to the end."[186]

Within two years Clarke was dead, and her death, like that of Elizabeth Long in 1907, was unanimously attributed to her arduous work for the WMS. Long's devotion to "her people" was praised at length; she was eulogized as a woman who realized "Ruskin's ideal of true womanhood in that 'she must be enduringly, incorrupt-ibly good, instinctively, infallibly wise – wise not for self-development but for self-renunciation; wise, not with the narrowness of insolent and loveless pride, but with the passionate gentleness of an infinitely variable, because infinitely applicable, modesty of service – the true changefulness of woman.'" According to Mrs Carman, the author of this screed, women like Long were irrefutable testimony to women's place in the Church; a Church that ignored "the value of woman's ministry in its missions" did so at its peril.[187] But this sort of praise lavished on Long and others who died in harness could not relieve the isolation and hardship of the women at Port Simpson and Kita-maat, whose brief careers attest to the severity of their experience.

Twenty-three (43 per cent) of the fifty-four women stationed among native peoples resigned within 3 years of joining the society's ranks. In total, thirty-seven women (68 per cent) worked for 5 years or less. While the average career length for all home missionaries was just over 12 years, women assigned to Indian missions worked an average of 7.5 years. Moreover, only five women remained in Indian missions until their retirement. They served an average of 30 years; among them was Lottie Deacon, who remained at Port Simpson until 1940. Two others were teachers; a fourth had been a nurse, and the fifth was Alice Jackson. Many women left for the same reasons as mis-sionaries in other fields: marriage, illness, and death. However, in nearly half (twenty-six, or 48 per cent) the cases, no reason was cited. Because the women were liable to repay some of their initial travel expenses to the society if they resigned during their first term, their decision was reached very carefully in the face of complete frustration and disappointment with Indian missionary work.

Some, like Kezia Hendrie and Sarah Hart, married missionaries and remained in the area, but others married ranchers or farmers whom they met while in northern British Columbia and severed their connections with missionary work in the area. The Board of Man-agers did not always approve of these alliances. A case in point is Dr Dorothea Bower, who has not been included in the statistical analysis of the WMS missionaries because of inadequate documentation of her career.[188] According to Elizabeth Varley, Bower, a recent graduate of Trinity Medical College, arrived in Kitamaat in 1904 as a WMS mis-sionary to practise medicine in the area and to take charge of the girls' home.[189] Bower became a close friend of the Anderson family. At their house she met Jack Fountain, one of "the stream of men who passed over the trail." Fountain, Varley recalled, "arrived at the ranch one night in desperate condition, ill and exhausted, with a forearm in an advanced state of blood poisoning from devil's club ... My father rowed over to the village and fetched Dr. Bower. Doctor and patient remained in the Anderson home until Mr. Fountain was recovered beyond the necessity of medical care ... Not only did Dr. Bower save the life of Jack Fountain but his arm as well." The couple became engaged and married, but "when news of the engagement leaked out, tongues wagged up and down the coast. Jack Fountain was much older than Dora, and not religious ... a real northern B.C. type,"[190] and hardly a suitable husband for a missionary.

Because Bower's behaviour was a discredit to the society, it appears that her name was dropped from the roster of missionaries after her morganatic marriage. Leda Caldwell, too, was disowned by the society when, several years after her resignation had been requested because the native community at Port Simpson complained about the way the school was being operated, she began privately to solicit funds for the Indians in British Columbia.[191] Another woman resigned from her work at Kitamaat in the midst of a bitter dispute between the two mission boards over the division of work and responsibility in the area. The struggle of "two societies with two distinct heads living in a very limited area, controlling 250 people at variance" created open hostility reminiscent of the Japan Affair between the WMS missionaries at the home and the General Board missionary.[192]

There were, then, a variety of circumstances contributing to the exodus of WMS personnel, but it appears that the exhausting nature of the work alone, without other complicating factors, was enough to discourage even the most buoyant recruit. As one General Board missionary at Kitamaat was provoked to write to a fellow minister, "had I a daughter qualified for mission work I should do all I could to dissuade her from entering the employ of any society whose policy it was to require of their workers what is required of [the WMS at Port Simpson]."[193]

For most of the women who staffed the WMS Indian missions, the reality of their careers was far removed from their expectations. That so many of them persisted less than three years and only five reached retirement seems ample proof that Indian missions were by far the most debilitating field at home or abroad. The few who endured the hardship of the environment and were able, at the same time, to shed some of their conventional middle-class attitudes and prejudices were exceptional women by any standards. They seemed to sense that they were capable of work that other women could not, and would not, attempt. In short, they perceived themselves as working women, not just do-gooders. As Alice Jackson wrote from Nelson House in 1922 at the age of fifty-nine, after she had plastered her sitting room, "As

I was working away at it I often thought of the tasks women did in war days. I thought we surely ought to be just as willing to do hard work for our beloved Missionary Society."[194] But Jackson, who was genuinely happy travelling with her dog team even in −50° temperatures to tend the sick, usually had no time to ponder the dimensions of her career.

Lizzie Donogh, who after much soul-searching resigned from the WMS after four years' service, was not as convinced as Jackson that working as a missionary in British Columbia was what God had intended or what she was suited for. In the final weeks before she left Kitamaat she felt "so wretched" but still managed to continue with her work. It eventually became "more and more of a drag tho', and [she felt] that it would be very unjust to the other workers as well as to the Society and to [herself] to continue too long."[195] In a gloomy letter to the society's president she related her sad encounters:

Sunday morning, while we were at church, a little girl 2 years old died, just choked with cold. I left here early, thinking I would call to see another sick child before [Sunday School] to find that the wee laddie had gone. There was great wailing and crying, but when on Monday night another little 3 year old girl died, and this morning a tiny baby, the whole village is panic stricken, five babies within a week, in a place this size, is awful ... Today I have attended two funerals and visited the house where the two other deaths were. It was awful, on one side of the stove, on a bed on the floor, sat one mother frantically trying to quiet her sick babe, near her on a table lay the body of the little girl who died last night ... on another bed on the floor sat the other mother and father nursing a child who was too sick to keep her eyes open, and near them on another table lay the little babe that had died a few hours before. The place was dirty and untidy as you can imagine and all around sat the old women wailing and mourning ...

March 6th 1912. on the SS "Vadao": ... I am really trying not to worry about things but it seems as tho we had just reached the limit at Kitamaat. Another child in the village died since I wrote the fore part of this letter ... Sunday 3rd about 7:30 we were startled by fire in the village. There are only 2 men of any strength in the village and three or four boys. So I left the Home brigade to go to carry water. I stayed to care for the little tots. They were so frightened ... all the homes were safe with the exception of one, but our church was burned to the ground ... Just as I came on board the body of a Kitamaat young man was carried ashore, being brought home from the logging camp, so the ladies will have a funeral to look after unless Mr. Anderson comes to the rescue.[196]

Donogh went home to Mount Forest, Ontario. The following year she returned to Kitamaat to marry a rancher and remained in the area for many more years, but she clearly had been disillusioned by her experiences with the wms.

In 1898 Alexander Sutherland referred an application from a missionary hopeful, Jennie Elliott, to Elizabeth Strachan with the observation that "her education seems to be rather defective, but that would not interfere with her particular work if she is competent to do it. Her health certificate is good, and she seems to be a pious girl, so I imagine you will run no serious risk in sending her to Pt. Simpson."[197] Elliott was hired and, typically, remained in Port Simpson five years before resigning. Twenty years later the Board of Managers continued to look to "college and normal school students and graduates" to work among "the young women of the East, who need the wealth of intellect and heart which you have to offer,"[198] but it never encouraged these same educated young women to remain in Canada as home missionaries.

The board failed to grasp that the self-confidence, independence, administrative skills, and social adaptability that usually accompanied a university degree were essential qualifications for success in any phase of missionary work. If certain aspects of home missionary work were less productive than the Board of Managers had anticipated, it can largely be attributed to the high turnover in the personnel of home missions. More bas cleaning the floors of home mission stations would, in the long run, have strengthened and stabilized wms home missionary work.

CHAPTER SIX

The elect sisterhood

In 1932 a wide-ranging and much debated critique of Protestant missions entitled *Re-Thinking Missions: A Layman's Inquiry after One Hundred Years* appeared. Arguing that the character of the agents affected the nature of the work, it assailed the spiritual and professional calibre of the men and women engaged in the world-wide missionary enterprise. The report contended that for every missionary "of conspicuous power, true saintliness and a sublime spirit of devotion," there were many more "of limited outlook and capacity ... whose vision of the inner meaning of the mission [had] become obscured by the intricacies, divisions, frictions and details of a task too great for their powers and their hearts."[1] In short, as William Hutchison has concluded from the report, the bid to "combine Christian service with the drive to make converts had too often led to the commissioning of second-rate doctors, educators, agronomists, and social workers, or else had distorted and deflected the energies of first-rate ones."[2]

The probe singled out unmarried women for particularly critical comment. Although some of them embodied "the highest values in the missionary field, and ... [were] contented in their work and healthfully adjusted to their environment ... breakdowns from emotional crises, the development of neurasthenic states and even more serious disturbances [were] by no means infrequent." The source of these "disturbances" was, the report argued, "the abnormality of the missionary's life ... [which] is accentuated, in the case of the unmarried women, by the lack of family ties and domestic responsibilities on the one hand, and of the social and recreational outlets of the professional woman ... on the other. There is little to shift the focus of her attention from routine mission work, and the consequence is a tendency to become mission-centric in a dangerous degree."[3] Based on the evidence of the foregoing chapters, the assumption that missionary work was an aberrant career for single women and that spinster missionaries were social misfits whose mental and physical problems were exacerbated by the isolation of the mission field seems wrong-headed.

The suggestion that women missionaries were anomalies seems scarcely applicable to the WMS professionals whose careers provided not only a satisfactory alternative to marriage but an opportunity afforded to few Canadian women of the time to develop professional and administrative skills. The close friendships within the individual mission stations and the widespread sense of sisterhood throughout the society forged, as the Japan Affair demonstrated, a strong and supportive women's network. In turn this solidarity, rooted in the female sphere, gave the women considerable leverage within the patriarchal religious institution from which they operated. By creating another separate sphere for themselves where neither their spinsterhood nor their gender was a bar to their success, they came much closer to equality with men inside and outside the Methodist Church than was permissible for most women of the same generation and background. WMS missionary work was respected, envied, and even feared by the women's male counterparts.

None the less, some of the concerns raised in the Layman's Report are relevant to the WMS experience. In its haste to be represented on the missionary stage the society not infrequently dispatched ill-prepared or unsuitable candidates, especially to its home mission stations. Although the society tried, as far as possible, to assign candidates to positions consistent with their talents and inclinations, recruits with the lowest qualifications were always overrepresented in Canada, to the detriment of the work. As well, the society's problems in attracting and retaining women doctors, top-rate or not, for the mission in West China determined the nature and course of WMS missionary work there. Equally, the missionaries' inability to jettison their middle-class convictions and Western cultural baggage seems in retrospect to have prevented them from extending the society's help to those most in need, that is, women at the very bottom of the social scale. Worse, the Canadian women could be thoughtlessly imperious. For example, Eliza Marshall and Dr Olive Rae were most grateful when an Englishman from the Customs House in Chengtu, on their behalf, kicked a "very troublesome" beggar into the gutter.[4] Their inability to bridge the gulf of social class also accounts for the strange indifference shown by WMS missionaries in Szechwan towards beggars dying by the roadside. The women pondered "what the Master would do," but assuming that their help would not be

understood, "like the Levite, [they passed] by on the other side."[5]
The report also censured the missionary's tendency to accentuate "the
unfavorable aspects of the culture in which he is placed, in part to
minimize the worth of the religions there prevalent,"[6] in order to
promote his own society rather than missions in general and to tie
Christianity to Western life, misdemeanours committed by virtually
all WMS employees.[7] In so doing, according to the report, missionaries
could not discharge their commitment as true ambassadors for
Christ.[8]

Although the WMS was unequivocal in its praise of the work of its
personnel, the society's overall success at home and abroad, and
indeed the effect of the missionary movement in general, remain
almost impossible to measure. Some historians, Kenton Clymer, for
instance, have concluded that because Western missionaries had so
few doubts about the validity of their work and "cultural relativism
was [a] ... foreign concept to [them],"[9] they were incapable of understanding why Oriental host cultures perceived missionaries as the
unwelcome agents of Western imperialism, as the menacing forerun-
ners of Western political domination and unwanted social change.
This may explain why the WMS, like other missionary organizations,
failed in its ultimate goal of regenerating Oriental society.

In the long run the WMS missionaries' direct impact was limited to
the relatively small number of women with whom they had personal
contact. In China girls and women received medical attention perhaps not otherwise available to them; in Japan the WMS girls' schools,
like other mission schools there, have been acknowledged for their
part in a gradual liberation of Japanese women. Wherever they were,
the WMS agents, like other North American women missionaries who
saw education as the key to any improvement in Oriental women's
status,[10] offered at least some academic or practical training for
women and they tried to convey an appreciation of women's own
worth in societies that placed little value on their well-being. Still at
issue, however, is the extent to which the missionaries' often self-
serving methods have tainted the beneficence of their crusade.

What Clymer's observation does not explain is the WMS's similar
lack of success among its Canadian native and immigrant clients. The
appropriate test case for the WMS missionaries may be their activities
in the home mission field, where they were no more successful and
where once again their effectiveness has to be measured in terms of
small victories on behalf of improving the quality of life of women
and children. On its home territory no less than in the Orient, the
WMS stubbornly clung to the cultural biases of middle-class evangelical Protestant Canada. Because of this institutional narrowness, the

efforts of individual missionaries became the ultimate determinant of success or failure.

There were none the less many occasions when the women were able, quite successfully, to transcend the strictures of class and gender. In the face of the revolutionary turmoil in China in 1911, Minnie Brimstin refused to abandon the twenty orphans in her care until she had provided a safe home for each of them, while in Victoria the missionaries tenaciously strove to rehabilitate women whom they would, except for their affiliation with the wms, never have encountered. But to survive in these trying situations, the women mustered all their determination and courage and, in the end, fell back on their unwavering religious faith and measureless confidence in Jesus and God as their personal protectors, sometimes virtually to the point of abdicating any responsibility for or control over their own actions. Christ was an omniscient presence in the missionary's life, an avuncular family member comparable to the "cozy person" to "nestle" up to whom Barbara Welter has observed in the nineteenth-century female hymnody.[11] The dying Hannah Lund looked to Jesus as her "Elder Brother": "without Him I am all weakness."[12] For Elizabeth Strachan, Christ was "the friend that sticketh closer than a brother," a familiar aphorism among Methodist women.[13] "What A Friend We Have in Jesus" was possibly the most frequently sung hymn at wms meetings.[14]

Some missionaries' relationships with God, and especially Christ, with his human form, suggest considerably more intense affection, intimacy, and even passion, emotions that evoke the powerful revivals that had aroused so many Methodist women. Elizabeth Graham believed the wms missionaries had "nothing to fear, so long as we are in full submission to God's will." Her sentiments were echoed by Elizabeth Dolmage, who advocated the "Surrendered life" as the best way to live.[15] If not in their temporal affairs then in spiritual matters at least, it seems that the wms missionaries could not escape from, and indeed accepted, some variant of patriarchal authority in their lives. Like their secular sisters, women missionaries observed the preachers' counsel to "endure what they could not cure,"[16] trusting in the wisdom and righteousness of God's will in all things. As Retta Gifford Kilborn put it during the 1895 Chengtu riots, "God makes no mistakes … If it is part of His Plan that we should suffer apparent defeat for a time, it is only that a more glorious triumph may crown the work in the end."[17] Paradoxically, then, the wms missionaries who, within the context of women's history, emerge as prototypes of independent women seem to have gained a degree of their liberation at the expense of free will, through their surrender to God. But then, paradoxes and contradictions were the very essence of the Victorian era, of the missionary movement and its champions, who steadfastly contended that the Christianization of the world was their paramount objective but who in the process became intent on realizing the more immediate goal of imposing the supposed material and cultural benefits of Western civilization on their charges and in the end were reduced to dispensing charity.

The strands of experience that were entangled in the minds and the unconscious of the WMS recruits, energizing them to become part of the impossible and irrational dream that aroused normally unromantic evangelical Protestants, are often perplexing. Paul Johnson has pointed out the difficulty for the historian in "trying to peer into a nineteenth-century mind, to decide exactly how important the Christian impulse was among so many others. Was David Livingstone, for instance, primarily a Christian evangelist, an imperialist – or an egoist?"[18] There can be no doubt that the WMS missionaries shared contemporary enthusiasm for Canada's appointed destiny to make "this world the home of freedom, of justice, and of peace" through the spread of Anglo-Saxon values.[19] Allied to their nationalist/imperialist impulses was a parallel vision of the Methodist Church as the pacesetter in the Christianizing process and Methodist women's own perception, given that they represented more than half of their Church's membership, that "whether the great work of the evangelization of the world ... is to be accelerated or retarded depends very largely upon us."[20] Those who followed the "word to the sisterhood ... to *live* and *serve*"[21] made a contract with God that, they anticipated, would be the means of their own salvation and perfection.

These emotional impulses must be weighed, however, against an equally strong material inducement steering single middle-class Methodist women towards a missionary career – that is, the necessity to support themselves, and in some cases their families. A missionary vocation offered an adequate salary, good employee benefits, likeminded colleagues, and status within one's community. It might even be argued, given the intimacy of existence in the mission field, that the WMS provided a surrogate for Victorian family life for its employees. Finally, there is the problem of trying to gauge the undercurrents of escapism, romance, and adventure pervading the women's correspondence. It was not a point a missionary would willingly concede because, like the professional Victorian women travellers of the day, women missionaries were open to the allegation that they were adventuresses, trying to avoid the obligations and restrictions of family life.[22] None the less, there is little doubt that the lure of the Orient

and venturing into the unknown, physically and mentally, taking
risks, even jeopardizing one's virginity,[23] but above all else having the
freedom to act independently – to do, within reason, what one
pleased without parental or social censure – appealed to these women
who, as members of the work-force, had already crossed one formidable barrier circumscribing female behaviour.

This brings the argument full circle. Where, then, does the balance
lie among religious conviction, social commitment, personal ambition, and material necessity as catalysts in the missionary-making
process? In view of the limited evidence to the contrary, the impression so zealously cultivated by the wms that its messengers were
prompted to become "soul winner[s]"[24] as the logical extension of
their intense Methodist piety must be taken at face value. The missionaries' individual explanations for their career choice are consistent with the society's popular versions. But usually, once they
reached their destinations in the mission field the women were simply too preoccupied with their commission and too anxious about
their own survival in alien territory to be excessively concerned for
their own souls. Questions about the depth and breadth of their
personal holiness and spiritual commitment, so critical to the wms
recruiting and assessment process, faded before the stark reality of
abandoned baby girls and bound feet in China, servile middle-class
women and overworked textile operators in Japan, lonely immigrant
mothers in Canada's inner-city slums, and child marriages among the
natives of British Columbia. For bona fide members of what Elizabeth
Strachan liked to call "the elect sisterhood,"[25] the intensity of their
own faith was no longer such a vital question. Success as a career
missionary was measured by other criteria – compassion, good
works, and social service. Long before their Church became officially
committed to the social gospel, wms missionaries, as products of a
deep Methodist tradition that stressed personal perfection and Christian responsibility for others, were already living it.

The period of the society's existence was, in fact, a time of great
change for Canadian Protestantism and for the Methodist Church.
The founders of the wms and the first employees of the society were,
as their testimonials affirm, steeped in the evangelicalism that
asserted "that man could do nothing, either by works or by wishes
for salvation, unless he was saved by Christ's freely offered grace."[26]
These religious convictions activated the wms work in the field, as
shown by the emphasis on the numbers of converts the women won
over as the ultimate proof of the society's success. Through the influence of the older missionaries who persisted with the society, especially in the Japan mission, this traditional desire "to win souls and

to present Christ to others"[27] continued to surface until well after the First World War, when, it is often assumed, the emphasis throughout the Methodist Church had shifted to wider concerns for society as embodied in the social gospel.[28]

After the turn of the century the society's appetite for ameliorating the material circumstances of their female constituents both at home and abroad became stronger as the increasingly middle-class Methodist Church shed the emotional hallmarks of evangelicalism for the restraint associated with respectability and assumed more obligation for the problems of an urbanized industrial Canada. As this awareness of social reality grew, "the individualism of the evangelical way seemed to many to be less and less appropriate. The demand 'save this man, now' became 'save this society, now' and the slogan 'the evangelization of the world in our generation' became 'the Christianization of the world in our generation.'"[29] Most women who joined the WMS as missionaries after the First World War were committed to the ideology and practice of the social gospel, which constituted a large segment of the curriculum of the Methodist Training School and drove the Student Volunteer Movement. But it seems equally important to remember that from the moment they arrived in the mission field, the first WMS missionaries attempted to relieve the human misery around them out of simple concern for the suffering of others and uneasiness about their own perfection and salvation if they did not try.

Whether their gestures smack of the civilizing or cultural rather than the purely evangelical aims of missionary endeavour, most women were able to move beyond their initial preoccupation with conversions to confront, albeit on their own terms and in their own ways, the reality of the circumstances they faced. Their outrage about the status and treatment of women in the mission fields the WMS serviced represents a feminist impulse, if not within the missionaries' own North American framework, certainly within the context of the traditional male-dominated cultures that were threatened by the missionaries' teachings.[30] One of the few explicit WMS missionary observations on the woman question seems remarkably current. It was drafted in 1922 by Evelyn Lackner, aged forty, stationed in Tokyo. "Ever since childhood," she wrote, "I learned 'Christianity has raised the position of women,' but now for the first time I fully realize what it means. It does not mean men offering women their seats in street cars, allowing them to be lawyers or preachers or even sanctioning their voting ... What it means is, that woman recognize that it is her right and her duty to call her body and soul her own and that man recognize her right."[31] Given traditional Christian sentiment on this issue during the preceding forty years, it is difficult not to speculate that Lackner's perception, if it was at all typical of some wide cross-section of Methodist women (it was published with the WMS's sanction in the *Missionary Outlook*), embodies an exceptionally radical strain of feminism within the Methodist Church. It would be interesting to understand how much of this opinion was attributable to the now well-established independence of the missionary professional, or to the missionaries' gradual articulation, in the absence of other effective voices, of the concerns of women within the Methodist Church. It would be equally instructive to know the extent to which this perception informed the WMS's workers' activities in the mission field.

Still, being a woman had its limitations, even when carrying out God's plans. Despite their determination to succeed in their chosen profession, the WMS missionaries often had to be content with limited accomplishments because of their sex. Specifically, while their efforts paved the way for the ultimate step in becoming a Christian, as women the WMS personnel could not perform the actual conversion as manifested in the sacrament of baptism. Their inability to complete the process they had set in motion may help to explain why, from the outset, the women were equally caught up in other less explicitly evangelical aspects of missionary activity: teaching and medical work, and transmitting Christian morality and the ideals of Western womanhood. They might more easily have pursued these philanthropic impulses at home as middle-class wives and mothers who confined their sense of social obligation to membership in a WMS auxiliary, fulfilling the normal expectations of their families and of Canadian society, which valued in women, above all else, adherence to the domestic virtues that characterized and promoted the "cult of true womanhood." But by enlisting instead as the paid employees of the WMS, the women were able to turn their passion for Christian social activism into an instrument to advance their own personal independence, professional development, and social standing.

The strength and the duration of the women's commitment to missionary work as a lifetime career depended very much, however, on the nature of their individual experiences in the field. Japan in the midst of its industrial revolution, China in the twilight of the Manchu dynasty, and Canada in its first great era of social transformation each presented unique demands, problems, and opportunities for the missionary. Not surprisingly, it was in Japan, where hostility and suspicion were tempered by a recognition of the missionaries' secular skills, that the pattern for institutional and individual success was established. Home missions, by contrast, proved to be the least fertile fields for cultivation of converts and this, together with the society's decision to staff them with the least qualified recruits, produced the highest rates of turnover.

In the end, however, degrees of commitment and dedication, even success, sometimes revolved around intangibles. Dr May Austen, forced to leave China because her mother was so lonely,[32] found her life "in the homeland ... empty, because no one [had her] Chinese experience."[33] She longed to return to the place where she had found pleasure and satisfaction. But for others, resignation, marriage, even death delivered them from responsibilities and environments that often threatened to – and sometimes did – destroy their physical, emotional, sexual, and, most critically for them, spiritual well-being. Considering the diversity of the missionary experience, what is important is that so many WMS employees persevered long enough to be identified as part of the growing number of Canadian women for whom a lifelong career had become an essential and rewarding alternative to marriage, home, and family. It is hard to disagree with Agnes Wintemute, who concluded, even before her first assignment was completed, that missionary work probably benefited her far more than those she sought to help.[34]

Notes

ARWMS *Annual Report Woman's Missionary Society*
MCC Methodist Church of Canada
UCA United Church Archives
UCAT United Church Archives, Toronto
UCC United Church of Canada
WMS Woman's Missionary Society

CHAPTER ONE

1 United Church Archives, Toronto (hereinafter UCAT), biographical file of Agnes Wintemute; Katherine Ridout, "A Woman of Mission," 208–44.

2 UCAT, Harper Coates family papers, box 2, extracts from Agnes Wintemute Coates, "Talks given in B.C., Canada during and Shortly after World War I on Our Attitudes towards Missionaries and Mission Work." Emphasis added.

3 Scott, *The Jewel in the Crown*, 19.

4 Clifton Phillips, "The Student Volunteer Movement and Its Role in China Missions, 1886–1920," 94.

5 Alice Kessler-Harris, *Out to Work*, 57.

6 See Grant, *A Profusion of Spires*, chap. 12, for an examination of the extent of religiously motivated activities in Ontario.

7 See Cohen, *Women's Work, Markets and Economic Developments in Nineteenth-Century Ontario*, 165, for statistics about the percentage of females married by age group in Ontario 1851–1911.

8 Austin, *Saving China*; S. Endicott, *James G. Endicott: Rebel Out of China*; Scott, *McClure: The China Years of Dr. Bob McClure*; Ion, *The Cross and the Rising Sun*.

9 See Juteau-Lee, "Les Religieuses du Québec," 22–33; Dumont-Johnson, "Les Communautés religieuses et la condition féminine," 79–102; Danylewycz, *Taking The Veil*.

10 Danylewycz, *Taking the Veil*, 160.

11 Brouwer, *New Women for God*, 7.

12 See Kealey, *A Not Unreasonable Claim*; Bacchi, *Liberation Deferred?*

13 Parr, "Nature and Hierarchy," 41.

14 Bacchi, *Liberation Deferred?* 38.

15 *Annual Report of the Woman's Missionary Society of the Methodist Church* [hereinafter ARWMS], 1893–94, xi.

16 Vicinus, *Independent Women*, 33.

17 Shortt and Doughty, *Canada and Its Provinces*, 11:313.

18 Graham, *Medicine Man to Missionary*, 14–20.

19 Grant, *Moon of Wintertime*, 101.

20 Ibid., 132–3.

21 Ibid., 151.

22 *Canada and Its Provinces*, 11:315–16.

23 Ibid., 316.

24 Magney, "The Methodist Church and the National Gospel, 1884–1914," 47.

25 *Christian Guardian*, 4 Sept. 1901.

26 Emery, "Methodist Missions among the Ukrainians," 9.

27 *Canada and Its Provinces*, 11:321.

28 Halpenny, *Our French Missions in Quebec*, 5.

29 Platt, *The Story of the Years*, 1:84.

30 *Canada and Its Provinces*, 11:320.

31 Sutherland, *Methodism in Canada: Its Work and Its Story*, 273.

32 Van Die, *An Evangelical Mind*, 64; UCAT, UCC, WMS Overseas Mission, Japan, missionaries' files, box 3, file of Martha Cartmell.

33 Ion, *The Cross and the Rising Sun*, 35.

34 *Fruits of Christian Missions in Japan*, 34–7; Ion, *The Cross and the Rising Sun*, 79–80.

35 Platt, *The Story of the Years*, 1:7.

36 Ibid., 13.

37 See Hunter, *The Gospel of Gentility*, 12–13, for a discussion of the circumstances leading to the emergence of women's missionary societies in the U.S.

38 Matthaei, *An Economic History of Women in America*, 114.

39 Peiss, *Cheap Amusements*, 7.

40 Matthaei, *An Economic History of Women in America*, 123.

41 Ibid., 173.

42 Donzelot, *The Policing of Families*, 45.

43 Rendall, *The Origins of Modern Feminism*, 77.

44 Mitchinson, "Canadian Women and Church Missionary Societies in the Nineteenth Century," 58; Blair, *The Clubwoman as Feminist*, 7–8.

45 Cott, *The Grounding of Modern Feminism*, 17.

46 Public Archives of Nova Scotia, MG20, vol. 1016, #1, *The Halifax Methodist Female Benevolent Society, Report, & c, 1828*; Linton, "WMS: 100 Years of Woman Power," 17.

47 Bush, "The Reverend James Caughey and Wesleyan Methodist Revivalism in Nineteenth-Century Canada," 245; Carwardine, *Trans-atlantic Revivalism*, 187.

48 Bentley, *Precious Stones for Zion's Wall*, 160.

49 See Smith, *Revivalism and Social Reform in Mid-Nineteenth Century America*, 43; Cross, *The Burned-over District*, 84–9.

50 James, ed., *Women in American Religion*, 7.

51 Gifford, "Sisterhoods of Service and Reform," 11.

52 Mitchinson, "Canadian Women and Church Missionary Societies in the Nineteenth Century," 60.

53 Ibid., 61; Headon, "Women and Organized Religion in Mid and Late Nineteenth Century Canada," 8–9; Brouwer, *New Women for God*, 10–36.

54 Prentice et al., *Canadian Women: A History*, 170–4.

55 Brown, "Women of the Word," 70–1; MacHaffie, *Herstory: Women in the Christian Tradition*, 95; Johnson, *Women in English Religion 1700–1925*, 63–5; Shiels, "The Feminization of American Congregationalism, 1730–1835," 46–50; Valenze, *Prophetic Sons and Daughters*, 278–9.

56 UCAT, Bay of Quinte Conference, Belleville Presbytery, Belleville, Ontario, Tabernacle Church WMS minutes, 1875–88, 20 June 1876.

57 UCAT, Methodist Episcopal Church in Canada, WMS minutes, 1881.

58 Hill, *The World Their Household*, 49.

59 UCAT, Methodist Episcopal Church in Canada, WMS minutes, 19 June 1878.

60 Ibid., WMS minutes, 1881.

61 Ibid., WMS Board of Managers report, 1883.

62 UCAT, Bay of Quinte Conference, Belleville Presbytery, Belleville, Ontario, Tabernacle Church WMS minutes, 26 Sept. 1884.

63 *Christian Guardian*, 2 Oct. 1878. Emphasis added.

64 Wallace, *The Macmillan Dictionary of Canadian Biography*, 800.

65 *Christian Guardian*, 2 Oct. 1878.

66 Ibid.

67 Platt, *The Story of the Years*, 1:19.

68 Ibid., 14; *Missionary Outlook*, Mar. 1881, 31.

69 *Missionary Outlook*, Mar. 1881, 32.

70 Platt, *The Story of the Years*, 1:15.

71 Katz, *The People of Hamilton, Canada West*.

72 Ibid., 343–8.

73 Morgan, *The Canadian Men and Women of the Time*, 668.

74 *Missionary Outlook*, Jan. 1881, 3.

75 *Christian Guardian*, 11 Oct. 1882.

76 Platt, *The Story of the Years*, 1:17.
77 UCAT, Hamilton Conference, Centenary Methodist Church, Hamilton, WMS minute book, 12 Feb. 1881, 45.
78 Platt, *The Story of the Years*, 1:20.
79 *Missionary Outlook*, May 1881, 54.
80 Ibid.
81 Ibid.
82 Hamilton Public Library, Norah Henderson scrapbook, 44, Norah Henderson, "In Feminine Forces," *The Herald* (Hamilton, Ont.), 7 July 1931.
83 Platt, *The Story of the Years*, 1:21–2.
84 Strachan, *The Story of the Years*, 3:327.
85 Platt, *The Story of the Years*, 1:23.
86 Ibid., 25.
87 *Ten Reasons Why I Should Belong to the Woman's Missionary Society*, 2.
88 Ibid., 2–3.
89 Sweet, *The Minister's Wife*, 34.
90 *Ten Reasons Why*, 3.
91 ARWMS, 1887–88, 23.
92 See, for example, Bacchi, *Liberation Deferred?* 59, for a discussion of the decline in the influence of Protestant churches 1880–1910.
93 ARWMS, 1884–85, 13.
94 *Missionary Outlook*, Mar. 1881, 32.
95 ARWMS, 1884–85, 13.
96 Platt, *The Story of the Years*, 1:24.
97 *Missionary Outlook*, Feb. 1882, 25.
98 Platt, *The Story of the Years*, 1:26; ARWMS, 1884–85, 39–40.
99 ARWMS, 1884–85, 40.
100 Mitchinson, "Aspects of Reform: Four Women's Organizations in Nineteenth-Century Canada," 74; Platt, *The Story of the Years*, 1:146.
101 Strachan, *The Story of the Years*, 3:333.
102 ARWMS, 1925–26, vii.
103 Ibid., xxxv.
104 Mitchinson, "Canadian Women and Church Missionary Societies," 59–60; Montgomery, *Western Women in Eastern Lands*, 35.
105 Kessler-Harris, *Out to Work*, 57.
106 Welter, "She Hath Done What She Could," 626–7.
107 Ibid., 631.
108 Garrett, "Sisters All," 221–4; Beaver, *All Loves Excelling*, chap. 3.
109 Hunter, *The Gospel of Gentility*, 13.
110 Ibid., 14.
111 Rev. I.B. Aylesworth, "Woman as Missionary," in Austin, *Woman: Her Character, Culture and Calling*, 191.
112 Welter, "She Hath Done What She Could," 637.

CHAPTER TWO

1 United Church Archives, Toronto [hereinafter UCAT], biographical file of Isabella Blackmore, Isabella Blackmore to Mrs Whiston, Claremont, NS, 12 Oct. 1888.

2 *Annual Report of the Woman's Missionary Society of the Methodist Church of Canada*, [hereinafter ARWMS], 1886–67, 125.

3 Ibid.

4 Ibid., 126.

5 Semmel, *The Methodist Revolution*, 17; Michael Gauvreau, "The Taming of History," 317.

6 See Van Die, *An Evangelical Mind*, 83.

7 ARWMS, 1886–67, 126.

8 Ibid., 125.

9 Ibid.

10 ARWMS, 1896–97, 199.

11 Cohen, *Women's Work, Markets and Economic Development in Nineteenth-Century Ontario*, 164; Urquhart and Buckley, *Historical Statistics of Canada*, 42.

12 Strachan, "Woman's Missionary Societies," *Canadian Methodist Magazine* 16 (1882): 228.

13 Emery, "Ontario Denied: The Methodist Church on the Prairies 1896 to 1914," 313.

14 Ibid., 313–14.

15 Ibid., 314.

16 Public Archives of Nova Scotia, MG100, vol. 248, #17a & b, "Women: Attitudes toward Female Breadwinners (1895)."

17 Conrad, Laidlaw, and Smyth, *No Place Like Home*, 15.

18 Emery, "The Origins of Canadian Methodist Involvement in the Social Gospel Movement 1890–1914," 105–6.

19 Hunter, *The Gospel of Gentility*, 28.

20 Magney, "The Methodist Church and the National Gospel, 1884–1914," 3; Semple, "The Impact of Urbanization on the Methodist Church in Central Canada, 1854–1884," 31.

21 Unless the parent was a minister, it was impossible to find parental occupations for women born after 1891 and whose names did not appear on the available census records. However, using Methodist Church records it was possible to locate all fathers who were ministers.

22 The term "daughter of the parsonage" appears frequently in WMS literature and reports.

23 Champion, *The Methodist Churches of Toronto*, 299.

24 UCAT, Methodist Church of Canada, WMS West China Mission papers, Mrs N.A. Powell to Mrs Hales, 12 May 1924. Sherritt, a member of the

West China Mission, left China when her father died. She promised to return but did not. It appears that the Board of Managers calculated the furlough salary and the costs of a postgraduate course that the society had paid for and sent the family a bill for $2,200 – hence the remark about the family's financial position.

25 Morgan, *Canadian Men and Women of the Time*, 845; Public Archives of Nova Scotia, MG100, vol. 172, 10–10a, Killams, "Brief Sketch of the Life of Thomas Killam 1st of Yarmouth."

26 Manuscript Census of Canada, 1881. According to E.J. Hobsbawm, "The widest definition of the middle class or those who aspired to imitate them was that of keeping domestic servants." Hobsbawm, *Empire and Industry*, 157. For the purposes of this study, the term middle class is used to refer generally to white-collar workers, businessmen, and members of the professions.

27 UCAT, biographical file of Florence Wickett.

28 Gorham, *The Victorian Girl and the Feminine Ideal*, 11.

29 Vicinus, *Independent Women*, 7.

30 Legendre, "The Baptist Contribution to Nineteenth Century Education for Women," 59–60.

31 Bacchi, *Liberation Deferred?* 19.

32 *Christian Guardian*, 25 Jan. 1888.

33 UCAT, biographical file of Margaret Armstrong.

34 See Gidney and Millar, *Inventing Secondary Education*, 265–73, for a discussion of the lack of a common standard for matriculation and university entrance in the province of Ontario.

35 Royce, *Landmarks in the Victorian Education of 'Young Ladies' under Methodist Church Auspices*, 3–24.

36 Public Archives of Ontario, Ontario Ladies' College papers, Education Department papers, school reports, 1850–1890, box 1, *Ontario Ladies' College, Whitby, Ontario, 1879–1880*, 16.

37 Ibid., 24.

38 *Report of the Massey Foundation Commission on the Secondary Schools and Colleges of the Methodist Church of Canada 1921*, 65.

39 Austin, *Woman: Her Character, Culture and Calling*, 443.

40 Urquhart and Buckley, *Historical Statistics of Canada*, 86.

41 Reid, "The Education of Women at Mount Allison, 1854–1914," 22–4.

42 Ibid., 24.

43 Public Archives of Ontario, *Ontario Ladies College*, 20.

44 Vicinus, "Distance and Desire," 47.

45 Ford, *A Path Not Strewn with Roses*, 5.

46 Bacchi, *Liberation Deferred?* 19.

47 Prentice et al., *Canadian Women: A History*, 156–61.

48 Kubat and Thornton, *A Statistical Profile of Canadian Society*, 130.

49 This sample consists of 182 women for whom both birth dates and educational histories were available.

50 Sissons, *A History of Victoria University*, 197.

51 Ten women, both married and single, employed by the Canadian Baptist mission in India had attended McMaster University, and another eight had attended Acadia University in Wolfville, NS, also a Baptist college. See Canadian Baptist Foreign Mission Board, *A Sketch of the Origin and Development of Our Mission Stations in India*, 187–97.

52 Ibid.

53 UCAT, biographical files of O. Markland and C. Sturdy; UCAT, MCC, WMS, WMS notebooks.

54 Bacchi, *Liberation Deferred?* 21.

55 Cowan, *It's Late and All the Girls Have Gone*.

56 Antler, "After College, What?," 410–11.

57 UCAT, biographical files of Florence Bird, Sybil Courtice, Ila Day, Etta deWolfe, Sarah Fullerton, and Olive Lindsay; MCC, WMS, WMS notebooks.

58 Gorham, *The Victorian Girl and the Feminine Ideal*, 27.

59 Jardine, "An Urban Middle-Class Calling," 178.

60 Coburn, "I See and Am Silent," 135–6.

61 "The Life of a Nurse," *The Globe*, 8 Oct. 1886, in Tausky, *Sara Jeannette Duncan, Selected Journalism*, 29.

62 Ibid., 28.

63 Jardine, "An Urban Middle-Class Calling," 179.

64 *Women of Canada*, 58.

65 Cohen, *Women's Work*, 215, n 120.

66 Coburn, "I See and Am Silent," 163.

67 See, for example, Grey-Bruce Regional Health Centre, Owen Sound, Ontario, papers of the Owen Sound General and Marine Hospital, Owen Sound, Ontario, "Owen Sound General and Marine Hospital School for Nurses. Requirements for Admission," ca 1903. Nurses were paid $196 over their three years of training and were given board and "a reasonable amount of laundry work."

68 Jardine, "An Urban Middle-Class Calling," 180.

69 UCAT, biographical files of Fannie Forrest, Caroline Wellwood, Martha Barnett, Violetta Shuttleworth, and Mary Assom.

70 Clarke, *A History of the Toronto General Hospital*, 94.

71 Ball, "A Perfect Farmer's Wife," 2–21.

72 Drachman, "Female Solidarity and Professional Success," 608.

73 UCAT, biographical files of May Austen, Mabel Cassidy, Anna Henry, Retta Gifford Kilborn, Maud Killam, Florence O'Donnell, Lily Snider, and Ada Speers.

74 UCAT, biographical files of Ada Speers and Lily Snider; E.M. Speers Meuser autobiography in biographical file of E.M. Speers Meuser.

75 Strong-Boag, "Feminism Constrained," 119.

76 *ARWMS*, 1897–98, vx.

77 UCAT, MCC, WMS, Executive minute books, 22 Oct. 1913.

78 Hacker, *The Indomitable Lady Doctors*, 93.

79 Ibid., 242–9. Until studies of other denominations appear, it is not possible to know whether the Presbyterians, Baptists, and others were more successful in attracting doctors. However, if Hacker's assertion is accurate, other women's missionary societies had far more missionary doctors in their ranks than did the Methodist WMS.

80 *Fifth Census of Canada, 1911*, 6:44.

81 Eliza Mosher, MD, "The Health of American Women," 242.

82 A.H. Reynar, "The 'New Woman' and the True Woman," *The Canadian Methodist Magazine* 16 (1882): 508.

83 See Cook, *The Regenerators*, chap. 5, for an extended discussion of the ideas of Benjamin Austin.

84 Austin, "Open Doors for the Women of To-day," 33.

85 Ibid., 35.

86 W. Withrow, "The Higher Education of Women," 330.

87 Graham, "Schoolmarms and Early Teaching in Ontario," 177; Danylewycz, Light, and Prentice, "The Evolution of the Sexual Division of Labour in Teaching," 89; Danylewycz and Prentice, "Teachers' Work," 79.

88 See Prentice, "The Feminization of Teaching," 49–65.

89 Mary McLeod Bethune, "How the Bethune-Cookman College Campus Started," excerpted from "Faith That Moved a Dump Heap," in *Who: The Magazine about People* 1 (June 1941): 31–5, 54, in Kerber and Mathews, *Women's America: Re-focusing the Past*, 260–2.

90 UCAT, biographical files of Elizabeth Alcorn, Muriel Hockey, May Inglis, Annie MacLean, Esther Ryan, Myra Veazey; Manuscript Census of Canada, 1861–81.

91 UCAT, biographical file of Martha Swann, Swann to Mrs Hardy, Wallace, Ont., 18 June 1900.

92 Davy, *Women, Work and Worship in the United Church of Canada*, 106.

93 Hensman, "The Kilborn Family," 1–13; UCAT, biographical file of Retta Gifford Kilborn.

94 Light and Parr, *Canadian Women on the Move 1867–1920*, 50.

95 UCAT, biographical file of E. Thompson, Thompson to E.S. Strachan, 17 June 1920.

96 Ross, *Miss Jessie K. Munro*, 4.

97 Van Die, *An Evangelical Mind*, 120.

98 Magney, "The Methodist Church and the National Gospel," 4.

99 Caldwell, "The Unification of Methodism in Canada," 7.

100 Magney, "The Methodist Church and the National Gospel," 4.

101 Ibid., 5.

102 Ibid., 4.

103 See Allen, "The Social Gospel and the Reform Tradition in Canada, 1890–1928," for a discussion of the shift to a more progressive viewpoint among Methodists.

104 UCAT, MCC, General Conference, *Journal of Proceedings*, 1906, 274–8.

105 Magney, "The Methodist Church and the National Gospel," 4.

106 See M.Gauvreau, *The Evangelical Century*, for an examination of the encounter of Methodist and Presbyterian theology with secular thought in the nineteenth century. Gauvreau argues that the evangelical creed retained its supremacy within these churches until the early twentieth century.

107 See Brouwer, "The Canadian Methodist Church and Ecclesiastical Suffrage for Women, 1902–1914."

108 Van Die, *An Evangelical Mind*, 23–5; McDannell, *The Christian Home in Victorian America, 1840–1900*, 18; Ryan, *Cradle of the Middle Class*, 187–97.

109 Sweet, *The Minister's Wife*, 33.

110 Blauvelt, "Women and Revivalism," 1–5; Bederman, "The Women Have Had Charge of the Church Work Long Enough," 435–8; Welter, "The Feminization of American Religion"; Douglas, *The Feminization of American Culture*.

111 See, Muir, "Petticoats in the Pulpit," for an examination of Canadian Methodist women's role as preachers in the early nineteenth century, and Whitely, "Modest, Retiring, and Fully Consecrated," for a discussion of Methodist women evangelists in late nineteenth-century Canada.

112 *Christian Guardian*, 14 Aug. 1889.

113 *Missionary Outlook*, Oct. 1908, 229.

114 Cott, *The Bonds of Womanhood*, 85–90; Sweet, *The Minister's Wife*, 32.

115 UCAT, Annie Allen papers, box 2, diaries, 23 Feb. 1919.

116 UCAT, biographical files for the Hart family members. Yet another daughter married J.C. Hennigar, a Methodist missionary in Japan. The remaining family members became a doctor, a minister, a dentist, and a nurse.

117 Van Die, *An Evangelical Mind*, 134.

118 UCAT, biographical files for members of the Woodsworth family.

119 UCAT, biographical file of E. Speers Meuser, autobiography of E. Speers Meuser.

120 Ibid.

121 Emery, "The Origins of Canadian Methodist Involvement in the Social Gospel Movement," 110.

122 Magney, "The Methodist Church and the National Gospel," 4.

123 Emery, "The Origins of Canadian Methodist Involvement in the Social Gospel Movement," 110; Langford, *Practical Divinity: Theology in the Wesleyan Tradition*, 39.

124 Airhart, "The Eclipse of Revivalist Spirituality," 63.

125 Johnston, *Shall We or Shall We Not?*, 94.

126 Ibid., 154.

127 *Christian Guardian*, 6 Jan. 1898.

128 Johnston, *Shall We or Shall We Not*, 147–9.

129 French, "The Evangelical Creed in Canada," 32.

130 Galbraith, *Methodist Manual*, 18.

131 McKillop, "Canadian Methodism in 1884," 19.

132 UCAT, Mary Lamb papers, Mary Lamb diaries, 8 Aug. 1920.

133 McKillop, "Canadian Methodism in 1884," 17.

134 Bacchi, *Liberation Deferred?* 59.

135 *Christian Guardian*, 4 Mar. 1891.

136 Semple, "The Nurture and Admonition of the Lord," 174.

137 *Christian Guardian*, 4 Mar. 1891.

138 UCAT, MCC, General Board of Missions, Young People's Forward Movement, Stephenson papers, box 1, F. Stephenson, *The Y.P.F.M. for Missions in the Methodist Church of Canada 1895–1925*, unpublished ms, n.d.

139 Sutherland, *The Methodist Church and Missions in Canada and Newfoundland*, 25.

140 UCAT, Stephenson papers, box 8, contains applications from college students who were prepared to join missionary societies after graduation.

141 *Student Mission Power*, 21; see also Robert, "The Origin of the Student Volunteer Watchword," 145–9.

142 *Student Mission Power*, 26–8.

143 Phillips, "The Student Volunteer Movement and Its Role in China Missions, 1886–1920," 94; S. Endicott, *James G. Endicott: Rebel Out of China*, 28.

144 See *Student Mission Power*, 110–12.

145 Phillips, "The Student Volunteer Movement and Its Role in China Missions," 98; *World-Wide Evangelization*, 625–8.

146 Ibid.

147 UCAT, Student Volunteer Movement papers (unsorted), *Suggestions Regarding Student Volunteer Groups*, 1.

148 Ibid.

149 *World-Wide Evangelization*, 571.

150 Phillips, "The Student Volunteer Movement and Its Role in China Missions," 101.

151 UCAT, SVM papers, "What It Means to be a Student Volunteer."

152 Ibid., declaration of Fern Scruton.

153 UCAT, biographical file of Mildred Armstrong, Armstrong to Mrs McMechan, London, 14 May 1902.

154 UCAT, biographical file of O. Lindsay, tribute to Rev. Olive Lindsay at her funeral, 24 Apr. 1965, by Fern Scruton.

155 UCAT, biographical file of Alice Jackson.

156 UCAT, biographical files.

157 UCAT, MCC, WMS, Executive minute books. These minutes report several instances where applications were withdrawn or not approved when it became clear that parents opposed their daughter's plans.

158 Pacey, "Fiction 1920–1940," 168–9.

159 Lambert, *The Romance of Missionary Heroism*, 8.

160 *ARWMS*, 1884–85, 9.

161 Ibid., 43.

162 *ARWMS*, 1920–21, vii.

163 Graham, "Schoolmarms and Early Teaching in Ontario," 194.

164 *Women of Canada*, 80.

165 UCAT, biographical file of Eliza Marshall, Marshall to WMS, 17 Dec. 1908.

166 McMaster University, Canadian Baptist Archives, *Beacon Lights*, Jan. 1922, 20.

167 In 1911 furlough salaries, which had previously been pegged at three-quarters salary, were raised to a standard $500. *ARWMS*, 1911–12, ix.

168 *ARWMS*, 1892–93, 195.

169 *Christian Guardian*, 12 June 1918.

170 UCAT, biographical file of M. Gormley.

171 UCAT, UCC, WMS Overseas Mission, Japan, Missionaries' Files, box 3, file of Martha Cartmell, Cartmell to Mrs S.J. Clare, Thornbury, 19 Aug. 1906. William Morley Punshon (1824–81) was a Wesleyan Methodist minister who came to Canada from England in 1868. A powerful preacher, he was influential in bringing about the 1873 unification of several branches of Methodism in Canada. In the same year he returned to England, where he died. Cartmell obviously heard Punshon preach before 1873, at least eight years before her ultimate decision to become a missionary was made. See Wallace, *The Macmillan Dictionary of Canadian Biography*, 611, for a reference to Punshon.

172 UCAT, Harper Coates family papers, box 2, Agnes Wintemute Coates diaries, 1 July 1886.

173 Ibid., July–Aug. 1886.

174 Ibid., 21 Aug. 1886.

175 UCAT, biographical file of Martha Swann, Swann to Mrs Hardy, 18 June 1900.

176 UCAT, biographical file of Jean Holt, Holt to Mrs Ferrie, Brandon, 3 Sept. 1912,

177 Ibid.

178 UCAT, biographical file of Uberta Steele, Steele to Mrs Briggs, 23 Apr. 1906.

179 UCAT, biographical file of Katharine Drake, Drake to Mrs J. Harrison, Hamilton, 11 Jan. 1909.

180 *Christian Guardian*, 11 Oct. 1916.

181 Welter, "The Feminization of American Religion," 91.

182 Sweet, *The Minister's Wife*, 38.

183 Lasch, *The New Radicalism in America*, 65.

184 Davies, "The People Called Methodists," 149.

185 French, "The People Called Methodists in Canada," 78.

186 *Christian Guardian*, 30 Jan. 1884.

187 Ibid., 4 Apr. 1894.

188 Thomas, "Servants of the Church," 379.

189 UCAT, biographical file of Louise Foster; E. Strachan to Foster, Toronto, 15 Oct. 1915.

190 UCAT, Alexander Sutherland papers, box 6, file 12, Sutherland to E.S. Strachan, 5 July 1894.

191 UCAT, biographical file of H. Paul.

192 UCAT, *Fifth Annual Report of the Toronto Deaconess Home and Training School of the Methodist Church of Canada*, 1899, 8.

193 Ibid.

194 Davies, "The People Called Methodists," 148.

195 ARWMS, 1894–95, 174.

196 ARWMS, 1898–99, 178.

197 ARWMS, 1917–18, 221; ARWMS, 1920–21, 239.

198 Bliss, "The Methodist Church and World War I," 213.

199 ARWMS, 1888–89, 12.

200 UCAT, MCC, WMS, Board of Management minute books, Sept. 1918.

201 UCAT, biographical file of M. Coon.

202 ARWMS, 1893–94, vi.

203 See, for example, UCAT, biographical files of N. McKim and M. Thompson, who became home missionaries because, according to medical reports, they had weak hearts.

204 UCAT, biographical files and WMS notebooks.

205 UCAT, Methodist Church of Canada, Strachan-Cartmell papers, box 1, file 3.

206 Ibid.

207 *Christian Guardian*, 20 Nov. 1882.

208 Ibid.

209 This term was often used by missionaries to refer to Japan. See, for example, Armstrong, *Progress in the Mikado's Empire*.

CHAPTER THREE

1 *Christian Guardian*, 21 Mar. 1883.

2 Longsworth, *Austin and Mabel*, 275.

3 *Christian Guardian*, 21 Mar. 1883.

4 Ibid., 14 Mar. 1883.

5 Ibid.

6 Yokoyama, *Japan in the Victorian Mind*, 78–82.

7 *Missionary Outlook*, Sept. 1893, 141.

8 Ion, *The Cross and the Rising Sun*, 102.

9 Beasley, *The Rise of Modern Japan*, 97. Beasley argues that many Japanese men and women with some social standing accepted Christianity, thus giving it a "more powerful voice in Japanese society than mere numbers might suggest." By 1907 there were 140,000 Christian converts, 50,000 of them Protestant.

10 Saunby, *Japan: The Land of the Morning*, 290–1.

11 Reischauer, *Japan: The Story of a Nation*, 135.

12 Morton, *Japan: Its History and Culture*, 156.

13 Yokoyama, *Japan in the Victorian Mind*, xxii.

14 Yanaga, *Japan since Perry*, 126.

15 Sanderson, *The First Century of Methodism in Canada*, 2, 365.

16 *Fruits of Christian Missions in Japan*, 70–1.

17 Beaver, *Ecumenical Beginnings in Protestant World Mission*, 117.

18 *Christian Guardian*, 11 Apr. 1883.

19 Platt, *The Story of the Years*, 1:9.

20 United Church Archives, Toronto [hereinafter UCAT], Strachan-Cartmell papers, box 1, file 4, E. Strachan to M. Cartmell, 13 Mar. 1883; *Annual Report of the Woman's Missionary Society* [hereinafter ARWMS], 1883–84, 10.

21 ARWMS, 1890–91, 175.

22 UCAT, Strachan-Cartmell papers, box 1, file 6, Mrs James Gooderham, Toronto, to M. Cartmell, 14 Apr. 1884; Linton, "WMS: 100 Years of Woman Power," 17.

23 *Missionary Outlook*, Apr. 1885, 56.

24 Platt, *The Story of the Years*, 2:9.

25 Hane, ed., *Reflections on the Way to the Gallows*, intro., 11.

26 Sievers, *Flowers in Salt*, 15.

27 Platt, *The Story of the Years*, 2:10.

28 Ibid, 10–11.

29 *Missionary Outlook*, Oct. 1884, 156.

30 See Platt, *The Story of the Years*, 2, and *Fruits of Christian Missions in Japan* for examples of this sort of hagiography.

31 *Fruits of Christian Missions*, 71.

32 Sievers, *Flowers in Salt*, 12.

33 Ibid., 14.

34 Hamilton Public Reference Library, Centenary Church, United Church of Canada, History 1868–1968, *Centenary Traditions*.

35 ARWMS, 1883–84, 12.

36 Platt, *The Story of the Years*, 2:20.

37 *Christian Guardian*, 19 May 1880.

38 Platt, *The Story of the Years*, 2:21.

39 *Christian Guardian*, 15 Aug. 1883.

40 *Missionary Outlook*, Oct. 1883, 156.

41 Gulick, *Working Women of Japan*, xi.

42 *Missionary Outlook*, Nov. 1884, 175.

43 *Fruits of Christian Missions*, 71.

44 Pharr, "Japan: Historical and Contemporary Perspectives," 229.

45 Paulson, "Evolution of the Feminine Ideal," 15.

46 Hane, ed., *Reflections*, 13.

47 Pharr, "Japan: Historical and Contemporary Perspectives," 228.

48 Hane, ed., *Reflections*, 12.

49 Platt, *The Story of the Years*, 2:21.

50 Sievers, "Feminist Criticism in Japanese Politics in the 1880s," 605.

51 Chafetz and Dworkin, *Female Revolt*, 141.

52 Sievers, "Feminist Criticism in Japanese Politics," 613.

53 Sievers, *Flowers in Salt*, 105.

54 Platt, *The Story of the Years*, 2:13.

55 *Missionary Outlook*, Jan. 1885, 7; Apr. 1885, 56.

56 Platt, *The Story of the Years*, 2:12–13; Gulick, *Working Women of Japan*, 24.

57 Platt, *The Story of the Years*, 2:16–17.

58 *ARWMS*, 1885–86, 12.

59 Platt, *The Story of the Years*, 2:17.

60 Ibid., 19.

61 *Christian Guardian*, 3 Feb. 1886.

62 Platt, *The Story of the Years*, 2:12.

63 *Missionary Outlook*, May 1886, 75.

64 Ibid., Sept. 1893, 141.

65 *Canadian Methodists in Japan 1911–1912*, 109.

66 See Powles, *Victorian Missionaries in Meiji, Japan*, 137, 145, n. 19.

67 *Missionary Outlook.*, Mar. 1886, 44.

68 Ibid., Feb. 1886, 29.

69 Ibid., May 1886, 92.

70 Ibid., Mar. 1887, 72.

71 UCAT, biographical file of M. Cartmell.

72 UCAT, UCC, WMS, Japan, box 3, Cartmell file, Cartmell to Mrs S. Clare, Thornbury, 19 Aug. 1906.

73 Platt, *The Story of the Years*, 2:14.

74 *Missionary Outlook*, Sept. 1887, 134.

75 Platt, *The Story of the Years*, 2:44.

76 UCAT, biographical file of M.J. Cunningham.

77 *Missionary Outlook*, Feb. 1888, 26.

78 UCAT, MCC, WMS, WMS Executive minute books, report of annual meeting, Sept. 1908.

79 UCAT, Harper Coates family papers, box 2, Agnes Wintemute diaries, diary 3.

80 UCAT, Norman, *One Hundred Years in Japan*, 1:83.

81 UCAT, Harper Coates family papers, box 2, Agnes Wintemute diaries, 21 Dec. 1886.

82 Ibid., 16 Feb. 1887.

83 Ibid., 23 Feb. 1887.

84 Ibid., 19 July 1887.

85 Gulick, *Working Women of Japan*, 19.

86 UCAT, Harper Coates family papers, box 2, Agnes Wintemute diaries, 19 July 1887.

87 UCAT, biographical file of Agnes Wintemute; see also Ridout, "A Life of Mission," 208–44, for an examination of Agnes Wintemute Coates's experience with missionary work in Japan until the First World War, and in particular for a discussion of her search for a religious identity.

88 *Christian Guardian*, 6 Feb. 1889.

89 Sievers, *Flowers in Salt*, 105–6.

90 Storry, *Japan and the Decline of the West in Asia, 1894–1943*, 17.

91 ARWMS, 1888–89, 39.

92 Ibid., 42.

93 UCAT, MCC, WMS, WMS Japan Council minutes, 3 June 1890, 44.

94 Ibid., 3 Sept. 1890, 49.

95 Sansom, *The Western World and Japan*, 481.

96 Yanaga, *Japan since Perry*, 128.

97 Ibid., 126–7; Reischauer, *Japan: The Story of a Nation*, 157.

98 Drummond, *A History of Christianity in Japan*, 200.

99 *Missionary Outlook*, Feb. 1893, 45.

100 Platt, *The Story of the Years*, 2:52.

101 Ibid., 53.

102 *Canadian Methodists in Japan*, 50.

103 *Christian Guardian*, 14 Sept. 1892; *Canadian Methodists in Japan*, 115–116.

104 *Missionary Outlook*, Sept. 1893, 14.

105 *Christian Guardian*, 17 Aug. 1887.

106 Ion, *The Cross and the Rising Sun*, 60. Hiraiwa, who was 31 at the time of the Spencer-Large wedding, became one of the leading Japanese preachers in the Canadian Methodist Japan mission.

107 UCAT, Harper Coates family papers, box 2, Agnes Wintemute diaries, 18–19 July 1887.

108 Ibid., 9 May 1887.

109 In September 1914, after several years of controversy, delegates to the General Conference voted to admit women to Methodist Church councils. *Christian Guardian*, 7 Oct. 1914.

110 UCAT, MCC, Japan Mission Collection, box 2, file 27, stenographic report of proceedings re Japan Affair at the annual meeting of the General

Board of Missions of the Methodist Church of Canada, Montreal, 3–11 Oct. 1895 (Toronto: Methodist Mission Room 1895), 75.

111 UCAT, MCC, WMS, Japan, box 1, Council minute books, 3 Sept. 1888, 3–4.

112 Ibid., 53.

113 Ibid., 60.

114 *Missionary Leaflet*, Apr. 1890, 3.

115 Ibid., July 1890, 3.

116 *Christian Guardian*, 28 May 1890.

117 UCAT, biographical file of E. Spencer Large; *Japan Daily Mail*, Yokohama, 7 Apr. 1890.

118 Ibid.

119 *Missionary Outlook*, June 1890, 84.

120 *Japan Daily Mail*, 7 Apr. 1890.

121 *Missionary Leaflet*, July 1890, 3.

122 *Christian Guardian*, 10 Dec. 1890.

123 Strachey, *Remarkable Relations*, 35–7.

124 *Christian Guardian*, 10 Dec. 1890; Showalter, *The Female Malady*, 138–9. *Christian Guardian*, 30 Apr. 1890, publicized the services provided at Clifton Springs and suggested that a similar institution should be opened in Canada.

125 *Christian Guardian*, 12 Aug. 1891.

126 UCAT, MCC, Japan Mission papers, box 1, file 1, F.A. Cassidy, St Catharines, Ont., to Dr Carman, Toronto, 29 Jan. 1898.

127 UCAT, WMS Japan Council minutes, Sept. 1891, 58–95.

128 Ibid., 3 Oct. 1891, 114.

129 UCAT, MCC, Japan Mission, box 2, file 27, stenographic report of proceedings re Japan Affair, 138.

130 Ibid., 134.

131 Ibid., 135.

132 UCAT, MCC, WMS Overseas Missions, Japan, Correspondence and Papers, 1883, 1909–25, box 2, file 1, "History of Herbie Bellamy Home, 1893," 6.

133 Ion, *The Cross and the Rising Sun*, 155.

134 UCAT, MCC, Newfoundland and Bermuda, WMS Correspondence, Miscellaneous, report of the board meeting of the WMS re Japan Affair, 13.

135 Ibid.

136 Ibid., 122.

137 UCAT, WMS Japan Council minutes, 13 July 1892, 120.

138 Ibid., 136.

139 Ibid., and *ARWMS*, 1892–93, 5.

140 UCAT, MCC, Japan Mission, box 2, stenographic report of proceedings re Japan Affair, 71.

141 UCAT, MCC, WMS, WMS Japan Council minutes, 10 Jan. 1893, 144–5.

142 Ibid., Macdonald to E.S. Large, 4 Mar. 1893. The letter from Macdonald is included in the WMS minutes.

143 Ibid., 148.

144 Ibid., 11 Mar. 1893, 152.

145 Ibid., Macdonald to E.S. Large, 4 Mar. 1893.

146 Ibid., 154.

147 UCAT, MCC, Japan Mission, box 2, file 27, stenographic report of proceedings re Japan Affair, 72.

148 Ibid., 73.

149 Ibid.

150 UCAT, MCC, WMS, WMS Japan Council minutes, 157.

151 UCAT, MCC, Japan Mission, box 2, file 27, stenographic report of proceedings re Japan Affair, 74.

152 Ibid., 76.

153 Ibid., 77.

154 Ibid., 78.

155 UCAT, MCC, Alexander Sutherland papers, box 6, file 11, Sutherland to E. Strachan, 4 Mar. 1893.

156 UCAT, MCC, WMS, WMS Japan Council minutes, 3 Dec. 1894, 25–6.

157 Ibid., 29.

158 Ibid.

159 *ARWMS*, 1894–95, vi.

160 UCAT, MCC, WMS, WMS Japan Council minutes, 18 July 1895, 52.

161 *The Globe*, Oct. 1895.

162 UCAT, MCC, WMS, WMS Correspondence, Miscellaneous, report of the board meeting of the WMS re Japan Affair, 16, 19.

163 Ibid.

164 Ibid., 21.

165 Ibid., 32.

166 UCAT, MCC, Japan Mission, box 2, file 27, stenographic report of proceedings re Japan Affair, 78.

167 UCAT, MCC, Japan Mission, General Correspondence, 1894–95, box 1, file 1, Alexander Sutherland to Albert Carman, 27 Dec. 1895. In this letter Sutherland quotes Cartmell.

168 UCAT, MCC, Japan Mission, box 2, file 27, stenographic report of proceedings re Japan Affair, 135–6.

169 Ibid., 136.

170 Ibid., 144.

171 Ibid., 146.

172 Ibid., 147.

173 Ibid., 189, 199.

174 Ibid., 145.

175 Ibid., 84.

176 UCAT, MCC, Bermuda and Newfoundland, UCC, Missions Pamphlets, box 1, confidential report of the general superintendent's official visit to the mission in Japan, Apr.-June 1898, 11.

177 Ibid., 17.

178 Ibid., 42.

179 UCAT, MCC, Japan Mission papers, box 11, file 3, Cassidy, St Catharines, to Albert Carman, Toronto, 19 Jan. 1898.

180 Ibid., file 1, Cassidy, St Catharines, to Carman, Toronto, 29 Mar. 1898.

181 UCAT, MCC, Japan Mission, box 2, file 27, stenographic report of proceedings re Japan Affair, 189.

182 ARWMS, 1896–97, vii.

183 Ibid.

184 UCAT, MCC, WMS, WMS Board of Managers minute books, 10 Oct. 1897; ARWMS, 1897–98, viii.

185 UCAT, biographical file of Eliza Spencer Large.

186 UCAT, MCC, Sutherland papers, box 10, file 196, E. Ross to Sutherland, 4 Sept. 1909.

187 ARWMS, 1895–96, 201.

188 Monthly Letter, May 1898, 1.

189 Missionary Outlook, Sept. 1897, 137.

190 Platt, The Story of the Years, 2:30.

191 UCAT, MCC, WMS, Miscellaneous Papers, Isabella Blackmore letterbooks, Blackmore to E. Strachan, 16 June 1898.

192 Platt, The Story of the Years, 2:33–6; UCAT, MCC, WMS, Miscellaneous Papers, Isabella Blackmore letterbooks.

193 UCAT, MCC, WMS, WMS Japan Council minutes, annual statement of the year ending 1899, 151–2.

194 Missionary Outlook, June 1899, 137.

195 Platt, The Story of the Years, 2:62.

196 Ibid.

197 Ibid., 64–5; Missionary Outlook, June 1892, 92.

198 ARWMS, 1898–99, lxi.

199 ARWMS, 1902–03, lvi.

200 Missionary Outlook, Oct. 1903, 239.

201 ARWMS, 1900–01, lxiv.

202 Missionary Outlook, Sept. 1893, 14.

203 Ibid., Dec. 1893, 190.

204 Ibid., May 1898, 112.

205 UCAT, MCC, WMS, Miscellaneous Papers, Blackmore letterbooks, Blackmore to Strachan, 2 Dec. 1897.

206 Ibid., Blackmore to Strachan. The letter is undated, but it probably was written in 1901.

207 UCAT, MCC, WMS, Board of Managers minute books, Mrs A. Carman, *The Rest Fund*, ca 1914.

208 UCAT, biographical file of I. Blackmore.

209 See Semple, "The Nurture and Admonition of the Lord," 157–76, for an examination of the shifting Methodist attitudes towards children.

210 *ARWMS*, 1911–12, lvi.

211 *Missionary Outlook*, June 1904, 145.

212 UCAT, MCC, WMS, Overseas Missions, Japan, Correspondence and Papers, 1893, 1909–25, file 1, "History of Herbie Bellamy Home, 1893."

213 Unmarried women employees dominated in the export industries, especially the production of silk and cotton. Between 1894 and 1912 women comprised 60 per cent of Japanese industrial labour. Their working conditions deteriorated as competition increased, and night shifts were added in many factories. Sievers, *Flowers in Salt*, 54–66.

214 *Missionary Outlook*, Apr. 1908, 87.

215 Ibid., June 1908, 139.

216 Ibid.

217 Lennox, *The Health and Turnover of Missionaries*, 120.

218 UCAT, MCC, WMS, Miscellaneous Papers, Isabella Blackmore letterbooks, Blackmore to E. Crombie, 2 May 1898.

219 Ibid., Blackmore to Strachan, 6 Oct. 1898.

220 See Ehrenreich and English, *For Her Own Good*, 103–4.

221 Chambers-Schiller, "The Single Woman," 346.

222 *Christian Guardian*, 21 Mar. 1894.

223 *Missionary Outlook*, July 1894, 107.

224 Ibid., Dec. 1904, 277.

225 UCAT, MCC, Sutherland papers, box 10, file 189, E. Strachan, Hamilton, to Sutherland, Toronto, 27 July 1907.

226 UCAT, MCC, WMS, Japan Council minutes, 19 July 1897, report of Outfit Committee, 95–6.

227 UCAT, Harper Coates family papers, Agnes Wintemute papers, E. Preston to her family, 31 Dec. 1891.

228 UCAT, MCC, WMS, Overseas Mission, Japan, Correspondence and Papers, box 2, file 6, Robertson to Mrs Powell, 4 Dec. 1919.

229 UCAT, Harper Coates family papers, Agnes Wintemute photo album.

230 *Missionary Outlook*, Dec. 1900, 286.

231 Ibid., July 1903, 166.

232 UCAT, MCC, Strachan-Cartmell papers, box 1, file 25, M.J. Cunningham to M. Cartmell, 14 Mar. 1906.

233 *Missionary Outlook*, Jan. 1905, 46.

234 *ARWMS*, 1904–05, li.

235 *Missionary Outlook*, Feb. 1905, 74.

236 Ibid., Apr. 1905, 94.

237 Ibid., Feb. 1910, 47.

238 Ibid., Dec. 1919, 280.

239 UCAT, biographical file of Annie Allen; UCAT, Annie Allen papers, Annie Allen diaries.

240 *Missionary Outlook*, Dec. 1919, 280.

241 Ibid., May 1913, 119.

242 Ibid., June 1917, 142.

243 Ibid., Nov. 1914, 270.

244 UCAT, MCC, WMS Overseas Missions, Correspondence and Papers, Japan, box 2, file 5, Hargrave to Wilkes, 21 June 1915.

245 MacLarren, *Canadians in Russia*, 203–4; UCAT, MCC, WMS, WMS Overseas Mission, Japan, box 2, file 6, Robertson to Powell, 2 Nov. 1918.

246 UCAT, MCC, WMS Overseas Mission, Japan, box 2, file 6, Robertson to Powell, 2 Nov. 1918.

247 Ibid., Powell to Robertson, 4 Mar. 1919.

248 *Christian Guardian*, 9 Apr. 1919.

249 UCAT, MCC, WMS, WMS Japan Mission papers, box 2, file 6, Robertson to Powell, 4 Dec. 1919.

250 Ibid., Robertson to Powell, 30 Dec. 1919.

251 Ibid., Robertson to Powell, 16 Feb. 1920.

252 Ibid., file 7, Blackmore to Robertson, 10 Dec. 1920.

253 Ibid., Robertson to Powell, 22 Dec. 1920.

254 Ibid., Blackmore to Powell, 1 Dec. 1921.

255 Ibid., file 9, Powell to Robertson, 14 Mar. 1923; 12 June 1923; 25 July 1923; 11 July 1924.

256 Ibid., Robertson to Powell, 28 July 1923.

257 Ibid., Robertson to Powell, 5 June 1924.

258 Seidensticker, *Low City, High City*, 3–9, 14–15.

259 UCAT, MCC, WMS, Japan Mission Correspondence and Papers, box 2, file 22, Powell to Robertson, 5 Dec. 1924.

260 *Missionary Outlook*, Jan. 1924, 15.

261 *Fruits of Christian Missions*, 77.

262 Ibid., 76.

263 UCAT, MCC, WMS, Japan Correspondence and Papers, box 2, file 10, Robertson to Powell, 9 Apr. 1925.

264 Ibid., Powell to Robertson, 7 May 1925.

265 Ibid., Robertson to Powell, 11 July 1924.

266 Strachan, *The Story of the Years*, 3:152.

267 UCAT, MCC, WMS, Executive notebooks, Ross to Miss G.A. Gollack, Edinburgh House, London, 6 Mar. 1922.

268 Strachan, *The Story of the Years*, 3:144.

269 UCAT, MCC, Strachan-Cartmell papers, box 1, file 23, A. Belton to Cartmell, 25 June 1898.

270 Ibid., file 26, Robertson to Cartmell, 1914.

271 UCAT, cassette of Sybil Courtice's recollection of her time spent in a Japanese internment camp.

272 UCAT, MCC, UCC, West China Mission papers, box 11, file 102, D.M. Perley to E. Shore, 29 Mar. 1912.

273 Ibid., Perley to Strachan, 17 June 1912. Ila Perley was examined by Dr C. Clarke in Toronto and was sent to the Barrie Sanatorium for treatment. She subsequently recovered and returned with her husband to China, where she raised a family. She died in Canada in 1963. UCAT, biographical file of D.M. Perley.

274 *Christian Guardian*, 21 Aug. 1921.

275 Ibid., 18 Jan. 1899.

CHAPTER FOUR

1 United Church Archives Toronto [hereinafter UCAT], Alexander Sutherland papers, box 4, file 8, Sutherland, Toronto, 14 Apr. 1890, to E.S. Strachan; see also Wallace, *The Heart of Sz-Chuan*, 20.

2 *Christian Guardian*, 20 Nov. 1898; Wallace, *The Heart of Sz-Chuan*, 29–32; Hartwell, *Granary of Heaven*, 4–5; Sutherland, *The Methodist Church and Missions in Canada and Newfoundland*, 222–3.

3 UCAT, Sutherland papers, box 4, file 7, Sutherland to Strachan, 14 Apr. 1890.

4 This decision was reached by the Committee of Consultation and Finance after discussions with Virgil Hart, former superintendent of the Central China Mission of the Methodist Episcopal Church of the United States, who was on furlough at his farm in Burlington, Ontario. See Wallace, *The Heart of Sz-Chuan*, 33; Hart, *Virgil C. Hart: Missionary Statesman*, 222–3; MacGillivray, *A Century of Protestant Missions in China 1807–1907*, 113.

5 Platt, *The Story of the Years*, 2:69.

6 Hartwell, *Granary of Heaven*, 6.

7 MacGillivray, *A Century of Protestant Missions in China 1807–1907*, 142; Latourette, *A History of Christian Missions in China*, 39.

8 Platt, *The Story of the Years*, 2:89.

9 Beaver, *All Loves Excelling*, 130; Brouwer, "Far Indeed from the Meekest of Women," 127.

10 Hacker, *The Indomitable Lady Doctors*, 242.

11 *Christian Guardian*, 7 Oct. 1891.

12 In *Saving China*, 52, Alvyn Austin notes that Amelia Brown was a registered nurse. There is no record of this in WMS files or United Church Archives biographical material.

13 Hartwell, *Granary of Heaven*, 6–10; Hart, *Virgil C. Hart*, 222–31.

14 *Missionary Outlook*, Jan. 1892, 15; Hart, *Virgil C. Hart*, 233; Hartwell, *Granary of Heaven*, 10.

15 UCAT, Sutherland papers, box 20, file 40, Sutherland to Hart, 1 Feb. 1892.

16 See the novel *The Call* by John Hersey, based upon his father's experiences in China, for a frank look at the pressure to marry *before* leaving for China.

17 Welter, "She Hath Done What She Could," 633.

18 UCAT, Alexander Sutherland papers, box 20, file 40, Sutherland to Hart, 1 Feb. 1892.

19 See UCAT, MCC, WMS West China Mission papers, box 3, file 11. Correspondence from China Inland Mission, Shanghai, 28 July 1908. This document is an agreement from the CIM to pay the WMS $550 in gold as recompense for the outfit of a WMS missionary who married one of their employees.

20 Hart, *Granary of Heaven*, 233.

21 Ward, *Courtship, Love, and Marriage in Nineteenth-Century English Canada*, 30–1.

22 Platt, *The Story of the Years*, 2:89.

23 Hartwell, *Granary of Heaven*, 26–7. The CIM had already set up mission stations in the area, but their employees wore Chinese-style clothing in order to appear less conspicuous.

24 UCAT, MCC, WMS, Executive minute books, 10 June 1892; UCAT, biographical file of R. Gifford Kilborn; see also Hensman, "The Kilborn Family," 1–13.

25 *Christian Guardian*, 18 Jan. 1893. Brackbill and Gifford seem to have become friends while they were in Owen Sound. At the farewell service for the two women, Brackbill acknowledged Gifford's influence on her decision to go to China. *Christian Guardian*, 1 Feb. 1893.

26 *Missionary Leaflet*, Nov. 1893, 4.

27 Ibid., July 1893, 7.

28 Esherick, *The Origins of the Boxer Rebellion*, 92.

29 Maxwell, *Assignment in China*, 192.

30 *Missionary Leaflet*, Nov. 1893, 5.

31 *Christian Guardian*, 12 Apr. 1893.

32 *Missionary Leaflet*, Sept. 1893, 3.

33 UCAT, MCC, WMS, Executive minute books, Apr. 1893.

34 *Monthly Letter*, Dec. 1893, 6.

35 Platt, *The Story of the Years*, 2:91–2.

36 Ibid., 92.

37 *Monthly Letter*, July 1894, 1; Aug.–Sept. 1894, 12; Platt, *The Story of the Years*, 2:92–3.

38 See Hunter, *The Gospel of Gentility*, 19.

39 *Monthly Letter*, Aug.–Sept. 1894, 12.
40 Ibid. Chinese women of the upper classes were physically unable to travel far by foot because of their bound feet.
41 *Monthly Letter*, Oct. 1894, 3.
42 Croll, "Rural China: Segregation to Solidarity," 48.
43 Bishop, *The Yangtze Valley and Beyond*, 2:315.
44 Ibid.
45 Ibid.
46 Hartwell, *Granary of Heaven*, 30.
47 Taylor, "Woman's Work in China," in Austin, ed., *Woman*, 180.
48 Withrow, *China and Its People*, 200.
49 See UCAT, Mary Lamb papers, Mary Lamb diaries; J.L. Stewart letters (author's possession).
50 *Monthly Letter*, Aug.–Sept. 1894, 12.
51 State Papers, Great Britain, Accounts and Papers, 1905, vol. CIII, vol. 60, report by Consul-General Hosie on the province of Such'uan.
52 See J.L. Stewart letters, Chengtu, to John Dunkin, London, Ont., 30 May 1910 (author's possession).
53 Kilborn, *Heal the Sick*, 71.
54 *Missionary Bulletin* 5 (1908): 121, letter written by Mrs Allen, 13 Jan. 1908.
55 UCAT, O. Jolliffe papers, Lena Jolliffe diaries, 7 June 1905.
56 See ibid., Lena Jolliffe diaries, for descriptions of typical meals served in missionary homes. For example, on 8 April 1919, dinner consisted of Tibetan duck and vegetables, cottage pudding, and fruit, and supper of cheese soup, cold duck, scalloped potatoes, peas, and chocolate pudding.
57 In one case, where the servants ate Chinese food and the missionary family Western food, it became so difficult to prepare two totally different menus that a Chinese caterer was hired to feed the servants. Lapp, *China Was My University*, 33.
58 *Missionary Outlook*, Apr. 1922, 339. This comment is from a letter written by E. Thompson on her way to Chungking.
59 *Methodist Magazine* 47 (1898): 157–8.
60 Platt, *The Story of the Years*, 2:94.
61 Ibid.
62 *Monthly Letter*, June 1895, 4–5.
63 UCAT, MCC, WMS, Executive minute books, 18 Apr. 1893.
64 Ibid.
65 UCAT, biographical file of Dr Retta Gifford Kilborn; UCAT, MCC, WMS, Executive minute books, 28 Oct. 1897.
66 *Monthly Letter*, June 1895, 5.
67 Ibid., Aug. 1895, 4.
68 Platt, *The Story of the Years*, 2:95; *Missionary Outlook*, July 1899, 191.

69 Gasster, *China's Struggle to Modernize*, 17–18.

70 Heren, Fitzgerald, Freeberne, Hook, and Bonavia, *China's Three Thousand Years*, 169.

71 Tuchman, *Stilwell and the American Experience in China, 1911–45*, 37–8.

72 *Monthly Letter*, June 1895, 1.

73 Paulsen, "The Szechwan Riots of 1895 and American 'Missionary Diplomacy,'" 287.

74 Report of Sir George Littledale, in O'Conor to Lord Roseberry, Peking, 3 November 1893, FO 17/1172, in Wehrle, *Britain, China and the Missionary Riots, 1891–1900*, 57.

75 UCAT, MCC, West China Mission papers, box 8, Sutherland to Hart, 8 July 1893.

76 Paulsen, "The Chengtu Anti-Missionary Riot May, 1895," 25–6; Hartwell, *Granary of Heaven*, 45.

77 Hartwell, *Granary of Heaven*, 44.

78 *Monthly Letter*, Apr. 1897, 2.

79 Hartwell, *Granary of Heaven*, 46.

80 *Monthly Letter*, Oct. 1895, 2.

81 Ibid.; Platt, *The Story of the Years*, 2:97–8.

82 *Monthly Letter*, Oct. 1895, 6.

83 Ibid.

84 Paulsen, "The Chengtu Anti-Missionary Riot," 29.

85 *Monthly Letter*, Oct. 1895, 7.

86 *Missionary Outlook*, Sept. 1895, 139.

87 UCAT, MCC, West China Mission papers, pamphlets, box 5, file 1, D.W. Stevenson, "The Riots at Chengtu," in Alfred Cunningham, *History of the Szechwan Riots, May–June, 1895*, 15.

88 Gay, *The Bourgeois Experience*, 1:459.

89 Platt, *The Story of the Years*, 2:99–100.

90 Strachan, *The Story of the Years*, 3:181.

91 Platt, *The Story of the Years*, 2:100.

92 Ibid., 101.

93 Forsythe, *An American Missionary Community in China, 1895–1905*, viii.

94 Ibid, vi.

95 Hunter, *The Gospel of Gentility*, 128–30.

96 See UCAT, Jolliffe papers, Lena Jolliffe diaries, 2 Jan. 1905, 10 Mar. 1905; and UCAT, biographical file of Grace Bedford. In a letter to her father dated 14 Sept. 1922, written "on a river," Bedford describes the trackers who pulled the boats. Their dress was "very picturesque, consisting of one very short jacket, for they are in & out of the water all the time. One of the other two girls is extremely modest (a very unfortunate affliction for China) & she is almost blinded every time she looks at the scenery & some of these trackers [get] within her range."

97 Feuerwerker, *The Foreign Establishment in China in the Early Twentieth Century*, 45–50; Forsythe, *An American Missionary Community in China, 1895–1905*, vi; Cohen, *China and Christianity*, 270–3.

98 UCAT, MCC, WMS West China Mission papers, box 3, file 11, letter to Mrs Hales, 22 May 1923.

99 Ibid.

100 Hunter, *The Gospel of Gentility*, 218–20.

101 Ibid., 206.

102 UCAT, MCC, WMS Executive minute books, letter to Miss Foster, Sept. 1908.

103 UCAT, MCC, West China Mission papers, box 9, file 83, Hartwell to Sutherland, 15 Nov. 1909.

104 Ibid.

105 Platt, *The Story of the Years*, 2:43.

106 Fairbank, "Missionary History as Fiction," 34.

107 See, for example, UCAT, biographical file of Edna Speers Meuser, autobiography of E.S. Meuser.

108 UCAT, Jolliffe papers, Lena Jolliffe diaries, 10 Mar. 1904.

109 *Missionary Outlook*, July 1901, 167.

110 Ibid., Mar. 1903, 69.

111 *ARWMS*, 1902–03, lxv.

112 *Missionary Outlook*, July 1903, 166.

113 UCAT, Jolliffe papers, Lena Jolliffe diaries, 26 Apr. 1905.

114 UCAT, Mary Lamb papers, Mary Lamb diaries, 27 Aug. 1922.

115 *Monthly Letter*, Dec. 1897, 4.

116 *Missionary Outlook*, Aug. 1899, 191.

117 Lee, "Female Infanticide in China," 169.

118 *Monthly Letter*, Apr. 1897, 2.

119 Platt, *The Story of the Years*, 2:102–3.

120 American women missionaries often placed their chosen children in the homes of Bible women. Hunter, *The Gospel of Gentility*, 191–7.

121 *Monthly Letter*, Feb. 1898, 5.

122 Ibid., Apr. 1898, 1.

123 Bishop, *The Yangtze Valley and Beyond*, 2:346–7.

124 Pruitt, *The Daughter of Han*, 22.

125 Bishop, *The Yangtze Valley and Beyond*, 2:348. See also Cameron, *Barbarians and Mandarins*, 363–6, for a discussion of the sexual connotations of footbinding.

126 Chafetz and Dworkin, *Female Revolt: Women's Movements in World and Historical Perspective*, 137.

127 Drucker, "The Influence of Western Women on the Anti-Footbinding Movement in 1840–41," 197.

128 Ibid., 199.

129 Strachan, *The Story of the Years*, 3:285.

130 Lang, *Chinese Family and Society*, 45.

131 Platt, *The Story of the Years*, 2:105.

132 Ibid., 106.

133 Strachan, *The Story of the Years*, 3:229–30.

134 UCAT, MCC, WMS West China Mission papers, box 3, file 1, inquiry from the Methodist Episcopal Mission Board about normal schools, n.d. The letter probably dates from the early 1920s.

135 Kazuko, *Chinese Women in a Century of Revolution, 1850–1950*, 28.

136 UCAT, UCC, West China Mission papers, pamphlets, box 1, file 28, Laura Hambly, *Our Girls' School in Chengtu*, 5.

137 Kazuko, *Chinese Women in a Century of Revolution, 1850–1950*, 28.

138 Strachan, *The Story of the Years*, 3:238.

139 *Monthly Letter*, Feb. 1899, 6.

140 *Missionary Outlook*, Feb. 1899, 41; June 1899, 142.

141 Ibid., Feb. 1899, 41.

142 Ibid., Oct. 1899, 237.

143 Ibid., Feb. 1900, 46.

144 *Christian Guardian*, 16 May 1900.

145 Wallace, *The Heart of Sz-Chuan*, 76; Esherick, *The Origins of the Boxer Rebellion*, 94–5.

146 Esherick, *The Origins of the Boxer Rebellion*, 95, 331; Purcell, *The Boxer Uprising*, 121; Hibbert, *The Dragon Wakes*, 328; Wehrle, *Britain, China and the Missionary Riots 1891–1900*, 110. Marilyn Blatt Young, in *Rhetoric of Empire*, 143, suggests that despite the atrocities they committed it is still possible to have some sympathy for the Boxers and their cause. American missionaries, however, generally supported expansionist ventures (189). Canadian missionaries, while not representatives of a nation with its own imperialist ambitions in China, certainly supported Britain. After each incident the Methodist Church of Canada pressed its claims for compensation from the Chinese government without any consideration that such losses might be part of the price that the church had to pay for establishing missions in China.

147 Heren, Fitzgerald, Freeberne, Hook, and Bonavia, *China's Three Thousand Years*, 174; See also Robert C. Forsythe, *The China Martyrs of 1900*, 67, for example, for a gruesome description of the fate of two women of the CIM in Shansi, who were "slowly battered to death while they remained in prayer. Their bodies were then stripped, exposed, and defiled. All their goods were piled in a heap in the courtyard, and gradually disappeared." Price, *China Journal 1889–1900*, contains an account of the Boxer attacks by a woman whom they killed. The Canadians killed in Shansi were William Peat of the Hamilton YMCA and Margaret Smith of New Hamburg. Austin, *Saving China*, 76.

148 Platt, *The Story of the Years*, 2: 114.

149 Haines, *Gunboats on the Great River*, 11–20.

150 *Missionary Outlook*, Nov. 1900, 262; Apr. 1901, 94.

151 Ibid., Apr. 1901, 94.

152 Ibid.

153 Ibid., Oct. 1901, 238.

154 Ibid.

155 Ibid., Jan. 1902, 22.

156 Ibid; Platt, *The Story of the Years*, 2:116; Esherick, *The Origins of the Boxer Rebellion*, 311. According to the ARWMS, 1901–02, vi, 5,680 *taels* was about $4,000 in gold. American mission societies generally did not keep the awards offered by the Chinese government but used the funds to create a scholarship fund for Chinese students who wished to study in the U.S. Austin, *Saving China*, 108.

157 ARWMS, 1901–02, lxiii.

158 Platt, *The Story of the Years*, 2:130–1.

159 Ibid., 132.

160 Ibid., 134–5.

161 Strachan, *The Story of the Years*, 3:185–6.

162 *Forward with China*, 255.

163 Ibid., 309.

164 Strachan, *The Story of the Years*, 3:255.

165 *Missionary Outlook*, May 1911, 118.

166 *Forward with China*, 306.

167 Latourette, *A History of Christian Missions in China*, 606.

168 *Canada's Missionary Congress, Report of the Committee on Statistics*, 323.

169 UCAT, China pamphlets, box 1, *A Call to Young Women from West China* (ca 1911), 1, 3.

170 *Christian Guardian*, 13 Nov. 1907.

171 Strachan, *The Story of the Years*, 3:245–6.

172 Gasster, *China's Struggle to Modernize*, 21.

173 *Christian Guardian*, 1 Apr. 1908.

174 Ibid., 22 July 1908.

175 Strachan, *The Story of the Years*, 3:197.

176 UCAT, MCC, West China Mission papers, box 9, file 94, T.E.S. Shore to Charles Murphy, 26 Jan. 1911.

177 Ibid., Joseph Pope to T.E.S. Shore, Ottawa, 31 Jan. 1911.

178 *Christian Guardian*, 20 Sept. 1911.

179 Seagrave, *The Soong Dynasty*, 121–3; Tuchman, *Stilwell and the American Experience in China, 1911–45*, 44.

180 *Forward with China*, 251; Heren, Fitzgerald, Freeberne, Hook, and Bonavia, *China's Three Thousand Years*, 177; Kapp, *Szechwan and the Chinese Republic*, 9–15.

181 Strachan, *The Story of the Years*, 3:198–200.
182 *Christian Guardian*, 22 Nov. 1911.
183 Ibid.
184 See *The Globe*, Sept. and Oct. 1911, and UCAT, MCC, West China Mission papers, box 10, file 94, Shore to Stuart Lyon, 12 Sept. 1911.
185 *The Globe*, 31 Oct. 1911.
186 Tuchman, *Stilwell and the American Experience in China, 1911–45*, 45.
187 UCAT, MCC, West China Mission papers, box 10, file 93, order no. 35 (51644), His Britannic Majesty's Consulate, Chungking, 31 Oct. 1911.
188 Great Britain, State Papers for China, China Papers, no. 3, 96, Consul General Wilkinson to Sir J. Jordan, Chengtu, 15 Oct. 1911.
189 Kapp, *Szechwan and the Chinese Republic*, 15.
190 *Missionary Outlook*, Apr. 1911, 89.
191 UCAT, MCC, West China Mission papers, box 10, file 97, O. Kilborn to Shore, 4 Dec. 1911.
192 *Missionary Outlook*, Apr. 1912, 89.
193 UCAT, MCC, West China Mission papers, box 11, file 99. This file contains a protest about the captain of the *Widgeon*. Ibid., file 102, contains a letter from J. Pope, Ottawa, 26 Jan. 1912, to Shore in which Pope would not support the missionaries' complaints. Pope concluded, after considerable investigation, that the missionaries had refused to board the steamer provided for them. If they had, the *Widgeon* would have escorted and protected them. As it was, the commander of the *Widgeon* was blameless.
194 UCAT, biographical file of E. McPherson, London *Advertiser*, ca Feb. 1912.
195 Ibid.
196 *Missionary Outlook*, Feb. 1912, 47.
197 UCAT, MCC, West China Mission papers, box 11, file 108, M.W. Hewlett to Rev. William Mortimore, Ichang, 29 Apr. 1912.
198 Ibid.
199 Ibid., file 107, O. Kilborn, Ichang, to Shore, 29 Apr. 1912.
200 Ibid., box 12, file 115, Shore to D.S. Kern, 12 Nov. 1912.
201 UCAT, biographical file of Violetta Shuttleworth. Shuttleworth withdrew at her own request from China to work as a nurse for the WMS at the General Board hospital, Lamont, Alberta.
202 UCAT, West China Mission papers, box 12, file 115, H.M. Consul, Ichang to D.S. Kern, 23 Sept. 1912.
203 Latourette, *A History of Christian Missions in China*, 610.
204 Mackerras, *Western Images of China*, 76.
205 *Christian Guardian*, 27 Nov. 1901.
206 Ibid.
207 Ibid., 7 Aug. 1908.

208 Austin, *Saving China*, 88.

209 Strachan, *The Story of the Years*, 3:211.

210 Ibid., 216–17.

211 *Missionary Outlook*, Nov. 1918, 262.

212 Ibid., Aug. 1913, 190.

213 Ibid., Mar. 1919, 71.

214 *Christian Guardian*, 25 Dec. 1918.

215 UCAT, MCC, WMS West China Mission papers, box 3, file 3, Harrison to Powell, Chengtu, 12 Dec. 1921.

216 Ibid.

217 Ibid., box 3, file 6, valuation of the property held by the WMS in West China.

218 Ibid., box 3, file 3, Harrison to Powell, 1 Oct. 1923.

219 Ibid., Harrison to Powell, 12 Jan. 1924.

220 *The Globe*, 29 Feb. 1924; Latourette, *A History of Christian Missions in China*, 817.

221 UCAT, WMS West China Mission papers, box 3, file 3, Harrison to Powell, 16 Sept. 1924.

222 *Missionary Outlook*, Feb. 1923, 70.

223 Tuchman, *Stilwell and the American Experience in China, 1911–45*, 73.

224 Austin, *Saving China*, 202. Bob Whyte, in *Unfinished Encounter: China and Christianity*, 153, suggests that most missionaries who "lived far from the great cities, were generally unaware of the ferment amongst Christian and non-Christian intellectuals, and they dismissed the anti-Christian movement of 1922 as the work of agitators."

225 UCAT, biographical file of Mary Lamb.

226 UCAT, Mary Lamb papers, Mary Lamb diary, Junghsien, 20 May 1920.

227 Ibid., 1 Aug. 1920.

228 Ibid., 2 Feb. 1921.

229 Ibid., 27 Aug. 1921.

230 Ibid.

231 Ibid., 24 Sept. 1921.

232 Ibid.

233 Ibid., 27 Apr. 1921.

234 Ibid., 26 Mar. 1924.

235 UCAT, biographical file of Mary Dallyn.

236 *West China Missionary News*, Apr. 1916, 31.

237 Ibid., Sept. 1923, 37.

238 UCAT, Lamb papers, Mary Lamb, Chengtu, to Anne Deware, 1 July 1923.

239 Ibid.

240 UCAT, MCC, West China Mission papers, box 11, file 107, Rev. J.R. Earle, Jenshow, to Shore, 28 Sept. 1912.

241 UCAT, Jolliffe papers, Lena Jolliffe diaries, 18 Oct. 1905.

242 *West China Missionary News*, June 1904, 128.

243 Ibid., Jan. 1918, 29–31; Lapp, *China Was My University*, 39.

244 UCAT, Jolliffe papers, Lena Jolliffe diaries, 1 Mar. 1915; 1 May 1915.

245 UCAT, W. Sheridan papers, box 1, file 15. The poems are not written in Sheridan's hand; there is, however, no indication of the source.

246 UCAT, MCC, WMS, Executive minute books, meeting of Executive Committee, Jan. 1912.

247 UCAT, biographical file of Dr Olive Rea.

248 Strachan, *The Story of the Years*, 3:220–3. The letters written by the medical practitioners often describe the unhealthy conditions in China, especially the night soil deposited on the fields and the sewage running down the urban streets.

249 Magney, "The Methodist Church and the National Gospel," 71.

250 UCAT, MCC, WMS, WMS notebooks.

251 *Missionary Outlook*, July 1924, 167.

252 Gay, *The Bourgeois Experience*, 1:11.

253 *Monthly Letter*, Aug.–Sept. 1897, 7, from a letter published after Ford's death. Ford wrote to the society as follows: "You could realize better how we are living face to face with the devil and his works daily, and how much we need the prayers of the home folk to help us keep sweet and unsullied, and from being hardened to it all. The misery and suffering, the vileness and crime, the lying and cheating, the idol worship! How true it is of China 'professing themselves to be wise they become fools, and changed the glory of the incorruptible God into an image made like to corruptible man,' and not only that, but lower things still 'and to birds and four-footed beasts and creeping things.' That first chapter of Romans never seemed so true before to me, and the book of 'the Acts of the Apostles never before read so like a real history of every-day living.'"

CHAPTER FIVE

1 Platt, *The Story of the Years*, 1:21–2.

2 *Annual Report of the Woman's Missionary Society* [hereinafter ARWMS], 1890–91, xiii.

3 ARWMS, 1918–19, xxiv, lix, lxxxviii.

4 Wallace, *The Macmillan Dictionary of Canadian Biography*, 800.

5 See chap. 2 for details of salaries.

6 Strachan, *The Story of the Years*, 3:334.

7 Data about parental occupation were available for thirty-seven (26 per cent) home missionaries. Sixteen fathers were professionals; nine were farmers; seven engaged in trade and commerce, while there were four labourers and one boarding-house keeper.

8 Sutherland, *The Methodist Church and Missions in Canada and Newfoundland*, 217.

9 Platt, *The Story of the Years*, 1:84.

10 Villard, *Up to the Light*, 170.

11 *Missionary Outlook*, June 1887, 85.

12 Miller, "Anti-Catholic Thought in Victorian Canada," 478.

13 *Christian Guardian*, 19 Oct. 1887.

14 *Missionary Outlook*, Mar. 1900, 70.

15 *Christian Guardian*, 24 Aug. 1882.

16 Platt, *The Story of the Years*, 1:87.

17 Ibid., 89.

18 *Missionary Outlook*, May 1892, 78.

19 Platt, *The Story of the Years*, 1:90–1.

20 Strachan, *The Story of the Years*, 3:43.

21 Platt, *The Story of the Years*, 1:93–4.

22 Strachan, *The Story of the Years*, 3:44–5.

23 Copp, *The Anatomy of Poverty*, 93–6.

24 Strachan, *The Story of the Years*, 3:46.

25 Copp, *The Anatomy of Poverty*, 43.

26 Strachan, *The Story of the Years*, 3:46.

27 UCAT, MCC, Missionary Society, Home Department, box 7, file 14, report of board of directors meeting, French Methodist Institute, 30 May 1919.

28 UCAT, MCC, WMS, Executive minute books, 20 Jan. 1909.

29 Sutherland, *The Methodist Church and Missions in Canada and Newfoundland*, 219.

30 United Church Archives, Vancouver School of Theology, Oriental Home and School Papers, Report 1887, J.E. Starr to E.S. Strachan; Oliver, *The Dominion of Canada*, 225; Platt, *The Story of the Years*, 1:103–4; UCAT, Albert Carman papers, box 26, file 157, copy of letter from Robson in "Work of the WMS, 1882–87," n.d.

31 This figure does not include the missionaries from Japan and China – Martha Cartmell, for instance, who occasionally worked for a year or two in the Victoria mission before returning to the Orient.

32 UCAT, biographical files of Lily McCargar, Margaret Eason, Grace Baker, and Elizabeth Staples.

33 Prochaska, *Women and Philanthropy in Nineteenth-Century England*, 188–93.

34 Walkowitz, *Prostitution and Victorian Society*, 117.

35 Platt, *The Story of the Years*, 1:105.

36 Ibid.

37 Ibid., 106.

38 *Missionary Leaflet*, Mar. 1890, 6.

39 Ibid., Feb. 1890, 7.

40 Morton, *In the Sea of Sterile Mountains*, 122.

41 *Missionary Leaflet*, Jan. 1891, 5.

42 Ibid., Aug. 1891, 3.

43 *Christian Guardian*, 21 Sept. 1887.

44 UCA, Vancouver School of Theology, Oriental Home and School Papers, Starr to Strachan.

45 *Christian Guardian*, 22 Jan. 1896.

46 See Hirata, "Free, Indentured, Enslaved: Chinese Prostitutes in Nineteenth-Century America."

47 *Missionary Leaflet*, Aug. 1892, 7.

48 *Missionary Outlook*, Feb. 1900, 46.

49 Ibid., Apr. 1900, 93.

50 Ibid., Sept. 1900, 216.

51 Reports from the rescue home indicate that Ah Yute was returned to Canton in 1913. She was admitted to the John Kerr Hospital for the Insane, where she died in 1923. UCA, Vancouver School of Theology, Oriental Home and School Papers, Victoria Oriental Home Record Book and Register 1881–1929.

52 Ward, *White Canada Forever*, 60–1.

53 Canada, House of Commons, Sessional Papers 1902, Paper 54, *Report of the Royal Commission on Chinese and Japanese Immigration*, 38.

54 Ibid.

55 Platt, *The Story of the Years*, 1:108–9.

56 Ibid., 110.

57 Strachan, *The Story of the Years*, 3:53.

58 Ibid., 61.

59 Ibid., 63–4.

60 Ibid., 65.

61 ARWMS, 1918–19, cxi.

62 UCA, Vancouver School of Theology, Oriental Home and School Papers, Victoria Oriental Home Record Book and Register 1881–1929.

63 *Missionary Outlook*, May 1919, 119.

64 Sugimato, *Japanese Immigration, the Vancouver Riots, and Canadian Diplomacy*, 232.

65 *Missionary Leaflet*, Aug. 1892, 6.

66 *Missionary Outlook*, Mar. 1889, 66.

67 Ibid., Sept. 1900, 216.

68 Ibid., July 1900, 167.

69 Ibid., Sept. 1905, 214.

70 UCAT, biographical file of Elizabeth Churchill.

71 UCAT, biographical file of Sarah Bowes.

72 Brown and Cook, *Canada, 1896–1921*, 323.

73 *Victoria Daily Colonist*, 14 Nov. 1942, as cited in Van Dieren, "The Response of the WMS to the Immigration of Asian Women 1888–1942," 94.

74 Grant, "The Reaction of Wasp Churches to Non-Wasp Immigrants," 3.

75 United Church Archives, Winnipeg, Conference of Manitoba and Northwestern Ontario, Women's Organizations, Special Collections, WMS Archives Conference WO13, Historical sketches and reprints, ts, "Some Facts re: The Beginnings of All People's Mission and Dolly Maguire Hughes"; see also Thomas, "Servants of the Church," for an examination of the work of Methodist deaconesses.

76 Grant, "The Reaction of Wasp Churches to Non-Wasp Immigrants," 3.

77 Palmer, *Patterns of Prejudice*, 28.

78 Emery, "Methodist Missions among the Ukrainians," 9; Laycock, *Bridges of Friendship*, 10.

79 *Missionary Bulletin*, 1908, 233.

80 Platt, *The Story of the Years*, 1:123.

81 Leonard, *The Austrian People*, 5.

82 Ibid.

83 UCAT, biographical files of Jessie Munro and Retta Edmonds.

84 *Missionary Outlook*, Sept. 1904, 208.

85 Emery, "Methodist Missions among the Ukrainians," 9.

86 Laycock, *Bridges of Friendship*, 9.

87 *Missionary Outlook*, June 1905, 143.

88 Ibid., Dec. 1904, 286.

89 Ibid.

90 Platt, *The Story of the Years*, 1:124.

91 *Missionary Outlook*, June 1905, 143.

92 UCAT, biographical file of E. Chace.

93 Emery, "Methodism Denied," 314.

94 UCAT, biographical files of E. Weekes and E. Chace.

95 Platt, *The Story of the Years*, 1:126.

96 Ibid., 5; Laycock, *Bridges of Friendship*, 9.

97 United Church Archives, Edmonton, Alta, letters from E. Chace to E. Weekes (probably written in the 1950s), 1 [photocopy].

98 Ibid., 6.

99 *Missionary Outlook*, Apr. 1911, 94.

100 Strachan, *The Story of the Years*, 3:71.

101 *Missionary Outlook*, Mar. 1912, 65.

102 UCA, Edmonton, Chace letters, 15.

103 Potrebenko, *No Streets of Gold*, 78.

104 UCA, Edmonton, Chace letters, 15.

105 Strachan, *The Story of the Years*, 3:73.

106 UCAT, United Church of Canada, WMS Home Missions, Boarding Schools, box 3, file 65, "The Story of the Move from Pakan to Wahstao, Alberta."
107 Strachan, *The Story of the Years*, 3:77.
108 Ibid., 78.
109 Ibid., 81.
110 Ibid., 82.
111 Ibid., 87.
112 See Peiss, *Cheap Amusements*, chap. 7, for a discussion of middle-class reformers' reactions to commercial recreation.
113 *Missionary Outlook*, Jan. 1910, 23.
114 Ibid., June 1910, 143.
115 Ibid., Jan. 1918, 23.
116 Ibid., Mar. 1909, 71.
117 UCA, Edmonton, Alta, Logbook kept at Wahstao, ca 1910 [photocopy].
118 UCAT, Methodist Church of Canada, Missionary Society, Home Department, box 9, file 10, Buchanan to Manning, 10 Apr. 1919.
119 Ibid., file 9, report of the sixth annual convention of Ruthenian workers, 1917.
120 Ibid., file 4, Buchanan to Manning, 10 Sept. 1919.
121 Ibid., file 6, Buchanan to Manning, 10 Sept. 1919.
122 Ibid., box 26, file 2, address of the Rev. J.A. Doyle, superintendent of Missions for Manitoba, given before the General Board of Missions, 18 Oct. 1921.
123 Ukrainian Pioneers' Association of Alberta, *Ukrainians in Alberta*, 2:81.
124 UCA, Edmonton, Chace letters, 23.
125 *Missionary Outlook*, Nov. 1911, 256.
126 Harney, "Chiaroscuro: Italians in Toronto, 1885–1915," 47.
127 Strachan, *The Story of the Years*, 3:90.
128 UCAT, Methodist Church of Canada, Home Missions, box 26, file 3, letter to E. Strachan from an unidentified WMS missionary, n.d.
129 Ibid., box 6, file 3, C.E. Manning, journal and reports, 1918–27, trip to the west, 1926, 13.
130 Ibid., box 6, file 2, Harvey Foster, Welland, Ont., to C.E. Manning, 13 May 1925.
131 See, for example, ibid., box 26, file 3, for a manuscript written by an unidentified WMS missionary that describes her attempts to contact the relatives of some of her constituents during a visit to eastern Europe.
132 UCAT, biographical file of Lottie Deacon.
133 Grant, *Moon of Wintertime*, 134.
134 Platt, *The Story of the Years*, 1:33–4.
135 UCAT, biographical file of Kezia Hendrie; UCAT, Young People's Forward Movement papers, box 24, "The True Story of Kezia Hendrie by a Friend," unpublished ms.

136 Platt, *The Story of the Years*, 1:34.

137 *Missionary Outlook*, Feb. 1885, 24.

138 UCAT, Hamilton Conference, Erie Presbytery, Brantford, Wellington Street Wesleyan Methodist Church Circuit Register, 1868.

139 "The True Story of Kezia Hendrie," 21.

140 United Church Archives, Vancouver School of Theology, BC Conference Papers, Bella Bella Mission, ms journal from 1880 sent by Rev. Arthur Barner to Dept. of Archives, Methodist Church of Canada, 8 Dec. 1880. This anonymous journal suggests that girls' homes were the only solution to the problem of child marriages.

141 "The True Story of Kezia Hendrie," 25.

142 Ibid., 19.

143 Ibid.

144 Ibid., 22.

145 Platt, *The Story of the Years*, 1:34.

146 Ibid.

147 UCAT, biographical files of H. Buehler and Margaret Laing. Laing returned to Canada after the death of her close friend and fellow missionary in Japan, Alice Belton.

148 Platt, *The Story of the Years*, 1:53.

149 Ibid., 54.

150 Ibid., 57.

151 It is hard to specify the number of women working at each Indian mission station at any given time because the women were shifted frequently from place to place.

152 Platt, *The Story of the Years*, 1:36.

153 *Missionary Outlook*, July 1899, 167.

154 *Monthly Letter*, May 1895, 5.

155 See UCAT, MCC, Endicott-Arnup papers, box 2, file 28. In a letter dated 15 May 1919, H. Whaley, a former missionary at Oxford House, reported "several instances where such clothing is either sold or traded out to the Indians for fur, moccasins, etc., etc." Whaley argued that missionaries should not "pauperize the Indians by giving such clothing gratis" and suggested that the money received should be returned to the mission societies.

156 Platt, *The Story of the Years*, 1:38.

157 Long, *How the Light Came to Kitamaat*, 18.

158 Platt, *The Story of the Years*, 1:71.

159 Ibid., 39.

160 Ibid., 40.

161 Ibid.

162 Strachan, *The Story of the Years*, 3:23.

163 *Missionary Outlook*, July 1902, 167.

164 Ibid., Jan. 1917, 22.

165 *Missionary Leaflet*, Aug. 1893, 8.

166 Ibid., May 1894, 4.

167 Ibid., Oct. 1893, 2.

168 UCA, Vancouver School of Theology, BC Conference, Bella Bella Missions, ms journal, 8 Dec. 1880.

169 *Monthly Letter*, Dec. 1895, 2.

170 *Missionary Outlook*, Feb. 1904, 47.

171 "The True Story of Kezia Hendrie," 21.

172 *Missionary Leaflet*, Jan. 1892.

173 *Monthly Letter*, July–Aug. 1896, 6.

174 Ibid., Oct. 1896, 6.

175 Strachan, *The Story of the Years*, 3:26.

176 See UCAT, WMS, Executive minute books, Sept. 1911.

177 *Missionary Outlook*, Nov. 1901, 262.

178 Strachan, *The Story of the Years*, 3:37.

179 Mangan, *The Games Ethic and Imperialism*, 191.

180 *Missionary Outlook*, Jan. 1902, 23; Varley, *Kitamaat, My Valley*, 130.

181 Ibid., 81.

182 Ibid., 93.

183 Ibid., 108.

184 Ibid., 109.

185 *Monthly Letter*, Jan. 1894, 2.

186 *Missionary Outlook*, Dec. 1905, 284.

187 Ibid., Apr. 1907, 85.

188 There is no biographical file for Dr Bower in the United Church Archives, nor is her name on any list of employees compiled by the society. WMS histories do not mention her, although other missionaries referred to her in their letters to WMS publications. A letter from C.S. Reddick, a missionary at Kitamaat, to the General Board of Missions, dated 23 April 1905, reported that the WMS intended to appoint a successor to Dr Bower, but there appear to be no further references to her. UCAT, Shore papers, box 1, file 115. In a letter from Elizabeth Strachan, 14 May 1908, to T.E.S Shore, general superintendent of Missions, inquiries were made about Bower's status, noting that she did not live in the WMS home although she was apparently paid by the WMS. Ibid., box 3, file 43, Strachan to Shore, 14 May 1908.

189 Varley, *Kitamaat, My Valley*, 51.

190 Ibid., 51–2.

191 *Christian Guardian*, 31 Mar. 1897. After Caldwell circulated a chain letter asking for prayers to help the Indians along with fifteen cents, the Board of Managers denied that she had any connection with the WMS.

192 UCAT, Shore papers, box 2, file 111, Rev. George Raley to Shore, 23 Jan. 1913.

193 Ibid., file 115, Reddick, Kitamaat, to Ferrier, 30 Dec. 1910.

194 *Missionary Outlook*, July 1922, 4.

195 UCAT, MCC, Shore papers, box 2, file 117, Lizzie Donogh to Elizabeth Ross, 13 Feb. 1912.

196 Ibid., L. Donogh, Kitamaat Mission, BC, to Elizabeth Ross, 12 Feb. 1912.

197 UCAT, MCC, Alexander Sutherland papers, box 8, file 16, Sutherland to E. Strachan, 15 Apr. 1898.

198 Ross, *Life Investment*.

CHAPTER SIX

1 Hocking, *Re-Thinking Missions*, 15.

2 Hutchison, *Errand to the World*, 163.

3 Hocking, *Re-Thinking Missions*, 300.

4 *Christian Guardian*, 4 May 1910.

5 Ibid., 14 Aug. 1907.

6 Hocking, *Re-Thinking Missions*, 16.

7 Ibid., 18–23.

8 Hutchison, *Errand to the World*, 162.

9 Clymer, *Protestant Missionaries in the Philippines, 1898–1916*, 191.

10 Flemming, *Women's Work for Women*, intro., 4.

11 Welter, "The Feminization of American Religion, 1800–1860," 89.

12 *Missionary Outlook*, July 1894, 107.

13 Strachan, "Woman's Missionary Societies," *Canadian Methodist Magazine* 16 (1882): 228.

14 See Sizer, *Gospel Hymns and Social Religion*, 33–9, for a discussion of the portrayal of Jesus in hymns. She argues that passion and passivity were the hallmarks of gospel hymns.

15 *Missionary Outlook*, Dec. 1921, 241.

16 Welter, "The Feminization of American Religion," 88.

17 *Missionary Outlook*, Sept. 1895, 133.

18 Johnson, *A History of Christianity*, 444.

19 G.M. Grant, "Current Events," *Queen's Quarterly* 5 (July 1897): 85, as cited in Berger, *The Sense of Power*, 218.

20 *ARWMS*, 1884–85, 16.

21 *Missionary Outlook*, Dec. 1905, 284.

22 See Birkett, *Spinsters Abroad*, 19–32.

23 See Vance, "Pleasure and Danger: Towards a Politics of Sexuality," for a discussion of the conflict between sexual danger and pleasure in women's lives.

24 *Christian Guardian*, 11 Oct. 1916.

25 UCAT, Strachan-Cartmell papers, box 1, file 12, E. Strachan to M. Cartmell, 1 Feb. 1886.

26 Best, "Evangelicalism and the Victorians," 39.

27 UCAT, biographical file of Constance Ward, answers to questions to candidates, ca 1917.

28 See Cook, *The Regenerators*, 20–3, for a discussion of the tension within the Methodist Church over the issue of higher criticism.

29 Allen, "The Social Gospel and the Reform Tradition in Canada 1890–1920," 384.

30 Garrett, "Sisters All: Feminism and the American Women's Missionary Movement," 228.

31 *Missionary Outlook*, Mar. 1922, 322.

32 UCAT, MCC, WMS, Executive notebooks, Board of Managers meeting, 25 Sept. 1917.

33 *Missionary Outlook*, July 1923, 158.

34 UCAT, Harper Coates family papers, Agnes Wintemute diaries, 23 Feb. 1887.

Bibliography

MANUSCRIPT COLLECTIONS

ARCHIVES OF ONTARIO
Ontario Ladies' College Papers

HAMILTON PUBLIC REFERENCE LIBRARY
Cartmell, Martha, and Strachan, Elizabeth Sutherland. Biographical material
Centenary Church, United Church of Canada. History 1868–1968
Henderson, Nora. Scrapbooks

OWEN GENERAL AND MARINE HOSPITAL, OWEN SOUND, ONTARIO
Papers of the Owen Sound General and Marine Hospital

PUBLIC ARCHIVES OF NOVA SCOTIA
Halifax Methodist Female Benevolent Society Papers

UNITED CHURCH OF CANADA ARCHIVES, EDMONTON
Correspondence between E. Chace and E. Weekes, Wahstao, Alberta [ts]
Diary kept by WMS missionaries, Wahstao, Alberta [ts]

UNITED CHURCH OF CANADA ARCHIVES, TORONTO
Allen, Annie. Personal Papers
Bay of Quinte Conference, Belleville Presbytery, Tabernacle Church. WMS Minutes
Biographical files of WMS missionaries, their families, and the elected officers of the society
Carman, Albert. Personal Papers
Centenary Methodist Church, Hamilton. WMS minute books
Harper Coates Family Papers
Endicott-Arnup Papers

Orlando Jolliffe Family Papers

Lamb, Mary. Personal Papers

Methodist Church of Canada. Deaconess Society Papers

Methodist Church of Canada. General Board of Missions. Young People's Forward Movement Papers

Methodist Church of Canada. Japan Mission Collection

Methodist Church of Canada. Missionary Society. Home Department

Methodist Church of Canada. United Church of Canada. Missions Pamphlets

Methodist Church of Canada. Woman's Missionary Society. Executive minute books

Methodist Church of Canada. Woman's Missionary Society. Miscellaneous correspondence

Methodist Church of Canada. Woman's Missionary Society. Notebooks

Methodist Church of Canada. Woman's Missionary Society. Overseas Missions. Japan

Methodist Church of Canada. Woman's Missionary Society. West China Correspondence and Papers

Methodist Episcopal Church in Canada. Woman's Missionary Society. Minutes and Reports, 1881–83

Sheridan, W.S. Personal Papers

Shore, T.E.S. Personal Papers

Strachan-Cartmell Papers

Student Volunteer Movement Papers

Alexander Sutherland Letterbooks and Papers

United Church of Canada. China Document Series

United Church of Canada. Missionary Society. Home Department

United Church of Canada. Woman's Missionary Society. Home Missions

United Church of Canada. Woman's Missionary Society. Overseas Mission. Japan

UNITED CHURCH OF CANADA ARCHIVES, UNIVERSITY OF WINNIPEG

Conference of Manitoba and Northwestern Ontario. Women's Organizations. Special Collections

UNITED CHURCH OF CANADA ARCHIVES, VANCOUVER SCHOOL OF THEOLOGY

Oriental Home and School Papers

GOVERNMENT DOCUMENTS

Canada. Census of Canada. 1851, 1861, 1871, 1881, 1891

5th Census of Canada, 1911. Ottawa: King's Printer, 1915

Dominion of Canada, House of Commons. *Sessional Papers*
Great Britain Parliamentary Papers. State Papers. China

NEWSPAPERS AND PERIODICALS

Annual Reports of the Missionary Society, Methodist Church of Canada 1881–1925
Annual Reports of the Woman's Missionary Society, Methodist Church of Canada 1881–1925
Canadian Methodist Magazine 1875–1906
Christian Guardian 1880–1925
Globe 1881–1925
Japan Daily Mail 1890
The Missionary Bulletin 1903–25
The Missionary Leaflet 1885–93
The Missionary Outlook 1881–1925
The Monthly Letter 1893–1925
The New Outlook 1925–39
The United Church Observer 1939–90
The West China Missionary News 1901–43

CONTEMPORARY SOURCES

A Call to Young Women from West China. Woman's Missionary Society of the Methodist Church, Canada.
Addison, Margaret. *Shaping a College Course with a View to Mission Work.* Woman's Missionary Society of the Methodist Church, Canada.
Armstrong, Robert C. *Progress in the Mikado's Empire.* Toronto: Missionary Society of the Methodist Church 1920.
Austin, B.F. "Open Doors for the Women of To-day." In Austin, ed., *Woman: Her Character, Culture and Calling.* 31–45.
– ed. *Woman: Her Character, Culture and Calling.* Brantford: Book and Bible House 1890.
Beach, Harlan. *A Geography and Atlas of Protestant Missions: Their Environment, Forces, Distributions, Methods, Problems, Results, and Prospects at the Opening of the Twentieth Century.* Vol. 2. *Statistics and Atlas.* New York: Student Volunteer Movement for Foreign Missions 1903.
Beaton, Kenneth J. *Serving with the Sons of Shuh: Fifty Fateful Years in West China, 1891–1941.* Toronto: United Church of Canada 1941.
Bentley, Eliza. *Precious Stones for Zion's Wall: A Record of Personal Experience in Things Connected with the Kingdom of God on Earth.* Toronto: William Briggs 1897.

Bishop, Isabella Bird. *The Yangtze Valley and Beyond.* 2 vols. New York: G.P. Putnam's Sons 1900.

Blackmore, I.S. *The Fiftieth Anniversary of the Founding of the Toyo Eiwa Jo Gakko.* 1934.

Bolton, A.E. *Medical Work among the Indians.* Woman's Missionary Society of the Methodist Church, Canada, 1895.

Brooks, Charlotte. *Work for Women in Chentu.* Woman's Missionary Society of the Methodist Church, Canada.

Canada's Missionary Congress: Addresses Delivered at the Canadian National Missionary Congress, held at Toronto, March 31 to April 4, 1909, with Reports of Committees. Toronto: Canadian Council, Laymen's Movement, 1909.

Canadian Baptist Foreign Mission Board. *A Sketch of the Origin and Development of our Mission Stations in India.* Toronto: Canadian Baptist Foreign Mission Board 1922.

Canadian Methodists in Japan 1911–1912. N. pub., n.d.

Carman, Mrs A. *The Rest Fund.* Woman's Missionary Society of the Methodist Church, Canada.

Chace, Edith. *Easter Day At Wahstao.* Woman's Missionary Society of the Methodist Church, Canada, 1909.

Champion, Thomas E. *The Methodist Churches of Toronto.* Toronto: G.M. Rose and Co. 1899.

Clarke, C.K. *A History of the Toronto General Hospital.* Toronto: William Briggs 1913.

Cornish, George, ed. *Cyclopaedia of Methodism in Canada.* 2 vols. Toronto: Methodist Book Room 1881, 1903.

Cowan, Kathleen. *It's Late and All the Girls Have Gone: An Annesley Diary, 1907–1910.* Ed. Aida Farrog Graff and David Knight. Toronto: Childe Thursday 1984.

Cunningham, Mary J. *Our Work in Japan.* N. pub., n.d.

Encyclopedia of Foreign Missions: Descriptive, Historical, Biographical, Statistical. New York: Funk and Wagnells Co. 1904.

Ferrier, Rev. Thompson. *Our Indians and Their Training for Citizenship.* Toronto: Methodist Book Room.

Forsythe, Robert C. *The China Martyrs of 1900: A Complete Roll of the Christian Heroes Martyred in China in 1900 with Narratives of Survivors.* London: Religious Tract Society 1904.

Galbraith, W. *Methodist Manual.* Toronto: William Briggs 1893.

Graham, E. *The Rest Fund.* Woman's Missionary Society of the Methodist Church, Canada.

Graham, Mrs W.H. *Forty-Five Years' Effort of the Woman's Missionary Society of the Methodist Church of Canada, 1881–1925.* Toronto: Woman's Missionary Society.

Gulick, Sidney L. *Working Women of Japan.* New York: Missionary Education Movement of the United States and Canada 1915.

Halpenny, Rev. W.T. *Our French Missions in Québec.*

Hambley, Laura. *Mission Stories from China.* Winnipeg 1944.

– *Our Girls' School in Chentu.* Woman's Missionary Society of the Methodist Church, Canada.

Hart, E.I. *Virgil C. Hart. Missionary Statesman.* Toronto: McClelland, Goodchild and Stewart 1917.

Hocking, William E. *Re-Thinking Missions: A Layman's Inquiry after One Hundred Years.* New York: Harper and Brothers 1932.

Johnston, Rev. Hugh. *Shall We or Shall We Not? A Series of Five Discourses Preached in the Pavilion Music Hall.* Toronto 1886.

Keenleyside, C.B. *A Day of Good Tidings.* Toronto: Young People's Forward Movement for Missions 1906.

– *God's Fellow Workers and the House To Be Built for Jehovah.* Toronto: The Missionary Society of the Methodist Church 1910.

Kilborn, O.L. *Heal the Sick.* Toronto: Missionary Society of the Methodist Church 1910.

Lambert, John C. *The Romance of Missionary Heroism.* London: Seeley and Co. 1907.

Latourette, K.S. *A History of Christian Missions in China.* New York: Macmillan 1929.

Lennox, William G. *The Health and Turnover of Missionaries.* New York: Foreign Mission Conference 1933.

Leonard, Edith Weekes. *The Austrian People.* Edmonton, n.d..

Long, Elizabeth E. *How the Light Came to Kitamaat.* N. pub., n.d.

MacGillivray, D., ed. *A Century of Protestant Missions in China 1807–1907.* New York: American Tract Society 1907; repr. San Francisco: Chinese Materials Centre 1979.

Maclean, John. *Canadian Savage Folk. The Native Tribes of Canada.* Toronto: William Briggs 1896; repr. Toronto: Coles 1971.

Methodist Church (Canada, Nfld., Bermuda). *Centennial of Canadian Methodism.* Toronto: William Briggs 1891.

– *Report of the General Superintendent's Official Visit to the Mission in Japan. April-June, 1898.* Toronto: Methodist Book and Publishing House 1898.

– *Doctrine and Discipline of the Methodist Church Canada, 1918.* Toronto: William Briggs 1919.

– *Our West China Mission.* Toronto: Missionary Society of the Methodist Church of Canada 1920.

– *Faith of Our Fathers. A Century of Victory 1821–1924.* Toronto: Methodist Missionary Society 1924.

Montgomery, Helen B. *Western Women in Eastern Lands: An Outline Study of Fifty Years of Woman's Work in Foreign Missions.* New York: Macmillan 1911.

Morgan, H.J., ed. *The Canadian Men and Women of the Time.* Toronto: William Briggs 1912.

Mosher, Eliza. "The Health of American Women." In Austin, ed., *Woman: Her Character, Culture, and Calling*. 235–45.

Oliver, Edmund H. *His Dominion of Canada: A Study in the Background, Development and Challenge of the Missions of the United Church of Canada*. Toronto: United Church Publishing House 1932.

Osterhout, S.S. *Orientals in Canada. The Story of the Work of the United Church with Asiatics in Canada*. Toronto: Ryerson Press 1929.

Platt, Mrs H.L. *The Story of the Years: A History of the Woman's Missionary Society of the Methodist Church of Canada 1881–1906*. Vol. 1. *Canada*. Vol. 2. *Beyond Seas*. Toronto: Woman's Missionary Society of the Methodist Church of Canada 1907.

Report of the Massey Foundation Commission on the Secondary Schools and Colleges of the Methodist Church of Canada, 1921. Toronto: Massey Foundation 1921.

Ross, Mrs E.W. *Life Investment*. Woman's Missionary Society of the Methodist Church, Canada.

– *Miss Jessie K. Munro*. Toronto: Woman's Missionary Society of the Methodist Church, Canada, 1923.

Sanderson, J.E. *The First Century of Methodism in Canada*. 2 vols. Toronto: William Briggs 1910.

Saunby, John. *Japan: The Land of the Morning*. Toronto: William Briggs 1895.

Smith, W.E. *A Canadian Doctor in West China: Forty Years Under Three Flags*. Toronto: Ryerson Press 1939.

Stauffer, Milton. *The Christian Occupation of China: A General Survey of the Numerical Strength and Geographical Distribution of the Christian Forces in China*. Shanghai 1923; repr. San Francisco: Chinese Materials Centre 1979.

Stephenson, Mrs F.C. *One Hundred Years of Canadian Methodist Missions. 1824–1924*. Toronto: Missionary Society of the Methodist Church 1925.

Strachan, Mrs E.S. *The Healing Hand of the Woman's Missionary Society in China 1894–1915*. Woman's Missionary Society of the Methodist Church, Canada.

– *The Story of the Years: A History of the Woman's Missionary Society of the Methodist Church, Canada*. Vol. 3. *1906–1916*. Toronto: Woman's Missionary Society of the Methodist Church, Canada, 1917.

Student Mission Power: Report of the First International Convention of the Student Volunteer Movement for Foreign Missions, Cleveland, Feb. 26—March 1, 1891. Repr. Pasadena, Calif., 1979.

Sutherland, Alexander. *Methodism in Canada. Its Work and Its Story*. London: Charles H. Kelly 1903.

– *The Methodist Church and Missions in Canada and Newfoundland*. Toronto: Young People's Forward Movement for Missions 1906.

Ten Reasons Why I Should Belong to the Woman's Missionary Society. Woman's Missionary Society of the Methodist Church, Canada.

The Cross in the East. Woman's Missionary Society of the Methodist Church, Canada.

United Church of Canada. *Forward With China. The Story of the Missions of the United Church of Canada in China.* Toronto: Board of Foreign Missions of the United Church of Canada 1928.

– *Fruits of Christian Missions in Japan.* Toronto: Woman's Missionary Society of the United Church of Canada.

Villard, P. *Up to the Light: The Story of French Protestantism in Canada.* Toronto: Board of Home Missions of the United Church of Canada 1928.

Wallace, Edward W. *The Heart of Sz-Chuan.* Toronto: Methodist Young People's Forward Movement for Missions 1903.

Weaver, E.P., A.E. Weaver, and E.C. Weaver, eds. *The Canadian Woman's Annual and Social Service Directory.* Toronto: McClelland, Goodchild and Stewart 1915.

Webster, Thomas. *History of the Methodist Episcopal Church in Canada.* Hamilton: Canada Christian Advocate Office 1870.

Withrow, W. "The Higher Education of Women." In Austin, ed., *Woman: Her Character, Culture, and Calling.* 325–31.

– *China and Its People.* Toronto: William Briggs 1894.

Women of Canada: Their Life and Work. National Council of Women of Canada 1900; repr. National Council of Women 1975.

Woodsworth, J. S. *Strangers within Our Gates or Coming Canadians.* Toronto: Missionary Society of the Methodist Church of Canada 1909.

World Missionary Conference 1910: To Consider Missionary Problems in Relation to the Non Christian World. Report of Commission I. Carrying the Gospel to the Non Christian World. New York: Oliphant, Anderson and Ferrier, F.H. Revell 1911.

World Missionary Conference 1910. Report of Commission VII. Missions and Governments. New York: Oliphant, Anderson and Ferrier, F.H. Revell 1911.

World-Wide Evangelization. The Urgent Business of the Church. New York: Student Volunteer Movement for Foreign Missions 1902.

SECONDARY SOURCES

Airhart, Phyllis. "The Eclipse of Revivalist Spirituality: The Transformation of Canadian Methodist Piety 1884–1925." PhD, University of Chicago 1985.

Allen, Richard. "The Social Gospel and the Reform Tradition in Canada, 1890–1928." *Canadian Historical Review* 49 (Dec. 1968): 381–99.

– *The Social Passion: Religion and Social Reform in Canada 1914–28.* Toronto: University of Toronto Press 1973.

Antler, Joyce. "'After College, What?': New Graduates and the Family Claim." *American Quarterly* 32, no. 4 (Fall 1980): 409–34.

Austin, Alvyn J. *Saving China: Canadian Missionaries in the Middle Kingdom 1888–1959*. Toronto: University of Toronto Press 1986.

Avery, Donald. *"Dangerous Foreigners": European Immigrant Workers and Labour Radicalism in Canada, 1896–1932*. Toronto: McClelland and Stewart 1979.

Bacchi, Carol Lee. *Liberation Deferred?: The Ideas of the English-Canadian Suffragists, 1877–1919*. Toronto: University of Toronto Press 1983.

Ball, Rosemary. "'A Perfect Farmer's Wife': Women in 19th–Century Rural Ontario." *Canada: A Historical Magazine* 3 (Dec. 1975): 2–21.

Barr, Pat. *To China with Love: The Lives and Times of Protestant Missionaries in China 1860–1900*. London: Seckert and Warburg 1972.

Beasley, W.G. *The Rise of Modern Japan*. London: Weidenfeld and Nicolson 1990.

Beaver, R. Pierce. *Ecumenical Beginnings in Protestant World Mission: A History of Comity*. New York: Thomas Nelson 1962.

– *All Loves Excelling: American Protestant Women Missionaries in World Mission*. Grand Rapids, Mich.: W.B. Eerdmanns 1968.

Bederman, Gail. "'The Women Have Had Charge of the Church Work Long Enough': The Men and Religion Forward Movement of 1911–1912 and the Masculinization of Middle-Class Protestantism." *American Quarterly* 41, no. 3 (Sept. 1989): 432–65.

Berger, Carl. *The Sense of Power*. Toronto: University of Toronto Press 1970.

Best, Geoffrey. "Evangelicalism and the Victorians." In Anthony Symondson, ed., *The Victorian Crisis of Faith*. London: Society for Promoting Christian Knowledge 1970, 37–55.

Birkett, Dea. *Spinsters Abroad: Victorian Lady Explorers*. London: Basil Blackwell 1989.

Blair, Karen. *The Clubwoman as Feminist: True Womanhood Redefined, 1868–1914*. New York: Holmes and Meier 1980.

Blauvelt, Martha. "Women and Revivalism." In Rosemary Ruether and Rosemary Keller, eds., *Women and Religion in America*. Vol. 1. *The Nineteenth Century*. San Francisco: Harper and Row 1981, 1–45.

Bliss, J.M. "The Methodist Church and World War I." *Canadian Historical Review* 49 (Sept. 1968): 213–33.

Boxer, Marilyn, and Jean Quaraert, eds. *Connecting Spheres: Women in the Western World, 1500 to the Present*. New York: Oxford University Press 1987.

Brouwer, Ruth Compton. "The Canadian Methodist Church and Ecclesiastical Suffrage for Women, 1902–1914," *Canadian Methodist Historical Society Papers* 2 (1977): 1–21.

– "Opening Doors through Social Service: Aspects of Women's Work in the Candian Presbyterian Mission in Central India, 1877–1914." In Leslie Flemming, ed., *Women's Work for Women: Missionaries and Social Change in Asia*. Boulder: Westview Press 1989, 11–34.

– *New Women for God: Canadian Presbyterian Women and India Missions 1876–1914.* Toronto: University of Toronto Press 1990.

Brown, Earl Kent. "Women of the Word." In Hilah Thomas and Rosemary Keller, eds., *Women in New Worlds: Historical Perspectives on the Wesleyan Tradition.* Nashville: Abingdon Press 1981, 69–87.

Brown, Robert Craig, and Ramsay Cook. *Canada 1896–1921: A Nation Transformed.* Toronto: McClelland and Stewart 1974.

Brumberg, Joan Jacobs. "Zenanas and Girlless Villages: The Ethnology of American Evangelical Women, 1870–1910." *Journal of American History* 69 (Sept. 1982): 347–71.

Bush, Peter George. "The Reverend James Caughey and Wesleyan Methodist Revivalism in Nineteenth-Century Canada." *Ontario History* 74 (Sept. 1987): 231–50.

Caldwell, J. Warren. "The Unification of Methodism in Canada, 1865–1884." *The Bulletin* (Committee on Archives of the United Church of Canada) 19 (1967): 3–61.

Caplan, Patricia, and Janet M. Burja. *Women United, Women Divided: Cross-cultural Perspectives on Female Solidarity.* London: Tavistock Publications 1978.

Carroll, Berenice A., ed. *Liberating Women's History: Theoretical and Critical Essays.* Urbana, Ill.: University of Illinois Press 1976.

Carroll, Theodora Foster. *Women, Religion and Development in the Third World.* New York: Praeger 1983.

Carter, Paul. *The Spiritual Crisis of the Gilded Age.* DeKalb, Ill.: Northern Illinois University Press 1971.

Carwardine, Richard. *Trans-atlantic Revivalism: Popular Evangelicalism in Britain and America, 1790–1865.* Westport, Conn.: Greenwood Press 1976.

Chafetz, Janet Saltzman, and Anthony Gary Dworkin. *Female Revolt: Women's Movements in World and Historical Perspective.* Totowa, NJ: Rowman and Allanheld 1986.

Chambers-Schiller, Lee. "The Single Woman: Family and Vocation among Nineteenth-Century Reformers." In Mary Kelley, ed., *Woman's Being, Woman's Place: Female Identity and Vocation in American History.* Boston: G.K. Hall 1977, 334–50.

Chappell, Constance and Mary. *Recollections of Japan.* Published privately 1978.

Christensen, Torben, and William R. Hutchison, eds. *Missionary Ideologies in the Imperialist Era: 1880–1920.* Copenhagen: Forlaget Aros 1982.

Clymer, Kenton. *Protestant Missionaries in the Philippines, 1898–1916: An Inquiry into the American Colonial Mentality.* Chicago: University of Illinois Press 1986.

Coburn, Judi. "'I See and Am Silent': A Short History of Nursing in Ontario." In *Women at Work: Ontario 1850–1930.* Toronto: Women's Press 1974, 127–163.

Cohen, Marjorie. *Women's Work, Markets, and Economic Developments in Nine-teenth-Century Ontario.* Toronto: University of Toronto Press 1988.

Cohen, Paul A. *China and Christianity: The Missionary Movement and the Growth of Chinese Antiforeignism, 1860–1870.* Cambridge, Mass.: Harvard University Press 1963.

Connelly, Mark. *The Response to Prostitution in the Progressive Era.* Chapel Hill, NC: University of North Carolina Press 1980.

Conrad, Margaret, Toni Laidlaw, and Donna Smyth, eds. *No Place Like Home: Diaries and Letters of Nova Scotia Women 1771–1938.* Halifax: Formac 1988.

Cook, Ramsay. *The Regenerators: Social Criticism in Late Victorian English Canada.* Toronto: University of Toronto Press 1985.

Copp, Terry. *The Anatomy of Poverty: The Condition of the Working Class in Montreal, 1897–1929.* Toronto: McClelland and Stewart 1974.

Cott, Nancy. *The Bonds of Womanhood: "Woman's Sphere" in New England, 1780–1835.* New Haven: Yale University Press 1977.

– *The Grounding of Modern Feminism.* New Haven: Yale University Press 1987.

Croll, Elisabeth. *Feminism and Socialism in China.* London: Routledge and Kegan Paul 1978.

– "Rural China: Segregation to Solidarity." In Patricia Caplan and Janet Burja, eds., *Women United, Women Divided: Cross-cultural Perspectives on Female Solidatiry.* London: Tavistock Publications 1978, 46–76.

Cross, Whitney. *The Burned-over District: The Social and Intellectual History of Enthusiastic Religion in Western New York, 1800–1850.* Ithaca: Cornell University Press 1950.

Curtin, Katie. *Women in China.* New York: Pathfinder Press 1975.

Danylewycz, Marta. *Taking the Veil: An Alternative to Marriage, Motherhood and Spinsterhood in Quebec, 1840–1920.* Toronto: McClelland and Stewart 1987.

Danylewycz, M., B. Light, and A. Prentice. "The Evolution of the Sexual Division in Labour in Teaching: A Nineteenth-Century Ontario and Québec Case Study." *Histoire sociale/Social History* 16 (May 1983): 81–110.

Danylewycz, M., and A. Prentice. "Teachers' Work: Changing Patterns and Perceptions in the Emerging School Systems of Nineteenth- and Early Twentieth-Century Central Canada." *Labour/Le Travail* 17 (Spring 1986): 59–82.

Davey, Ian. "Trends in Female School Attendance in Mid-Nineteenth Century Ontario." *Histoire sociale/Social History* 8 (Nov. 1975): 238–54.

Davies, Rupert. "The People Called Methodists: 1. Our Doctrines." In Rupert Davies and Gordon Rupp, eds., *A History of the Methodist Church in Great Britain.* London: Epworth Press 1965, 1:147–79.

Davy, Shirley, ed. *Women Work and Worship in the United Church of Canada.* Toronto: United Church of Canada 1983.

Donzelot, Jacques. *The Policing of Families*. New York: Pantheon 1979.

Douglas, Ann. *The Feminization of American Culture*. New York: Alfred Knopf 1977.

Drachman, Virginia. "Female Solidarity and Professional Success: The Dilemma of Women Doctors in Late Nineteenth-Century America." *Journal of Social History* (Summer 1982): 607–19.

Drucker, Alison. "The Influence of Western Women on the Anti-Footbinding Movement in 1840–41." In Richard Guisso and Stanley Johannesen, eds., *Women in China: Current Directions in Historical Scholarship*. Youngstown, NY: Philo Press 1981, 179–200.

Drummond, Richard H. *A History of Christianity in Japan*. Grand Rapids, Mich.: William B. Eerdmann 1970.

Dumont-Johnson, Micheline. "Les Communautés religieuses et la condition féminine." *Recherches sociographiques* 19 (Jan.–Apr. 1978): 79–102.

Dyhouse, Carol. *Girls Growing Up in Late Victorian and Edwardian England*. London: Routledge and Kegan Paul 1981.

Ehrenreich, Barbara, and Dierdre English. *For Her Own Good: 150 Years of the Experts' Advice to Women*. Garden City, NY: Anchor Books 1979.

Eisenstein, Zillah, ed. *Capitalist Patriarchy and the Case for Socialist Feminism*. New York and London: Monthly Review Press 1979.

Emery, G.N. "Methodist Missions among the Ukrainians." *Alberta Historical Review* 19 (Spring 1971): 8–19.

– "Ontario Denied: The Methodist Church on the Prairies 1896–1914." In F.H. Armstrong, H.A. Stevenson, and J.D. Wilson, eds., *Aspects of Nineteenth-Century Ontario: Essays Presented to James J. Talman*. London, Ont.: University of Western Ontario Press 1974, 312–26.

– "The Origins of Canadian Methodist Involvement in the Social Gospel Movement 1890–1914." *The Bulletin* (Committee on Archives of the United Church) 26 (1977): 104–19.

Endicott, S. *James G. Endicott: Rebel Out of China*. Toronto: University of Toronto Press 1980.

Epstein, Barbara. *The Politics of Domesticity: Women, Evangelization and Temperance in Nineteenth-Century America*. Middleton, Conn.: Wesleyan University Press 1981.

Esherick, Joseph W. *The Origins of the Boxer Rebellion*. Berkeley: University of California Press 1986.

Faderman, Lillian. *Surpassing the Love of Men: Romantic Friendship and Love between Women from the Renaissance to the Present*. New York: Wm Morrow 1981.

Fairbank, John K., ed. *The Missionary Enterprise in China and America*. Cambridge: Harvard University Press 1974.

– and Edwin O. Reischauer. *China: Tradition and Transformation*. Boston: George Allen and Unwin 1979.

- "Missionary History as Fiction." In Fairbank, ed., *China Watch*. Cambridge, Mass.: Harvard University Press 1987, 27–41.
Feuerwerker, Albert. *The Foreign Establishment in China in the Early Twentieth Century*. Ann Arbor, Mich.: Univ. of Michigan Press 1976.
Flemming, Leslie A., ed. *Women's Work for Women: Missionaries and Social Change in Asia*. Boulder, Col.: Westview Press 1989, intro, 2–27.
Ford, Anne R. *A Path Not Strewn with Roses: One Hundred Years of Women at the University of Toronto, 1884–1984*. Toronto: University of Toronto Press 1985.
Forsythe, Sydney A. *An American Missionary Community in China, 1895–1905*. Cambridge, Mass.: Harvard University Press 1971.
Foster, John W. "The Imperialism of Righteousness: Canadian Protestant Missions and the Chinese Revolution, 1925–1928." PhD, University of Toronto 1977.
Freedman, Estelle B., Barbara Gelpi, Susan Johnson, and Kathleen Weston, eds. *The Lesbian Issue: Essays from Signs*. Chicago: University of Chicago Press 1985.
French, Goldwin. *Parsons and Politics: The Role of the Wesleyan Methodists in Upper Canada and the Maritimes from 1780 to 1855*. Toronto: Ryerson Press 1962.
- "The People Called Methodists in Canada." In John W. Grant, ed., *The Churches and the Canadian Experience*. Toronto: Ryerson Press 1963, 69–80.
- "The Evangelical Creed in Canada." In W.L. Morton, ed., *The Shield of Achilles: Aspects of Canada in the Victorian Age*. Toronto: McClelland and Stewart 1968, 15–35.
Friedman, Jean E., and William G. Shade. *Our American Sisters: Women in American Life and Thought*. Lexington, Mass.: D.C. Heath 1982.
Garrett, Shirley S. "Sisters All: Feminism and the American Women's Missionary Movement." In Torben Christensen and William R. Hutchison, eds., *Missionary Ideologies in the Imperialist Era: 1880–1920*. Copenhagen: Forlaget Aros 1982, 221–28.
Gasster, Michael. *China's Struggle to Modernize*. New York: Alfred A. Knopf 1972.
Gauvreau, Michael. "The Taming of History: Reflections on the Canadian Methodist Encounter with Biblical Criticism, 1830–1900." *Canadian Historical Review* 65 (Sept. 1984): 315–46.
- *The Evangelical Century: College and Creed in English Canada from the Great Revival to the Great Depression*. Montreal and Kingston: McGill-Queen's University Press 1991.
Gay, Peter. *The Bourgeois Experience: Victoria to Freud*. 2 vols. New York: Oxford University Press 1984, 1986.
Getty, Ian, and Antoine Lussier, eds. *As Long as the Sun Shines and the Water Flows*. Vancouver: University of British Columbia Press 1983.

Gidney, R.D., and W.P.J. Millar. *Inventing Secondary Education: The Rise of the High School in Nineteenth-Century Ontario*. Montreal and Kingston: McGill-Queen's University Press 1990.

Giele, Janet, and Audrey Smock, eds. *Women's Roles and Status in Eight Countries*. New York: John Wiley and Sons 1977.

Gifford, Caroline DeSwart. "Sisterhoods of Service and Reform: Organized Methodist Women in the Late Nineteenth Century, An Essay on the State of the Research." Paper presented to Canadian Methodist Historical Society, Toronto, June 1985.

Gillett, Margaret. *We Walked Very Warily: A History of Women at McGill*. Montreal: Eden Press 1981.

Gorham, Deborah. *The Victorian Girl and the Feminine Ideal*. London: Croom Helm 1982.

Graham, Elizabeth. "Schoolmarms and Early Teaching in Ontario." In *Women at Work: Ontario 1850–1930*. Toronto: Women's Press 1974, 165–209.

– *Medicine Man to Missionary: Missionaries as Agents of Change among the Indians of Southern Ontario, 1784–1867*. Toronto: Peter Martin 1975.

Grant, John W. *The Canadian Experience of Church Union*. Richmond, Va.: John Knox Press 1967.

– "The Reaction of Wasp Churches to Non-Wasp Immigrants." *Canadian Society of Church History Papers* 10 (1968): 1–11.

– *The Church in the Canadian Era: The First Century of Confederation*. Toronto: McGraw-Hill Ryerson 1972.

– *Moon of Wintertime: Missionaries and the Indians of Canada in Encounter since 1534*. Toronto: University of Toronto Press 1984.

– *A Profusion of Spires*. Toronto: University of Toronto Press 1988.

Gregg, Alice H. *China and Educational Autonomy: The Changing Role of the Protestant Educational Missionary in China, 1807–1937*. Syracuse: Syracuse University Press 1946.

Hacker, Carlotta. *The Indomitable Lady Doctors*. Toronto: Clarke, Irwin 1974.

Haines, Gregory. *Gunboats on the Great River*. London: Macdonald and Jane's 1976.

Halevy, Elie. *The Birth of Methodism in England*. Chicago: University of Chicago Press 1971.

Hane, Mikiso, ed. *Reflections on the Way to the Gallows: Rebel Women in Prewar Japan*. Berkeley: University of California Press 1988, intro., 1–28.

Harney, Robert F. *Italians in Canada*. Toronto: Multicultural History Society of Ontario 1978.

– "Chiaroscuro: Italians in Toronto 1885–1915." *Polyphony* 6 (Spring—Summer 1984): 44–9.

Harris, Barbara J. *Beyond Her Sphere: Women and the Professions in American History*. Westport, Conn.: Greenwood Press 1978.

Hartwell, George E. *Granary of Heaven*. Toronto: Woman's Missionary Society of the United Church of Canada 1941.

Haycock, Ronald Graham. *The Image of the Indian*. Waterloo, Ont.: Wilfrid Laurier University 1971.

Headon, Christopher. "Women and Organized Religion in Mid- and Late-Nineteenth-Century Canada." *Journal of the Canadian Church Historical Society* 20 (1978): 3–18.

Hensman, Bertha. "The Kilborn Family: A Record of a Canadian Family's Service to Medical Work and Education in China and Hong Kong." *Canadian Medical Association Journal* 97 (Aug. 1967): 1–13.

Heren, Louis, C.P. Fitzgerald, Michael Freeberne, Brian Hook, and David Bonavia. *China's Three Thousand Years: The Story of a Great Civilization*. New York: Collier 1973.

Hersey, John. *The Call*. New York: Penguin 1985.

Hibbert, Christopher. *The Dragon Wakes: China and the West 1793–1911*. London: Longmans 1970.

Hill, Patricia R. *The World Their Household: The American Woman's Foreign Mission Movement and Cultural Transformation, 1870–1920*. Ann Arbor: University of Michigan Press 1985.

Hirata, Lucie. "Free, Indentured, Enslaved. Chinese Prostitutes in Nineteenth-Century America." *Signs* 5(Autumn 1979): 3–29.

Hobsbawm, E.J. *Industry and Empire*. Harmondsworth: Penguin 1977.

Hockin, Katharine. *Servants of God in People's China*. New York: Friendship Press 1962.

Hughes, E.R. *The Invasion of China by the Western World*. New York: Barnes and Noble 1961.

Hunter, Jane. *The Gospel of Gentility: American Women Missionaries in Turn-of-the-Century China*. New Haven: Yale University Press 1984.

Hutchison, William R. *Errand to the World: American Protestant Thought and Foreign Missions*. Chicago: University of Chicago Press 1987.

Hyatt, Irwin. *Our Ordered Lives Confess: Three Nineteenth-Century American Missionaries in East Shantung*. Cambridge, Mass.: Harvard University Press 1976.

Ion, A. Hamish. *The Cross and the Rising Sun*. Waterloo: Wilfrid Laurier University Press 1990.

Isaacs, Harold R. *Images of Asia: American Views of China and India*. New York: Capricorn Books 1962.

James, Janet Wilson. "Women and Religion: An Introduction." *American Quarterly* 30, no. 5 (Winter 1978): 579–81.

– ed. *Women in American Religion*. Philadelphia: University of Pennsylvania Press 1980.

Jansen, Marius, ed. *Changing Japanese Attitudes towards Modernization*. Princeton: Princeton University Press 1964.

Jardine, Pauline. "An Urban Middle-Class Calling: Women and the Emergence of Modern Nursing Education at Toronto General Hospital 1881–1914." *Urban History Review* 17 (Feb. 1989): 177–90.

Jeffreys, Sheila. *The Spinster and Her Enemies: Feminism and Sexuality 1880–1930.* London: Pandora Books 1985.

Johnson, Dale. *Women in English Religion 1700–1925.* New York; Edwin Mellen Press 1983.

Johnson, Paul. *A History of Christianity.* Harmondsworth: Penguin 1976.

Juteau-Lee, Danielle. "Les Religieuses du Québec: Leur influence sur la vie professionnelle des femmes, 1908–1954." *Atlantis* 5 (Spring 1980): 22–33.

Kapp, Robert A. *Szechwan and the Chinese Republic: Provincial Military and Central Power, 1911–1938.* New Haven: Yale University Press 1973.

Katz, Michael. *The People of Hamilton, Canada West: Family and Class in a Mid-Nineteenth-Century City.* Cambridge, Mass.: Harvard University Press 1975.

Kazuko, Ono. *Chinese Women in a Century of Revolution, 1850–1950.* Stanford: Stanford University Press 1989.

Kealey, Linda, ed. *A Not Unreasonable Claim: Women and Reform in Canada, 1880s-1920s.* Toronto: Women's Press 1979.

Kelley, Mary, ed. *Woman's Being, Woman's Place: Female Identity and Vocation in American History.* Boston: G.K. Hall 1979.

Kerber, Linda, and Jane Mathews. *Women's America: Re-focusing the Past.* New York: Oxford University Press 1983.

Kessler-Harris, Alice. *Out to Work: A History of Wage-Earning Women in the United States.* New York: Oxford University Press 1982.

Kowalski, Kenneth. "The West China Mission of the Methodist Church of Canada, Szechwan, China, 1891–1911." MA, University of Alberta 1970.

Kubat, Daniel, and David Thornton. *A Statistical Profile of Canadian Society.* Toronto: McGraw-Hill Ryerson 1974.

Lang, Olga. *Chinese Family and Society.* New Haven: Yale University Press 1946, repr. 1968.

Langford, Thomas A. *Practical Divinity: Theology in the Wesleyan Tradition.* Nashville: Abingdon Press 1983.

Lapp, Eula C. *China Was My University: The Life of Hulda May Carscallen.* Agincourt, Ont.: Generation Press 1980.

Lasch, Christopher. *The New Radicalism in America, 1889–1963: The Intellectual as a Social Type.* New York: Alfred A. Knopf 1965.

LaViolette, Forest. *The Struggle for Survival: Indian Cultures and the Protestant Ethic in British Columbia.* Toronto: University of Toronto Press 1961.

Lawrie, Bruce. "An Historical Overview of the Canadian Methodist Mission in West China 1891–1925." *Canadian Methodist Historical Society Papers* 2 (1978): 1–8.

Laycock, Mae. *Bridges of Friendship.* Published privately 1976.

Lebra, Joyce, Joy Paulson, and Elizabeth Powers, eds. *Women in Changing Japan*. Boulder, Col.: Westview Books 1976.

Lee, Bernice. "Female Infanticide in China." In Richard Guisso and Stanley Johannesen, eds., *Women in China: Current Directions in Historical Scholarship*. Youngstown, NY: Philo Press 1981, 163–77.

Leechman, Douglas. *Native Tribes of Canada*. Toronto: W.J. Gage, n.d.

Legendre, Anne Carmelle. "The Baptist Contribution to Nineteenth Century Education for Women: An Examination of Moulton College and McMaster University." MA, McMaster University 1981.

Liao, Kuang-Sheng. *Antiforeignism and Modernization in China 1860–1980: Linkage between Domestic Politics and Foreign Policy*. Hong Kong: Chinese University Press 1984.

Light, Beth, and Joy Parr, eds. *Canadian Women on the Move, 1867–1920*. Toronto: New Hogtown Press and the Ontario Institute for Studies in Education 1983.

Linton, Marilyn. "WMS: 100 Years of Woman Power." *United Church Observer* (June 1976):16–19.

Liu, Kwang-Ching, ed. *American Missionaries in China: Papers from Harvard Seminars*. Cambridge, Mass.: Harvard University East Asian Research Center 1966.

Longsworth, Polly. *Austin and Mabel: The Amherst Affair and Love Letters of Austin Dickinson and Mabel Loomis Todd*. New York: Farrar, Strauss, Giroux 1984.

Lubove, Roy. *The Professional Altruist: The Emergence of Social Work as a Career 1880–1930*. Cambridge, Mass.: Harvard University Press 1965.

Lutz, Jessie C., ed. *Christian Missions in China: Evangelists of What?* Boston: D.C. Heath 1965.

Lyall, Leslie T. *The China Inland Mission 1865–1965*. Chicago: Moody Press 1965.

McDannell, Colleen. *The Christian Home in Victorian America, 1840–1900*. Bloomington: Indiana University Press 1986.

McDowell, John Patrick. *The Social Gospel in the South: The Woman's Home Mission Movement in the Methodist Episcopal Church South, 1886–1939*. Baton Rouge: Louisiana State University Press 1982.

MacHaffie, Barbara. *Herstory: Women in the Christian Tradition*. Philadelphia: Fortress Press 1986.

Mackerras, Colin. *Western Images of China*. Oxford: Oxford University Press 1989.

McKillop, Brian. *A Disciplined Intelligence: Critical Inquiry and Canadian Thought in the Victorian Era*. Montreal: McGill-Queen's University Press 1979.

– "Canadian Methodism in 1884." *Canadian Methodist Historical Society Papers* 4 (1984): 1–33.

MacLarren, Roy. *Canadians in Russia, 1918–1919*. Toronto: Macmillan of Canada 1976.

McLoughlin, William G. *Revivals, Awakenings, and Reform: An Essay on Religion and Social Change in America, 1607–1977*. Chicago: University of Chicago Press 1976.

Magney, William H. "The Methodist Church and the National Gospel, 1884–1914." *The Bulletin* (Committee on Archives of the United Church of Canada) 20 (1968): 3–95.

Mangan, J.A. *The Games Ethic and Imperialism: Aspects of the Diffusion of an Ideal*. London: Viking 1986.

Matthaei, Julie A. *An Economic History of Women in America: Women's Work, the Social Division of Labour and the Development of Capitalism*. Brighton: Harvester Press 1982.

Maxwell, Grant. *Assignment in China: 71 Canadians in China 1902–1954*. Scarboro: Scarboro Foreign Mission Society 1982.

Middleton, Dorothy. *Victorian Lady Travellers*. London: Routledge and Kegan Paul 1965.

Miller, J.R. "Anti-Catholic Thought in Victorian Canada." *Canadian Historical Review* 66 (Dec.1985): 474–94.

Miller, Stuart C. *The Unwelcome Immigrant: The American Image of the Chinese, 1785–1882*. Berkeley: University of California Press 1969.

Minden, Karen. "Missionaries, Medicine and Modernization: Canadian Medical Missionaries in Sechuan, 1925–1952." PhD, York University 1981.

Mitchinson, Wendy. "Aspects of Reform: Four Women's Organizations in Nineteenth-Century Canada." PhD, York University 1977.

– "Canadian Women and Church Missionary Societies in the Nineteenth Century: A Step Towards Independence." *Atlantis* 2 (Spring 1977): 57–75.

Moir, J.S., and C.T. McIntire, eds. *Canadian Protestant and Catholic Missions, 1820–1960s: Historical Essays in Honour of John Webster Grant*. New York: Peter Land 1988.

Moorhouse, Geoffrey. *The Missionaries*. London: Eyre Methuen 1973.

Morton, James. *In the Sea of Sterile Mountains*. Vancouver: J.J. Douglas 1974.

Morton, W. Scott. *Japan: Its History and Culture*. New York: Thomas Y. Cromwell 1975.

Muir, Elizabeth. "Petticoats in the Pulpit: Early Nineteenth Century Methodist Women Preachers in Upper Canada." PhD, McGill University 1990.

Neill, Stephen. *Colonialism and Christian Missions*. New York: McGraw-Hill 1966.

Newton, Judith, Mary Ryan, and Judith Walkowitz, eds. *Sex and Class in Women's History*. London: Routledge and Kegan Paul 1983.

Norman, Gwen. *One Hundred Years in Japan*. Unpublished ms 1979.

Norwood, Frank A. *The Story of American Methodism: A History of the United Methodists and Their Relations*. Nashville, Tenn.: Abingdon Press 1974.

Pacey, Desmond. "Fiction (1920–1940)." In Carl Klinck, ed., *Literary History of Canada: Canadian Literature in English*. Toronto: University of Toronto Press 1965, 1:168–204.

Palmer, Howard. *Patterns of Prejudice: A History of Nativism in Alberta*. Toronto: McClelland and Stewart 1982.

Parr, Joy. "Nature and Hierarchy: Reflections on Writing the History of Women and Children." *Atlantis* 11 (Fall 1985): 39–44.

Paulsen, George E. "The Szechwan Riots of 1895 and American 'Missionary Diplomacy.'" *Journal of Asian Studies* 28 (Feb. 1969): 285–98.

– "The Chengtu Anti-Missionary Riot May, 1895." *Methodist History* 7 (Apr. 1969): 24–31.

Paulson, Joy. "Evolution of the Feminine Ideal." In Joyce Lebra, Joy Paulson, and Elizabeth Powers, eds., *Women in Changing Japan*. Boulder, Colo.: Westview Press 1976, 13–18.

Peiss, Kathy. *Cheap Amusements: Working Women and Leisure in Turn-of-the-Century New York*. Philadelphia: Temple University Press, 1986.

Pharr, Susan J. "Japan: Historical and Contemporary Perspectives." In Janet Giele and Audrey Smock, eds. *Women's Roles and Status in Eight Countries*. New York: John Wiley and Sons 1977, 219–55.

Phillips, Clifton. "The Student Volunteer Movement and Its Role in China Missions." In John K. Fairbank, ed., *The Missionary Enterprise in China and America*. Cambridge, Mass.: Harvard University Press 1974, 93–109.

Pivar, David J. *Purity Crusade: Sexual Morality and Social Controls, 1868–1900*. Westport, Conn.: Greenwood Press 1973.

Potrebenko, Helen. *No Streets of Gold: A Social History of Ukrainians in Alberta*. Vancouver: New Star Books 1977.

Powles, Cyril. *Victorian Missionaries in Meiji Japan: The Shiba Sect, 1873–1900*. Toronto: University of Toronto–York University Joint Centre on Modern East Asia 1987.

Prentice, Alison. "The Feminization of Teaching." In Susan Trofimenkoff and Alison Prentice, eds., *The Neglected Majority*. Toronto: McClelland and Stewart 1977, 1:49–65.

Prentice, Alison, Paula Bourne, Gail Cuthbert Brandt, Beth Light, Wendy Mitchinson, and Naomi Black. *Canadian Women: A History*. Toronto: Harcourt Brace Jovanovich 1988.

Prentice, Alison, and Susan Houston, eds. *Family School and Society in Nineteenth-Century Canada*. Toronto: Oxford University Press 1975.

Price, Eva Jane. *China Journal 1889–1900: An American Missionary Family during the Boxer Rebellion*. New York: Scribners 1989.

Prochaska, F.K. *Women and Philanthropy in Nineteenth-Century England*. Oxford: Clarendon Press 1980.

Pruitt, Ida. *The Daughter of Han: The Autobiography of a Chinese Working Woman*. Stanford, Calif.: Stanford University Press 1945, repr. 1967.

Purcell, Victor. *The Boxer Uprising: A Background Study*. Cambridge: Cambridge University Press 1963.

Rabe, Valentin H. *The Home Base of American China Missions 1880–1920*. Cambridge, Mass.: Harvard University Press 1978.

Reid, John. "The Education of Women at Mount Allison, 1854–1914." *Acadiensis* 12 (Spring 1983): 3–33.

Reischauer, Edwin O. *Japan: The Story of a Nation*. New York: Alfred A. Knopf 1974.

Rendall, Jane. *The Origins of Modern Feminism: Women in Britain, France and the United States*. London: Macmillan 1985.

Reuther, Rosemary, and Rosemary Skinner, eds. *Women and Religion in America*. Vol. 1. *The Nineteenth Century*. San Francisco: Harper and Row 1981. Vol. 3. *1900–1968*. San Francisco: Harper and Row 1986.

Ridout, Katherine, "A Woman of Mission: The Religious and Cultural Odyssey of Agnes Wintemute Coates." *Canadian Historical Review* 71 (June 1990): 204–44.

Robert, Dana. "The Origin of the Student Volunteer Watchword: The Evangelization of the World in This Generation." *International Bulletin of Missionary Research* 10 (Oct. 1986): 146–9.

Rosenberg, Carroll Smith. *Religion and the Rise of the American City: The New York City Mission Movement 1812–1870*. Ithaca, NY: Cornell University Press 1971.

– "The Female World of Love and Ritual: Relations between Women in Nineteenth-Century America." *Signs* 1 (1975): 1–29.

Roy, Patricia. "British Columbia's Fear of Asians, 1900–1950," *Histoire sociale/ Social History* 13 (May 1980): 161–72.

Royce, Marion. "The Contribution of the Methodist Church to Social Welfare in Canada." MA, University of Toronto 1940.

– *Landmarks in the Victorian Education of 'Young Ladies' under Methodist Church Auspices*. Toronto: Ontario Institute for Studies in Education 1977.

Ryan, Mary. *Cradle of the Middle Class: The Family in Oneida County, New York, 1790–1865*. Cambridge: Cambridge University Press 1981.

Sansom, G.B. *The Western World and Japan: A Study in the Interaction of European and Asiatic Cultures*. New York: Alfred A. Knopf 1958.

Scott, Munroe. *McClure: The China Years of Dr. Bob McClure*. Toronto: Canec Publishing and Supply House 1977.

Scott, Paul. *The Jewel in the Crown*. London: Granada 1973.

Seagrave, Sterling. *The Soong Dynasty*. New York: Harper and Row 1985.

Seidensticker, Edward. *Low City, High City: Tokyo from Edo to the Earthquake*. New York: Alfred A. Knopf 1983.

Semmell, Bernard. *The Methodist Revolution*. New York: Basic Books 1973.

Semple, Neil A. "The Impact of Urbanization on the Methodist Church in Central Canada, 1854–1884." PhD, University of Toronto 1979.

- "'The Nurture and Admonition of the Lord': Nineteenth-Century Canadian Methodism's Response to 'Childhood.'" *Histoire sociale/Social History* 14 (May 1981): 157–76.

Shenkichi, Eto, and Harold Z. Schreffen, eds. *The 1911 Revolution in China: Interpretive Essays*. Tokyo: University of Tokyo Press 1984.

Shiels, Richard D. "The Feminization of American Congregationalism, 1730–1835." *American Quarterly* 33. no. 1 (Spring 1981): 46–62.

Shortt, Adam, and Arthur G. Doughty, eds. *Canada and Its Provinces*. Vol. 11. Toronto: Glasgow, Brook and Company 1914.

Showalter, Elaine. *The Female Malady: Women, Madness, and English Culture, 1830–1980*. New York: Pantheon 1985.

Sievers, Sharon. "Feminist Criticism in Japanese Politics in the 1880s: The Experience of Kishida Toshiko." *Signs* 6 (Summer 1981): 602–16.

- *Flowers in Salt: The Beginnings of Feminist Consciousness in Modern Japan*. Stanford, Calif.: Stanford University Press 1983.

Sissons, C.B. *A History of Victoria University*. Toronto: University of Toronto Press 1952.

Sizer, Sandra. *Gospel Hymns and Social Religion: The Rhetoric of Nineteenth-Century Revivalism*. Philadelphia: Temple University Press 1978.

Smith, Timothy L. *Revivalism and Social Reform in Mid-Nineteenth Century America*. New York: Abingdon Press 1957.

Snitow, Ann, Christine Stansell, and Sharon Thompson, eds. *Powers of Desire: The Politics of Sexuality*. New York: Monthly Review Press 1983.

Spicer, Jean. *The Woman's Missionary Society in Manitoba 1884–1959*. Toronto: United Church of Canada 1959.

Storry, Richard. *Japan and the Decline of the West in Asia 1894–1943*. London: Macmillan 1979.

Strachey, Barbara. *Remarkable Relations: The Story of the Pearsall Smith Women*. New York: Universe Books 1982.

Strong-Boag, Veronica J. *The Parliament of Women: The National Council of Women of Canada, 1893–1929*. Ottawa: National Museums of Canada 1976.

- "Canada's Women Doctors: Feminism Constrained." In Linda Kealey, ed., *A Not Unreasonable Claim: Women and Reform in Canada, 1880s-1920s*. Toronto: Women's Press 1979, 109–29.

- ed. *'A Woman with A Purpose': The Diaries of Elizabeth Smith 1872–1884*. Toronto: University of Toronto Press 1980.

Sugimato, Howard H. *Japanese Immigration, The Vancouver Riots and Canadian Diplomacy*. New York: Arno Press 1978.

Sweet, Leonard. *The Minister's Wife. Her Role in Nineteenth-Century American Evangelization*. Philadelphia: Temple University Press 1985.

Sweet, William Warren. *Revivalism in America: Its Origin, Growth and Decline*. Gloucester, Mass.: Peter Smith 1944; repr. 1965.

Tausky, Thomas E., ed. *Sara Jeanette Duncan: Selected Journalism*. Ottawa: Tecumseh Press 1978.

They Went Forth in the Church's Mission. Bruce Presbytery United Church Women 1967.

Thomas, Hilah, and Rosemary Skinner Keller, eds. *Women in New Worlds. Historical Perspectives on the Wesleyan Tradition*. Nashville: Abingdon Press 1981.

Thomas, John. "Servants of the Church: Canadian Methodist Deaconess Work." *Canadian Historical Review* 65 (Sept. 1984): 371–95.

Thomson, James C., Peter W. Stanley, and John Curtis Perry. *Sentimental Imperialists: The American Experience in East Asia*. New York: Harper and Row 1981.

Trofimenkoff, Susan Mann, and Alison Prentice, eds. *The Neglected Majority: Essays in Canadian Women's History*. Vol. 1. Toronto: McClelland and Stewart 1977.

Trollope, Joanne. *Britannia's Daughters: Women of the British Empire*. London: Hutchinson 1983.

Tuchman, Barbara. *Stilwell and the American Experience in China 1911–45*. New York: Bantam 1971.

Tucker, Ruth. *Guardians of the Great Commission: The Story of Women in Modern Missions*. Grand Rapids, Mich.: Zondervan 1988.

Ukrainian Pioneers' Association of Alberta. *Ukrainians in Alberta*. Vol. 2. Winnipeg: Ukrainian Pioneers' Association of Alberta 1981.

Urquhart, M.C., and K. Buckley. *Historical Statistics of Canada*. Toronto: Macmillan 1965.

Valenze, Deborah. *Prophetic Sons and Daughters: Female Preaching and Popular Religion in Industrial England*. Princeton: Princeton Univrsity Press 1985.

Vance, Carole. "Pleasure and Danger: Towards a Politics of Sexuality." In Vance, ed., *Pleasure and Danger: Exploring Female Sexuality*. London: Routledge and Kegan Paul 1984, 1–27.

Van Die, Marguerite. *An Evangelical Mind: Nathanael Burwash and the Methodist Tradition in Canada, 1839–1918*. Montreal and Kingston: McGill-Queen's University Press 1989.

Van Dieren, Karen. "The Response of the wms to the Immigration of Asian Women 1888–1942." In Barbara Latham and Roberta J. Pazdro, eds., *Not Just Pin Money: Selected Essays on the History of Women's Work in British Columbia*. Victoria, bc: Camosun College 1984, 79–97.

Varg, Paul A. *Missionaries, Chinese and Diplomats: The American Protestant Missionary Movement in China 1890–1952*. Princeton, nj: Princeton University Press 1958.

Varley, Elizabeth. *Kitamaat, My Valley*. Terrace, bc: Northern Times Press 1985.

Vicinus, Martha. "'One Life To Stand Beside Me': Emotional Conflicts in First-Generation College Women in England." *Feminist Studies* 8 (Fall 1982): 603–28.

- "Distance and Desire: English Boarding-School Friendships." In Estelle Freedman, Barbara Gelpi, Susan Johnson, and Kathleen Weston, eds., *The Lesbian Issue: Essays from Signs*. Chicago: Univ. of Chicago Press 1985, 43–65.
- *Independent Women: Work and Community for Single Women 1850–1920*. London: Virago Press 1985.
Walkowitz, Judith R. *Prostitution and Victorian Society*. Cambridge: Cambridge University Press 1980.
Wallace, W. Stewart, ed. *The Macmillan Dictionary of Canadian Biography*. Toronto: Macmillan 1963.
Walsh, Mary Roth. *"Doctors Wanted: No Women Need Apply": Sexual Barriers in the Medical Profession*. New Haven: Yale University Press 1977.
Ward, Peter. "The Oriental Immigrant and Canada's Protestant Clergy, 1858–1925." *BC Studies* 22 (Summer 1974): 40–55.
- *White Canada Forever: Popular Attitudes and Public Policy towards Orientals in British Columbia*. Montreal: McGill-Queen's University Press 1978.
- *Courtship, Love, and Marriage in Nineteenth-Century English Canada*. Montreal and Kingston: McGill-Queen's University Press 1990.
Warren, Max. *Social History and Christian Mission*. London: SCM Press 1967.
Wehrle, Edmund S. *Britain, China and the Missionary Riots 1891–1900*. Minneapolis: University of Minnesota Press 1966.
Wein, Roberta. "Women's Colleges and Domesticity, 1875–1918." *History of Education Quarterly* (Spring 1974): 31–47.
Welter, Barbara. "The Feminization of American Religion: 1800–1860." In *Dimity Convictions: The American Woman in the Nineteenth Century*. Athens: Ohio University Press 1976, 83–102.
- "She Hath Done What She Could: Protestant Women's Missionary Careers in Nineteenth-Century America." *American Quarterly* 30 (1978): 624–38.
Whitely, Marilyn. "'Doing Just About What They Please': Ladies' Aids in Ontario Methodism." *Ontario History* 82, no. 4 (Dec. 1990): 289–304.
Whyte, Bob. *Unfinished Encounter: China and Christianity*. London: Fount Paperbacks 1988.
Wiebe, Robert H. *The Search for Order 1877–1920*. New York: Hill and Wang 1967.
Wilson, J.D. "'No Blanket To Be Worn in School': The Education of Indians in Early Nineteenth-Century Ontario." *Histoire sociale/Social History* 7 (Nov. 1974): 293–305.
Wolf, Margery, and Roxane Walker, eds. *Women in Chinese Society*. Stanford, Calif.: Stanford University Press 1975.
Yanaga, Chitoshi. *Japan since Perry*. New York: McGraw Hill 1949.
Yokoyama, Toshio. *Japan in the Victorian Mind*. London: Macmillan 1987.
Young, Marilyn Blatt. *The Rhetoric of Empire: American China Policy, 1895–1901*. Cambridge, Mass.: Harvard University Press 1968.

Index